The Humanity of Christ

Princeton Theological Monograph Series

K. C. Hanson, Charles M. Collier, D. Christopher Spinks,
and Robin A. Parry, Series Editors

The Humanity of Christ

The Significance of the Anhypostasis *and* Enhypostasis *in Karl Barth's Christology*

JAMES P. HALEY

PICKWICK *Publications* · Eugene, Oregon

THE HUMANITY OF CHRIST
The Significance of the *Anhypostasis* and *Enhypostasis* in Karl Barth's Christology

Princeton Theological Monograph Series 227

Pickwick Publications
An Imprint of Wipf and Stock Publishers
199 W. 8th Ave., Suite 3
Eugene, OR 97401

www.wipfandstock.com

PAPERBACK ISBN: 978-1-5326-1415-6
HARDCOVER ISBN: 978-1-5326-1417-0
EBOOK ISBN: 978-1-5326-1416-3

Cataloguing-in-Publication data:

Names: Haley, James P.

Title: The Humanity of Christ : The Significance of the Anhypostasis and Enhypostasis in Karl Barth's Christology / James P. Haley.

Description: Eugene, OR: Pickwick Publications, 2017 | Series: Princeton Theological Monograph Series 227 | Includes bibliographical references.

Identifiers: ISBN 978-1-5326-1415-6 (paperback) | ISBN 978-1-5326-1417-0 (hardcover) | ISBN 978-1-5326-1416-3 (ebook)

Subjects: LCSH: Barth, Karl, 1886–1968. | Jesus Christ—Person and offices.

Classification: BT203 .H37 2017 (print) | BT203 .H37 (ebook)

Manufactured in the U.S.A.   08/18/17

Dedication

This work is dedicated to my wife Tina, and my four sons James, Johnathan, Mitchell, and Joseph. They have lived with this project in our home with great love and patience. Thank you. I love you.

This work is also dedicated to my mother Montez, and to the memory of my father whose name I bear with great humility and thankfulness to Almighty God. I am richly blessed to call them mother and father.

Finally, this work is dedicated to my Savior Jesus Christ in whose magnificence as the mediator of the covenant and our reconciliation to a holy God overwhelms me in my feeble attempts to fathom His greatness.

Contents

Acknowledgments

I WOULD LIKE TO express my great appreciation and thanks to Professor Robert Vosloo for his warm and insightful direction during the course of my dissertation work. It has indeed been a great pleasure to work with, and get to know Dr. Vosloo.

Many thanks also go to the Faculty of Theology at the University of Stellenbosch for their gracious reception, and their commitment to world class theological discourse with a view towards impacting the world with the gospel of Christ. My experience at Stellenbosch was life-changing and one in which the Lord continues to use in my theological pursuits.

I would also like to thank my dissertation review committee. It was their careful and thoughtful comments on my dissertation that compelled me to add the final chapter to this work, which I trust will enhance the project as a whole.

Introduction

The Issue at Hand

WHY DO WE STILL read Karl Barth? One reason, I believe, is because even when we disagree with Barth, he forces upon us a deep consideration into his way of thinking, which in turn forces upon us a deeper consideration into our own theological point of view. This is especially true with respect to Barth's Christology given its undulating hills and unpredictable valleys through which he journeys in search of what it means to say the *Word became flesh*. It was in this search, this pursuit, that Barth discovered the concepts of *anhypostasis* and *enhypostasis*, which he uniquely combines together as a way to describe the union of divine and human natures in the person of Jesus Christ. For Barth, this was not an attempt to break away from orthodox Christology, but his way to more fully explore how the Logos of God became a human being in one person, without doing violence to the true essence of divinity and humanity in their union together. One of the most striking aspects of Barth's Christology is how he labors to personally understand the being of Jesus Christ as the Word became flesh given Barth's genuine desire to discover the revealed Christ according to the testimony of sacred Scripture. In fundamentals, Barth determines that Jesus Christ is both the subject and object of divine revelation as the mediator of reconciliation between God and humanity, in whose being is the indissoluble union of human being with the Logos made manifest as Jesus of Nazareth.

> "Jesus Christ very God and very man" does not mean that in Jesus Christ God and a man were really side by side, but it means that Jesus Christ, the Son of God and thus Himself true God, is also a true man. But this man exists inasmuch as the Son of God is this man—not otherwise . . . Thus the reality of Jesus Christ is that God Himself in person is actively present in the flesh. God Himself in person is the Subject of a real human being and

acting. And just because God is the Subject of it, this being and acting are real.[1]

It is Barth's ardent and enduring expression of Jesus Christ as God's revelation in this world that marks his move away from the anthropocentric influences of his early theological training to a Christ-centered understanding of the revelation of God.[2] I would venture to say that Barth's pursuit of the revelation of God in Christ was not simply an academic or ecclesiastical endeavor, but a personal pursuit. It was by no happenstance that Barth's change in theological direction came not as a result of his research as a university professor of theology, but as a pastor in a small village in Safenwil, Switzerland. For Barth, the theological reality of a people who lived in a real world, beset with real problems, had no small impact on his thinking as he sought out a new theological course, the impetus of which was found in the Word of God. As Barth himself describes it, he began to be: "increasingly preoccupied with the idea of the kingdom of God in the biblical, real, this-worldly sense of the term. This raised more and more problems over the way in which I should use the Bible in my sermons, which for all too long I had taken for granted."[3]

With Barth's turn to the Scriptures came his serious attention to its exegesis, which found significant expression in *The Epistle to the Romans*. In Barth's *Romans* we do not simply find a turning away from liberal theology, but Barth's absolute turning to the Scriptures as the "witness to the Word of God" made manifest in the person of Jesus Christ.[4] This marks Barth's theological grounding—that true knowledge of God first demands the revelation of God—which can only be made manifest in God's movement towards humanity. This is the act of God in the person of Jesus Christ.[5] This is God making a great promise to Mary that she would have a son, and that:

1. Barth, *CD* I/2, 150–51.

2. See Hart, "Was God in Christ?," 3. Hart singles out Karl Barth as the systematic theologian whose writings most seriously take up the themes of Christology and the knowledge of God in the twentieth century. That is, Barth tackles head on the themes of Christology together with the humanity of Christ as the mediator of reconciliation, in whose person manifests the true knowledge of God.

3. Busch, *Karl Barth*, 92–97.

4. Barth announced to the theological world his dramatic shift in thinking with his commentary on *The Epistle to the Romans*, which was first published in 1919, and published in its revised version (*Romans* II) in 1921. Moreover, it is interesting to note that Barth's first major theological work is an exegesis of the Scriptures.

5. Joseph Mangina identifies another important component of Barth's break with liberal theology with respect to his rejection of "Cartesianism," or an anthropological philosophy that depicts any human capacity for self transcendence. That is, Barth attacks liberal theology from above in the realization that the God of the Bible cannot be defined in terms of the world. See Mangina, *Karl Barth on the Christian Life*, 12–13.

"You shall call his name Jesus!" This is something which theologically as well as practically cannot be elucidated enough, that indeed the whole content of the Bible from A to Z including everything we call the Christian Church and Christian dispensation absolutely depends on this name Jesus. The *name* is the last thing that could still be said about someone, and everything now centers around this someone himself. Through this "someone," through Jesus, the Holy Scriptures is distinguished from other good and serious and pious books. Through Jesus that which in the Holy Scripture is called revelation, is distinguished from what surely can also be said about the other great ones, gods and men.[6]

In *Romans* Barth expresses the revelation of God dialectically in the veiling and unveiling of God in the flesh of Jesus the Nazarene. Barth uses the language of paradox to describe the revelation of God in the true humanity of Jesus, the same human essence that is enjoined to all human beings. And yet, this true humanity does not exist in isolation, but is joined to God himself in its union with the Logos. This is the ontological paradox that Barth expresses as the dialectic of veiling and unveiling of Christ's human nature. This is important to understand because the language of veiling and unveiling in *Romans* anticipates the language of *anhypostasis* and *enhypostasis* that Barth would soon discover, which would in turn provide the ontological frame of reference to more precisely express the revelation of God in the person of Jesus Christ as *vere Deus* and *vere homo*. In Barth's *Romans* the revelation of God in Jesus Christ clearly emerges with the force of God's movement toward humanity. This is the faithfulness of God revealed in Christ who as the truth of eternity encounters this world as the light of redemption, forgiveness, and resurrection.

In Him we have found the standard by which all discovery of God and all being discovered by Him is made known as such; in Him we recognize that this finding and being found is the truth of the order of eternity. Many live their lives in the light of redemption and forgiveness and resurrection; but that we have eyes to see their manner of life we owe to the One. In His light we see light. That it is the Christ whom we have encountered in Jesus is guaranteed by our finding in Him the sharply defined, final interpretation of the Word of the faithfulness of God to which the Law and the Prophets bare witness. His entering within the deepest darkness of human ambiguity and abiding

6. Barth, *Great Promise*, 27–28.

within it is THE faithfulness. The life of Jesus is perfected obedience to the will of the faithful God.[7]

Barth's commentary on Romans resulted (ironically enough) in his appointment as Honorary Professor of Reformed Theology at the University of Göttingen. It was at Göttingen that Barth first embarked upon his study of dogmatics which would occupy him for the rest of his life. With Barth's theological bearings now firmly established in the Scripture (which attests to the revelation of God in Jesus Christ rather than being understood as revelation itself),[8] the *reality* of Barth's theology finds its basis in the *reality* of Jesus Christ. While for Barth philosophy may still have a place in drawing attention to the great dichotomy between God and humanity, philosophy in itself has no power to stake a claim to the revelation of God.[9] The human condition is absolutely dependent upon God's willingness to move towards us and reveal himself to us in a way that we can fully embrace; that is, in the revelation of the man Jesus of Nazareth.

> For this reason theology can think and speak only as it looks at Jesus Christ and from the vantage point of what He is. It cannot introduce Him. Neither can it bring about that dialogue, history, and communion. It does not have the disposition of these things. It is dependent upon the Holy Scripture, according to which the covenant is *in full effect* and in which Jesus Christ *witnesses to Himself*. It hears this witness. It trusts it and is satisfied with it.[10]

As Barth's theological course began to change in earnest (and quite literally in his move from the pastorate in Safenwil to Honorary Professor of Reformed Dogmatics in Göttingen), he prepared for his first lectures

7. Barth, *Epistle to the Romans*, 97.

8. Barth's interpretation of the Scripture as the Word of God has long been debated. A. M. Fairweather argues that Barth's view of the Scriptures as revelation denudes it from that Word which is indeed God's Word. As such, Barth's view of Scripture only bears witness to the possible operation of the Spirit where unity of God with His Word is achieved, where this unity as a secondary and instrumental factor has nothing to do with its content. See Fairweather, *Word as Truth*, 42–43.

9. Amy Marga notes that for Barth "revelation means reconciliation." For example, in Barth's response to Erich Przywara and what he learned about catholic theology in his study of Thomas Aquinas, Barth begins his response by using the philosophical category of realism claiming that without it the doctrine of revelation would not be possible. That is, "without the philosophical perspective of realism, theology would not be able to affirm God's existence. As such, if theology claims that God is real, that "God *is*," then it must speak to God's participation in creaturely 'being.'" See Marga, *Barth's Dialogue with Catholicism*, 136–37.

10. Barth, *Humanity of God*, 55.

on dogmatics given at Göttingen. It was here that Barth made a significant discovery while reading Heinrich Heppe's *Reformed Dogmatics*, together with Heinrich Schmid's *The Doctrinal Theology of the Evangelical Lutheran Church*. In these texts Barth first came across the concepts of *anhypostasis* and *enhypostasis* to explain how the human nature of Christ exists in union with the Logos.[11] *Anhypostasis* expresses the human nature of Jesus as having no subsistence (an-hypostasis) apart from its union with the Logos. *Enhypostasis* is used to express the human nature of Jesus as having its being "in" the subsistence (en-hypostasis) of the incarnate Son of God.

While it is generally recognized that the concepts of *anhypostasis* and *enhypostasis* have a place in Karl Barth's Christology, there is little consensus as to the extent and significance that these concepts have in Barth's Christology as a whole. Nevertheless, Barth scholarship with respect to his adoption of these concepts reveals some interesting observations. Bruce McCormack identifies Barth's discovery of *anhypostasis* and *enhypostasis* as a momentous event in his Christology.[12] Barth now has at his disposal the ontological language necessary to more precisely express the revelation of God in the ontological event of Jesus Christ. McCormack's observation began a theological debate of sorts over Barth's adoption of these concepts into his Christology, and whether or not Barth had misinterpreted *anhypostasis* and *enhypostasis* as first developed by the patristic Fathers, and subsequently adopted by the scholastics.

F. LeRon Shults argues that Barth misinterprets *anhypostasis* and *enhypostasis* contrary to the patristic Church Fathers as he received it through the dogmatic compilations of Heinrich Schmid and Heinrich Heppe.[13] Following Shults, U. M. Lang[14] and Matthias Gockel[15] argued that the protestant scholasticism that Barth worked through to develop his own understanding

11. Bruce McCormack notes that in May 1924 while preparing for his first lectures in dogmatics in Göttingen, Barth came upon the anhypostatic-enhypostatic christological dogma of the ancient Church in Heinrich Heppe's post-Reformation textbook entitled *Reformed Dogmatics*, which became Barth's foundational text. See McCormack, *Critically Realistic Dialectical Theology*, 327, 337.

12. McCormack argues that Barth saw in it "an understanding of the incarnate being of the Mediator which preserved that infinite qualitative distinction between God and humankind which had been at the forefront of his concerns throughout the previous phase." The similarity to the dialectic of veiling and unveiling that Barth expressed in *Romans* was obvious. In taking human nature to himself in the flesh of Jesus, God veils himself in this creaturely form. See McCormack, *Critically Realistic Dialectical Theology*, 327.

13. See Shults, "Dubious Christological Formula."

14. See Lang, "*Anhypostasis–Enhypostasis.*"

15. See Gockel, "*Anhypostasis–Enhypostasis* Theory."

of these concepts was very much in line with traditional orthodoxy. Lang, however, states that if Barth adopted *anhypostasis* and *enhypostasis* as a dual formula, it is an innovation all his own.[16] Paul Dafydd Jones argues that while Barth's adoption of *anhypostasis* and *enhypostasis* marked a defining moment in his early theological development, Barth departs from the "older dogmatics" in favor of his own reflections in his mature Christology.[17]

In this book I argue against Shults that Barth's interpretation of *anhypostasis* and *enhypostasis* as a dual ontological formula not only differs with the patristic Church Fathers, but with the scholastics and post-scholastics as well; all of which interpreted *anhypostasis* and *enhypostasis* as autonomous concepts to describe the human nature of Christ. Moreover, while I agree with Lang that Barth's adoption of these concepts as a dual formula is an innovation all his own, I push this argument forward by demonstrating that Barth's ontological innovation proves to be foundational to his Christology as a whole. That being said, this books seeks to examine Barth's adoption of *anhypostasis* and *enhypostasis* which he uses to explain how the human of Christ exists in union with his divine nature. But more than that, this book seeks to understand the *significance* that Barth's adoption of these concepts have on his Christology from the early stages of his christological development—to his mature Christology. Like many aspects of Barth's theology, what appears on the surface does not necessarily reflect the substance that settles much deeper beneath.

I acknowledge that my use of the term *ontology* to describe Barth's understanding of how the human nature of Jesus exists in union with the Logos is not a term that Barth himself used in this particular context. However, I argue that while Barth did not use the strict language of ontology, we should not reject the ontological development in Barth's understanding of the humanity of Christ, especially in view of his unique coupling of *anhypostasis* and *enhypostasis*.[18] In other words, I argue that the christological innovation that Barth develops out of his adoption of these concepts is grounded in ontology; that is, in the existent being of the Word of God that became flesh. In my view, the ontological union of the humanity of Christ (as the Son of Man) with the Logos (as the Son of God) proves to be the central and fundamental point of contact/union between Jesus Christ and his people

16. Graham Ward notes the development of this debate and the "dialectical character" of Barth's adoption of *anhypostasis* and *enhypostasis* as a dual formula. See Ward, *Christ and Culture*, 10.

17. See Jones, *Humanity of Christ*, 147.

18. We take notice here of Thomas F. Torrance's statement that Karl Barth's theological conceptions were not logically, but ontologically derived. See Torrance, *Karl Barth*, 128.

(the Church), which naturally flows out of Barth's Christology. Moreover, as I will show, Barth does in fact use the language of ontology to develop the union of Jesus Christ as the royal man—with his church—which in turn brings about the union of the triune God with his people. Beginning with the *Göttingen Dogmatics* and progressing through the *Church Dogmatics* Barth uniquely expresses the humanity of Christ ontologically as both *anhypostasis* and *enhypostasis* in its union with the Logos. For Barth, this is the act of God revealing himself in the man Jesus of Nazareth.

Karl Barth's Innovative Adoption of *Anhypostasis* and *Enhypostasis*

The concepts of *anhypostasis* and *enhypostasis* first emerged in the writings of patristic church Fathers who defended the Chalcedon definition of the two natures of Christ against attacks from the Eutychians on one side—who claimed that Chalcedon separated Jesus Christ into two persons; and the Nestorians on the other side—who claimed that Chalcedon merged the two natures of Christ into one.[19] In response, Chalcedon apologists developed language that distinguished between the concepts of person (*hypostasis*) and nature (*physis*) in explaining how the human nature of Christ exists in union with the Logos. In so doing the language of *anhypostasis* and *enhypostasis* emerged to explain how Jesus Christ can subsist as one distinct person who encompasses in his being two natures; divine and human, which are "unconfused, immutable, and indivisible, inseparable" in their union. Following the patristic writers, Lutheran and Reformed scholastics also took up these concepts to explain the subsistence of Christ's human nature in union with the Logos.

Barth, however, adopted *anhypostasis* and *enhypostasis* in a way that moves beyond both the patristic Fathers and scholastics. What protestant orthodoxy adopted as autonomous concepts to express the union of Christ's human nature with the Logos, Barth uniquely expresses as a dual ontological formula. For Barth, the human nature of Christ is both *anhypostasis* and *enhypostasis* in its union with the Logos. I argue that Barth's formulation of these concepts is not simply his unique way to express the incarnation of Christ, but in fact becomes the ontological basis for Barth's expression of the revelation of the triune God—in the person of Jesus Christ—as the mediator of reconciliation between God and humanity. Moreover, Barth's

19. In this book the term orthodox refers to agreement with the Council of Chalcedon's definition of Jesus Christ who exists as one person with two natures, which are unconfused and indivisible; that is, very God and very man.

construction of the humanity of Christ as *anhypostasis* and *enhypostasis* provides the ontological grounding to express the convergence of time and eternity in Jesus of Nazareth in whom the reconciliation of humanity with God is accomplished *in his revelation.*

> The unity of God and man in Christ is, then, the act of the Logos in assuming human being. His becoming, and therefore the thing that human being encounters in this becoming of the Logos, is an act of God in the person of the Word . . . This man Jesus Christ is identical with God because the Word became flesh in the sense just explained. Therefore He does not only live through God and with God. He is God Himself. Nor is He autonomous and self existent. His reality, existence and being is wholly and absolutely that of God Himself, the God who acts in His Word.[20]

One of the most striking aspects of Barth's adoption of both *anhypostasis* and *enhypostasis* as attributes of Christ's human nature (i.e., in their coupling together) is that Barth never acknowledges this configuration departs from the same orthodoxy from which he received them. Whereas historical orthodoxy used *anhypostasis* strictly in a negative sense to explain what the humanity of Christ was not (i.e., without subsistence), Karl Barth adopts as the negative side of the *enhypostasis* to explain the humanity of Christ—in both senses. Barth in fact relies upon the orthodox use of these terms in his own unique appropriation of them. It is this coupling together of both the positive and negative aspect of these terms—which Barth clearly adopted with vigor—that draws our attention.

The Significance of *Anhypostasis* and *Enhypostasis* in Barth's Christology

Barth's adoption of *anhypostasis* and *enhypostasis* is significant to his Christology for a number of reasons. First it allows him to transition from the motif of veiling and unveiling used in the paradoxical language of *Romans* to a more ontologically dynamic and precise language; language that for Barth is theologically and historically validated as orthodox to express the union of divine and human natures in Christ. Second, Barth can now use ontological language to more forcefully express how the Word became flesh in the revelation of Jesus Christ. That is, *anhypostasis* and *enhypostasis* ground the humanity of Christ in his union with the Logos of God—in the

---

20 Barth, *CD* I/2, 162.

Word *becoming* flesh. Third, these concepts open up for Barth a fluid range of theological motion to express the revelation of God in the humanity of Christ as the coalescence of divine and human natures which remain immutable and unconfused in this union. Fourth, *anhypostasis* and *enhypostasis* provide the ontological impetus for Barth to express the act of God's revelation in the union of divinity with humanity made manifest in Jesus of Nazareth as the exaltation of the Son of Man. Fifth—and a much neglected point—Barth applies the conceptual union of *anhypostasis* and *enhypostasis* to explain Christ's relationship with his church. This point in fact solidifies the ontological *significance* of these concepts in Barth's Christology.

I argue that Barth's unique adoption of *anhypostasis* and *enhypostasis* as a dual ontological formula demonstrates quite clearly that Barth makes this doctrine his own to express the humanity of Christ as the revelation of God. I further argue that Barth's adoption of these concepts does not mark a change in his theological thinking per se, but simply provides the ontological language for Barth to express with more precision the event of God's revelation in Jesus Christ which carries through to Barth's mature Christology. Methodologically, I approach this work with the intent to first clarify how Barth interprets the historical development of the *anhypostasis* and *enhypostasis* of Christ's human nature; and second to demonstrate the significance of Barth's appropriation of these terms into his Christology. As such, this book is developed in six separate but interrelated chapters.

Chapter 1 follows the historical orthodox development of the concepts *anhypostasis* and *enhypostasis* to explain the humanity of Christ. An examination of the historical development of these terms as *separate* and *unrelated* terms is presented to establish the interpretive dichotomy when compared with Karl Barth's own interpretation of these concepts as *congruent* and *interrelated* terms. Four patristic writers are first reviewed: John of Caesarea, Leontius of Byzantium, Leontius of Jerusalem, and John of Damascus, all of whom used the concept of *enhypostasis* to explain that the human nature of Christ exists as a real subsistence in the hypostasis of the Logos. The concept of *anhypostasis*, however, is used exclusively as a negative description to explain that Christ's human nature has no reality in itself outside of its union with the Logos. Lutheran and Reformed scholastic writers, as well as the eighteenth century dogmatic compilations of Heinrich Schmid (Lutheran) and Heinrich Heppe (Reformed) are reviewed, which demonstrates a consistency in their understanding of these concepts together with that of the patristic fathers. All of this will show that historically, orthodox writers understood *anhypostasis* and *enhypostasis* as autonomous concepts. Moreover, any interpretation of these terms as a dual formulation to explain Christ's human nature was foreign to their thinking.

Chapter 2 examines Karl Barth's unique appropriation of *anhypostasis* and *enhypostasis* as a dual formula to express the human nature of Christ. Barth is first introduced to these concepts through the dogmatics compilations of Heinrich Schmid (Lutheran) and Heinrich Heppe (Reformed), which Barth came across as he prepared for his dogmatic lectures at the University of Göttingen. Barth's adoption of these concepts is first expressed in the *Göttingen Dogmatics*, and then more fully developed over the course of his work in the *Church Dogmatics*. Our main concern here is to understand how Barth interprets these concepts as a dual formula to express the existence of the human nature of Christ in union with the Logos, and how his interpretation differs from that of historical protestant orthodoxy. Indeed, for Barth, the *anhypostasis* and *enhypostasis* of Christ's human nature establishes ontologically the indissoluble union of the Logos with Christ's human nature, which is necessary to accomplish the reconciliation of God with humanity. As such, Barth insists that the *enhypostasis* of Christ's human nature must be understood in relation to the *anhypostasis* of the same human nature. Citing the scholastics, Barth argues that:

> Their negative position asserted that Christ's flesh in itself has no existence, and this was asserted in the interests of their positive position that Christ's flesh has its existence through the Word and in the Word, who is God Himself acting as Revealer and Reconciler. Understood in this its original sense, this particular doctrine, abstruse in appearance only, is particularly well adapted to make it clear that the reality attested by the Holy Scriptures, Jesus Christ, is the reality of a divine act of Lordship, which is unique and singular as compared with all other events, and in this way to characterize it as a reality held up to faith by revelation. It is in virtue of the eternal Word that Jesus Christ exists as a man of flesh and blood in our sphere, as a man like us, as an historical phenomenon.[21]

Barth's coupling together of these opposite perspectives creates in his Christology a unique and dynamic understanding of the humanity of Christ where God and humanity are united in such a way that: to say Jesus of Nazareth is to say very God, and to say the Logos of God is to say very man. For Barth, while they are separate in their essence, they are never distinct in this union of God and humanity. They are indeed one.

Chapter 3 follows the development of *anhypostasis* and *enhypostasis* in Karl Barth's Christology as his ontological grounding for expressing the revelation of God in Jesus Christ as the Word became flesh. This is important to

21. Ibid., 164.

understand because although the language of *anhypostasis* and *enhypostasis* did not appear in Barth's Christology until the *Göttingen Dogmatics*, Barth's theology of the revelation of God in Jesus Christ was firmly grounded in his turn to the Scripture as the basis for theology, in tandem with his turning away from liberal theology. While Barth does not divorce himself from philosophical reflection in his theology, he clearly argues that philosophy has no proper place in realizing the revelation of God. Revelation is strictly a work of God made manifest in the person of Jesus Christ. Barth's discovery of the *anhypostasis* and *enhypostasis* simply gave ontological expression to his understanding that Jesus of Nazareth exists in indissoluble union with the Logos as the God-man.

Moreover, the concepts of *anhypostasis* and *enhypostasis* provide the theological function for Barth's development of the revelation of Jesus Christ as the Word became flesh—in the εγενετο. For Barth, in the εγενετο, the human nature of Christ dialectically veils and unveils the revelation of God. Yet, in the humanity of Christ, in his birth, crucifixion, and resurrection, is revealed the reality of God in the Logos taking to himself real human essence. Moreover, as a natural connection to the εγενετο, Barth employs *anhypostasis* and *enhypostasis* as a dialectical argument in his dialogue with Lutheran and Reformed Christology in working through the ontological character of the union of very God with very man. However, Barth leaves unresolved the differences between the Lutheran and Reformed understanding of the *logos asarkos*. Yet, in this dialectic Barth establishes ontologically that there must be a separate, but not distinctive attribute of the human nature of Christ in union with the Logos.

Chapter 4 identifies the themes of coalescence in the divine and human natures of Christ grounded in the ontology of the *anhypostasis* and *enhypostasis*. Barth develops Jesus Christ as the revelation of God in whose being realizes the convergence of eternity and time as the mediator of reconciliation. His revelation as very God and very man becomes the unifying cord that binds together the ontological essence of the God-man with his role as the mediator of reconciliation. This may be described as the *ontological event* of the God-man, the absolute coalescence of very God and very man in Jesus Christ, who as the keeper of the covenant is both the subject and object of divine election. "It is the name of Jesus Christ which, according to the divine self-revelation, forms the focus at which the two decisive beams of the truth forced upon us converge and unite: on the one hand the electing God and on the other the elected man."[22] As the mediator of the covenant Jesus Christ humbles himself as the Son of Man. And yet, even

22. Barth, *CD* II/2, 59.

in his humiliation as Jesus of Nazareth, Jesus Christ is exalted as the Son of Man. For Barth, in this event there is no distinction in time between Jesus Christ's humiliation and exaltation. To do so would split apart the divine nature from the human nature in their absolute union, which in Barth's thinking is an ontological impossibility given the *anhypostasis* and *enhypostasis* of Christ's human nature in its union with the Logos.

> Where in Paul, for example, is He the Crucified who has not yet risen, or the Risen who has not yet been crucified? Would He be the One whom the New Testament attests as the Mediator between God and man if He were only the one and not the other? And if He is the Mediator, which one of the two can He be alone and without the other? Both aspects force themselves upon us. We have to do with the being of the one and entire Jesus Christ whose humiliation adds nothing. And in this being we have to do with His action, the work and event of the atonement.[23]

In the revelation of Jesus Christ genuine humanity is exalted in its indissoluble union with the Logos. This is the action, the movement of grace in God's self-revelation in Jesus of Nazareth as genuine humanity. Consequently, the reality of Christ's humanity is the light that the humanity of the first Adam can only reflect. In fact, Jesus of Nazareth is the *genuine* first Adam, where life in Christ helps to explain life in Adam. Fundamentally Barth argues that real and genuine humanity is the humanity of Christ where the human nature that we share with Adam is preserved as a *provisional copy* of the real humanity assumed by Christ. As Adam's heirs, as sinners and enemies of God, we are still in this provisional way humanity whose nature reflects the true human nature of Christ. "Paul does not go to Adam to see how he is connected with Christ; he goes to Christ to see how *He* is connected with Adam."[24]

The absolute union of *very God* and *very man* in Jesus Christ mirrors the absolute union of the *person* and *work* of Jesus Christ as the mediator of reconciliation. Barth does not distinguish between Christ as the revelation of God, and the event of Jesus Christ as the mediator of reconciliation. Christ exists as the mediator of reconciliation between God and humanity in the sense that in him the reconciliation of God and humanity are event. And in this event: "God encounters and is revealed to all men as the gracious God and in this event again all men are placed under the consequence and outworking of this encounter and revelation."[25] In this con-

23. Barth, *CD* IV/1, 133.
24. Barth, *Christ and Adam*, 60.
25. Barth, *CD* IV/1, 125.

vergence of time and space, the eternal Word claims time and creation as his own. As the Word of God who became flesh in time, in every moment of his temporal existence, and every point before or after his temporal existence as true God and true man—*Jesus Christ is the same*. To understand Barth's vantage point here in view of the *anhypostasis* and *enhypostasis* is to start with the eternal Logos, but the Logos that is not isolated from the humanity that he is elected to assume. The union between divine and human natures is an eternal union. "For Jesus Christ—not an empty *Logos*, but Jesus Christ the incarnate Word, the baby born in Bethlehem, the man put to death at Golgotha and raised again in the garden of Joseph of Arimathea, the man whose history this is—is the unity of the two. He is both at one and the same time."[26]

Chapter 5 evaluates Barth's critique of Chalcedon's definition of the two natures of Christ as very God and very man through the ontological lenses of the *anhypostasis* and *enhypostasis* of Christ's human nature. While Barth does not disagree with the Chalcedon definition in essentials, he is interested to develop a more precise definition and understanding of the union of divine and human natures in Christ as the act of God's revelation as the Son of Man in his exaltation. Barth uses the dynamic of *anhypostasis* and *enhypostasis* to more precisely explain the union of divine and human natures as the *hypostatica unio* in the act of God's revelation made manifest in the exaltation of the Son of Man.

Karl Barth's expression of the humanity of Christ as *anhypostasis* and *enhypostasis* reaches its apex in the Doctrine of Reconciliation where he develops Jesus Christ as the *Servant as Lord*. It is in the *Homecoming of the Son of Man*—in Christ's exaltation as the true man—where Barth emphasizes the human nature of Christ being brought into union with the divine nature in dialogue with the Chalcedon definition of the two natures. For Barth, the *anhypostasis* and *enhypostasis* of Christ's human nature undergird his insistence that the person of Jesus Christ must not be viewed statically in his being as the God-man, but dynamically in the event of God's movement of grace towards humanity.

Moreover, for Barth, the exaltation of human essence in the Son of Man is expressed in the language of *communicatio idiomatum* (the *impartation* of the human essence to the divine and the divine to the human, as it takes place in Jesus Christ), which Barth understands to be more deeply expressed in the *communio naturarum* (the *communion* of the human and divine essence in the one Jesus Christ without change and admixture, but also without cleavage and separation). But more deeply still, the exaltation

26. Barth, *CD* IV/1, 53.

of the Son of Man is expressed in the *unio hypostatica*, where the union of the divine and human essence in Christ *constitutes one personal life*, and yet they remain distinct. This is the movement of God's grace towards humanity (the *communicatio gratiarum*) in his willing condescension in the union of divine essence with human essence in the person of Jesus Christ.

> In all this we are again describing the *enhypostasis* or *anhyposta-sis* of the human nature of Jesus Christ. We may well say that this is the sum and root of all grace addressed to Him. Whatever else has still to be said may be traced back to the fact, and depends upon it, that the One who is Jesus Christ is present in human nature is the Son of God, that the Son is present as this man is present, and that this man is none other than the Son. We can and should state this as follows. It is only as the Son of God that Jesus Christ also exists as man, but He does actually exist in this way. As a man, of this human essence, He can be known even by those who do not know Him as the Son of God.[27]

Chapter 6 develops the climatic significance of the *anhypostasis* and *enhypostasis* in Karl Barth's Christology expressed quite vividly in the royal man and his relationship to his church. In view of the royal man we are now able to peer more deeply into the dynamic relationship between the ontological union of divine and human natures in Christ, and Christ's ontological relationship with his church. I argue that one ontological relationship cannot be properly understood without the other, both of which are centered in the royal man. The royal man plays a pivotal role in Barth's understanding of the eternal Word in action, who freely takes to himself the true flesh of humanity in his movement towards humanity—in their ontological union.

Barth understands that in the *objective* sense this is a union with all humanity by virtue of his becoming true humanity. However, in a more *subjective* sense, it is Christ's particular union with his church. Out of this dynamic relationship between the ontological union of divine and human natures in Christ—based upon the *anhypostasis* and *enhypostasis*—emerges Christ's ontological relationship with his church. Not only does Barth's development of the royal man give us better insight into the union of Christ with his church, but we also see in this *anhypostasis* and *enhypostasis* dynamic how Barth develops true humanity in Jesus of Nazareth and the sanctification of his church in its exaltation—in union with him.

27. Barth, *CD* IV/2, 91.

I

Anhypostasis and *Enhypostasis*
Historical Formulation and Interpretation

Introduction

IN HIS *CHURCH DOGMATICS* Karl Barth relentlessly develops and inter-
prets the person of Jesus Christ as the necessary *subject* and *object* of
divine revelation whose fingerprints touch upon every nuance of sacred
Scripture.[1] For Barth, Jesus Christ is the central figure and focus of the
Word of God manifested in time and space as the Word became flesh.[2]
Barth explains that:

> This fulfilled time which is identical with Jesus Christ, this ab-
> solute event in relation to which every event is not yet event or
> has ceased to be so, this "It is finished," this *Deus dixit* for which
> there are no analogies, is the revelation attested to in the Bible.
> To understand the Bible from beginning to end, from verse to
> verse, is to understand how everything in it relates to this as its
> invisible-visible centre.[3]

Grounded in the reality of the Word became flesh Barth expresses Jesus Christ as the absolute center of God's revelation of himself whose advent

---

1. Throughout his *Church Dogmatics* Barth works within a wide scope of historical/
theological church doctrine that finds its nucleus in the person of Jesus Christ. In so
doing Barth integrates Christology throughout his *Church Dogmatics*, which flows out
of his development of (1) *The Doctrine of the Word of God*, (2) *The Doctrine of God*, (3)
The Doctrine of Creation, and (4) *The Doctrine of Reconciliation*; all of which find their
impetus in the revelation of Jesus Christ as *very God* and *very man*. However, I do not
understand Barth's integration of Christology throughout the *Church Dogmatics* to be
done in a way that isolates Christ from his relationship within the Triune Godhead,
because in Christ is made manifest the revelation of the Triune God.

2. Barth, *CD* I/2, 159. For Barth, the historical event realized in the Word became
flesh points to the center, to the unveiling mystery of the revelation of God being among
us and with us in the person of Jesus Christ.

3. Barth, *CD* I/1, 116.

marks the fullness of God's free grace bestowed upon humanity,[4] and in whose person manifests the confluence of "very God and very man."[5] That being said, any honest investigation into Karl Barth's ontological and theological development of Jesus Christ as the God-man must recognize Barth's insistence that the human nature of Christ exists in absolute union with his divine nature. One in fact can argue that Barth understands the ontological essence of Jesus Christ as he understands the ontological essence of the triune God; that is, just as the Son exists in perfect union with the Father and the Holy Spirit as one God, so too the divine nature of Christ exists in perfect union with his human nature as one person.[6] In this way both ontological formulations of (1) the Triune God and (2) the person of Jesus Christ manifest perfect union together with perfect distinctiveness in their being.[7]

Given this ontological presupposition Barth works out his understanding of the fundamental/biblical truth undergirding the essence of Jesus Christ, which he encapsulates in the statement the Word became flesh.[8] In this event—eternal God in the second person of the Trinity reveals in this world *true* God by taking upon himself the nature of *true* humanity. And in this event, in the eternal Word taking upon himself the nature of created humanity, Barth could not conceive ontologically the person of Jesus Christ in whose being separates (in any sense) true God from true humanity.[9] Whatever argument one makes with respect to Barth's understanding of Jesus Christ as the God-man, that argument must grant that Barth worked within a christological system that understands Jesus Christ as one person who perfectly unites in his being the natures of *true* God and *true* humanity—*given his understanding of Christ's human nature as true humanity.*

---

4. In this book men and women are referred to jointly as humanity, humankind, etc. I will, however, remain true to the language as received when quoting Karl Barth and his use of the terms "man" or "men" to refer to men and women jointly.

5. Barth, CD I/2, 153. Barth understands Jesus Christ to be *very God* and *very man* who as the eternal Son of God (the Logos) assumed a nature like ours, the same nature subject to sin (yet without sin) in which we stand before God as condemned and lost sinners.

6. Barth, CD I/2, 136. Barth stresses that the human existence of Jesus is possible only through his union with the eternal Word, a union which is accomplished in every respect as *very God* and *very man*. The emphasis here is placed on the inseparable unity of divine and human essence while maintaining the distinctiveness between the two.

7. Barth, CD I/1, 362. Barth uses the term "mode" (not to be understood as modalism) to describe the distinctions between Father, Son, and Holy Spirit as his way to emphasize the perfect union within the Godhead relative to his being and work.

8. Barth CD I/2, 159. Barth's development of the Word became flesh becomes the major theme for explaining the act of God's self-revelation in the person of Jesus Christ.

9. Ibid., 161.

Throughout his *Church Dogmatics* and development of the person who is Jesus Christ, Barth moves deliberately (one may even say cautiously) as he considers the objectives of *Church Dogmatics* as an investigational study within the context of Biblical exegesis, historical church councils, and the works of theologians whose influence lay heavy upon orthodox Christology.[10] In view of Barth's approach to dogmatics, one of the critical questions we raise with respect to Barth's understanding of the human nature of Christ is how he interprets the historical/theological development of Christ's human nature as evidenced by his adoption of the dual formula *anhypostasis* and *enhypostasis*.[11] For Barth, this dual formulation was historically validated as a legitimate theological expression of how the person of Christ embodies both divine and human natures ontologically. This is not an insignificant point of theological reference because it enabled Barth to cite this formula as both historical and authoritative support for his own ontological development of the God-man. That is, Barth cites the use of *anhypostasis* and *enhypostasis* by earlier dogmaticians to argue how the human nature of Christ comes into union with the divine nature of the Logos. Barth explains that:

> The earlier dogmaticians tried even more explicitly to distinguish from every other kind of unity, and in that way to characterize, the uniqueness of the unity of the Word and human nature . . . But from the utter uniqueness of this unity follows the statement that God and Man are so related in Jesus Christ, that He exists as Man so far and only so far as He exists as God, i.e. in the mode of existence of the eternal Word of God. What we therefore express is a doctrine unanimously sponsored by early theology in its entirety, that of the *anhypostasis* and *enhypostasis* of the human nature of Christ. *Anhypostasis* asserts the negative . . . Apart from the divine mode of being whose existence it acquires it has none of its own; *Enhypostasis* asserts the positive. In virtue of the εγενετο, i.e., in virtue of the *assumptio*, the human nature acquires existence (subsistence) in the existence of God, meaning in the mode of being (hypostasis, "person") of the word.[12]

---

10. Barth gives significant consideration to patristic and scholastic scholars, as well as historical church council proclamations in developing his interpretation and understanding of the ontology of Christ.

11. Barth's own interpretation of the historical/theological development of the terms *anhypostasis* and *enhypostasis* prove to be a major point of interest in his own appropriation of these terms as a "dual" formula in his Christology.

12. Barth, *CD* I/2, 163.

The genesis of Barth's appropriation of *anhypostasis* and *enhypostasis* is found in the *Göttingen Dogmatics* where Barth provides an early glimpse into his understanding of the term *anhypostatos*, which he uses negatively to express the human nature of Christ having no reality in itself, and the *enhypostatos*, which he uses positively to express the human nature of Christ as having real subsistence in its union with the Logos.[13] We note also in the *Göttingen Dogmatics* that Barth primarily treats *anhypostasis* and *enhypostasis* as two independent concepts in describing the human nature of Christ in its ontological union with God the Son.

> Nevertheless—and this is where the emphasis falls—this indi-
> vidual that incorporates human nature has never existed any-
> where as such. The humanity of Christ, although it is body and
> soul, and an individual, is nothing subsistent or real in itself.
> Thus it did not exist prior to its union with the Logos. It has
> no independent existence alongside or apart from him . . . This
> idea, the idea of humanity, and this individual who incorporates
> it, cannot for a single moment be abstracted from their assump-
> tion into the person of the Logos. The divine subject who unites
> Himself with them makes them revelation. The human nature
> of Christ has no personhood of its own. It is anhypostatos—the
> formula in which the description culminates. Or, more posi-
> tively, it is *enhypostatos*. It has personhood, subsistence, reality,
> only in its union with the Logos of God.[14]

In the *Church Dogmatics*, however, Barth clearly transitions from the incongruity of *anhypostasis* and *enhypostasis* expressed in the *Göttingen Dogmatics*, to an understanding of the interrelationship between these concepts which are now developed as a congruent/dual formula to express ontologically how the human nature of Christ exists in union with the Logos. Furthermore, we see in the *Church Dogmatics* Barth's mature development of *anhypostasis* and *enhypostasis* as ontological terms, together with the significance of his appropriation of these concepts in his Christology that becomes foundational in *The Doctrine of Reconciliation* with a specific view to Christ's union with his church.[15] Given therefore the breadth and significance of Barth's appropriation of *anhypostasis* and *enhypostasis* in

13. Barth's dogmatics work first began with his lectures at the University of Göttingen where he became the Honorary Professor of Reformed Theology in 1921.

14. Barth, *Göttingen Dogmatics*, 157.

15. The breadth of Karl Barth's usage of *anhypostasis* and *enhypostasis* extends from *Die Lehre vom Wort Gottes* (*KD* I/2) published in 1939, to *Die Lehre von der Schöpfung* (*KD* III/2) published in 1945, to *Die Lehre von der Versöhnung* (*KD* IV/2) published in 1955.

his Christology, we will review the historical/theological development and interpretation of these terms used to express the human nature of Christ considering three historical periods:

1. Orthodox Patristic Greek writers during the sixth through the eighth centuries.

2. Lutheran and Reformed Scholastic writers during the sixteenth through the eighteenth centuries.

3. Lutheran and Reformed dogmatics compilations of Heinrich Schmid and Heinrich Heppe (respectively) written during the nineteenth century (post-scholastic period).

We will review how the anhypostatos and *enhypostatos* (together with other formulations of these terms) were used by orthodox writers throughout these periods of christological development to express ontologically the human nature of Christ in union with the Logos. This analysis will also serve as a frame of historical reference for understanding these concepts and their use by orthodox theologians juxtaposed against Barth's own understanding and appropriation in his Christology. This will in turn provide a theological gauge to measure Barth's understanding of these concepts compared to the orthodox tradition.

Anhypostasis and *Enhypostasis*: Patristic Period Formulation

Prelude

The Council of Chalcedon's ontological formulation of Jesus Christ as "one hypostasis with two natures," coupled with the theological opposition raised against it became the impetus for orthodox patristic writers to explain and defend Christ's human nature consistent with the Chalcedonian definition.[16] The Council's language expressing the person of Jesus Christ as *very God* and *very man* is concise and decisive:

16. In view of the Chalcedon language describing Jesus Christ as one hypostasis with two natures, both the Alexandrians and Antiochenes were concerned with finding language that adequately describes the center of Christ's will and action. The two sides, however, disagreed over the identity of the primary agent in Christ. Cyril's focus centered on the Logos in Christ, whereas Nestorius focused on the man assumed in Christ. The Antiochenes preferred to describe the stability and unity of Christ by using prosopon (person); that is, a legal person (*persona*). In contrast, Cyril of Alexandria preferred the language of physis (nature), which implied the unity of the acting and encountered Logos. However, when Cyril of Alexandria used his trademark phrase

Following the holy Fathers we teach with one voice that the Son [of God] and our Lord Jesus Christ is to be confessed as one and the same [Person], that he is perfect in Godhead and perfect in manhood, very God and very man, of a reasonable soul and [human] body consisting, consubstantial with the Father as touching his Godhead, and consubstantial with us as touching his manhood; made in all things like unto us, sin only excepted; begotten of his Father before the worlds according to his Godhead; but in these last days for us men and for our salvation born [into the world] of the Virgin Mary, the Mother of God according to his manhood. This one and the same Jesus Christ, the only–begotten Son [of God] must be confessed to be in two natures, unconfusedly, immutably, indivisibly, inseparably [united], and that without the distinction of natures being taken away by each union, but rather the peculiar property of each nature being preserved and being united in one Person and subsistence, not separated or divided into two persons, but one and the same Son and only–begotten, God the Word, our Lord Jesus Christ, as the prophets of old time have spoken concerning him, and as the Lord Jesus Christ hath taught us, and as the Creed of the Fathers hath delivered to us.[17]

The Chalcedon definition set out to establish a true incarnation of the Logos which denied both the conversion of God into humanity and the conversion of humanity into God—and the consequent absorption of the one into the other. That is, the Council was concerned with the actual and abiding union of two natures—*very God* and *very man*—in the one personal life of Jesus Christ. Nature or substance (*ousia*) represents the totality of powers and qualities that constitute a being; whereas, person or hypostasis (*prosopon*) is the self-asserting and acting subject.[18] That being said, Chalcedon's formulation of Jesus Christ as "one hypostasis in two natures" shows the Council's concern with determining the levels of unity and distinction in Christ. It is the differentiation between hypostasis and physis that developed out of this problem.[19] In spite of the almost unanimous declaration of the

---

"one incarnate nature (mia physis) of God the Logos," he could still distinguish the intact divine and human natures (physeis, plural) that are united in Christ. See Driver, *Christ at the Center*, 219. We note also that as the Nicene doctrine of the Trinity marks the half way point between Tritheism and Sabellianism, so the Chalcedonian formula marks the mid-way point between Nestorianism and Eutychianism. See Schaff, *Creeds of Christendom*, 130.

17. Percival, *Nicene* and *Post-Nicene Fathers*, 14:264–65.

18. See Schaff, *Creeds of Christendom*, 30.

19. See Grillmeier, "Christological Definitions," 75. See Wesche, "Christology of

bishops in favor of Chalcedon's formulation (as was true for all new councils that differed from previous tradition), reception was not an instant event. In fact, the Council's formulation was met by clearly delineated opponents. Depending on the spiritual or psychological presuppositions of the parties, the result could be fruitful dialogue, or irreconcilable opposition. Both cases are found in the aftermath of Chalcedon.[20]

In response to Chalcedon the Monophysites voiced their opposition to the Council's formulation[21] and branded it as nothing more than a thinly veiled Nestorianism.[22] Ongoing Monophysite rejection of Chalcedon precipitated debate over the ontological union of Christ's divine and human natures well into the eight century. Chalcedon apologists who argued against the co-mixture of Christ's natures (as purported by the Monophysites) faced the challenge of balancing their argument against the conclusion that distinguishing between the divine and human natures logically issues two separate persons (as purported by the Nestorians). In the Monophysite opposition to Chalcedon, Severus of Antioch argued that "there is no nature without prosopon," i.e., concrete individual ("ουκ εστι φυσις απροσωπος").[23] This axiom was often used by miaphysites in their attacks on Chalcedonian Christology claiming that the doctrine of one prosopon or hypostasis in two natures is merely a disguised Nestorianism because it necessarily implies two prosopa (persons).[24]

Leontius," who points to Chalcedon's use of the terms hypostasis and nature (*physis*) as a way to synthesize the language and thought of Pope Leo I and Cyril.

20. See Grillmeier, *Christ in Christian Tradition*, 2.4:1.

21. See Lohse, *Short History of Christian Doctrine*, 94. Rather than bringing unity to the Christological debate over the two natures of Christ, the Chalcedonian Creed revived the conflict between the Monophysites and the Nestorians. Many followers of Alexandrian Christology believed that Chalcedon did not sufficiently take into account their concern to emphasize more the unity of the two natures in the person of Christ.

22. See Young, *From Nicea to Chalcedon*, 239. The Nestorians argued that the two natures of Christ presupposed two persons. Nestorius himself was chiefly concerned with the sharp division between the human and divine; that is, between the creator and the created. This was an axiomatic principle that he defended at all costs, a distinction that Chalcedon made no attempt to resolve except simply to affirm two natures in one, and one in two without separation or mixture. This in fact was the confession that Nestorius was trying to establish.

23. Severus, also known as the Patriarch of Antioch (512–18), was a leading opponent of Chalcedon's formula defining the person of Christ as one hypostasis with two natures. See Grillmeier, *Christ in Christian Tradition*, 2.2:19. Severus claimed that his opponents argued: "it was in his ousia that the Logos of God endured the saving cross and took upon himself the passion on our behalf," and that they "would not consent to call the one Lord and our God and Savior Jesus Christ homoousios with us in the flesh"; see Pelikan, *Christian Tradition*, 1:269.

24. Lang, "*Anhypostasis–Enhypostasis*," 636.

It was during this critical period of christological development that the terms *enypostaton* and *anypostaton* found expression from the pens of Chalcedon apologists in their defense of the human nature of Christ against Monophysite and Nestorian protagonists.[25] It is in consideration of these arguments and the use of the terms *anypostaton* and *enypostaton* to define the human nature of Christ that we turn our attention toward the following questions:

1. Was there a consensus agreement among orthodox patristic writers in their use of the terms *anypostatos* and *enypostatos* to describe the human nature of Christ?

2. If there were any distinctions in the use of these terms, what were they, and what impact did they have in this area of Christology?

3. Did those who used the language of *anypostatos* and *enhypostatos* depart in any significant way from the language and orthodox interpretation of Chalcedon?

Our analysis of the terms *anypostatos* and *enypostatos* used by Chalcedon apologists to express the human nature of Christ in the patristic period will consider four theologians whose writings were influential and authoritative: (1) John of Caesarea, (2) Leontius of Byzantium, (3) Leontius of Jerusalem, and (4) John of Damascus.

John of Caesarea

John of Caesarea (early sixth century theologian also known as John the Grammarian) is recognized by scholars as an early and leading defender of the Chalcedon formula defining Christ as one person with two natures. An opponent of Severus, John developed a more structured defense of Chalcedon's definition of the two natures of Christ citing Cyril as a supporter of his argument.[26] John is also recognized as the first theologian to give prominence to the term *enhypostatos* in Christology.[27] In his work entitled *Apologia Concilii Chalcedonensis* John responds to Severus's claim that there

25. The term *enypostaton* is the adjectival form of hypostasis, and is used to describe a being with subsistence in itself. Some scholars such as Aloys Grillmeier use the more traditional transliteration *enhypostaton* (with an "h"). Other forms of this terminology include *enhypostatos* and anhypostatos as noted in the text of this chapter. The term *anypostaton* is the adjectival form of hypostasis, and is used to describe a being without subsistence in itself.

26. See Grillmeier, *Christ in Christian Tradition*, 2.2:24–25.

27. See Lang, "Anhypostasis–Enhypostasis," 632.

is no nature without prosopon, where Severus argues that Chalcedon's definition of Christ as "one prosopon/hypostasis with two natures" is simply a
disguised Nestorianism because it implies two prosopa.[28] In his response
to Severus, John introduces the term ενυποστατος to explain the human
nature of Christ. Interestingly, John argues that Severus (who himself held
that the union in Christ came out of two natures) would be forced to admit
that this union came out of two prosopa following his own line of logic.[29]
John, however, does not develop his argument against Severus using the
well known Cyrillian formula "ενωσις καθ υποστασιν" to express the human nature of Christ, but instead coins a new term ενυποστατος, which he
uses to describe a sense of "existing" or being "real" to explain the Christology of Chalcedon.[30] This is evident in his interpretation of Athanasius's
exegesis of υπαρσις in Jeremiah 9:9 (LXX). John explains:

> Therefore if someone according to this comment speaks of the
> substances as *enhypostatoi,* that is existing, not even we would
> deny that. For the hypostasis is not different from the substance
> as for existence, but insofar as the one exists as common, namely
> the substance, the hypostasis, however, as proper, whenever to-
> gether with that which is universal it is also in possession of that
> which is proper.[31]

John uses *physis* in relation to *nature* to explain the Chalcedon formula
of "one hypostasis with two natures" via the concept of *ousia.* For Chalcedon
and Severus alike, the controversy about concepts revolved around the word
physis and its meaning. In his effort to "prove the legitimacy of the "two *physeis*" of Chalcedon, John called in the concept *ousia.* By precise definition he
attempted to contrast *ousia* with the concept hypostasis and to give it its own
function in establishing the two-nature formula."[32] In so doing John clarifies
the term *ousia* to express the "real existence" of Christ's human nature and
its relation to hypostasis while being careful to show that being real in this
sense does not make the humanity of Christ into a hypostasis, nor a second

28. Ibid., 636.

29. Ibid. Baillie notes with respect to the fifth century controversy with Nestorius,
that Cyril of Alexandria "worked out the idea, which passed into Catholic dogma, that
there was no man Jesus existing independently of the Divine Logos: the human element
in the Incarnation was simply human *nature* assumed by the second person of the Trinity. There was no human *hypostasis* or *persona*: the *persona* was the Divine Son, while
the human nature was ανυποστατος;" see Baillie, *God was in Christ,* 85–86.

30. Lang, "*Anhypostasis–Enhypostasis,*" 636.

31. Ibid., 637. Lang cites John of Caesarea, *Apologia Concilii Chalcedonensis,*
55.200–56.211.

32. Grillmeier, *Christ in Christian Tradition,* 2.2:54.

person. John argues (with reference to Cyril of Alexandria and Athanasius), the closeness of the hypostasis concept to "reality" or "existence."[33] In this way John introduces into the discussion a new concept—*enhypostaton*— "through which what is common to *ousia* and *hypostasis* is brought into relief and what is special, which differentiates both, is bracketed."[34]

Furthermore, in John's use of the term *enhypostaton* to defend the reality of Christ's human nature (by its existence in the hypostasis of the person of Christ) we see its fundamental meaning: "it is existence, reality, in the sense of υπαρσις." This emerges out of John's struggle for his "formula of two *ousiai*." With respect to reality, ousia is equivalent to hypostasis. Therefore, the distinction is not determined by a sense of reality, but in the mode of existing: "the *ousia* exists as the universal in the individuals, while the hypostasis signifies the final, concrete individual substance." It is therefore clear that the *enhypostaton* is definitely present in the hypostasis. This means: "to be real as hypostasis. The prefix *en* does not refer to another being in which this hypostasis would inexist, but rather to the proper reality of this concrete *enhypostaton*."[35] John, however, is hesitant to express both divine and human substances (natures) of Christ as *enypostatos*, evidently out of concern that this might imply two separate (proper) individuals, i.e., hypostases. Rather, he argues that ενυποστατος, if applied to substance or nature simply indicates real existence without reference to mode. Therefore, being ενυποστατος does not imply that it is a proper hypostasis over the common substance.[36] John concludes that:

> Consequently we do not say that our [i.e. the human] substance is *enhypostatos* in Christ, as a characteristic hypostasis on its own and being a prosopon, but insofar as it has a concrete existence and is. For sometimes hypostasis, i.e., substance, indicates having a concrete existence, as is shown when it is deprived of the properties characteristic of it and seen as belonging to the prosopon.[37]

John's point of emphasis with respect to ενυποστατος simply means that the humanity of Christ enjoys real existence, but an existence separate from that which characterizes the individual (prosopon). John furthermore argues that "το υφεστηκεναι" (i.e., concrete existence) can be attributed

33. Ibid., 58.

34. Ibid. Grillmeier cites John's *Apologia*.

35. Grillmeier, *Christ in Christian Tradition*, 2.2:63. Grillmeier cites John's *Apologia*.

36. Lang, "*Anhypostasis–Enhypostasis*," 637.

37. Ibid. Lang cites John of Caesarea, *Apologia Concilii Chalcedonensis*, 55.203–56.208.

to the ousia even if it does not contain the properties necessary to make it a prosopon. *Ousia*, therefore, may be called ενυποστατος. The question remains, however, in what way can the ousia (Christ's human nature) exist concretely if not as a hypostasis or prosopon of its own? John's response is that the human nature is ενυποστατος in Christ.[38]

John responds to Severus's argument that there is no nature without hypostasis by explaining how the human ousia (nature) of Christ is united (ενυποστατως) with the divine hypostasis of the Logos. Specifically, John argues that which belongs to the flesh becomes the property of the Logos since it is his own flesh. Based on John's interpretation of Cyrillian Christology, this appropriation of the ousia implies that the human nature of Christ is taken up into the hypostasis of the Son of God in a way that individual existence is communicated to it as the ensouled flesh that becomes proper to him.[39] John emphasizes the reality of the two natures of Christ and dismisses Severus's charge of Nestorianism by arguing that both divinity and humanity are proper to Christ. The divine nature belongs to Christ by virtue of His divine essence τη φυσει, whereas the human nature belongs to him by virtue of its union with the Logos ενυποστατος ενωσις. John's use of the term ενυποστατος therefore allows him to avoid any notion that each nature has a hypostasis of its own.[40] John concludes that: "Two or more natures can be seen in one and the same prosopon, when there is an *enhypostatos* union of them. For if they were divided, each would be recognized in a person of its own hypostasis."[41]

Furthermore, John uses the term ενυποστατος to express the reality of Christ's human nature whose mode of existence is realized in an individualized hypostasis, and dismisses any thought of existence as an accident—which is properly speaking, ανυποστατα. Therefore, based on John's use of the formula ενυποστατος ενωσις, which indicates that both the divinity and humanity of Christ exist in one hypostasis of the Logos, they can be realized in the same prosopon. Moreover, John's argument is peculiar to the person of Christ; that is, the human nature exists in a real and distinct essence in the person of Christ as *enhypostatos*. While John uses the term *enhypostatos* to primarily mean "having a concrete existence," it implies that a common

38. Ibid., 637–38.

39. Ibid., 638. Lang cites John of Caesarea, *Apologia Concilii Chalcedonensis,* 57.259–61, and explains that "This is the way in which the human nature of Christ is to be conceived as individualized. The Grammarian's formula ενωσις ενυποστατος serves the purpose to denote this unique manner of existence."

40. Ibid., 639.

41. Ibid. Lang cites John of Caesarea, *Capitula XVII contra Monophysitas:* CCG 1, 64.107–10, cf. 122–24.

nature or substance always exists as being individualized *in* a hypostasis. This describes the peculiarity of the incarnation where the ensouled flesh is taken up into the hypostasis of the Son of God, and as such, is given individual existence in this unique manner.[42]

Leontius of Byzantium

Perhaps the most controversial of the patristic orthodox writers is Leontius of Byzantium (490–544) whose use of the term *enypostaton* to describe the human nature of Christ has spawned considerable theological debate. Virtually all scholars today agree that Leontius of Byzantium is the same sixth century monk who wrote *Contra Nestorianos et Eutychianos* (*CNE*) in his defense of Christ's human nature against the Eutychian heresy. Moreover, Leontius took part in several important theological discussions, including a formal conference between the Chalcedonians and Monophysites in 533 where he worked to balance the emphasis of Leo and Chalcedon on the distinctiveness of Christ by further exploring the unity of Christ.[43]

Leontius wrote *Contra Nestorianos et Eutychianos* to demonstrate that the formula of Chalcedon is the "golden" mean between two diametrically opposed but equally heretical positions. That is, Leontius set out to refute the Nestorian and Monophysite arguments that question the viability of the Chalcedon position.[44] Moreover, as a harmonizer of Cyril and Chalcedon, Leontius uses the term *enhypostatos* to explain how the human nature of Christ exists in the hypostasis of the Logos (not being an accident) and how two natures can exist concretely together while having only one hypostasis between them.[45] Leontius argues that when the Word became flesh and dwelt among us he received into his own hypostasis a human nature that was perfect and entire, the result of which is that both the divine and human natures exist together without division or confusion in the one pre-existent hypostasis of the Logos. While the human nature does not possess a separate hypostasis of its own, it is united with the divine nature in the hypostasis of the Logos. In other words, the human nature is "enhypostatic."[46]

The principle question raised with respect to Leontius is: did he use the term *enypostaton* to develop a new philosophical understanding of the human nature of Christ (reaching beyond Chalcedon) or simply as a means to

---

42. Ibid., 639–40.

43. See Hardy and Richardson, *Christology of the Later Fathers*, vol. 3, 375.

44. See Krausmüller, "Making Sense of the Formula of Chalcedon," 486.

45. See Lynch, "Leontius of Byzantium," 459.

46. See Rees, "Byzantium and His Defense," 111–12.

affirm the Chalcedon definition of Christ's human nature? This question of interpretation is centered on the sixth-century monk's alleged redefinition of the term *enypostaton* to represent a nature that does not have existence in its own hypostasis, but in the hypostasis of another nature. This opinion presupposes that Leontius formulated a philosophical theory with the help of a new meaning for *enypostaton* as a way to help explain how two natures can exist in a single hypostasis.[47] A proper understanding of Leontius's use of the term *enypostaton* therefore becomes the crucial factor in interpreting his ontological view of the human nature of Christ. With this in mind, we take notice that Leontius's aim in Book 3 of *CNE* was to oppose the Monophysites without compromising with the Nestorians as he sought to clarify the use of the terms hypostasis and ousia to describe the human nature of Christ.[48] Leontius states as his purpose in the prologue:

> [Since] the definition of [the terms] hypostasis and ousia . . .
> remains confused and vague among those now counted wise,
> I have undertaken to elucidate and clarify [them]. This is the
> christological exigency that Leontius is addressing.[49]

Given therefore the aim of Leontius in Book 3 of *CNE* is to develop a polemic against anti-Chalcedonian views of Christ's human nature, the question is how did Leontius use the term *enypostaton* to define the human nature of Christ? The traditional reading of Leontius understood him to give the term "enhypostasized" a new and nontraditional metaphysical meaning that enabled him to avoid the heresy that Jesus Christ existed in two hypostases. This interpretation is commonly attributed primarily to the influence of Friedrich Loofs, and became a critical factor in influencing how contemporary theologians viewed Leontius's development of the human nature of Christ.[50] Loofs interpreted Leontius in a way that reached beyond the Chalcedonian formula as he asked if one can speak of a terminological progress in understanding the person of Jesus Christ after the Council of Chalcedon and the ongoing conflicts between defenders and opponents of its formula. Loofs claimed that Leontius used the term *enhypostatos* to express the human nature of Christ as existing not "in itself" but "within something else," namely the incarnate Logos.[51]

47. See Shults, "Dubious Christological Formula," 431.

48. Ibid., 434.

49. Ibid., 431. Shults cites David Evans's translation of *Leontius of Byzantium* 15.

50. Ibid., 436.

51. See Gockel, "A Dubious Christological Formula," 517. Gockel notes that it was Loofs's study entitled *Leontius von Byzanz und die gleichnamigen Schriftsteller der griechischen Kirche*, which began a revival of scholarship on Leontius.

Loofs claimed that Leontius developed the concept of something having a hypostasis "not in itself," but in the hypostasis of "another nature." If this translation proved to be accurate it would indeed suggest a dramatic departure from the language of Chalcedon. Moreover, based upon the influence of Loofs, this reading of Leontius was almost unanimously accepted as playing a special role in the development of Christian doctrine.[52] Loofs interprets Leontius to say: "The human nature in Christ is not *anypostatos*, nor itself an hypostasis, but *enypostatos* (1277D), that is, it has its *hypostenai* εν το λογο."[53] Loofs, however, misinterpreted Leontius's use of the term *enhypostaton* to mean that which exists within *something else*, rather than that which has concrete existence *in itself*. Therefore, given that Chalcedon refers to one hypostasis only, and that Leontius did not find another meaning for hypostasis, he did not advance much beyond Chalcedon in his ontology of the human nature of Christ.[54]

The proper interpretation of the term *enhypostaton* is to possess concrete existence. In other words, that which is *enhypostaton* enjoys actual being in itself. As such, the prefix *en* in this compound word is the opposite of the alpha privatiuum (e.g., a-hypostaton) and precisely means to possess that property which was denied by the negation. Therefore, *enhypostaton* simply means to have *concrete existence* or *actuality*.[55] Loofs, however, misinterpreted a passage in Leontius's *CNE* where Leontius introduces the distinction between hypostasis (referring to an individual) and *enhypostaton* (referring to substance). In *CNE* Leontius explains that *hypostasis* and the *enhypostatized* (ενυποστατον) are not the same thing. Where hypostasis refers to the *individuum*, hypostatic refers to the essence. Moreover, hypostasis defines the person (*prosopon*) by means of particular characteristics. The *enhypostatized* (ενυποστατον), however, means that it is not an accident.[56] The debated sentence in Leontius's *CNE* reads: "the enhypostasized means, however, that it is not an accident; [the latter] has its being in another and is not perceived in itself; of this kind are all qualities."[57]

Loofs's error was in attributing the phrase "has its being in another" to *enhypostaton* instead of συμβεβηκος. However, contrary to Loofs's

52. See Shults, "Dubious Christological Formula," 436.

53. Ibid., 437.

54. Ibid. Aloys Grillmeier also notes that precisely at the time of Leontius the old meaning of *enhypostatos* as "in its own reality" still held. See Grillmeier, *Christ in Christian Tradition*, vol. 2, 195.

55. Ibid., 438.

56. See Grillmeier, *Christ in Christian Tradition*, vol. 2 194. Grillmeier cites Leontius in *Contra Nestorianos et Eutychianos (CNE)*.

57. Ibid.

interpretation, Leontius emphasizes that although the *enhypostaton* is not the same as a hypostasis; it exists as its own reality and is not an accident.[58] Moreover, Leontius distinguishes between hypostasis and physis.[59] A nature is not a hypostasis because there is no reversal in this relationship. While a hypostasis is also a nature, a nature is not yet a hypostasis. A nature satisfies the definition of being (ειναι), and a hypostasis also satisfies the definition of being by itself (καθ εαυτο ειναι). Nature fits the definition of species, while hypostasis signifies individuality. Nature shows the character of a general object, while hypostasis distinguishes what is particular from the common.[60]

Leontius explains that in Christ the human nature does not possess a separate hypostasis of its own, but is united with the divine nature in the hypostasis of the Logos. Leontius argues against the Nestorians that the human nature of Christ did not exist in a hypostasis peculiar to it alone, but in the hypostasis of the Logos, which existed before it. Although the hypostasis of the Logos has a divine nature and its properties, it does not stand in these alone, but also supplies those characteristics resulting from the assumption of a more recent nature (i.e., human nature).[61] Moreover, Leontius draws the ontological distinction between *enhypostaton* and *anhypostaton* arguing against the notion that a human nature in Christ must either exist as a separate human hypostasis or else admit that this human nature is merely a figment of the imagination.[62] Leontius argues that *enhypostaton* indicates that something is not an accident, but has being in another. To say that a nature as *anhypostaton* does not exist is a true statement. However, it is not correct to conclude from this statement that the opposite of anhypostatos is a hypostasis. As anhypostatos, a nature (or substance) will therefore never exist in itself. Nature is not hypostasis because the argument is not reversible: "hypostasis is also nature, but nature is not yet also hypostasis."[63]

Although Leontius's understanding of the ontological relationship between hypostasis and physis applies to the human nature of Christ, he leaves unclear the distinction between hypostasis and physis . . . "it follows that the manhood of Christ would also have to be characterized as *hypostasis*. For Jesus of Nazareth is a concrete individual human being; he has his *notao characteristicae* which distinguish him as a human being from other human

---

58. See Gockel, "A Dubious Christological Formula," 518.

59. Ibid.

60. Ibid., 518–19.

61. See Rees, "Byzantium and His Defense," 112.

62. See Krausmüller, "Making Sense of the Formula of Chalcedon," 487.

63. Ibid., "Making Sense of the Formula of Chalcedon," 487. Krausmüller cites Leontius of Byzantium, *CNE*.

beings."[64] Furthermore, throughout *CNE* Leontius fails to realize the consequence of his distinction between nature and *hypostasis*. "Not even once does he ask himself whether the human nature of Christ is individualized through the *idia* [of a human being]."[65]

In contrast to his work in *CNE*, Leontius does not distinguish between hypostasis and *enhypostasis* in his work entitled *Epilyseis*. While he relates nature (*physis*) to substance (*ousia*), he does not further develop the relationship between *enhypostasis* and being. In *CNE* he relates hypostasis to being as "being in itself"; however, in *Epilyseis* hypostasis is simply characterized by the ratio of accidents. In both works hypostasis is somehow related to the individual, but is also characterized by accidents in the *Epilyseis*. In the end, the relation between nature and hypostasis remains unexplained by Leontius. Furthermore, the distinction between substance and hypostasis confuses rather than clarifies the idea of hypostasis in relation to the *enhypostasis*. Perhaps this lack of clarity can be attributed to Leontius' desire to avoid the charge of Nestorianism in his debate with a miaphysite. Notwithstanding this difficulty, in both treatises Leontius argues that the properties of the natures are preserved in their union in the one hypostasis of Christ.[66]

We note here that F. LeRon Shults claims (and rightly so) that Karl Barth appropriated *anhypostasis* and *enhypostasis* as a dual formula to describe the human nature of Christ, which moves beyond the autonomous treatment of these terms by Leontius of Byzantium.[67] In this way Barth understands the *anhypostasis* to express (negatively) that the human nature of Christ has no subsistence outside its union with the Logos, but realizes its subsistence positively as *enhypostasis* in this union. Shults, however, further argues that Barth appropriated *anhypostasis* and *enhypostasis* as a dual formula based upon the invention of Protestant Scholasticism through his reading of Heinrich Heppe and Heinrich Schmid. I argue against Shults and will show that the Protestant Scholastics appropriated *anhypostasis* and *enhypostasis* consistent with the patristic Fathers (including Leontius of Byzantium) as autonomous concepts to explain the human nature of Christ. U. M. Lang makes this point and notes that Barth's appropriation of *anhypostasis* and *anhypostasis* as a dual formula is an innovation all is own.[68] I agree with Lang, but will further argue throughout this book that Barth's adoption of *anhypostasis* and *enhypostasis* is not only unique to his

---

64. Grillmeier, "Christological Definitions," 80.

65. Grillmeier, *Christ in Christian Tradition*, vol. 2, 193.

66. See Gockel, "A Dubious Christological Formula," 522.

67. See Shults, "Dubious Christological Formula," 431.

68. See Lang, "*Anhypostasis–Enhypostasis*," 632.

Christology, but in fact becomes the ontological foundation of his Christology as a whole.

Leontius of Jerusalem

Leontius of Jerusalem is recognized as the sixth century contemporary of Leontius of Byzantium who as a member of Justinian's court wrote between the years 538–544. According to manuscript tradition, "the all-wise monk lord Leontius of Jerusalem" wrote two theological treatises called "Against the Nestorians" and "Against the Monophysites." As indicated by the titles, Leontius used these treatises to defend the Chalcedon definition of the two natures of Christ against both Nestorian and Monophysite attacks.[69] Moreover, in his polemic Leontius sought to synthesize the writings of Cyril and Chalcedon in his defense of the human nature of Christ.[70] Compared to Leontius of Byzantium, Leontius of Jerusalem introduces a more distinctive version of the one subject in Christ using the concept of one hypostasis with two natures.[71]

The sixth century concept of hypostasis was generally understood to be a nature with properties, where nature is understood as the foundation of being, and properties being added to render an individual (or hypostasis). Leontius, however, marks a distinct shift in this thinking by arguing that the hypostasis is conceptually distinguished from natures and not produced by them. We see therefore in Leontius of Jerusalem an important transition in the ontological expression of Christ where the hypostasis takes priority over nature as the foundation of nature's existence. For Leontius, "the hypostasis itself is the foundation and not the product of being: it is the υττοκειμενον πραγμα, 'the underlying reality', or if you will, the 'real subject.'"[72]

The conceptual problems confronted by Leontius of Byzantium with respect to nature and hypostasis were dealt with more successfully by Leontius of Jerusalem who understands *enhypostaton* as "having a concrete existence." The divine and human natures are said to be "enhypostasized," or realized, in one hypostasis.[73] With this in view the first advance of Leontius of Jerusalem is that he consciously distinguished between a union of natures (*unio in natura et secundum naturam*) and a union of *hypostasis* (*unio in hypostasi et secundum hypostasim*) in the incarnation of Christ. That is, "the

69. See Krausmüller, "Leontius of Jerusalem," 637.

70. See Wesche, "Christology of Leontius," 65.

71. See Grillmeier, *Christ in Christian Tradition*, vol. 2, 276.

72. See Wesche, "Christology of Leontius," 73.

73. See Gockel, "A Dubious Christological Formula," 523.

Logos does not assume an additional *hypostasis* in order now to attain the perfection of the hypostasis; he possesses only the (hypostasis) which he also had after the addition of the *nature* which he did not have."[74] Moreover, and perhaps just as important in this context is Leontius's claim that the human nature of Christ does not exist *anhypostaton*, nor does it exist idio-hypostaton (of its own) because it possesses its hypostasis in the Logos.[75] Leontius states that:

> The two natures, we say, subsist in one and the same hypostasis, admittedly not as if one of the two could be in it anhypostati-cally, but rather that both can subsist in the common hyposta-sis . . . whereby each of the two natures is enhypostatic. For in order to be something, it is necessary that this same thing is also wholly on its own. If the natures have being, they must also subsist υφιστημι and be enhypostatic. But because they are not independent of each other . . . it is not necessary that each of the two exists on its own. Thus it is clear that the two *enhypostata* must not be *heterohypostata* (=hypostasis beside hypostasis), but are thought of as being in one and the same *hypostasis*.[76]

Leontius clearly distinguishes the human nature of Jesus from the hypostasis in which it exists (the pre-existent Logos) because the divine act affects both the creation (ουσιωσις) of the human nature and its unification (συνουσιωσις) with the divine hypostasis.[77] In the polemical treatise *Adversus Nestorianos* Leontius attributes ενυποστατος to (ουσια/ φυσις) in the sense of "having concrete existence" while also being indi-vidualized in a hypostasis. He explains whereas in the Trinity there are "τρεις υποστασεις ενουσιους εν μια ουσια," so in Christ there are "φυσεις . . . ενυποστατους δυο εν μια υποστασει." With this explanation Leon-tius first denies that the two natures of Christ are ανυποστατοι (without concrete reality), and secondly denies that two hypostases exist in Christ. Much like John of Caesarea, Leontius is responding to the misconceived interpretation of the Chalcedon definition of two natures in Christ as being ετερουποστατοι or ιδιουποστατοι, implying a doctrine of two hypostases.[78] Furthermore, Leontius (again like John of Caesarea before

74. See Grillmeier, *Christ in Christian Tradition*, vol. 2, 276–77. Grillmeier also cites Leontius of Jerusalem in *Contra Nestorianos*.

75. See Gockel, "A Dubious Christological Formula," 523.

76. See Grillmeier, *Christ in Christian Tradition*, vol. 2, 285. Grillmeier translates Leontius of Jerusalem in *Contra Nestorianos*.

77. See Gockel, "A Dubious Christological Formula," 524.

78. See Lang, "*Anhypostasis–Enhypostasis*," 640–41.

him) draws attention to the necessary ontology of the divine and human natures of Christ existing concretely as ενυποστατοι.The term *enhypostatos*, therefore, represents the two natures of Christ existing in one and the same hypostasis.[79] Leontius explains:

> For we say that the two natures concretely exist in one and the same hypostasis, not as if one of them could exist without a hypostasis in it, but as if both could subsist in the one common hypostasis; and so each of the two is *enhypostatos* according to one and the same hypostasis. Thus it is evident that the *enhypostaton* cannot be *heterohypostaton*, but must be thought of in one and the same hypostasis for both of them.[80]

Therefore, with respect to development of the hypostatic union in Christ we see in Leontius of Jerusalem a clear transition in ontological thought from that of Leontius of Byzantium. Furthermore, Leontius of Jerusalem achieves a clearer interpretation of the hypostatic union in affirming that the Logos "hypostatically inserted (ενυπεστησεν) the flesh into his own hypostasis (τη ιδια υποστασει) and not into that of a simple human being." Leontius therefore ushers in a great christological concept where the verb (υφιστημι/υποσταναι) with the prefix εν becomes the technical expression for "to cause to subsist in" and in the second aorist for "to subsist in." The theological result is Leontius can propose that simultaneous with the creation of Christ's human nature and its physical existence, the human nature of Christ becomes subsistent in the hypostasis of the Logos. It therefore exists strictly as the existence of the Logos in the world. As such, the human nature of Christ never exists separately as an independent human subject."[81]

Moreover, Leontius defines hypostasis as that which underlies the union of one or more natures, but not the union of natures themselves. Rather, the hypostasis is an invisible point that can be made more complex by additions, but also cannot be diminished to nothing because in its simplicity it is not comprised of parts. Leontius anticipates the trinitarian implications given this ontological context by distinguishing hypostasis from physis (or nature); in that hypostasis is a particular, but not a particular *nature*.[82] Leontius concludes that because the hypostasis of Christ is separated from all human beings who exist outside of him, and natures can

---

79. Ibid., 641.

80. See Gockel, "A Dubious Christological Formula," Gockel cites Leontius of Jerusalem in *Adversus Nestorianos*.

81. See Gockel, "A Dubious Christological Formula," 525.

82. See Wesche, "Christology of Leontius," 73–74. Wesche cites Leontius of Jerusalem in *Adversus Nestorianos*.

be united in the same hypostasis without confusion, the hypostasis is that essence governing a nature existing in distinction from another nature. The human nature therefore maintains its own individual and distinct nature even in union with the nature of the divine Logos. However, it is not possible for a hypostasis to be united to another hypostasis comprising two hypostaseis because the hypostasis being separate from others is the most intimate property of individuals.[83] That Leontius distinguishes between hypostasis and nature, where hypostasis is the foundation rather than the product of its constitution, allows him to defend charges that his Christology purports the production of a new composite physis or hypostasis. Leontius makes this point clear:

> The union is of natures in the hypostasis, that is to say, there is a union of one nature with the other, but from these natures there has not been produced a composite nature, since they are not united by confusion, nor is there a union of hypostaseis since the union is not of hypostaseis. But the properties of the hypostasis of the Logos have become more composite, since it accumulates more properties in itself along with its own simple properties after the incarnation, which proves that neither his nature nor his hypostasis is composite or mutable.[84]

Leontius also understands that the divine hypostasis of the Logos is a composite, which possesses more than one property, and becomes more composite through the addition of the properties of humanity. As such, the simple hypostasis of the Logos combines properties of the divine and human natures. The hypostasis itself, however, remains simple, indivisible, and immutable. Being the foundation and principle of the existence of natures, the hypostasis is distinguished conceptually from its own constitution of natures, being able to receive new natures without being altered. But the hypostasis—as one subject—cannot be united with another hypostasis without either becoming a juxtaposition of two subjects, which is not a true union, or becoming another subject altogether resulting in its alteration. The hypostasis therefore is open to receive other natures and properties, but not another hypostasis. That being said, Leontius does not view the human nature of Christ as being absorbed into the hypostasis of the Logos, but remains as a "particular nature" in this union.[85] Leontius states that: "We say the Logos assumed a certain particular nature from our nature into

---

83. Ibid., 75–76. Wesche cites Leontius of Jerusalem in *Adversus Nestorianos*.

84. Ibid., 79. Wesche cites Leontius of Jerusalem in *Adversus Nestorianos*.

85. Ibid., 79–80.

his own hypostasis."[86] In this context Leontius uses the analogy of an iron immersed in fire to explain how a nature can be particular without being a hypostasis.[87] Leontius argues:

> But we say that just as the iron which is made red–hot in the furnace does not lose any part of its hypostasis from the species of the fire, but admits only the nature into its own hypostasis—for likewise the hypostasis of the fire in the furnace remains, lacking nothing, even after the iron becomes red–hot—so also we say that the Logos assumed from our nature a somewhat particular nature (φυσιν ιδικην τινα) into his own hypostasis.[88]

Leontius uses the term "particular" (ιδικη) to explain how the particularity of Christ's human nature does not extend to its separation from his divine nature in union with the divine hypostasis.[89] Leontius argues that the humanity in Christ is not particular in itself, but it shares with the divine nature the one hypostasis of the Logos (αντι γαρ ιδικης, κοινην). That is, instead of a human hypostasis, the human nature of Christ has acquired the divine hypostasis of the Logos, which becomes the ultimate blessedness for humanity in Christ.[90] Because the human nature remains particular in its union with the hypostasis—not mingled or confused with the divine nature—it therefore sustains its own natural definition in union with the Logos. Nature, however, does not exist except in a hypostasis. There is no such thing as nature by itself.[91] "In all other mere men, there is no nature of man that can be observed by itself, but each nature belongs to a particular someone, and is seen as an enhypostasized nature."[92]

Leontius further argues that the clearest evidence that demonstrates the human nature maintains its full reality in unity with the Logos is that in its union—the existent mode of the Logos changes—but not his divine nature. This is evidenced in the virgin birth where the hypostasis of the Logos (not the divine nature) exists in a different mode; that is, in the flesh.[93] Leontius states that: "When he was born of the woman in time he was not brought into existence, but into a certain mode of existence (ουκ ες το ειναι,

---

86. Ibid., 80. Wesche cites Leontius of Jerusalem in *Adversus Nestorianos*.

87. Ibid., 80–81.

88. Ibid., 81. Wesche cites Leontius of Jerusalem in *Adversus Nestorianos*.

89. Ibid., 81.

90. Ibid. Wesche cites Leontius of Jerusalem in *Adversus Nestorianos*.

91. Ibid., 82.

92. Ibid.

93. Ibid., 88.

αλλ εις το τοιωσδε ειναι)."[94] Ontologically speaking, Leontius explains that the hypostasis of Christ is not the mode of existence (being immutable) but that which experiences the change in the mode of existence when it assumes the human nature.[95] Regarding Christ Leontius explains:

> He is born by a certain type of generation, not by being trans-
> formed, but at the same time, he does not remain absolutely
> simple as before (ουδε απλως μενων γυμνος), nor does he re-
> main in his simple existence (εις το ειναι), nor does he remain
> in the manner of existence which describes him before, but he is
> now with the flesh; and henceforth I dare to say his hypostasis is
> altered in its manner of being in this way (εις το τοιωσδε ειναι
> το λοιπον αλλοιωθεντα πως τμν υποστασιν), not because there
> is a change of the Logos' properties, or because there is a change
> of the properties as God; but because he receives and acquires
> the other properties of Jesus, and he acquires the properties of
> the human nature (τον ανθρωπον) in the same one hypostasis of
> the Logos himself which increases and receives more properties,
> both hypostatic and natural, which surpass all prosopa on either
> side and make it consubstantial [to God and man]. Therefore,
> in no way is he formed as the Logos, but the Logos himself is
> formed as the Christ; and this happens only in reference to one
> of his parts, the flesh."[96]

For Leontius, the hypostasis is the foundation of existence and union of natures that are real and whose properties exist only in the hypostasis, and not in each other. In the person of Jesus Christ the human nature contributes its properties to the hypostasis of the Logos making it now visible and corporeal. Even so, the hypostasis itself remains unchanged as the foundation of being.[97] Leontius explains that there was not a different hypostasis before and after the incarnation. However, the Logos appears differently in his different states (αλλως δε και αλλως εμφαινομενος ο Λογος). Before his incarnation the hypostasis of the Logos was invisible only, but now it is made visible having assumed to itself a covering in the humanity of Christ.[98]

Leontius of Jerusalem understands all natures to be *enypostaton*.[99] As the foundation and principle of existence the hypostasis becomes more

94. Ibid.
95. Ibid.
96. Ibid. Wesche cites Leontius of Jerusalem in *Adversus Nestorianos*.
97. Ibid., 89.
98. Ibid.
99. See Shults, "Dubious Christological Formula," 438.

composite in receiving natures and their properties into its being. Through the union of human nature with the divine nature of the Logos, the incarnate Logos is now able to do in union what he cannot do in either nature by itself.[100] Furthermore, while for Leontius the union of the human nature renders the divine Logos truly incarnate, the human nature is in no way lost or merged into the immensity of the divine Logos. The Logos therefore becomes full humanity through the assumption of a complete and particular human nature.[101]

John of Damascus

In the eight century John of Damascus wrote *De fide orthodox* as a concise theological treaty against heresy. Incorporating the thinking of orthodox thinkers, which included Cyril of Alexandria and Leontius of Byzantium, John's aim in this work was not to submit novel views of his own, but to collect into one theological work the thinking of the ancients.[102] John also worked to reformulate the Christology of Chalcedon by setting out his understanding of the terms anhypostatos, *enhypostatos*, and hypostasis.[103] As such, John uses the terms *anypostaton* and *enypostaton* similar to Cyril and Leontius of Byzantium to explain the human nature of Christ. In Book 3, Chapter 9, of *De fide orthodox*, John refers directly to Leontius's argument in Chapter 1 of *Contra Nestorianos et Eutychianos*, and asserts that the flesh and the Word have one and the same substance. Moreover, the Damascene argues that one cannot speak of either nature as being *anypostaton*.[104] Responding to the question whether there is any nature that does not have subsistence, John states:

> For although there is no nature without subsistence, nor essence apart from person (since in truth it is in persons and subsistences that essence and nature are to be contemplated), yet it does not necessarily follow that the natures that are united in subsistence should have each its own proper subsistence. For after they have come together in one subsistence, it is possible that neither should they be without subsistence, nor should each have its own peculiar subsistence, but that each should have one and the same subsistence . . . For the flesh of God the Word

---

100. See Wesche, "Christology of Leontius," 90–91.

101. Ibid., 92.

102. See Schaff and Wace, *Nicene* and *Post Nicene Fathers*, vol. 9, Prologue, viii.

103. See Lang, "*Anhypostasis–Enhypostasis*," 649.

104. See Shults, "Dubious Christological Formula," 438.

did not subsist as an independent subsistence, nor did there arise another subsistence besides that of God the Word, but as it existed in that it became rather a subsistence which subsisted in another, than one which was an independent subsistence. Wherefore, neither does it lack subsistence altogether, nor yet is there thus introduced into the Trinity another subsistence.[105]

John's development of the Chalcedon formula demonstrates a more explicit explanation of Christ's humanity as *enhypostatos*, which denotes being in-existence in the hypostasis of the Logos.[106] The Damascene argues that the nature which has been assumed by another hypostasis exists in this hypostasis as *enhypostaton*. Therefore, the flesh of the Lord does not subsist by itself as a hypostasis, but rather *enhypostatos*. That is, the humanity of Christ "came to subsist in the hypostasis of the Logos, having been assumed by it, and has obtained and still has this very hypostasis."[107] In this way John seeks to clarify the terminological ambiguity left by the *De Sectis* and introduces another sense of *enhypostatos* which describes a nature that has been taken up by another hypostasis through which it exists.[108] This explains why the human nature does not subsist by itself and is not considered a hypostasis, but rather *enhypostatos* in relation to the Logos. This thinking is also put forward in the Damascene's work entitled the *Expositio Fidei*.[109] John explains:

For the flesh of the God-Logos did not subsist with its own subsistence, nor has it become another hypostasis in addition to the hypostasis of the God-Logos, but it has rather become *enhypostatos*, subsisting in it [i.e., the hypostasis of the God-Logos] and not a hypostasis for itself with its own subsistence. Therefore it is neither without hypostasis nor has it introduced another hypostasis into the Trinity.[110]

The interpretation of this passage has been disputed among scholars. While the late nineteenth century German theologian Josef Bach[111]

---

105. See Schaff and Wace, *Nicene* and *Post Nicene Fathers*, 9:53.

106. See Lang, "Anhypostasis–Enhypostasis," 648–49.

107. Ibid., 649–50.

108. Ibid. The work entitled *De Sectis* was written by an unknown author in the defense of the Chalcedonian formula of two natures in one hypostasis.

109. See Lang, "Anhypostasis–Enhypostasis," 650.

110. Ibid. Lang cites John of Damascus in *Expositio fidei*.

111. Ibid. Lang cites Josef Back in *Die Dogmengeschichte des Mittelalters vom christologischen Standpunkte oder Die mittelalterliche Christologie vom achten bis sechzehnten Jahrhundert*.

understands *enhypostatos* to mean "inexistent," Daley argues that such a translation is not necessary here.[112] The use of the term *enhypostatos* in combination with the phrase "εν αυτη υποστασα" suggests that its use denotes the human nature's existence in the hypostasis of the Logos.[113]

In John's work entitled *Contra Jacobitas* he cites a passage from Leontius of Byzantium's *CNE* where Leontius formulates the difference between hypostasis and *enhypostaton* by defining a person as having characteristic properties. That is, the substance is distinct from an accident because it does not exist in another subject. John further develops Leontius's definition as he draws the distinction between that which is in something (το εν τινι) and that which is (το εν ω). Whereas, the ενουσιον is that which is in the substance as a collection of accidents indicating a hypostasis (but not itself the substance), the ενυποστατον is not identical with the hypostasis, but is rather seen in the hypostasis. John's definition of ousia or "whatever exists" as that "which exists in what manner soever, whether on its own, whether with another thing or in another thing" certainly allows for its existence in another hypostasis. In this respect John gives two examples for in-existence: that of fire in a wick and that of the flesh of Christ in the eternal hypostasis of the Logos.[114]

We see also in another passage in *Contra Jacobitas* where John uses more explicit language related to *enhypostatos* to describe the in-existence of the humanity of Christ in the hypostasis of the Logos.[115] The Damascene explains that the human nature of Christ is *enhypostatos* (in-existent) because it does not exist as a proper hypostasis of its own. However, as *enhypostatos*, it has concrete existence *in* the hypostasis of the Logos.[116] Furthermore, John avoids identifying nature (or substance) with hypostasis to forestall the false conclusion drawn from the Chalcedon definition that two natures imply two separate hypostases (concrete individuals), which was charged by the miaphysites against the "Nestorianism" of the Council.[117] We see the same argument in a passage taken from John Damascene's treatise entitled *De Natura Composita contra Acephalos*, which illustrates his application of the term ενυποστατος to the union of divinity and humanity of Christ.[118] John states:

112. Ibid. Lang cites Daley in *The Christology of Leontius of Byzantium*.

113. Ibid., 650–651.

114. Ibid., 651.

115. Ibid.

116. Ibid., 652. Lang cites John of Damascus in *Contra Jacobitas*.

117. Ibid.

118. Ibid., 653.

> In some cases the *enhypostaton* means the substance, as it is seen in the hypostasis and exists on its own, while in other cases it denotes each of the individual components that have come into union in order to compose a single hypostasis. It is patent to which particular cases the second usage applies: as soul and body are united in human beings to compose one hypostasis, so the divinity and the humanity of Christ have come into union and effect one common composite hypostasis. In this respect both natures may be said to be ενυποστατος.[119]

The material point here is that John of Damascus understands ενυποστατος to represent real substance with respect to the union of divinity and humanity in Christ as one composite hypostasis. Just as the divine nature exists as real substance, so also the human nature exists as real substance.

Conclusion

We have examined the writings of four patristic Fathers who used the terms *anypostaton* and *enypostaton* to express the human nature of Christ in their defense of the Chalcedon formula: "one person with two natures." In so doing we noted the problem facing all Chalcedon apologists during this period to explain how Christ's human nature exists in its own reality in union with the Logos, yet not as a separate person within this union. We also noted in each of these patristic Fathers continuity in understanding Christ's human nature to have real and separate existence as *enypostaton* in its union with the person of the Logos, and not *anypostaton*, which suggests the absence of real existence in this union.

John of Caesarea developed the concept of *ousia* as having reality in its own substance much like the hypostasis enjoys reality in its own substance, which in turn allowed John to appropriate to *ousia* its own function in establishing the two nature formula. In this way John uses *ousia* to describe the human nature of Christ and introduces the term *enypostaton* to explain the human nature of Christ as "existing" or "real" in the hypostasis of Christ. As such, John explains how two natures can be seen in the same person, being united *enypostaton* together in Christ.

Despite the theological debate over Leontius of Byzantium with respect to the term *enypostaton*, we concluded that he did not use *enypostaton* as a way to develop a new philosophical concept of the human nature of Christ having a hypostasis "not in itself," but in the hypostasis of another

---

119. Ibid. Lang cites John of Damascus from his treatise entitled *De Natura Composita contra Acephalos.*

nature. Rather, he simply used *enypostaton* as a way to affirm the Chalcedon definition of human nature as a real substance in its being. While Leontius leaves unanswered the relationship between nature and hypostasis, he argues that the properties of the divine and human natures are preserved in their union in the one hypostasis of Christ.

Leontius of Jerusalem deals more successfully with the conceptual problems confronted by Leontius of Byzantium with respect to nature and hypostasis. Because "*enhypostaton*" means having concrete existence, the divine and human natures are "enhypostasized," or realized in one hypostasis. Leontius asserts that Christ's human nature does not exist as *anhypostaton* because it possesses its hypostasis in the Logos. In this way the two natures subsist as individual realities in one and the same hypostasis. Following the thinking of John of Caesarea, Leontius of Jerusalem emphasizes that the divine and human natures of Christ both exist concretely as *enopostatoi*; that is, in one and the same hypostasis. Moreover, John develops a clearer interpretation of the hypostatic union as he transitions from Leontius of Byzantium by arguing the Logos hypostatically inserted the flesh into his own hypostasis and not into that of a simple human being. The theological result is that Christ's human nature becomes subsistent and exists only as the existence of the Word, never as a separate existence of an independent human subject. Even so, the human nature of Christ is not absorbed into the hypostasis of the Logos, but remains a particular nature in this union. The hypostasis therefore is the foundation of existence and union of the divine and human natures that are real and exist only in the hypostasis, and not in each other.

John of Damascus cites Leontius of Byzantium in his use of the terms *anypostaton* and *enypostaton* to affirm that the flesh and the Word have one and the same substance, and argues that neither one can be understood as *anypostaton* (having no subsistence in itself). John further develops the Chalcedon formula by expressing a more explicit explanation of Christ's human nature as *enhypostatos*, which denotes being in-existence in the hypostasis of the Logos. In this way the nature which has been assumed by another hypostasis has its existence in this so called *enhypostaton*. John also describes *enhypostatos* in the sense of a nature being taken up by another hypostasis through which it has its existence. This nature therefore lacks no hypostasis nor has it introduced another hypostasis into the Trinity. John further develops *enypostaton* from Leontius of Byzantium's definition by drawing the distinction between that which is in something and that which is (exists).

Based upon our analysis of these patristic Fathers we can therefore conclude that there is indeed consensus agreement in their use of the terms *anhypostaton* and *enhypostaton* to describe the human nature of Christ. We also see a historical progression of ontological development in the use of these terms rather than disagreement over the substance of the human nature of Christ. Furthermore, we find no departure or disparity from the language and thinking of Chalcedon in the use of these terms, but an affirmation of its definition: "one person with two natures." In addition, the concept of *anhypostaton* is not used in a negative sense to describe the existence of Christ's human nature, but simply as a way to assert that its substance exists not in itself but in the person (hypostasis) of the Logos. Therefore, the use of the terms *anhypostaton* and *enhypostaton* as a dual formula to describe the human nature of Christ is not a valid doctrinal expression of these patristic Fathers.

Finally, as I have noted, F. LeRon Shults argues that Karl Barth appropriated *anhypostasis* and *enhypostasis* as a dual formula to describe the human nature of Christ, which moves beyond the autonomous treatment of these terms by the patristic Fathers based upon the invention of Protestant Scholasticism that Barth received through his reading of Heinrich Heppe and Heinrich Schmid. I argue against Shults and will show that the Protestant Scholastics appropriated *anhypostasis* and *enhypostasis* consistent with the patristic Fathers as autonomous concepts to explain the human nature of Christ. I also noted U. M. Lang's statement that Barth's appropriation of *anhypostasis* and *anhypostasis* as a dual formula is an innovation all his own. I agree with Lang, but will further argue that Barth's adoption of *anhypostasis* and *enhypostasis* is not only unique to his Christology, but in fact becomes the ontological foundation to his Christology as a whole. We now turn to the scholastic and post-scholastic writers and their understanding of *anhypostasis* and *enhypostasis* to express the human nature of Christ.

Scholastic and Post-scholastic Period Formulation

Prelude

In view of the patristic writers and their formulation of the terms *anypostatos* and *enypostatos* to explain the human nature of Christ, we now turn our attention to the scholastic and post-scholastic period writers. In so doing we will consider how Lutheran and Reformed scholastics appropriated these terms, together with Thomas Aquinas, whose Christology weighed heavily upon this period as well. In the post-scholastic period we will focus on the dogmatic compilations of Heinrich Schmid (Lutheran) in *The Doctrinal Theology of the Evangelical Lutheran Church*, and Heinrich Heppe

(Reformed) in *Reformed Dogmatics*, both of whom cite the scholastics in their own appropriation of *anhypostasis* and *enhypostasis*. It is from these texts that Barth first gained acquaintance with the terms *anhypostasis* and *enhypostasis*.[120]

Historically speaking, F. LeRon Shults posits that the scholastics misappropriated *anhypostasis* and *enhypostasis* to explain the human nature of Christ, and employed these terms in a way that contradicted their usage by the Greek Fathers.[121] While agreeing with Shults that the use of *anhypostasis* and *enhypostasis* as a christological formula cannot be found in the Church Fathers, U. M. Lang argues that neither can these terms be found in Protestant orthodoxy as a dual formula to describe the human nature of Christ.[122] Therefore, the question before us is: how did orthodox Lutheran and Reformed writers of the scholastic and post-scholastic periods formulate the terms *anhypostasis* and *enhypostasis* to explain the human nature of Christ? Furthermore, did their formulation of these terms depart from the patristic Fathers (as Shults suggests), or did their ontological understanding of Christ's human nature mirror the patristic Fathers in explaining the human nature of Christ? Or, more specifically:

1. Was there a consensus among Lutheran writers in their use and application of the terms *anhypostasis* and *enhypostasis* to explain the human nature of Christ?

2. If there was disagreement, what was it, and how did it impact their Christology?

3. Was there consensus among Reformed writers in their use and application of the terms *anhypostasis* and *enhypostasis* to explain the human nature of Christ?

4. If there was disagreement, what was it, and how did it bear upon on their Christology?

---

120. In his work entitled *The Doctrinal Theology of the Evangelical Lutheran Church* (1875) Heinrich Schmid develops a compilation of theological statements taken from the writings of fourteen prominent Lutheran theologians in the sixteenth and seventeenth centuries. Schmid uses these quotations to support and clarify the Christian faith developed in the early Lutheran tradition up through the time of Rationalism. Heinrich Heppe's work entitled *Reformed Dogmatics* (1861) is a compendium of Reformed dogmatic writers with the expressed intent to transmit the thinking of acknowledged representatives of Reformed orthodoxy.

121. See Shults, "Dubious Christological Formula," 443.

122. See Lang, "Anhypostasis–Enhypostasis," 631.

5. Did the Lutheran and Reformed writers differ in their Christology with regard to their formulation and application of the terms *anhypostasis* and *enhypostasis*?

Lutheran Interpretation and Development

We include with the scholastic writers Thomas Aquinas (1225–1274) and his ontological development of Christ's human nature in view of Chalcedon.[123] Aquinas agrees with the Chalcedon formula of the two natures and argues that in Christ "human nature is so united to the Word that the Word subsists in it."[124] For Aquinas this implies that human nature is more dignified in Christ than in us. This is so because in us—human nature exists by itself as its own personality. However, in Christ human nature exists in the person of the Word.[125] Aquinas understands Christ's human nature to be an individual substance, "yet because Christ's human nature does not exist separately by itself but in something more perfect, namely in the person of the Word of God, it follows that it does not have its own personality (*non habeat personalitatem propriam*)."[126] Aquinas, however, concludes that concerning the subsistence of the human nature of Christ "the assumed nature does not have its own proper personality, not because of the lack of something pertaining to the perfection of human nature, but because of the addition of something surpassing human nature, which is union to a divine person (*unio ad divinam personam*)."[127] While Aquinas does not use the technical term *enhypostaton* to describe the human nature of Christ, like the patristic Fathers before him, Aquinas argues that the human nature of Christ does not exist *idiohypostaton,* but in its own reality in the person of Christ.[128]

---

123. Thomas Aquinas develops his understanding of Chalcedon and Christ's human nature in *Summa Theologiae* and his response to the question whether "the union of the incarnate Word was wrought in one person?;" see Gockel, "A Dubious Christological Formula," 526. We include Aquinas in this section as an important point of contact between the patristic Fathers and the Protestant Scholastics with respect to understanding the Chalcedon definition of Jesus Christ who exists as one person with two natures. After Aquinas we transition to Johann Gerhard as the first Lutheran scholastic theologian in our discussion.

124. See Gockel, "A Dubious Christological Formula," 526. Gockel cites Thomas Aquinas in *Summa Theologiae.*

125. Ibid.

126. Ibid.

127. Ibid.

128. Ibid.

... the person or hypostasis of Christ can be viewed in a twofold way. On the one hand, as it is in itself, it is always simple, as in the nature of the Word too. On the other hand, it is considered under the aspect of person or hypostasis, which means subsisting in some nature, and according to this the person of Christ subsists in two natures. Hence, although there is one subsisting reality, there are nonetheless two different aspects of its subsisting. Thus, it is called a subsisting person, as far as one [person] subsists in two [natures].[129]

Aquinas's understanding of Christ's human nature is consistent with the patristic Fathers and the Protestant scholastics that followed him. Although Aquinas did not employ the terms *anhypostasis* and *enhypostasis* in his writings, he used the concept of *impersonalitas* to describe Christ's human nature as existing only in the person of the Word.[130] The Protestant scholastics would later use this term as a coherent translation of ανυποστασια and reflect further upon the relation between the terms *anhypostaton* and *enhypostaton*. Moreover, when Aquinas states that Christ's human nature exists only in the person of the Word and does not have a personality of its own, he translates the patristic idea that Christ's human nature is not *idiohypostaton*.[131]

In his work entitled *Loci Theologici*, early seventeenth century Lutheran theologian Johann Gerhard (1582—1637)[132] uses the terms ανυποστατος and ενυποστατος to explain the human nature of Christ and its relationship to the Logos.[133] Gerhard uses a two-fold (negative and positive) explanation of Ανυποστατον in relationship to Christ's human nature:

Ανυποστατον has a twofold meaning. Absolutely and simply, that is called ανυποστατον which subsists neither in its own nor in another υποστασις . . . but is purely negative. In this sense, the human nature of Christ cannot be said to be ανυποστατον. Relatively and secondarily, that is called ανυποστατον which does not in fact subsist in its own but in the ὑπόstasiς of another; which indeed has essence yet not in its own personality and

129. Ibid., 527. Gockel cites Aquinas in *Summa Theologiae*.

130. Ibid.

131. Ibid.

132. Johann Gerhard, professor of theology at the academy to Jena, was a leading 17th century German Lutheran theologian and polemicist, and author of the standard Lutheran dogmatic treatise *Loci Theologici*.

133. See Gockel, "A Dubious Christological Formula," 528.

> subsistence. In this sense, Christ's flesh is called ανυποστατος, because it is ενυποστατος, subsistent in the Λογος himself.[134]

In this passage Gerhard argues that the human nature of Christ cannot be understood as ανυποστατον in a purely negative sense, having no substance in itself or in another υποστασις. Rather, Gerhard describes the humanity of Christ positively as ανυποστατον, that is, it simply does not subsist on its own, but enjoys real subsistence in union with the Λογος.

The focus of Gerhard's argument dismisses the notion that Christ's human nature existed before it was brought into union with the Logos by insisting that the anhypostasia of Christ's human nature must be understood in the order of its constitution (*ordo naturae*) rather than the order of its temporal state (*ordo temporis*). Gerhard uses the concept of in-subsistence to emphasize that there never was a time when the human nature of Christ subsisted outside the hypostatic union.[135] We therefore see in Gerhard the concept of *anhypostasis* not in a negative sense to describe the human naturSe of Christ, but in a positive way to deny his existence prior to the incarnation. Moreover, we see the apparent influence of John of Damascus on Gerhard's thinking, given that in Gerhard's posthumous work entitled *Patrologia* he cites a fairly exhaustive list of John of Damascus's works published in Greek and Latin.[136]

The seventeenth century theologian Andreas Quenstedt (1617–1688) follows Thomas Aquinas in explaining the Chalcedon formula of one hypostasis in two unconfused natures.[137] For Quenstedt the terms anhypostatos and *enhypostatos* illustrate two sides of the same coin. He explains that the Logos unites human nature with himself in his person, so that the proper hypostasis of the human nature and its place of subsistence is in something higher, i.e., the divine. So too, out of the anhypostatos comes the *enhypostatos*.[138] Quenstedt understands *anhypostasis* as "*carentia propriae subsistentiae*." Quenstedt himself cites John of Damascus in his use of *anhypostatos* and *enhypostatos*, which Quenstedt describes as being somewhat ambiguous, and notes that the expression *anhypostasis* is used to describe things that simply do not exist. *Enhypostasis* on the other hand describes

---

134. Ibid. Gockel cites Gerhard in *Loci Theologici*.

135. Ibid.

136. See Lang, "Anhypostasis–Enhypostasis," 655–56.

137. Andreas Quenstedt is recognized by many historians as a leading and influential post reformation Lutheran theologian, whose work includes the *Theologia Didactio-Polemica Sive Systema Theologicum*, which was written to address and debate significant doctrinal issues of his day.

138. See Gockel, "A Dubious Christological Formula," 528–29.

things which either exist *per se* or inhere in another thing such as an accident in a subject.[139] Quenstedt, who in subscribing to the Damascene's view of Christ's human nature "takes Damascene's *Expositio fidei* III 9 as a *locus classicus* for the doctrine of the subsistence of Christ's human nature: εν του Λογου υποστασει, quae αμφοτερων των φυσεων υποστασις."[140]

David Hollaz (1648–1713) understands Christ's human nature to be ανυποστασια because it subsists only in the hypostasis of the Logos.[141] In this context Hollaz notes that if the human nature of Christ retained its own subsistence, this would result in the union of two persons and thus two mediators, which is contrary to the teaching of I Timothy 2:5. For Hollaz, a person is one formally constituted in its being as an entirely complete and unified subsistence.[142] With respect to Christ, Hollaz concludes that one of the two natures that come together in one person must be without its own subsistence. Since the *divine* nature is the same as its subsistence in the person of the Logos, it cannot be without it. It is therefore evident that "the absence of a proper subsistence (*carentia propriae subsistentiae*) must be attributed to the human nature."[143]

More specifically Hollaz argues that when Christ's human nature is considered strictly in itself, it "does not possess its own actual subsistence (*propriam subsistentiam actu non habet*)." However, when it is considered in its union with the divine nature, it is rightly called ενυποστατος. In other words, the human nature of Christ is "subsistent in the Logos."[144]

In the nineteenth century Lutheran theologian Heinrich Schmid (1811–1885) wrote *The Doctrinal Theology of the Evangelical Lutheran Church* (1875), which is a compilation of Lutheran dogma taken from the sixteenth and seventeenth centuries. In it Schmid works with the concepts *anhypostasis* and *enhypostasis* to express the human nature of Christ, and affirms as a theological principle the existence of the human nature of Christ as a real substance in union with his divine nature. With respect to the divine and human natures of Christ, Schmid states that: "Each of these natures is to be regarded as truly genuine and entire."[145] Schmid acknowledges the peculiar ontological relationship between Christ's human and

139. See Lang, "Anhypostasis–Enhypostasis," 656.

140. Ibid.

141. David Hollaz is regarded by historians as the last of the so-called silver age of Lutheran orthodoxy, whose work entitled *Examen* was an important and influential Lutheran dogmatics.

142. See Gockel, "A Dubious Christological Formula," 529.

143. Ibid. Gockel sites Hollaz in *Examen theologicum acroamaticum*.

144. Ibid.

145. See Schmid, *Doctrinal Theology*, 294.

divine natures, and uses the term ανυποστασια to explain that there is a significant difference between the mode of Christ's human nature and the human nature of other men. Schmid explains that in view of the peculiar circumstances connected with the birth of Christ, together with the unique relationship in which the Logos sustains this human nature, certain peculiarities must be granted to the human nature of Christ which distinguishes it from other human beings. Schmid explains this as the ανυποστασια (lack of personality).[146] In explaining ανυποστασια relative to the human nature of Christ and the time of its subsistence, Schmid argues both negatively and positively that the human nature of Christ possesses no hypostasis outside its union with the divine nature:

> The first results from the peculiar relation with the divine Λογοσ entered into with the human nature; for this latter is not to be regarded as at any time subsisting by itself and constituting a person by itself, since the Λογος did not assume a human person, but only a human nature. Therefore there is negatively predicated of the human nature the ανυποστασια, inasmuch as the human nature has no personality of its own; and there is positively predicated of it the ανυποστασια, inasmuch as this human nature has become possessed of another hypostasis, that of the divine nature.[147]

The fundamental point of emphasis is that Christ's human nature does not have personality in its subsistence (outside its union with the Logos) because his human nature is not a human person—*it is a human nature.* As an axiomatic point of orthodox ontology Schmid explains that in the union of divine and human natures the Logos imparts personality to the human nature of Christ. As the second person of the Godhead, the Logos acts to unite human nature to himself thereby imparting his own personality to this human nature—in this union. The Logos therefore "sustains an active relation to the human nature, which He assumes, while the human nature stands in a passive relation to Him."[148]

While arguing that the divine and human natures of Christ are absolutely united in the Logos, Schmid in no way denies the individual and real subsistence of the human nature in this union. He cites Hollaz in affirming the integrity of both human and divine natures in their personal union and subsistence in the hypostasis of Christ, and concludes that "The personal union is a conjunction of the two natures, divine and human, subsisting

146. Ibid., 294–95.
147. Ibid., 295.
148. Ibid., 295–96.

in one hypostasis of the Son of God, producing a mutual and an indissoluble communion of both natures."[149] Schmid is deliberate in his use of term ανυποστασια to demonstrate that Christ's human nature cannot be understood as an individual person, and he cites Hollaz's use of the term ανυποστασια to argue that the human nature of Christ enjoys real subsistence in union with the divine person. If on the other hand, the human nature retained a particular subsistence, by definition it would be considered a second person. Schmid explains:

> To the human nature of Christ there belong certain individual designations, by which, as by certain distinctive characteristics or prerogatives, He excels other men; such are (a) ανυποστασια, the being without a peculiar subsistence, since this is replaced by the divine person (υποστασις) of the Son of God, as one far more exalted. If the human nature of Christ had retained its peculiar subsistence, there would have been in Christ two persons, and therefore two mediators, contrary to I Tim. 2:5. The reason is, because a person is formally constituted in its being by a subsistence altogether complete, and therefore unity of person is to be determined from unity of subsistence. Therefore, one or the other nature, of those which unite in one person, must be without its own peculiar subsistence; and, since the divine nature, which is really the same as its subsistence, cannot really be without the same, it is evident that the absence of a peculiar subsistence must be ascribed to the human nature.[150]

Schmid also distinguishes between ανυποστατον and ενυποστατον, not as a dual formula, but to substantiate that Christ's human nature does not exist as a separate reality outside its union with the Logos. Therefore, the term ανυποστατον is not used to describe a negative characteristic of Christ's human nature. Neither Schmid nor scholastic Lutheran orthodoxy thought in these terms—unlike Barth. The material point for the Lutherans was to ensure that the human nature of Christ did not exist outside its union with the Logos so as to construe another person in this union. Following this line of thinking Schmid cites Quenstedt who emphasizes that ανυποστατος—with respect to Christ's human nature—simply means that it does not exist in itself as a peculiar personality (hypostasis). Rather, the human nature of Christ is ενυποστατος because it exists as real substance by partaking in the hypostasis in the Logos.

---

149. Ibid., 296.
150. Ibid., 300.

> That is ανυποστατον which does not subsist of itself and accord-
> ing to its peculiar personality; but that is ενυποστατον which
> subsists in another, and becomes the partaker of the hypostasis
> of another. When, therefore, the human nature of Christ is said
> to be ανυποστατος, nothing else is meant than that it does not
> subsist of itself, and according to itself, in a peculiar personality;
> moreover, it is called ενυποστατος, because it has become a par-
> taker of the hypostasis of another, and subsists in the Λογος.[151]

Anticipating objections to the peculiar subsistence of Christ's human nature in union with the divine hypostasis, Schmid cites Hollaz
who responds to the question: "If the human nature is without a peculiar
subsistence, the same will be more imperfect than our nature, which is
αυθυποστατος, or subsisting of itself" by arguing "The perfection of an
object is to be determined from its essence, and not from its subsistence."[152]
Moreover, Schmid cites Gerhard who emphasizes that Christ's human nature is not ανυποστατον in the sense of having no subsistence on its own;
but rather, it is ανυποστατον relatively because it enjoys real subsistence in
its union within the divine Logos:

> **Ανυποστατον** has a twofold meaning. Absolutely, that is said to
> be ανυποστατον, which subsists neither in its own υποστασις,
> nor in that of another, which has neither essence nor subsis-
> tence, is neither in itself, nor in another, but is purely negative.
> In this sense, the human nature of Christ cannot be said to be
> ανυποστατον. Relatively, that is said to be ανυποστατον, which
> does not subsist in its own, but in the υποστασις of another,
> which indeed had essence, but not personality and subsistence
> peculiar to itself. In this sense, the flesh of Christ is said to
> be ανυποστατος, because it is ενυποστατος, subsisting in the
> Λογος.[153]

Schmid also cites Gerhard's argument that the ανυποστασια of Christ's
human nature affirms the genesis of its existence and subsistence at the incarnation, and not before. Once again the point is made that ανυποστατος
is not a term used to express what the human nature of Christ is in relation
to its union with the Logos, but rather, what it is not.

> The statement of some, that the starting-point of the incarna-
> tion is the ανυποστασια of the flesh intervening between that
> subsistence, on the one hand, by which the mass whereof the

151. Ibid., 300.
152. Ibid., 301.
153. Ibid.

body of Christ was formed subsisted as a part of the Virgin, not by its own subsistence and that of the Virgin; and the subsistence, on the other hand whereby the human nature, formed from the sanctified mass by the operation of the Holy Ghost in the first moment of incarnation, began to subsist with the very subsistence of the Λογος, communicated to it, is not to be received in such a sense *as though the flesh of Christ was at any time entirely* ανυποστατος; but, because in our thought, such an ανυποστασια is regarded prior to its reception into the subsistence of the Λογος, not with regard to the order of time, but to that of nature. *The flesh* and *soul were not first united into one person; but formation of the flesh, by the Holy Ghost, from the separated* and *sanctified mass, the giving of a soul to this flesh as formed, the taking up of the formed* and *animated flesh into the subsistence of the Λογος,* and *the conception of the formed, animated,* and *subsisting flesh in the womb of the virgin, were simultaneous.*[154]

The point that Schmid drives home here is that the concept of *anhypostasis* serves to mark the non-existence of the human nature of Christ prior to the incarnation. In other words, *anhypostasis* is not a concept of reality that is applied to the human nature of Christ, but it is the antithesis of *enhypostasis* which explains how human essence exists in union with the divine person of the Logos.

Reformed Interpretation and Development

Similar to the Lutherans, the Reformed scholastics also worked with the concepts of *anhypostasis* and *enhypostasis* to explain the human nature of Christ in its union with the Logos. Reformed theologian Bartholomaeus Keckermann (1571–1609)[155] distinguishes between two concepts of substance (much like Johann Gerhard), and explains that while the human nature of Christ is not a distinct person, it is an individual, or, "as the Logicians say," a primary substance.[156] Keckermann explains:

But someone may say: 'Every substantial individual subsists by itself: if therefore Christ's human nature, considered by itself, is an individual, it therefore subsists by itself.' I answer: Subsisting

154. Ibid.

155. Bartholomaeus Keckermann was a Reformed Calvinist theologian and philosopher (University of Heidelberg) whose writings included works in systematic theology and rhetoric.

156. See Gockel, "A Dubious Christological Formula," 529–30.

> by itself is sometimes opposed to that which subsists in some-
> thing else, and so human nature always subsists by itself, because
> it is a substance and not an accident, which is characterized as
> existing in something else. But if subsisting by itself means the
> same as subsisting separately, outside the union and sustenance
> by the other, then it is false to say that the human nature subsists
> by itself, since it is sustained by the Logos, to which it is united
> in such a way that outside the Logos it could not have existence
> for a moment.[157]

However, we see in Keckermann's language (quite similar to Leontius of Byzantium) a failure to adequately distinguish between nature and hypostasis. Even so, he emphasizes that Christ's human nature is not an accident, but has real subsistence and contemporaneous existence in its union with the Logos.[158]

Johann Heinrich Alsted (1588–1638) explains "that Christ's human nature never subsisted on its own, but was an instrument ενυποστατος εν τω Λογω."[159] Alsted argues that Jesus Christ is similar to us with respect to *physis*, but not with respect to *hypostasis*. That is, the human nature of Christ is similar to us in its essence, not in its subsistence."[160] Also, the Reformed scholastic Heinrich Heidegger (1633–1698) argues that because there is one mediator in Christ, there must also be one hypostasis that is Christ.[161] Because the human nature must subsist in the divine, it becomes ενυποστατος through its subsistence in the Logos. That Jesus Christ exists as a man predicates that fact that he exists as one subsistent person (hypostasis). "Either the divine nature subsists in the human nature or the human in the divine. That the divine nature should subsist in the human, and be sustained by it, is opposed to its infinite perfection. Therefore, the human is ανυποστατος by itself (*per se*) and becomes ενυποστατος in the Logos."[162]

---

157. See Gockel, "A Dubious Christological Formula," 529–30. Gockel cites Kecker-mann in *Systema SacroSanctae Theologiae, tribus libris adornatum.*

158. Ibid., 530.

159. Johann Heinrich Alsted was a Reformed Calvinist theologian who is regarded as one the most influential encylopedists of all time. His theological works included polemics on trinitarian and christological doctrine.

160. See Gockel, "A Dubious Christological Formula," 530. Gockel cites Alsted in *Theologia scholastica didactica.*

161. Heinrich Heidegger was a Swiss born Reformed dogmatician and ecclesiastical writer.

162. See Gockel, "A Dubious Christological Formula," 531. Gockel cites Heidegger in *Corpus Theologiae Christianae.*

The nineteenth century Reformed theologian Heinrich Heppe (1820–1879) wrote the *Reformed Dogmatics* (1861) as a compilation of Reformed dogmatics in order to expound the orthodox system of Reformed faith. In the *Reformed Dogmatics* Heppe worked with the terms *anhypostasis* and *enhypostasis* (similar to the Lutheran Schmid) to explain the human nature of Christ given is union and individuality within the Logos. Heppe explains that:

> In essentials all Reformed dogmaticians are agreed that the divinity of Christ is not really the divine nature (common to the three persons of the Trinity) but the person of the Logos, the Logos-determination of the Trinity, the deity thought of under the personal determination of the Logos; and that the humanity of Christ is the human nature common to all human personalities, thought of in abstraction (and so not personally) but individually.[163]

In the *Reformed Dogmatics* Heppe cites Amandus Polanus who explains that the substance of Christ's human nature is assumed by the eternal Word—the person, not the nature of Christ—in its union with the Logos as stated in John 1:14. That is, the expression that Christ exists in the union of two natures as both divine and the human must be understood in a figurative sense. "It is not strictly the nature but the person or subsistence of the Word existing eternally in the form or nature of God, that has assumed the human nature and united it to itself. Exactly as John 1:14 does not say, the divine nature became flesh, but the Word became flesh."[164] Using similar language Heinrich Heidegger argues that the human nature of Christ was not assumed into the divine nature, but into the person of the divine Logos. As such this assumption took place into the person (not nature) of the Son. "Whence it was not deity but the Λογος or sermo that is said to have become flesh, John 1:14 to be God manifested in the flesh."[165]

Heppe explains that the human nature of Christ subsists in union with the Logos while maintaining its own individuality.[166] Therefore, humanity taken up into the person of the Logos is not a personal man, but a human nature without personal subsistence. However, this human essence must be understood to exist in "its full spirit-body essentiality and individuality." This explains why the incarnation of the Logos does not result in a new "third thing" arising out of this union. The infinite mode of being of the

163. Heppe, *Reformed Dogmatics*, 414.
164. Ibid., 414.
165. Ibid., 415.
166. Ibid., 416.

Logos assumed to itself the finite mode of human being by taking up into his personal subsistence human nature. "The Logos thus exists alike without and within the humanity of Christ. The Logos is still pre-existent, the Trinity is still complete. Christ's human nature had hypostatic subsistence only by its being taken up into the hypostasis of the Logos."[167]

Moreover, the humanity of Christ exists as an individual of substance in view of the form of its essence as the determining factor of its individuality, not its personality. His human nature is a "prime intelligent substance perfect in the *esse* of its substance" (i.e., an individual). Ontologically speaking, the reality of human nature is measured "by its matter, form and essential attributes," and not by "its personality."[168] Christ's human nature exists as "an individumm distinct from the divine nature, though not a distinct person," and is sustained by its union within the divine Logos.[169] The term ενυποστατον explains that the substance of the Christ's human nature exists as an individuum in its subsistence in the divine Logos. "He assumed not a person but a nature, and it considered as an individuum. The reason for the former statement is that Christ's human nature never subsisted per se but has always been an instrument ενυποστατον εν τω λογω."[170] Similarly speaking—the Leiden Synopsis (1625) refers to the ανυποστατος of Christ's human nature to affirm that it came into existence at conception, and not to imply its lack of individuality in its union within the Logos:

> The manner in which the only-begotten Son of God became flesh is by the direct union of the person of the Son of God with the human nature or the assumption of the human nature into one and the same person, Phil 2:7; Heb 2:16 (. . . He taketh hold of the seed of Abraham); so that the Son of God, the second person of the sacrosanct Trinity, assumed into the unity of His person right from the moment of conception not a pre-existent person but one ανυποστατος of its own hypostasis or devoid of subsistence, and make it belong to himself.[171]

In the end Heppe portrays the Reformed use of the concepts *anhypostasis* and *enhypostasis* as a way to affirm the reality of the human nature of Christ in its assumption by the person of the Logos. Positively, the human nature exists in the Logos as a distinguishable human essence that enjoys hypostasis strictly in its union with the Logos (*enhypostasis*).

167. Ibid., 416.
168. Ibid., 416. Heppe cites Francis Turretin.
169. Ibid., 417. Heppe cites Keckermann.
170. Ibid. Heppe cites Alsted.
171. Heppe, *Reformed Dogmatics*, 418.

Negatively, the human nature did not exist prior to the incarnation. It was in fact *anhypostasis* because it had no hypostasis to call its own before the *Word became flesh.*

Conclusion

We examined the writings of Lutheran and Reformed scholastics, as well as Thomas Aquinas, with respect to their use and understanding of the concepts *anhypostasis* and *enhypostasis* to express the human nature of Christ. We also considered the writings of post-scholastic theologians Heinrich Schmid (Lutheran) and Heinrich Heppe (Reformed) in view of their apparent influence on Barth in providing his first acquaintance with these terms.

The Lutheran scholastics understood the concept of *anhypostasis* to describe something that subsists neither in its own or in another hypostasis. Moreover, it was not a term used to describe the human nature of Christ negatively, but as a way to describe the humanity of Christ positively as having its subsistence and genesis of existence in union with the hypostasis of the Logos. The terms *anhypostasis* and *enhypostasis* therefore are not used as contrasting concepts to describe the human nature of Christ, but to illustrate two sides of the same coin. Because the human nature is united into the person of the Logos—and therefore cannot be thought of as *anhypostasis*—it becomes *enhypostasis* in this union. *Anhypostaton* is used simply to describe things that don't exist, and *enhypostaton* to describe things that exist per se or inhere in another thing. The human nature of Christ therefore subsists not as a separate person, but in the hypostasis of the Logos.

Nineteenth century Lutheran theologian Heinrich Schmid consistently cites the Lutheran scholastics and uses the term ανυποστασια to argue both negatively and positively that Christ's human nature possesses no hypostasis outside its union in the Logos. Because the Logos assumed a human nature (not a person), this human nature is ενυποστασια, having become possessed by the hypostasis of the Logos. Christ's human nature is not ανυποστατον in the sense of having no subsistence of its own, but rather, is ανυποστατον relatively because it enjoys real subsistence in its union with the divine Logos.

Consistent with their Lutheran brethren, the Reformed scholastics distinguish between two concepts of substance and note that the human nature of Christ exists as a real substance, and is therefore not an accident. This subsistence, however, does not preclude the fact that the human nature of Christ is sustained by its union in the Logos. Nineteenth century Reformed theologian Heinrich Heppe agrees with and cites the Reformed scholastics in explaining that the human nature of Christ was not assumed into the divine nature, but into the person of the Logos. The Logos therefore assumed a nature and not a person, which never subsisted per se, but has always been an instrument ενυποστατον in the divine Logos.

We therefore conclude that there was consensus agreement among Lutheran and Reformed writers (in the scholastic and post-scholastic periods) in their use and application of the concepts *anhypostasis* and *enhypostasis* to explain the human nature of Christ. Furthermore, we understand that their use and application of these terms was consistent with the orthodox patristic Fathers. Moreover, we see throughout these historical periods of orthodox christological development that the concept of *anhypostaton* was not used in a negative sense to describe the existence of Christ's human nature, but simply as a way to assert that its substance exists not in itself, but in its subsistence in the Logos. Therefore, the terms *anhypostasis* and *enhypostasis* are not used as a dual formula to describe the human nature of Christ, nor is it a valid doctrinal expression of orthodox writers. This stands in rather dramatic contrast to Karl Barth's appropriation of *anhypostasis* and *enhypostasis* as a dual formula to explain the union of Christ's human nature with the Logos. Barth understands the *anhypostasis* to describe the negative aspect of Christ's human nature—having no subsistence in itself—which clearly differs with historical orthodoxy. Moreover, Barth's construction of *anhypostasis* and *enhypostasis* as a dual formula is an innovation unique to his Christology; and as we will show, becomes the ontological foundation for Barth's Christology as a whole.

2

Karl Barth's Interpretive Construal
of *Anhypostasis* and *Enhypostasis*

Introduction

KARL BARTH'S INTERPRETATION OF *anhypostasis* and *enhypostasis* cannot simply be stated as a matter of theological course without first giving close consideration to the context from which he adopts these terms into his Christology. That is, Barth appropriates the formula *anhypostasis* and *enhypostasis* as orthodox christological terms which he uses to express ontologically how the human nature of Christ comes into union with the Logos—*made manifest in the person of Jesus Christ*. Moreover, Barth's adoption of these terms marks a significant transition in his Christology,[1] which provides the ontological grounding to express the revelation of God in the person of Jesus Christ in the texture of his humanity.[2]

In the *anhypostasis* and *enhypostasis* Barth finds a fluid range of christological motion to explain how the revelation of God is effected in the humanity of Christ both in its veiling and unveiling. Once appropriated into his Christology, these concepts form the ontological foundation by which Barth expresses the person of Jesus Christ as *very God* and *very man*,[3] which in turn allows him to express the incarnation as the eternal Son of God who

1. See McCormack, *Dialectical Theology*, 327. McCormack recognizes the significance of Barth's "momentous discovery" of the "anhypostatic-enhypostatic Christological dogma" and argues that Barth saw in this dogma an understanding of the incarnate mediator that preserved the "infinite qualitative distinction" between God and humanity that concerned Barth up to this point. Moreover, as I will show, this infinite qualitative distinction demonstrated by the *anhypostasis* and *enhypostasis* is developed throughout the *Church Dogmatics* in Barth's ontological development of Jesus Christ.

2. See Jones, *Humanity of Christ*, 23. Jones observes that in the anhypostatic and enhypostatic sense of Christ's human nature Barth found a way to "stabilize and to render more precise his understanding of revelation."

3. See McCormack, *Dialectical Theology*, 327–28. McCormack argues that the significance of Barth's adoption of the *anhypostasis* and *enhypostasis* model is that it enables the time-eternity dialectic to be built into the very structure of Barth's Christology, while giving the incarnation its proper emphasis.

takes to himself a human nature without altering in any respect his divinity as the second person of the Trinity.[4]

We note also that Barth's ontology of the union of divine and human natures in Jesus Christ matures over the long course of his christological development. While *anhypostasis* and *enhypostasis* did not become a part of Barth's christological language until the *Göttingen Dogmatics*, we see the groundwork for his adoption of these terms being laid in his dialectic of time-eternity and veiling-unveiling expressed in *Romans* II. In his book on *Romans*, the question that Barth struggled to answer was how the veiling and unveiling of the triune God in the person of Jesus Christ—the one in whom time and eternity converge in the incarnate Son of God—can be expressed ontologically as such. It was in Göttingen, as Barth wrestled with this theological question that he was introduced to the concepts of *anhypostasis* and *enhypostasis* through the dogmatics works of Heinrich Schmid and Heinrich Heppe. And it is in the *Göttingen Dogmatics* that Barth first expressed these terms as the ontological grounding and framework to explain how the Logos assumes to himself human nature in the person of Jesus Christ. Thereafter, Barth develops more fully the *anhypostasis* and *enhypostasis* of Christ's human nature as a dual formula throughout the *Church Dogmatics*.

Given this background, my objective in this section is to examine Karl Barth's interpretation of *anhypostasis* and *enhypostasis* to explain how divinity and humanity are united ontologically in the person of Jesus Christ, and how this interpretation compares with historical protestant orthodoxy. I will do so by considering Barth's development of human nature in union with the divine Christ given:

1. Barth's development of the human nature of Christ in *Romans* II.

2. The influence of Lutheran and Reformed Christology with respect to the *anhypostasis* and *enhypostasis*.

3. Barth's introduction of *anhypostasis* and *enhypostasis* in the *Göttingen Dogmatics*.

4. Barth's mature development of *anhypostasis* and *enhypostasis* in the *Church Dogmatics*.

I will also evaluate Barth's interpretation of *anhypostasis* and *enhypostasis* juxtaposed against the protestant orthodox interpretation of these terms as a way to determine the points of agreement and variation.

4. See McCormack, *Dialectical Theology*, 361. McCormack identified Barth's dialectical understanding of the incarnation as the "unity of differentiation," with the kenosis of the Son becoming a positive rather than negative act in the Logos assuming human nature to himself.

Anhypostasis and *Enhypostasis*: Interpretative Development in Barth's Christology

The Humanity of God in *Romans II*

Notwithstanding the distinction that Karl Barth makes between the revelation of God as the Word became flesh in the person of Jesus Christ, and the Scriptures which attest to that revelation,[5] Barth's Christology consistently rests upon and finds its impetus in his exegesis of the Word of God.[6] That being said, Barth develops his system of dogmatics recognizing the Holy Scriptures as its foundational component from which all theological musings must flow.[7] Barth's reliance on the Scriptures as the basis for his Christology[8] finds early and dramatic expression in *The Epistle to the Romans*, which he wrote, and then wrote again, while serving as a pastor in Safenwil, Switzerland not long after the onset of World War I.[9]

Moreover, it is no coincidence that Barth developed his expositions on Romans in close proximity to the First World War. The devastating impact of the war on continental European culture—together with the complicity of liberal theology in the war effort—changed forever how Barth viewed theology in relationship to its historical and cultural context.[10] Moreover,

5. See Barth, *CD* I/1, 108–9. Barth distinguishes between the revelation of God realized in the person of Jesus Christ and the Holy Scriptures which attest to that revelation. Barth understands the Scriptures to be the word of men who yearned for Immanuel, and who saw, heard, and handled it in Jesus Christ. For Barth, the Scriptures declare, attest, and proclaim this revelation of God manifested in Jesus Christ and actually become the Word of God to the extent that God causes it to be his Word—to the extent that he speaks through it.

6. Despite his qualified view of Holy Scripture, Barth's *Church Dogmatics* is replete with his expositional treatment of Scripture as the foundation and authority by which he holds his dogmatics accountable.

7. See Burnett, *Karl Barth's Theological Exegesis*, 23. Burnett attributes Barth's willingness to continue his biblical exegesis amidst the "torrent" of criticism he received after *Romans* I and II to the importance that Barth placed upon exegesis. Burnett argues that throughout Barth's theological career he claimed that biblical exegesis remained the presupposition and goal of all his work.

8. Geoffrey Bromiley argues that Barth's biblical exegesis and understanding of the Bible became a dominant emphasis in his theology and opened the door to theological exegesis and biblical theology. "He focused on the inner subject matter of Scripture rather than on the external circumstances. He did this, not by repudiating the historical question, but by redefining it." Bromiley, "The Karl Barth Experience," 65.

9. Barth served as pastor in the parish of Safenwil from 1911–1921, where his turn to the Scriptures became foundational to his preaching and theological thinking. Eberhard Busch explains that: "It was the discovery of the Bible which held his attention." Busch, *Karl Barth*, 98.

10. Timothy Gorringe argues that from beginning to end Barth's theological work

for Barth, the historicity of the man Jesus clearly speaks to the shift in German theological, political, and social culture following the First World War. For Barth, it is the reality of the revelation of God in Jesus of Nazareth that directly confronts the cultural upheaval that dominated the landscape of the day because—in Jesus humanity is filled with the voice of God.[11] Barth's book on *Romans* not only provides valuable insights into his early development of the humanity of Christ, but it also sets the stage for a more robust Christology, which Barth develops in his dogmatics works through his adoption of *anhypostasis* and *enhypostasis* to explain the human nature of Christ. In this section I will examine Barth's development of the humanity of Christ in *Romans* II, which demonstrates his early ontological grounding of the relationship between divine and human natures in the eternal Logos.

In October of 1920 Barth decided to rewrite his first version of *Romans*.[12] Amazingly, Barth wrote his second version during the eleven month period between the autumn of 1920 and the summer of 1921 while still serving as pastor in his parish in Safenwil. This revision, coming hard on the heels of his first edition of *Romans* published in 1919, was not a simple revision, but a complete re-write of his first edition—*page by page*. In Barth's own estimation of his second version he says that "even now there will be all kinds of oversights and dislocations, but I think that I am a *bit* nearer to the truth of the matter than before."[13] We also observe in *Romans* II an important motivation with respect to Barth's theology that he attributes primarily to his greater study of *Paul's Epistle to the Romans*.[14] Barth explains that

---

is "against hegemony," which above all distinguishes it as a "contextual theology" developed in response to his context, Gorringe, *Karl Barth*, 1. While I certainly do not disagree with the obvious cultural relevance of Barth's theology, I would add that while the cultural changes of Barth's day may have been the impetus of much of Barth's theology; it was his pursuit of a relevant and biblical theology, centered in the person of Jesus Christ, which determined Barth's theological course.

11. Timothy Gorringe argues that in *Romans* Barth speaks to the spirit of the age, where there was a definite shaking of the foundations in science, art, music, and philosophy, as well as theology, Gorringe, *Karl Barth*, 69.

12. Evidently, it was after a visit from his friend Friedrich Gogarten that Barth decided to re-write his first commentary on *Romans*. "And now a strange and decisive bit of news: when Gogarten, with whom I had so many good conversations by day and night, was gone, suddenly the *Letter to the Romans* began to shed its skin; that is, I received the enlightenment that, as it now stands, it is simply impossible that it should be reprinted; rather it must be reformed root and branch."; see *Barth-Thurneysen Correspondence*, 53.

13. Busch, *Karl Barth*, 118.

14. See McCormack, "Historical Criticism and Dogmatic Interest," 322–26. Bruce McCormack identifies in Barth's *Romans* what he describes as a "revolution in biblical hermeneutics." That is, Barth sought to demonstrate the limits of a historical-critical

the impetus for his revision was: "First and most important: the continued study of Paul himself. My manner of working has enabled me to deal only with portions of the rest of the Pauline literature, but each fresh piece of work has brought with it new light upon the Epistle to the Romans."[15]

Romans II not only marks a pivotal movement in Barth's theology, but it also provides a sharpened view into his maturing development of the humanity of Christ and establishes the christological grounding that we first see demonstrated in the *Göttingen Dogmatics,* and then more fully developed throughout the *Church Dogmatics.*[16] In *Romans* II Jesus Christ is the *paradoxical* revelation of God in this world in whose being manifests both the humiliation of a sinner in Jesus and the exaltation of Christ as the light of the last things. Barth sees in the person of Jesus Christ the convergence of: humiliation and exaltation, veiling and unveiling, time and eternity, and God and humanity. And yet, the conflicting realities of time and eternity find absolute unity in Jesus Christ, who manifests in his person the faithfulness of God in his righteousness, in whose advent is realized the second and final Adam, and in whom the Word becomes flesh in the form of a servant.[17]

Barth understands that the faithfulness of God—witnessed by the Law and the Prophets—is revealed in both the humiliation and exaltation

---

study of the Bible in favor of a more theological exegesis approach.

15. Barth, *Epistle to the Romans,* 3. John Webster argues that despite wide and continual speculation over Barth's motivation for writing his *Romans,* Barth simply wanted to write a commentary on Paul's Epistle to the Romans. Webster further argues that "Even though we may judge that on occasions Barth did not achieve the right sort of subservience of his text to the biblical text, the intention of his method is beyond doubt." Webster, "Karl Barth," 205, 221.

16. Bruce McCormack suggests that "the gains made in *Romans* II are everywhere presupposed throughout the *Church Dogmatics*; that the continuity in theological perspective between these two great works so greatly outweighs the discontinuity that those who wish to read the dogmatics without the benefit of the lens provided by *Romans* II will understand everything in the wrong light."; see McCormack, *Dialectical Theology,* 244–45. Friedrich-Wilhelm Marquardt further notes that in both of Barth's Romans commentaries is found not only the exposition of Scripture in general, but also the "real prolegomena of the Church Dogmatics" where the concept of God is explained in preliminary form. See Marquardt, "The Idol Totters," 176. I argue that we can also say *Romans* II serves as a prolegomena to Barth's mature ontological development of Christ's human nature which will find its grounding in the *anhypostasis* and *enhypostasis.*

17. Herein presents a brief compendium of Barth's development of the revelation of God in Jesus Christ taken from his exegesis of Romans chapters 3, 5, and 8, in whose being the dialectic of time and eternity, and veiling and unveiling converge and find personal unity. We note already in this language Barth's sharpened sense of union between divine and human natures in Christ.

of Jesus Christ.[18] The reality of Jesus as *very man* is evidenced in his being made a sinner like those with whom he dwells in a sin-drenched earth, as Jesus gives himself to the judgment of God on behalf of his people. We witness here Barth's emphasis on the cross and death of Jesus that mark his life. As God's servant, Jesus sacrifices himself. His life becomes one of *negation* as he gives up every legitimate claim to personal achievement. Yet, even in his humiliation, God exalts him as the light of the last things. As the servant of God the humiliation of Christ becomes his exaltation.[19]

> Jesus stands among sinners as a sinner; He sets Himself wholly under the judgment under which the world is set; He takes His place where God can be present only in questioning about Him; He takes the form of a slave; He moves to the cross and death; His greatest achievement is a negative achievement. He is not a genius, endowed with manifest or even occult powers; He is not a hero or leader of men. He is neither poet nor thinker:—*My God, my God, why hast thou forsaken me?* Nevertheless, precisely in this negation, He is the fulfillment of every possibility of human progress, as the Prophets and the Law conceive of progress and evolution, because He sacrifices to the incomparably greater and to the invisibly Other every claim to genius and every human heroic or aesthetic or physic possibility, because there is no conceivable human possibility of which He did not rid Himself. Herein He is recognized as the Christ; for this reason God hath exalted Him; and consequently He is the light of the last things by which all men and all things are illuminated. In Him we behold the faithfulness of God in the depths of Hell. The Messiah is the end of mankind, and here also God is found faithful. On the day when mankind is dissolved the new era of the righteousness of God will be inaugurated.[20]

The paradoxical revelation of God's faithfulness in Jesus Christ, however, is not revealed as a self-evident truth in this world. The revelation of God is by definition a paradox because it cannot be naturally discerned

18. Barth lays the groundwork here for the ontological scheme of Jesus of Nazareth (more fully developed in the *Church Dogmatics*), in whose person manifests the righteousness of God in His humiliation and exaltation. "The faithfulness of God is the divine patience according to which He provides, at sundry times and at many divers points in human history, occasions and possibilities and witnesses of the knowledge of His righteousness. Jesus of Nazareth is the point at which it can be seen that all the other points form one line of supreme significance . . . The faithfulness of God and Jesus the Christ confirm one another." Barth, *Romans*, 96.

19. Barth, *Romans*, 96–97; *Der Römerbrief*, 136–37.

20. Ibid., 97.

(of the world), but must be supernaturally revealed (by the Spirit of God) through faith. The divine nature of Christ is a secrecy clothed in the flesh of Jesus that can only be revealed by the exercise of faith in the faithfulness of God. It is Jesus Christ who makes manifest the active movement of God's revelation to the world, but revelation dictated by his own terms. That is, the revelation of Jesus Christ is the act of God's grace in the event of his supernatural intersection with the natural realm of his creation.

> In Jesus revelation is a paradox [paradoxes], however objective and universal it may be. That the promises of the faithfulness of God have been fulfilled in Jesus the Christ is not, and never will be, a self-evident truth, since in Him it appears in its final hiddenness and its most profound secrecy. The truth, in fact, can never be self-evident, because it is a matter neither of historical nor of psychological experience, and because it is neither a cosmic happening within the natural order, nor even the most supreme event of our imaginings.[21]

The dialectic of veiling and unveiling emerges quite forcibly in the paradoxical revelation of the righteousness God in Jesus, who in his flesh veils the incomprehensibility of eternal God from anyone who seeks him in the name of human religion. This marks the absolute necessity for the revelation of faith—demonstrated by the mercy of God in the flesh of Jesus—in whose advent manifests the supernatural intercourse of eternity with time. This time-eternity dialectic can only be described as a miracle—*vertical from above*. As such, genuine and permanent righteousness in possible based solely upon the righteousness of God.[22]

Barth's dialectic of veiling and unveiling finds its fullest expression in the flesh of Jesus Christ. Not only is he a historical possibility, he is *the* possibility of the revelation of eternal God in time and space. Jesus lived as real humanity in real history. Yet as a real man, Jesus of Nazareth is not simply humanity, but the man in whom time and eternity converge in the revelation of God in the flesh. This is important for Barth because the life of Jesus Christ must be understood historically within the framework of human history as an actual event in the midst of other events limited by the boundaries of time. His life belongs to the texture of human life, who in the time-eternity dialectic is *the* man who is filled with the voice of God.[23]

As the possibility of humanity, Jesus is the man who died and was resurrected from that death by God the Father. This forms the impetus of

21. Ibid., 97–98; *Der Römerbrief,* 137.
22. Ibid., 98–102.
23. Ibid., 103–4.

new humanity being born from above—the dialectic of God and humanity manifested in Jesus Christ—wrought by the revelation of faith. This dialectic of God and humanity reveals the movement of God to humanity in the man Jesus Christ. Barth connects the death and resurrection of Christ with the "new man" who comes into being; that is, one who is born from above. This is God giving life to the dead, calling those to life as if they were not dead. Moreover, this calling to life in Jesus Christ cannot be realized apart from faith in Jesus Christ. "If there be no gamble of faith, if faith be forgotten or for one moment suspended, or if it be thought of as anything but a hazard, this identity is no more than an entirely trivial enterprise of religious or speculative arrogance. Speaking dialectically: this identification must always be shattered by the recognition that man is not God."[24]

As humanity, the life of Jesus Christ is marked by his death. It is in fact the death of Jesus that becomes the priority of his life and testifies to his reality as humanity. Barth emphasizes that the Scripture bears witness to the life of Jesus through his death, which in fact illumines his life. "Everything shines in the light of His death, and is illuminated by it. No single passage in the Synoptic Gospels is intelligible apart from the death."[25] Therefore, as true humanity, Jesus stands in juxtaposition with Adam, but always as a contrast to Adam, not as a counter-balancing existence. Like Adam, Jesus dies as the result of sin. But unlike Adam, Jesus is resurrected from his death as the second and last Adam; the one who has overcome the death wrought by the first Adam. And yet, while the death of Jesus presupposes his being as humanity; it is in his resurrection that the Father declares Jesus to be the Son of God as well. "Christ is contrasted with Adam as the goal and purpose of the movement. Hence between them there can be no equipoise. As the goal, Christ does not merely expose a dis-tinction. He forces a de-cision between the two factors. By doing this, He is not merely the second, but the *last* Adam (1 Cor 15:45)."[26]

Barth expresses the time-eternity dialectic manifested in Jesus Christ as very man; but very man as the Son of God. Although he was born of the seed of David in the flesh, Jesus is also non-concrete, unobservable, and non-historical. Flesh and blood alone cannot reveal to us what God alone reveals out the secret counsel of his eternal will, through the power of the resurrection in the man Jesus Christ:

24. Ibid., 149.

25. Ibid., 159.

26. Ibid., 166. As we shall see, Barth corrects himself on this point in the *Church Dogmatics* where he develops Jesus Christ as the *first* Adam.

But Christ is the 'new' subject, the EGO of the coming world. This EGO receives and bears and reveals the divine *justification* and election—*This is my beloved Son, in whom I am well pleased.* This qualification of man, this appointing as the Son of God, through the power of the resurrection (i.3.4), of Him who was born of the seed of David, is also non-concrete, unobservable, and non-historical. Flesh and blood cannot reveal it unto us. Here also hath our knowledge and the object of our knowledge proceed from the secret of divine predestination, by which all human history is constituted anew and given a pre-eminent and victorious meaning.[27]

Once again, dialectically speaking, Barth draws time and eternity together in Jesus, the Christ; as the one who stands at these cross-roads as *very God* and *very man*. In this way the eternal glory of God invades the realm of this world, which in its sinfulness has separated itself from a Holy God. This separation, however, is bridged by God who sends his own Son into this world of regression and estrangement. In this way, *very God* and *very man* is revealed as the Word became flesh.

To this, Jesus, the Christ, the eternal Christ, bears witness. At these cross-roads, then, God's own Son stands, and He stands nowhere else. God SENDS HIM—from the realm of the eternal, unfallen, unknown world of the Beginning and the End. Therefore, He is 'born of the Virgin Mary'—that is, He is our protest against assigning eternity to any Humanity or Nature or History which we can observe. Therefore, He is 'very God and very Man'—that is, He is the document by which the original, lost-but-recoverable union of God and man is guaranteed. God sends Him—into this temporal, fallen world with which we are only too familiar; into this order which we can finally interpret only in biological categories, and which we call 'Nature'; into this order which we can finally interpret only from the point of view of economic materialism, and which we call 'History'; in fact, into this humanity and into this flesh. Yes— the Word became flesh, became as we shall hear later,—sin controlled flesh.[28]

Barth further expresses the *very God* and *very man* motif in describing the *kenosis* of the eternal Christ, the Son of God, who took the form of a servant. That is, Jesus appears on the scene as the Son of God incognito.

27. Ibid., 181–82.

28. Ibid., 277.

He humbled himself and surrendered all of himself as the servant of God. Therefore, Christ cannot be recognized in his true identity except as he is revealed by the eternal Father which reaches beyond mere human comprehension. "It is imperative that the incognito [Inkognito] of the Son of God should increase and gain the upper hand, that it should move on to final self-surrender and self-abandonment; imperative that we, from the human point of view, should be scandalized; imperative that we should recognize that not flesh and blood but only the Father which is in heaven can reveal that there is more to be found here than flesh and blood."[29]

To sum up, in *Romans* II the revelation of God in Jesus Christ is a paradox, which Barth expresses as the dialectic of time-eternity and veiling-unveiling. As the revelation of God, Jesus is clothed in a secrecy that cannot be revealed by the flesh, but strictly through the supernatural revelation of faith. However, the revelation of God in Jesus Christ is not a *natural* revelation, so that the humanity of Christ becomes a veiling of his being. Yet this veiling in no way negates the true humanity of Jesus who lived in history as the *true* revelation of eternal God in time and space. Dialectically speaking, Jesus stands at the crossroads as *very God* and *very man* who is revealed supernaturally as the Word became flesh, who even in the kenosis is exalted as the Son of God.

The stage is therefore set for Barth's more precise ontological development of Jesus Christ that explains dialectically how the human nature of Christ can both veil and unveil the revelation of God in this world. That is, the essence of the person of Jesus Christ that so uniquely and paradoxically unites the eternal with the time and space of this world will find more tangible expression in Barth's adoption of *anhypostasis* and *enhypostasis*.

Reformed and Lutheran Influence

In the early part of 1921, while still working to complete his second edition of *Romans*, Karl Barth received an invitation to become Honorary Professor of Reformed Theology at Göttingen University.[30] In a letter dated January 29, 1921, Johann Adam Heilmann, who had been pastor of the Reformed congregation in Göttingen from 1891 to 1920, wrote to Karl Barth in Safenwil:

29. Ibid., 281; *Der Römerbrief,* 386.

30. The Chair of Reformed Theology at Göttingen was founded with the help of American Presbyterians, and was awarded to Barth (as he understood it) based upon his first edition of *Romans* and his passionate concern with the Bible. See Busch, *Karl Barth,* 123.

For years I have been striving to establish a Reformed professorate in Göttingen. The Reformed Church had five universities and academies at the beginning of the nineteenth century. All of them were taken away from it, and the result is that its scholarly work has remained underdeveloped to an extent that we should be ashamed of. There is insufficient education of the ministers of the Reformed Church, a confusion, in many cases a deadening effect on the Reformed congregations, and great damage to the entire Protestant Church. I do not want to recreate something old and past, nor even less conjure up any confessional narrowness, but what I would like is that the charismata that the Lord has given to the Reformed branch of the church should not remain unused, forgotten, and scorned. Reformed Protestantism has a calling and should fulfill it to the blessing of German Christianity.[31]

Such was the genesis of Barth's invitation to become the Honorary Professor of Reformed Dogmatics at Göttingen. And it was in Göttingen, as Barth prepared for his lectures on dogmatics that he first encountered the terms *anhypostasis* and *enhypostasis* in the dogmatics compilations of Heinrich Heppe and Heinrich Schmid.[32] The impact on Barth was profound. The dialectic of veiling and unveiling that so forcibly emerges in Barth's Christology in *Romans* II can now lay claim ontologically to a historical/theological framework that provides more precise (and flexibly) language through Barth's adoption of these terms.[33] Barth describes his encounter with Heinrich Heppe and Heinrich Schmid given their approach to dogmatics where the Scriptures take a high priority in understanding the revelation of God.

Then it was that, along with the parallel Lutheran work of H. Schmid, Heppe's volume just recently published fell into my hands . . . I read, I studied, I reflected; and found that I was rewarded with the discovery, that here at last I was in the atmosphere in which the road by way of the Reformers to H.

31. Barth, *The Theology of the Reformed Confessions*, Preface, vii.

32. "Barth's discovery of the *anhypostasis* and *enhypostasis* came in the form of the Post Reformation text books of the Lutheran, Heinrich Schmid and the Reformed, Heinrich Heppe while Barth was first developing his dogmatics lectures in Göttingen." McCormack, *Dialectical Theology*, 337.

33. In identifying the christological breakthrough of Barth's discovery of the *anhypostasis* and *enhypostasis*, Bruce McCormack notes that, "The proximity to Barth's dialectic of veiling and unveiling was obvious. In that God takes to God's self a human nature, God veils God's self in a creaturely medium . . . God can only be known in Jesus where He condescends to grant faith to the would-be human knower; where He unveils Himself in and through the veil of human flesh." McCormack, *Dialectical Theology*, 327.

Scripture was a more sensible and natural one to tread, than the atmosphere, now only too familiar to me, of the theological literature determined by Schleiermacher and Ritschl. I found a dogmatics which had form and substance, oriented upon the central indications of the Biblical evidences for revelation, which it also managed to follow out in detail with astonishing richness—a dogmatics which by adopting and sticking to main lines of the Reformation attempted alike a worthy continuation of the doctrinal constructions of the older Church, and yet was also out to cherish and preserve continuity with the ecclesiastical science of the Middle Ages.[34]

The significance of these works lay in their historical compilations of Reformed and Lutheran theology together with their expression of *anhypostasis* and *enhypostasis* to explain the ontology of Christ's human nature. This marks the place where Barth first breathed in deeply these concepts as a legitimate dogma to explain how the human nature of Christ came into union with the Logos. That being said, my objective in this section is to examine the Reformed and Lutheran dogma of *anhypostasis* and *enhypostasis* and their influence on Barth's own adoption of these terms as presented in the dogmatics works of Heinrich Heppe and Heinrich Schmid. I will also examine Barth's departure from both the Reformed and Lutheran understanding of *anhypostasis* and *enhypostasis* in his unique interpretation of these terms as a dual formula.

Heinrich Heppe—Reformed Theology and the Anhypostasis/Enhypostasis

Heinrich Heppe was born in March 1820 in Kassel, Germany, the son of a soldier and court musician of the Hessian government. Given the influence of his mother and grandmother, the young Heppe enrolled at the Kassel Gymnasium at Marburg University to study theology.[35] Heppe completed his theological studies at Marburg in 1843, and was awarded the degree of doctor of philosophy in 1844. After holding a pastorate in Kassel from 1845 through 1849, Heppe was appointed Privatdozent at Marburg in 1849, where at age 32 (in 1852) he became the youngest person in Germany to hold the doctor of theology degree. Heppe's published works from 1844 to

34. Barth qualifies his acceptance of Heppe's *Reformed Dogmatics* with respect to the doctrine of Scripture, especially the mystery of revelation. See Heppe, *Reformed Dogmatics*, Barth's Foreword, v.

35. It is Heppe's able editing of Reformed scholastic dogmatics works for which he is known today, Zuck, "Heinrich Heppe," 419.

until the end of his life in 1879 were significant in both quality and quantity.[36] Heppe's classic textbook on Reformed dogmatics was published in 1861 where he states in the foreword to the first edition that his aim was to expound the orthodox system of the doctrine of the Reformed Church faithfully and without addition.

> All the written sources I could lay hands on, I have carefully researched and compared, in order to transmit the thought material brought to light and disseminated by the acknowledge representatives of Reformed orthodoxy. Where differences were found, I have given an account of them and have at the same time attempted to set forth, which view is to be regarded as that truly corresponding to the spirit of Reformed Church doctrine.[37]

In view of the fact that Barth's first acquaintance with the concepts of *anhypostasis* and *enhypostasis* came through Heppe's *Reformed Dogmatics*, the question before us is did Heppe use these concepts to explain the Reformed doctrine in a way that construes a dual formulation that Barth appropriated into his own Christology? In the *Reformed Dogmatics* Heinrich Heppe takes up the subject of the incarnation in the context of Jesus Christ as the mediator of the covenant of grace, where he presents the incarnation of the Logos as the Word became flesh. Heppe clearly argues that this does not mean the Word turned into flesh or was confusedly mixed with flesh, but "he who was the Son of God became the Son of Man: not by confusion or essence but by the unity of the person."[38]

Moreover, the humanity of Christ taken up into the personality of the Logos is not a separate man, but human nature without personal subsistence (i.e., without individual personhood). The Logos therefore assumes a human nature, not a person, into its personal subsistence. In this way the Logos—the eternal mode of being—takes into his personal subsistence a finite mode of being. This finite being (human nature), however, is understood to exist essentially and individually by virtue of its union with the Logos.[39]

Heppe's emphasis is grounded in the fact that Christ's humanity is an *individuum*, an exposition of human nature in individual form. "It has real existence only in the person of the Logos, not itself." Interestingly, Heppe's specific reference to the concepts of *anhypostasis* and *enhypostasis* in the

---

36. Zuck cites his own unpublished chronological bibliography of Heppe, which includes 92 items, many of which are multi-volume works. See Zuck, *Heinrich Heppe*, 421.

37. Heppe, *Reformed Dogmatics*, Preface, vi.

38. Ibid., 414.

39. Ibid.

Reformed Dogmatics is rather sparse. He cites Alsted that the Logos assumed not a person but a nature, which subsisted ενυποστατον εν τω λογω. That is, the human nature of Christ enjoyed its subsistence strictly based upon its union with the Logos. Whereas, in the context of the Leiden Synopsis Heppe states that the second person of the Trinity assumed at the moment of conception not a pre-existent person, but one ανυποστατος of its own hypostasis, or devoid of substance prior to its union with the Logos.[40]

Despite the paucity of Heppe's use of the specific terms ανυποστατος and ενυποστατον in the *Reformed Dogmatics,* he is clear to explain that the human nature of Christ exists in personal subsistence in the Logos, which can be defined as ενυποστατον. However, the human nature assumed by the Logos was devoid of subsistence prior to the incarnation—it is ανυποστατος. In other words, these concepts express opposing views of Christ's human nature with respect to its substance in relationship to its union with the Logos. We understand therefore that Heppe expresses ανυποστατος and ενυποστατον as autonomous terms to explain how the human nature of Christ exists in union with the Logos.

Heinrich Schmid—Lutheran Theology and *the* Anhypostasis/Enhypostasis

Heinrich Schmid (1811–1886) was a Doctor and Professor of Theology at the University of Erlangen whose work entitled *The Doctrinal Theology of the Evangelical Lutheran Church* (1875) is considered a classical compendium of Lutheran dogmatics. Schmid draws upon the writings of prominent Lutheran theologians who lived during the sixteenth and seventeenth centuries which he employs to support and clarify the Christian faith as developed in the early Lutheran tradition.[41]

In Schmid's work he uses the concepts of *anhypostasis* and *enhypostasis* to explain how the Logos comes into union of the human nature of Christ, and cites a number of Lutheran scholastics to support his use of these terms specific to the ontology of Christ's human nature. *Anhypostasis* and *enhypostasis* prove to be particularly helpful in Lutheran dogma, which emphasizes that the human nature of Christ has no existence prior to its union with the Logos. While Schmid acknowledges the peculiar ontological relationship between Christ's divine and human nature, he also

---

40. Ibid., 416–17.

41. As a compiler of Lutheran theology in the sixteenth and seventeenth centuries, Heinrich Schmid's work takes on a historical character rather than a final or resolute definition of Lutheran theology. See Schmid, *Doctrinal Theology,* 3.

affirms that Christ's human nature enjoys real subsistence (in itself) in its union with the Logos.

Lutheran dogma states that Christ's humanity has no existence prior to the incarnation. This is the driving principle of Schmid's use of ανυποστασια, which he employs to explain how the human nature of Christ is sustained by the person of the Logos, rather than in its own capacity. In other words, the humanity of Christ does not exist as a separate person in its own being, but derives that personhood from its union with the Logos. This is the strict context in which Schmid refers to Christ's human nature in a negative sense as ανυποστασια. That is; the negative aspect of ανυποστασια is applied to the human nature of Christ prior to the incarnation, not subsequent to it, having been assumed by the Logos in this union. To emphasize this point Schmid makes the counter argument that the ανυποστασια can also be understood *positively* because the human nature of Christ has become possessed by the hypostasis of the Logos. The Logos imparts personality to the human nature of Christ in their union, and actively sustains this union as an indissoluble communion of divine and human nature subsisting in one hypostasis of the Son of God.

Schmid also notes that the human nature of Christ existing as ανυποστασια (i.e. without individual personhood), does not negate individual essence in the human nature's being, but simply precludes any notion that Jesus Christ exists as two persons in the Logos. In this way, in its peculiar union with the divine Logos, the human nature of Christ excels other human beings. We note here also the emphasis on the *union between divine* and *human natures* in the Logos, which so richly characterizes Lutheran christological dogma.

Karl Barth's Reception of Reformed and Lutheran Interpretation of Anhypostasis *and* Enhypostasis

It is important to understand that Barth approaches the concepts of *anhypostasis* and *enhypostasis* given the backdrop of Reformed and Lutheran doctrine regarding the human nature of Christ and its union with the Logos. Barth in fact develops these terms dialectically in the *Church Dogmatics* in direct relationship to Reformed and Lutheran Christology. We therefore see the clear influence of both Reformed and Lutheran perspectives of the *anhypostasis* and *enhypostasis* expressed in Karl Barth's adoption of these terms as he was introduced to them by Heppe and Schmid.[42] Barth cites

42. Barth writes to Thurneysen on May 28, 1924: "Take a look in an old book on Dogmatics and see what they understood by "An-Hypostasia" in regard to the nature of

Hollaz in his use of the term *anhypostasis* (or *impersonalitas*) to describe the human nature of Christ having no personality in his own being.

> Hollaz defines the term as follows (ex. Theol. Acroam., 1707, III, 1, 3, qu. 12): *carentia propriae subsistentiae, divina Filii Dei hypostasi tanquam longe eminentiori compensata.* By υποστασις, *persona*, was meant the independent existence (the *propria subsistentia*) of His humanity. Its υποστασις is, longe eminentior, that of the Logos, no other. Jesus Christ exists as a man because as this One exists, because as He makes human essence His own, adopting and exalting it into unity with Himself. As a man, therefore, He exists directly in and with the one God in the mode of existence of His eternal Son and Logos—not otherwise or apart from this mode.[43]

We note here Barth's emphasis on the Logos, who assuming human essence to himself makes it his own. As such, this mode of human existence is possible only through the existence of the eternal Son—the Logos. Barth cites Polanus and Heidegger (via Heppe) emphasizing the human nature being elected, but not existing autonomously.

> He certainly does not exist only εν ιδεα, but εν ατομω, *in uno certo individuo* (Polanus, Synt. Theol. Chr., 1609, VI, 15, col. 2406), in the one form of human nature and being elected and prepared and actualised by God, yet not autonomously, as would be the case if that with which God unites Himself were a *homo* and not *humanitas*. With a more emphatic regard for this *anhypostasis* of the human nature of Jesus Christ, H. Heidegger (Corp. Theol. Chr., 1700, XVII, 36, quoted from Heppe, 2nd edition, 325) defined the incarnation as the *assumptio* . . . [44]

Barth argues that this theologoumenon, which purports that Christ's human nature has no true independent existence like us (being indirectly maintained by the *enhypostasis*), in no way denies the true humanity of Christ, nor gives any allusion to a concealed or blatant Docetism. The issue therefore for Barth is not to deny the true humanity of Christ, but the autonomous existence of His humanity.[45]

Christ. That was forceful teaching—which should now be put back on the lamp-stand . . ." Barth-Thurneysen Correspondence, 185.

43. Barth *CD* IV/2, 49. We take notice here that Barth cites Hollaz and his understanding of the *impersonalitas* of Christ's human nature to complement Barth's own argument for the *anhypostasis* of Christ's human nature.

44. Ibid.

45. Ibid.

But to this objection we may reply with Hollaz (loc. Cit.): Perfectio rei ex essential, non ex subsistentia aestimanda est. It is true enough that the humanum exists always in the form of actual man. This existence is not denied to the man Jesus, but ascribed to Him with the positive concept of *enhypostasis*. But it is hard to see how the full truth of the humanity of Jesus Christ is qualified or even destroyed by the fact that as distinct from us He is also a real man only as the Son of God, so that there can be no question of a peculiar and autonomous existence of His humanity.[46]

Although Reformed and Lutheran theology played a major role in Barth's familiarity with the concepts of *anhypostasis* and *enhypostasis*, he did not adopt these concepts in the strictest sense as they were characterized by this dogma. Recognizing the historical/theological legitimacy of *anhypostasis* and *enhypostasis*, Barth adopted these concepts as he saw their place in the revelation of Jesus Christ expressed by the time-eternity and veiling-unveiling dialectic. In essentials, Barth agreed that Christ's human nature came into existence in the incarnation of the Logos; whereupon the Logos assumed to himself human nature in the flesh of Jesus. In this sense Barth agreed with Heppe and Schmid that in the humanity of Christ's union with the Logos, his humanity is understood to exist as ενυποστατον, having subsistence in the hypostasis of the Logos.

Barth also agreed with Heppe and Schmid that the human nature of Jesus was ανυποστατος, having no existence before its union with the Logos in the incarnation. It is in the *anhypostasis*, however, where Barth demonstrates an interesting ontological dexterity in his interpretation of the *anhypostasis* of Christ's human nature. Whereas both the Reformed and Lutherans isolate the *anhypostasis* of Christ's human nature to that point prior to the incarnation (being non-existent), Barth continues to embrace *anhypostasis* as a negative characteristic of Christ's human nature even in its union with the Logos. This aspect of Barth's Christology first emerged in the *Göttingen Dogmatics* and thereafter was more fully developed in the *Church Dogmatics*.

The *Göttingen Dogmatics*

Having completed his first edition of *Der Römerbrief* in 1919, and in the midst of his first revision in 1921 (*Romans* II), Barth accepted the Honorary Professorship of Reformed Theology at Göttingen where he devoted his first

46. Ibid.

years lecturing on the Heidelberg Catechism, John Calvin, Ulrich Zwingli, the Reformed Confessions, and Friedrich Schleiermacher.[47] As Barth took up German theological academic life at Göttingen, the Weimar Republic was approaching the two year point coming on the heels of Germany's defeat in the First World War. Post war reconstruction brought with it significant changes to German political, social, and theological thinking in an effort to break with the *old way of thinking*. Theologically speaking this included a renewed interest in *deep meaning* in the world, as well as dialectical theology. Barth's theological development in Germany clearly engages these dynamic cultural changes as well as the contemporary theological thinking that surrounded him.[48] Indeed, this period in German history proved to be invaluable to Barth as he worked through the impact of Jesus of Nazareth upon human history. During his academic career in Germany Barth taught at Göttingen between 1921 and 1925, at Münster from October 1925 to 1930, and at Bonn from March 1930 to June 1935. By the time Barth was forced to leave Bonn for Basel in 1935, his theology had clearly engaged the German theological and political/social thinking of his day as Barth worked out what it means that the revelation of Jesus Christ actively confronts individuals in his person.

The *Göttingen Dogmatics* (originally entitled: *Unterrichte in der christlichen Religion*)[49] was born out of Barth's lectures on dogmatics given at Göttingen during the period April 1924 to October 1925, and provides helpful insights into his earliest theological thinking. Viewed in its historical context, the *Göttingen Dogmatics*, this *Urdogmatik*, is the forerunner to Barth's *Christliche Dogmatik* of Münster[50] and the *Church Dogmatics* of Bonn and

47. See Webster, *Barth's Earlier Theology*, 42. Although Barth arrived in Göttingen less than fully equipped for the task of teaching Reformed theology, he was no stranger to academic theological work having grown up in a household where his father was a Professor of Theology. Moreover, Barth himself had worked on a leading liberal theological journal while a student at Marburg, not to mention his exegetical work on *Romans*, as well as publishing a number of public articles for which he was well known. His lectures at Göttingen not only immersed him into the Reformed theological world, but also produced an early glimpse into his Reformed theological development.

48. See Gorringe, *Karl Barth*, 78.

49. See Bromiley, *Göttingen Dogmatics*, Translator's Preface. Barth agreed to this title under compulsion. The Lutheran theological faculty at Göttingen insisted that Barth's lectures be restricted to Reformed Dogmatics. Barth disagreed because he did not want to be restricted to any "ecumenical tags" in his lectures. When Barth's appeal to the Minister of Culture at Berlin was denied, his compromise was to use the title *Unterrichte in der christlichen Religion*, which in reality served only as a cover to his lectures on Church Dogmatics.

50. Barth was Professor of Dogmatics and New Testament Exegesis in Münster during the period October 1925 to March 1930. At Münster Barth penned his second

Basel.[51] Interestingly, the Göttingen work is the only larger dogmatics that Barth ever completed. Although the volume of material covered in this work is obviously much smaller than that developed in the *Church Dogmatics*, we see enough similarity in basic structure to gain an understanding into Barth's line of thinking at this point of his christological development.

Barth's lectures at Göttingen, which were given on the heels of his *Romans* commentaries, provide the impetus for his quest for a new theology capable of responding to the ongoing cultural shift in the Weimar Republic. The ecstatic and abstract approach of Expressionism that had first dominated German thinking after the War began to give way to the "Neue Sachlichkeit" (the new objectivity), which brought with it a spirit of resignation in the face of the stark reality of German life.[52] With the German cultural realities in clear view, we see in the *Göttingen Dogmatics* that Barth begins to lay significant groundwork for explaining the objective reality of Jesus Christ that directly confronts this sense of resignation.[53]

Barth first adopts the terms *anhypostasis* and *enhypostasis* to explain how the human nature of Christ exists in union with the Logos in the *Göttingen Dogmatics* where he generally treats these terms as autonomous concepts rather than coupling them together to form an ontological unit.[54] In

---

Dogmatics work entitled *Die Christliche Dogmatik im Entwurf.* Bruce McCormack argues that Barth wrote this book with the "Göttingen material before him," resulting in little change in fundamental decisions made in the Göttingen material. See McCormack, *Dialectical Theology*, 376.

51. Barth taught at Bonn from March 1930 to June 1935 where he wrote *Die Kirchliche Dogmatik* I/1. In June 1935 Barth returned to Basle, Switzerland where he taught until his retirement, writing the remaining volumes of *Die Kirchliche Dogmatik*.

52. See McCormack, *Dialectical Theology*, 329.

53. Timothy Gorringe makes an important observation here. In Göttingen Barth begins in earnest to wrestle with the questions of God's Word and preaching (i.e., How can it be said in preaching that "God has spoken?"). In his pursuit of answering these questions Barth focused on the canon, the authority and freedom in the Church, and the doctrines of the Trinity and incarnation. Gorringe argues that the characterization of Barth's theology as "neo-orthodox" came out of Barth's "affirmation of the canon, or the ancient doctrines of the *an-*and *enhypostasis*" where Barth elaborated Dogmatic Prolegomena in a new way. In other words, Barth is not retreating back beyond the enlightenment but actually takes up these ideas in his arduous confrontation with hegemony. See Gorringe, *Karl Barth*, 101–102. I agree with Gorringe, but would add that it is Barth's unique adoption of *anhypostasis* and *enhypostasis* that actually moves beyond seventeenth century theology, which grounds his antithesis toward hegemony in the person and revelation of Jesus Christ.

54. Given that fact that Barth first came across the concepts of *anhypostasis* and *enhypostasis* in the old protestant theological compilations of Heppe and Schmid, some critics were convinced that Barth's theology represented a return to orthodoxy. See Gorringe, *Karl Barth*, 95.

other words, there is no compelling evidence in the *Göttingen Dogmatics* that Barth expresses *anhypostasis* and *enhypostasis* as a congruous ontological formula to explain the subsistence of Christ's human nature. At the same time we see here (and in the *Church Dogmatics* as well) Barth's polemic use of *anhypostasis* and *enhypostasis* as a dialectic between Reformed and Lutheran Christology, buttressed by a historical/theological frame of reference in his appropriation of these terms. With this in view I will consider Barth's argument for the *anhypostasis*, which becomes the dominant theme of his ontological argument for Christ's human nature in the *Göttingen Dogmatics*. The *enhypostasis* on the other hand, although an important ontological concept in Christ's human nature, plays a relatively small role at this stage of Barth's christological development.

Barth approaches the *anhypostasis* of Christ's human nature given his presupposition that both the Reformed and Lutherans affirm the "historical phenomenon" that as the form of revelation, Jesus is a "creature of the triune God." From this mutual point of christological agreement, however, there emerges an ontological dichotomy with respect to Christ's human nature that sharply distinguishes the Reformed from the Lutherans. Whereas the Lutherans understand that, as a *creature*, Jesus is inviolably united to the Logos without qualification; the Reformed understand that, as a *creation*, Jesus is united to the Logos subject to the rule that "the finite is not capable of the infinite."[55] What is particularly interesting in this context is Barth's presupposition that both the Reformed and Lutherans appropriate the term *anhypostasis* in a *negative* sense to describe the human nature of Christ, having no real personality or subsistence of its own given its union with the Logos. Moreover, while assuming a *paradoxical* view of the *anhypostasis* with respect to Christ's human nature, Barth judges that both the Reformed and Lutherans confused the meaning of *anhypostasis* so as to deny the personality of Christ's human nature altogether.[56]

> Both Lutherans and Reformed, so as to obviate any possible misunderstanding, even went so far as to deny to Christ's human

---

55. Barth, *Göttingen Dogmatics*, 90. In this context Barth develops the principle of God's self-revelation in the person of Jesus of Nazareth set against the historicity of Jesus that emerged in eighteenth century theology. That is, Barth sharply distinguishes between the "content" of revelation as God alone versus the "form" of revelation in Jesus of Nazareth. In this way Barth speaks against a "deifying of the creature" in the revelation of God.

56. Barth introduces his transition to the *anhypostasis* of Christ's human nature by stating: "The content of revelation is God *alone*." Although the form is not the content, it is here that one hears: Deus dixit. That is, "in the humanity of Christ the content of revelation as well as the subject is God alone." Barth, *Göttingen Dogmatics*, 89–90.

nature any personality at all. The person of the God-man is exclusively the Word, the Logos of God. No matter what we think
of this paradoxical thesis, the so-called *anhypostasis* of Christ's
human nature, it would certainly be wiser to consider its content
instead of getting worked up about it.[57]

This seemingly innocuous passage in fact reflects the high priority
that Barth places upon the God-man. That is, Jesus of Nazareth exists as
very man, but a man who in his humanity is inseparable from his union
with the second person of the Trinity. Put another way, in his union with
the Logos, Jesus of Nazareth in fact becomes one with the Logos of God.
This is the christological principle upon which Barth works out his understanding of the *anhypostasis* of Christ's human nature. For Barth, no
ground can be given here. Jesus Christ is not simply a historical figure (as
purported by liberal theology), but he himself—in his person—is indeed
the revelation of God. This ontological grounding becomes foundational
for Barth given the *paradoxical* nature of the *anhypostasis*. The question
therefore that emerges is: how can a human nature, which has no personality or reality in its own being, become very man (i.e., real being) in union
with the Logos? Barth anticipates and meets this question in his ontology
of the incarnation, and makes a fundamental statement with respect to the
union of divine and human natures when he says that: "The incarnation
implies that the Son assumes human nature."[58] It is Christ's assumption
of human nature that explains "how revelation is effected." That is, the
eternal Christ, who is unchangeable in his divine nature, unites with his
"divine mode of being" a "human mode of existence."[59] Barth describes
the function of this union by explaining:

> It is not, then, a changing or alteration of the divine nature of the
> Son, but with His divine mode of existence the Son takes a hu-
> man mode of existence, uniting it—the "grace of union"—to His
> person, just as the divine mode of existence is eternally united
> to His person, yet without in any way altering His divine mode
> of existence.[60]

Given this context, it is in the kenosis of the incarnate Son that Barth
emphasizes the union of the Logos with human nature, rather than the
union of *divine* and *human natures* in the person of Christ. That is, even

57. Ibid., 90.
58. Ibid., 156.
59. Ibid.
60. Ibid.

in the Son's *emptying* of his divine majesty in his incarnation, Christ does not wholly or partially cease to be the eternal Son of the Father; otherwise, the incarnation would not be the revelation of God. Rather, in the kenosis, the Son of God becomes the Son of Man, an uncompromising unity of the Logos and human nature in the person of Jesus Christ.[61] And yet, Barth's adoption of the kenosis leads to an open ended expression of this union leaving unanswered how the human nature comes into this union with the Logos. In other words, if in his emptying Christ retains his full essence of divinity, how is the union of human nature with the Logos affected? Barth works through this problem dialectically as he examines Reformed and Lutheran orthodoxy of the incarnation.

In his analysis Barth points to an inaccuracy in the "older Lutherans"[62] and their understanding of the union of divine and human natures—in contrast to the older Reformed (and more dynamic view), which stresses the *person* as the divine *subject*.[63] Barth describes the incarnation as "a personal, not a natural work," and clearly favors the Reformed view that the Logos (not deity or divine essence per se), was made flesh in the incarnation.[64] That is, it is not the substance of the Father, the Son, and the Spirit as deity that became flesh, but the Son, who became human without ceasing to be deity in the second person of the Trinity. In this way the Son assumes and unites human nature to his person.[65]

The question that must be raised at this point is given that the Son assumes human nature, how does Barth understand this human nature to subsist in this union? In response, I would first say that Barth clearly understands the human nature of Christ to be common to all humanity, yet without sin. He cites Philippians 2:7 in affirming that Jesus subsists in the form of a servant, as a being with a human body and human soul.[66] Barth further describes the human nature of Christ as being "compressed" into one individual.[67] He emphasizes that the human nature of Christ "has never existed anywhere as such" (consistent with both Lutheran and Reformed doctrine). "The humanity of Christ, although it is a body and soul,

61. Ibid.

62. Ibid.

63. Ibid.

64. Ibid.

65. Ibid.

66. See Barth, *Epistle to the Philippians*, 63. In the explaining the kenosis Barth emphasizes it is the Son who wills to perform this act of renunciation. "He *wills* it so." The Son willingly puts himself in a place where he alone knows himself in the way the Father knows him.

67. Barth, *Göttingen Dogmatics*, 157.

and an individual, is nothing subsistent or real in itself. Thus it did not exist prior to its union with the Logos. It has no independent existence alongside or apart from him."[68]

This compression of human nature into the Logos rejects any notion of a separate subsistence either "alongside or apart" from its union with the Logos. As such, this ontological framework establishes the revelation of God not in the human individuality of Jesus, but in the individual person of the Logos. It is the eternal Son who takes to himself human nature in Jesus—not the man Jesus who unites himself with the Son. "This idea, the idea of humanity, and this individual who incorporates it, cannot for a single moment be abstracted from their assumption into the person of the Logos. The divine subject who unites Himself with them makes them revelation."[69]

This is the context in which Barth first appropriates anhypostatos to describe the human nature of Christ as having no subsistence in itself. While he argues that Christ's human nature is not an individual person (consistent with Protestant orthodoxy), Barth uses anhypostatos as a negative construct that delimits the *very man* of Christ in union with the Logos (inconsistent with protestant orthodoxy). Barth's thinking emerges more forcibly if we simply ask why he places so much emphasis on the anhypostatos of Christ's human nature in this ontological argument. As previously shown, this was clearly not the emphasis of Reformed or Lutheran doctrine.[70] The concept of *anhypostasis* was used to argue that Christ's human nature had no existence prior to the incarnation. In other words, it was never understood as a concept to describe the human nature of Christ. Furthermore, *anhypostasis* was never accepted by protestant orthodoxy as one side of a two-sided formula in describing the ontology of Christ's human nature—as Barth suggests. Granted, in the *Göttingen Dogmatics* Barth does not postulate a dual ontological formula in his own language, but he refers to an "assumed" formula with anhypostatos serving as the negative side of the *enhypostasis*. Describing Christ's human nature as anhypostatos, Barth refers to the, "formula in which the description culminates. Or,

68. Ibid.

69. Ibid.

70. Baillie argues that "even among theologians who profess to accept the full catholic doctrine of the hypostatic union there is a manifest unwillingness to distinguish Christ's manhood from that of other men by speaking of His 'impersonal humanity'. In view of the time-honored phrase 'Though Man, He is not, strictly speaking, a Man.'" Baillie goes on to say, "But most divines to-day, whether 'Catholic' or 'Dialectical-Protestant' in their orthodoxy, and even while professing to accept in some sense the *anhypostasia* of Ephesus and Chalcedon, would shrink from such a statement, and would quite naturally and without embarrassment speak of Jesus Christ as a man, just as the New Testament writers surely do." Baillie, *God was in Christ*, 15–16.

more positively, it is *enhypostatos*. It has personhood, subsistence, reality, only in its union with the Logos of God."[71]

There is a gentle subtlety in Barth's language here as he moors the terms: personhood, subsistence, and reality into the same mode of existence. When we consider Barth's thinking juxtaposed against the Lutheran and Reformed Fathers (who asserted that in its essence the reality of existence is not bound by personhood per se), we discover an ontological cleavage between Barth's argument and historical orthodoxy. As we have seen, the orthodox Fathers did not use *anhypostasis* to describe Christ's human nature negatively; that is, as having no subsistence of its own, but strictly as a way to describe what Christ's human nature *is not*. In other words, Christ's human nature is not *anhypostasis* because it enjoys real subsistence in its union with the Logos. Therefore, in this respect Barth's use of *anhypostasis* to describe Christ's human nature in a negative sense moves beyond the orthodox Fathers.[72] Even so, I do not believe that it is Barth's intent to move beyond the limits of an orthodox ontology of Christ's human nature, but simply to emphasize that as the subject of divine revelation the Logos assumed to himself a human nature—*in the man named Jesus of Nazareth.*[73]

Interestingly, the passage cited above is the only one in the *Göttingen Dogmatics* where Barth refers specifically to the *enhypostatos* of Christ's human nature. As we have seen, the thrust of Barth's development of *anhypostasis* and *enhypostasis* in the *Göttingen Dogmatics* centers on the *negative*—on the idea that Christ's human nature, being anhypostatos, has no real subsistence (in itself) in its union with the Logos. This is somewhat counter-balanced by Barth's adoption of *enhypostatos*, which he uses to describe how Christ's human nature (positively) has personhood, subsistence, and reality in union with the person of the Logos.[74] As a result, the anhypostatos and *enhypostatos* manifest opposite sides of the same christo-

---

71. Barth, *Göttingen Dogmatics*, 157.

72. With respect to Barth's understanding of *anhypostasis*, Baillie observes that "Barth is quite clear that the Word became not merely Man, but *a* Man, and insists that the *anhypostasia*, the 'impersonality', never meant that the humanity of Christ had no 'personality' in the modern sense (for which the Latin word would be *individualitas*), but that it had no independent existence." Baillie further observes, "But still more notable is the answer that Barth gives to the question whether it was fallen or unfallen human nature that Christ assumed in the incarnation. He knows very well that the orthodox tradition, whether Catholic or Protestant, has always most explicitly answered: 'Unfallen human nature.' But Barth himself quite boldly answers: 'Fallen human nature', and maintains that this is what is meant by the Word becoming not only *man* but *flesh*." Baillie, *God was in Christ*, 16.

73. Barth, *Göttingen Dogmatics*, 157.

74. Ibid.

logical coin in explaining how Christ's human nature is united ontologically with the Logos. In this way Barth grants that Christ's human nature enjoys subsistent reality in union with the Logos, while providing an ontological counter balance to the anhypostatos.

Barth further argues for the orthodoxy of his adoption of anhypostatos by citing both the Reformed and Lutherans in their affirmation of the early church description of Mary as the mater Domini, theotokos, deipara, the God-bearer.[75] Barth reasons that the incarnation bears witness to the reality of Mary giving birth to God's Son, who although he was born in the flesh of human nature, manifested reality as a human being in the person of God's Son.[76] It is this reality, Barth's uncompromising emphasis that the Logos takes to himself human nature—defined as *anhypostasis*—which Barth believes should be apparent given the very nature of the incarnation. This anhypostatos, however, remains paradoxical as Barth stresses the reality of Christ's human nature in Jesus, yet always with the caveat that this reality is reality only in the Logos who assumed to himself the flesh of humanity. But it must be noted here that Barth's emphasis on the *anhypostasis* does not portray docetic sympathies, but is simply used to explain how Christ's human nature exists in its union with the Logos.[77]

> A further inference is that those who saw and heard and handled Jesus did not see and hear and handle a mere appearance or vesture or dwelling of the Logos but the Logos himself in the flesh of Christ. To be sure, it was the servant form of the human nature—and this means here, too, the indirectness of revelation, the possibility of offense, the demand for faith—but it was still the Logos himself, not a second alongside him.[78]

While Jesus was indeed a real human being with a real body, mind, and soul, the revelation of God in Jesus Christ is not derived strictly in the flesh, which in Barth's thinking is nothing more than a "divinization of the creature."[79] Rather, as anhypostatos, the human being of Jesus exists only in and through Christ. This principal emphasis governs Barth's thinking with

75. Ibid.

76. Ibid.

77. Barth's Christology remains consistent in its abject denial of a docetic view of Christ's human nature. This ontological presupposition takes on a fervent expression particularly in the *Church Dogmatics* where Barth emphasizes the realness of Christ's human nature as the absolute and necessary reality in Christ's role as mediator between God and humanity.

78. Barth, *Göttingen Dogmatics*, 158.

79. Ibid.

respect to this doctrine such that "apart from the Logos he could not consist for a moment."[80]

In view of our consideration of Karl Barth's development of the *anhypostasis* and *enhypostasis* of Christ's human nature in the *Göttingen Dogmatics,* we can identify four key points that summarize Barth's adoption of these terms at this stage of his christological development:

1. Barth adopts the term anhypostatos to describe the human nature of Christ negatively, having no separate reality of being in its union with the Logos.

2. There is a theological cleavage between Barth's understanding of *anhypostasis* and orthodox protestant Christology with respect to the reality of Christ's human nature in its union with the Logos.

3. Barth adopts the term *enhypostatos* to describe the human nature of Christ positively, having subsistent reality in its union with the Logos.

4. Barth develops *anhypostasis* and *enhypostasis* as autonomous, rather than congruent ontological concepts to explain Christ's human nature.

In the *Göttingen Dogmatics,* the emphasis of Barth's adoption of *anhypostasis* and *enhypostasis* rests upon the *anhypostasis,* which he interprets as protestant orthodox dogma in denying the subsistent reality of Christ's human nature (in itself) in union with the Logos. In this way Barth moves beyond both Reformed and Lutheran orthodox Christology, which does not use *anhypostasis* to deny the separate reality of Christ's human nature, but simply to affirm its non-existence prior to the incarnation, so as to preclude any notion of two persons being united in the Logos. We note here that when Barth once again begins to take up these concepts in the *Church Dogmatics* in the late 1930s, he does so in the midst of a German culture vastly removed from the one in which he wrote his dogmatics in Göttingen. With this shift in German political and social climate emerges Barth's further development of *anhypostasis* and *enhypostasis* in the humanity of Christ. What emerges is a fuller synthesis of these concepts—not only with respect to the union of human nature with the Logos—but Barth's ground breaking expression of Jesus Christ's union with his church.

80. Ibid.

The *Church Dogmatics*

Karl Barth's fullest development of *anhypostasis* and *enhypostasis* to express the human nature of Christ occurs in the *Church Dogmatics,* which he presents in three distinct sections:

1. *Die Lehre vom Wort Gottes—KD* I/2 (1939); ET, *The Doctrine of the Word of God—CD* I/2

2. *Die Lehre von der Schöpfung—KD* III/2 (1945); ET, *The Doctrine of Creation—CD* III/2

3. *Die Lehre von der Versöhnung—KD* IV/2 (1955); ET *The Doctrine of Reconciliation—CD* IV/2

By 1939 the uncertain and shifting sands of the Weimar Republic[81] had given way to the Third Reich's reorientation of German culture—together with its perverted view of humanity—evidenced by its persecution of the Jewish people and instigation of the Second World War.[82] Barth was dismissed from his professorship in Bonn in 1935 for his refusal to give the oath of loyalty to the Führer. However, within three days of his dismissal Barth was offered a special chair at the university at Basle where he wrote and lectured his *Church Dogmatics* for the remaining years of his life. In Basle, fourteen years after Barth first adopted *anhypostasis* and *enhypostasis* to explain the human nature of Christ in the *Göttingen Dogmatics,* these terms once again find expression throughout the *Church Dogmatics* where Barth transitions from a rather incongruous treatment of these concepts to their ontological union in expressing the subsistence of Christ's human nature. Nevertheless, in this movement Barth does not waver ontologically in his understanding of Christ's human nature as a non-subsistent being, having been assumed by its union with the Logos. In other words, Barth continues to express the human nature of Christ negatively as *anhypostasis*—as not being self-subsistent—which is counter-balanced by the subsis-

---

81. See Hoffmann, *The History of the German Resistance 1933–1945,* 3. Succeeding the Prussian/German government after its defeat in the First World War, the Weimar Republic was unable to overcome its external and internal weaknesses and challenges. That is, it failed to successfully cope with the continuous attacks of its national political opponents, both left-wing and national. This was compounded by the economic burdens of post war reparations and national inflation. Even as the reviving republic began to show signs of survival, it was rocked by the 1929 economic crisis from which it could not recover.

82. Ibid., 100. After the announcement of Hitler's pact with Stalin in August 1939, Hitler unleashed a vast anti-Jewish campaign "such as had not been seen since the middle ages." Thousands of Jewish businesses and synagogues were looted, destroyed, or set on fire.

tent reality of the *enhypostasis* enjoined through its union with the Logos. In this analysis of the *Church Dogmatics* I will consider Barth's interpretation of the *anhypostasis* and *enhypostasis* in each of the three sections where he uses these terms to explain the ontology of Christ's human nature.

The Doctrine of the Word of God—CD I/2

Despite his extrication from Germany, Barth still felt a close kinship with the German people who had played such an important role on his theological development. This feeling of kinship was exacerbated in light of the German theological struggles that came with the rise of the Nazi Party. Karl Barth was deeply concerned with opposing the Nazis and their rejection of the first commandment, which for him was no less than a matter of preserving the true church.[83] In the summer of 1937 Barth completed the second half of the prolegomena (*KD* I/2) where he transitions from his development of the Trinity (in *KD* I/1) and the subject of revelation to the reality of this revelation in the person of Jesus Christ. That is, Barth now addresses the objective reality that God's freedom for humanity is realized in the incarnate Word as an event, which provides the basis for "the *possibility* that God *can* become a man."[84]

The stage is therefore set for Barth's most precise treatment of *anhypostasis* and *enhypostasis* in the *Church Dogmatics* which is found in the second half-volume of *Doctrine of the Word of God*, the impetus of which emerges from Barth's desire to explain in tangible language—supported by historical/theological orthodoxy—how the Logos comes into union with human nature in the person of Jesus Christ *as a real person*. The underlying ontological principle expressed by the use of these terms is that the eternal Logos assumes to himself human nature, which is made manifest in Jesus Christ. Barth emphasizes this point in his introductory comments to this section when he says: "But from the utter uniqueness of this unity follows the statement, that God and man are so related in Jesus Christ, that He exists as Man so far and only so far as He exists as God, i.e., in the mode of existence of the eternal Word of God."[85]

Barth argues for the historical orthodoxy of *anhypostasis* and *enhypostasis* by stating: "What we therefore express is a doctrine unanimously sponsored by early theology in its entirety, that of the *anhypostasis* and

---

83. Busch, *Karl Barth*, 271.

84. Ibid., 282.

85. Barth, *CD* I/2, 163.

enhypostasis of the human nature of Christ."[86] In citing "early theology" and its "unanimous agreement" Barth suggests that both *anhypostasis* and *enhypostasis* were historical/orthodox christological terms used to explain the ontology of Christ's human nature.[87] Barth's understanding here is consistent with the *Göttingen Dogmatics*, and sets the stage for his further development of the interrelationship of these terms demonstrated by his coupling them into one ontological statement (i.e., as expressed by the formula *anhypostasis* and *enhypostasis*).[88] Herein, Barth lays down more concrete language to first explain the *anhypostasis* as the negative characteristic of Christ's human nature, having no existence prior to the incarnation and union with the Logos in the event of the εγενετο.

> *Anhypostasis* asserts the negative. Since in virtue of the εγενετο, i.e., in virtue of the *assumptio*, Christ's human nature has its existence—the ancients said, its subsistence—in the existence of God, meaning in the mode of being (hypostasis, "person") of the Word, it does not possess it in and for itself, *in abstracto*. Apart from the divine mode of being whose existence it acquires it has none of its own; i.e., apart from its concrete existence in God in the event of the *unio*, it has no existence of its own, it is ανυποστατος.[89]

I observe two key components in this statement to explain the *anhypostasis* of Christ's human nature. First, Barth notes that the Logos assumes to himself a human nature that did not exist prior to its union with the Logos. In other words, this human nature does not possess being in and of itself (*in abstracto*), but strictly in its union with the Logos, which Barth accurately notes was the argument of the ancients (patristic Fathers). Secondly, Barth concludes that ontologically the absence of being outside its union with the Logos logically demands the human nature to be understood

86. Ibid.

87. Barth refers here to the patristic Fathers who worked with the terms *anhypostasis* and *enhypostasis* (and variations thereof) in defense of Chalcedon. In chapter 2, I examined four significant figures of the patristic era who were actively engaged in this debate.

88. Torrance recognizes Barth's adoption of *anhypostasis* and *enhypostasis* as a couplet formulation, but also attributes this coupling to earlier theology: "In particular I was gripped by the way in which he resurrected and deployed the theological couplet anhypostasia and enhypostasia to throw into sharp focus 'the inner logic of grace' (as I called it) embodied in the incarnation, with reference to which, not least as it had taken paradigmatic shape in the Virgin Birth of Jesus, all the ways and works of God in His interaction with us in space and time may be given careful formulation." Torrance, *Karl Barth Biblical* and *Evangelical Theologian*, 125.

89. Barth, *CD* I/2, 163.

negatively as ανυποστατος in this union. As previously shown, this is at variance with the patristic Fathers, as well as scholastic and post-scholastic orthodoxy, who did not apply ανυποστατος to Christ's human nature as a negative characteristic of his being.

Barth then applies the second half of the ontological statement (or formula) as the positive aspect of Christ's human nature. In describing Christ's human nature as ενυποστατος Barth grants that it has concrete existence of its own by virtue of the εγενετο.

> *Enhypostasis* asserts the positive. In virtue of the εγενετο, i.e. in virtue of the *assumptio*, the human nature acquires existence (subsistence) in the existence of God, meaning in the mode of being (hypostasis, "person") of the Word. This divine mode of being gives it existence in the event of the *unio*, and in this way it has a concrete existence of its own, it is ενυποστατος.[90]

The material point that I take away from this statement is that positively the ενυποστατος of Christ's human nature is ontologically joined—*in the event of its union with the Logos*—to the negative ανυποστατος of the same human nature. Even so, one must ask if this formulation of the positive aspect of Christ's human nature legitimately represents the fullness of his existence. This is the question that Barth repeatedly addresses throughout the *Church Dogmatics* in his use of this theologoumenon.[91]

90. Ibid. With respect to the "negative" and "positive" aspects of the an-*enhypostasis* in Barth's definition, Oliver Crisp suggests: "This way of speaking about the *anhypostatos physis* and *enhypostatos physis* is, it seems to me, somewhat misleading, for it could be taken to mean that the two aspects of the an-enhypostasia distinction are negative and positive ways of stating the same thesis. But this is not the case." see Crisp, *Divinity and Humanity*, 74. I argue that this is precisely what Barth does in joining both *anhypostasis* and *enhypostasis* into one congruent clause to describe the human nature of Christ.

91. Torrance understands the negative *anhypostasis* to be appropriately counter balanced by the positive *enhypostasis* in Barth's development of Christ's human nature: "Karl Barth's participation in this struggle for the unity and integrity of the faith is particularly evident in his rich understanding and deployment of the theological couplet *anhypostasia* and *enhypostasia*, which was designed to carry the doctrine of the hypostatic union in Christ further in a positive way. The negative term an-hypostasia asserts that apart from the incarnation of the Son of God Jesus would not have come into being and exists as a completely human person in the full hypostatic reality of the incarnate Son of God. It asserts that Jesus Christ did not have an independent hypostasis which was then adopted into union with the divine hypostasis of the Son of God, but that thanks to the pure act of God's grace, in coming into being Jesus Christ was given a complete human hypostasis in, and in perfect oneness with, the divine hypostasis of the Son. The theological couplet *anhypostasia/enhypostasia* expresses in succinct hypostatic terms the essential logic in the irreversible movement of God's grace . . . However, by grace alone does not in any way mean the diminishing far less the excluding of the

Barth affirms that as ενυποστατος the human nature of Christ enjoys concrete existence of its own in union with the Logos, and cites the Second Council of Constantinople (553) in which "this doctrine was erected into dogma."[92] In this way Barth demonstrates that the Council's aim was to guard against the idea of a double existence of Christ as God and humanity. Barth concludes: "what the eternal Word made His own, giving it thereby His own existence, was not a man, but man's nature, man's being, and so not a second existence but a second possibility of existence, to wit, that of a man."[93]

In his argument, the *paradoxical* fence that Barth struggles to climb over is explaining how the "lack" of subsistence embodied by the *anhypostasis* does not deny true humanity to the human nature of Christ in spite of the assumed counter-balancing of the *enhypostasis*. Having established the formula of *anhypostasis* and *enhypostasis* as an orthodox understanding of Christ's human nature, Barth argues that the absence of the human nature's self existence does not deny true humanity to Jesus Christ because such an argument misunderstands the Latin term impersonalitas used occasionally for *anhypostasis*.[94]

> But what Christ's human nature lacks according to the early doctrine is not what we call personality. This the early writers called individulatis, and they never taught that Christ's human nature lacked this, but rather that this qualification actually belonged to true human being. Personalitas was their name for what we call existence or being. Their negative position asserted

human but on the contrary its full and complete establishment. The archetypal instance of that was the virgin birth of Jesus. The realisation that anhypostasia and enhypostasia are essentially complementary and must be used together as a double concept derives ultimately from Cyril of Alexandria, but Barth himself seems to have taken it from seventeenth century Reformed theologians. As Barth used it, however, this was a technically precise way of speaking of the reality, wholeness and integrity of the human nature of Jesus Christ in the incarnation, without lapsing into adoptionism, and of speaking of its perfect oneness with the divine nature of Christ without lapsing into monophysitism. Through maintaining the proper differentiation between God and the creation, the negative term is made to serve the positive term in such a way as to stress the indivisible union of the divine and human natures in their undiminished reality in the one person of Jesus Christ. It was thus the strongest way devised by Patristic theology after the Council of Chalcedon to reject any form of schizoid understanding of Jesus Christ such as had been put forward not only in Nestorian heresy, but in the post-Chalcedonian dualism attacked so strongly by Severus of Antioch on the basis of the teaching of Cyril of Alexandria." see Torrance, *Karl Barth*, 199–200.

92. Barth, *CD* I/2, 163.

93. Ibid.

94. Barth, *CD* I/2, 164.

that Christ's flesh in itself has no existence, and this was asserted
in the interests of their positive position that Christ's flesh has
its existence through the Word and in the Word, who is God
Himself acting as Revealer and Reconciler.[95]

Reflecting on Barth's comments cited above brings to mind that the
patristic Fathers, the Lutheran and Reformed scholastics, Heinrich Schmid,
and Heinrich Heppe never understood the human nature of Christ to lack
anything in its existence in union with the Logos. If there was any negative
connotation in their ontology of the human nature of Christ it was simply to
affirm that it did not exist prior to its union with the Logos at the moment of
incarnation. Hence, there was never any reason to express *anhypostasis* and
enhypostasis in juxtaposition with each other as a way to explain how the
positive counter-balances the negative. Barth clearly moves beyond historical orthodoxy in this respect.

It is this counter-balancing of the paradoxical union of *anhypostasis*
and *enhypostasis* that Barth uses to argue how the revelation of God is made
manifest in the person of Jesus Christ, which Barth understands to square
with the reality of Christ attested to by the Scriptures.

Understood in this its original sense, this particular doctrine,
abstruse in appearance only, is particularly well adapted to make
it clear that the reality attested by Holy Scripture, Jesus Christ
is the reality of a divine act of Lordship which is unique and
singular as compared will all other events, and in this way to
characterize it as a reality held up to faith by revelation.[96]

Using the language of *anhypostasis* and *enhypostasis* Barth's allusion to the dialectic of veiling and unveiling is readily apparent. The end
point for Barth is not to develop an ontological model to explain how the
negative feature of Christ's human nature is balanced by the positive. But
rather, Barth wants to provide an ontological basis—supported by orthodox
Christology—to explain how eternal God reveals himself in the flesh of real
humanity. Nevertheless, Barth's argument reverts to a negative grounding of
Christ's human nature that exists passively in union with the divine Word.

It is in virtue of the eternal Word that Jesus Christ exists as a man
of flesh and blood in our sphere, as a man like us, as an historical
phenomenon. But it is only in virtue of the divine Word that He
exists as such. If He existed in a different way, how would He be
revelation in the real sense in which revelation is intended in

95. Ibid.
96. Ibid., 164–65.

> Holy Scripture? Because of this positive aspect, it was well worth making the negative a dogma and giving it the very careful consideration which it received in early Christology.[97]

True to his uncompromising commitment to the revelation of God in the humanity of Christ, Barth emphasizes that the existence of this humanity is made possible only by virtue of its union with the Logos. This is a crucial point to grasp in Barth's thinking here. Although Barth holds on to the negative aspect of *anhypostasis*, he also holds on firmly to the fact that Jesus of Nazareth is *real humanity* who exists as flesh and blood like us (as *enhypostasis*) as a *historical figure*. For Barth, it is in the historical person of Jesus Christ that the revelation of God is actually realized according to Holy Scripture. Consequently, the coupling of *anhypostasis* and *enhypostasis* must be maintained.

The Doctrine of Creation—CD III/2

In 1945 Karl Barth published the *Doctrine of Creation* (*CD* III/2) approximately six years after the *Doctrine of the Word* (*CD* I/2).[98] Although Barth makes only a brief reference to the *anhypostasis* and *enhypostasis* in this context, it gives us important insight into his understanding of God's creation of—and the relationship to—human nature created in Jesus Christ. The fact that the humanity of Christ is a creation of God does not diminish the fact of his indissoluble union with the Logos.

> This man is there in and by the sovereign being of God which He is born and by which He is sustained and preserved and upheld. Not two juxtaposed realities—a divine and then a human, or even less a human and then a divine—constitute the essence of man, this man, but the one, divine reality, in which as such the human is posited, contained, and included. Man, this man, is the immanent kingdom of God, nothing more and nothing in and for Himself. Similarly, the kingdom of God is utterly and unreservedly this man. He is as He is in the Word of God. And the fact that this is so lifts Him above all other creatures. This is the distinction which is His and His alone.[99]

We see in this passage perhaps the true essence of how Barth understands the humanity of Jesus in union with the Logos. The person of Jesus

97. Ibid., 165.

98. Originally published as *Die Lehre vom Wort Gottes—KD* I/2 (1939) and *Die Lehre von der Schöpfung—KD* III/2 (1945) respectively.

99. Barth, *CD* III/2, 69–70.

Christ is not, ontologically speaking, the simple joining together of divine and human natures. Rather, he is divine reality manifested in a man; not just any man, but the man lifted above all created men as the Word of God. As such, Jesus exists as he is—only as he is the Word of God.[100] Based upon this thesis Barth draws heavily upon the formula *anhypostasis* and *enhypostasis* to express the ontological union of God with humanity.

> In this we are repeating in other words the doctrine of the Early Church concerning the anhypostasia or enhypostasia of the human nature of Christ by which John 1:14 ("the Word became flesh") was rightly interpreted: ut caro illa nullam propriam subsistentiam extra Dei Filium habeat sed ab illo et in eo vere sustentetur et gestetur (Syn. Pur. Theol. Leiden, 1624, Disp. 25, 4). The correctness of this theologoumenon is seen in the fact that its negative statement is only the delimitation of the positive. Because the man Jesus came into being and is by the Word of God, it is only by the Word of God that He came into being and is. Because He is the Son of God, it is only as such that He is real man.[101]

Interestingly, we notice that Barth describes the human nature of Christ as "anhypostasia *or* enhypostasia." The counter-balancing of this positive/negative dynamic is seamlessly interwoven into Christ's human nature as Barth explains that the negative only delimits the positive. Moreover, it is here that the *anhypostasis* and *enhypostasis* of Christ's human nature converge in the dialectic of both time-eternity and veiling-unveiling. This is the paradox of the creation of Christ's human nature. This is the mystery of Jesus Christ existing as *very God* and *very man.*

The Doctrine of Reconciliation—CD IV/2

Barth's final expression of *anhypostasis* and *enhypostasis* is found in the *Doctrine of Reconciliation* (CD IV/2), which was published in 1955, thirty

---

100. William Stacy Johnson argues that Barth agreed with Schleiermacher that Jesus constitutes the first instance in history of a completed human existence. Nevertheless, Barth rejected the idea that Jesus accomplished this task through a realization of his own inherent capacity for God. For Barth Jesus Christ is both fully human and fully divine. "Every act of Jesus is thoroughly human and divine at once. This double agency occurs in such a way that the divinity does not abrogate the humanity, nor vice versa, for Jesus is completely like us in his human nature, differing from us only in the fact that his is a human nature now exalted to its true destiny." Johnson, *The Mystery of God*, 110-11.

101. Barth, *CD* III/2, 70.

years after his first adoption of these terms in Göttingen.[102] This is important to note for two reasons. First, the significance of the *anhypostasis* and *enhypostasis* had not lost its theological fervor in Barth's thinking, and in fact becomes axiomatic to his Christology. Second, this language becomes indispensible for Barth to express the union of divinity and humanity in God's reconciliation with humanity, as well as his dialogue with Chalcedon in working out the union of divine and human natures in the person of Christ. As such, Barth appeals historically to the older dogmatics and the use of the *anhypostasis* (or impersonalitas) to describe the negative aspect of Christ's human nature having no personality by virtue of its own being.

> At this point we reached what the older dogmatics—using the language of later Greek philosophy—described by the term *anhypostasis*, the impersonalitas of the human nature of Christ. Its ὑpostasiς is, longe eminentior, that of the Logos, no other. Jesus Christ exists as a man because as this One exists, because as He makes human essence His own, adopting and exalting it into unity with Himself. As a man, therefore, He exists directly in and with the one God in the mode of existence of His eternal Son and Logos—not otherwise or apart from this mode.[103]

Barth then argues the other side of the formula that Christ's human nature is also *enhypostasis*, which describes the positive aspect. As such, Barth states that it is the attribute of *enhypostasis* that affirms true humanity to Christ—even in view of the fact that he is distinct from us (as humanity) because his humanity exists only as the Son of God. Moreover, Barth rejects any notion of a concealed or blatant Docetism. Rather, he emphasizes here that true humanity exists in union with the Logos, but not as an autonomous existence.[104]

> It is true enough that the humanum exists always in the form of actual man. This existence is not denied to the man Jesus, but ascribed to Him with the positive concept of *enhypostasis*. But it is hard to see how the full truth of the humanity of Jesus Christ is qualified or even destroyed by the fact that as distinct from us He is also a real man only as the Son of God, so that there can be no question of a peculiar and autonomous existence of His humanity.[105]

---

102. Originally published as *Die Lehre von der Versöhnung—KD* IV/2 (1955).

103. Barth, *CD* IV/2, 49.

104. Ibid.

105. Ibid.

It is in God's reconciliation of humanity to himself in Jesus Christ—in the absolute union of human essence with divine essence in the person of Christ—that undergirds Barth's understanding of Christ's humanity. This is the christological principle that grounds Barth's understanding and appropriation of *anhypostasis* and *enhypostasis*. The eternal Christ takes true humanity to himself as our representative in Jesus, but humanity that is unique to all humanity in his union with the eternal Christ.

> We have seen what depends on it: no less than the fact that in Jesus Christ we do not have to do with a man into whom God has changed Himself, but unchanged and directly with God Himself; no less than the unity in which as man He is the Son of God, and as the Son of God man; and finally no less than the universal relevance and significance of His existence for all other men.[106]

Interestingly, Barth uses *enhypostasis* to address the question of how the humanity of Jesus Christ can exist in union with the eternal Logos as the ruler and sustainer of the world. With this question in view Barth distinguishes the existence of the human essence joined to Christ in Jesus of Nazareth from the eternal and divine essence of Christ as the eternal Logos. The eternal Word of God spoke creation into existence and maintains creation as its ruler and sustainer. Therefore, the eternal existence of God is differentiated from the existence of his creation, much like the Logos is differentiated from the human essence of Jesus of Nazareth. In other words, the humanity of Christ (as all creation) exists relative to the existent divinity of Christ.

> The answer to this question is that the *enhypostasis* of the human being of Jesus Christ, His existence in and with the Son of God, is sufficiently sharply differentiated from the *sustentatio generalis* in which God maintains and accompanies and rules the whole world by the fact that the existence of God is not in any sense identical with that of the world, or the existence of the world with that of God, in virtue of His creative action, but God has and maintains His own existence in relation to the world, and the world in relation to God.[107]

In this context Barth also explains that the union of humanity with the Logos is not to be compared to human relationships understood as two self-existent beings. This must be so because the humanity of Christ is also

106. Ibid.
107. Barth, *CD* IV/2, 53.

anhypostasis. "For one thing, two self-existent persons are presupposed in those unions, which is not at all the case in respect of the latter [Jesus Christ], in the relationship between the divine Logos and human flesh (*anhypostasis*)."[108] The *anhypostasis* therefore provides a clear ontological distinction between the self-existent divine nature of Christ as creator God and the created human essence of Jesus of Nazareth whose subsistence is strictly derived based upon its union with the Logos.

Finally, Barth uses *anhypostasis* and *enhypostasis* to describe the relationship of the church to Jesus Christ as its head.[109] As the (earthly) body of Christ, the church is brought into union with Christ's earthly-historical form. In describing the essence of the church Barth states: "It is of human essence—for the Church is not of divine essence like its Head. But it does not exist in independence of Him. It is not itself the Head, nor does it become such. But it exists (ανυποστατος and ενυποστατος) in and in virtue of His existence."[110] Barth's allusion to the existence of the church in Christ as both *anhypostasis* and *enhypostasis* is striking. Just as the humanity of Christ negatively has no existence outside of its union with the Logos, so the church negatively has no existence outside its union with its head, Jesus Christ. However, as his church it enjoys the realty of existence in this union. As I will later show, the significance of Barth's adoption of *anhypostasis* and *enhypostasis* is brought to bear in its brightest form in Christ's union and relationship with his church.

In summary, we see in the *Church Dogmatics* Karl Barth's transition from a somewhat autonomous treatment of *anhypostasis* and *enhypostasis* previously developed in the *Göttingen Dogmatics*, to an ontological formula of *anhypostasis* and *enhypostasis* which he uses to express the human nature of Christ both negatively and positively. In this transition, however, it should be noted that Barth leaves unaltered his understanding that as *anhypostasis*, the human nature of Christ does not exist by virtue of its own reality in union with the Logos. By definition this is the negative characteristic of Christ's human nature. At the same time, as *enhypostasis*, Barth argues that Christ's human nature enjoys real subsistence by virtue of its union with the Logos. The *anhypostasis* and *enhypostasis* therefore becomes an axiomatic statement to define Christ's human nature both negatively as being non-subsistent (*anhypostasis*), while at the same time being subsistent (*enhypostasis*) in its union with the Logos. Consequently, by interpreting

---

108. Ibid.

109. This is a largely ignored aspect of Barth's adoption of these concepts, which I explore in chapter 6 in Barth's development of the royal man.

110. Barth, *CD* IV/2, 59.

and joining *anhypostasis* and *enhypostasis* in this way, Barth moves beyond protestant orthodoxy with respect to the ontology of Christ's human nature.

Conclusion

Having considered Karl Barth's adoption of *anhypostasis* and *enhypostasis* to express the human nature of Christ, I recognize that these terms are not pervasive (per se) in his christological language. However, the significance of Barth's assumption of these terms as the ontological grounding for understanding Christ's human nature in union with the Logos is unmistakable. As has been shown, Barth's dialectic of veiling-unveiling and time-eternity in *Romans* II anticipates the paradox of Christ's human nature, through which Barth's adoption of *anhypostasis* and *enhypostasis* in his dogmatics provides a more precise ontological frame of reference in his Christology. With this in mind I note two particular points with respect to these terms that Barth uniquely claims for himself—*whether he realized it or not*.

First, Barth's adoption of *anhypostasis* as a negative characteristic of Christ's human nature in its union with the Logos is a clear departure from historical protestant orthodoxy, which viewed *anhypostasis* strictly in the pre-incarnate sense. The patristic Fathers, Lutheran and Reformed scholastics, Heinrich Heppe, and Heinrich Schmid all agreed that the human nature of Christ was a subsistent being in its union with the Logos notwithstanding their use of *anhypostasis*. Historically speaking, the predominant thinking was to demonstrate that as *anhypostasis*; the human nature of Christ did not exist prior to the incarnation thereby precluding any argument that the Logos was comprised of two, rather than one person in the advent.

Second, Barth's coupling of *anhypostasis* and *enhypostasis* as an ontological expression of Christ's human nature is unique to his Christology. If we consider closely enough the ontological implications of Barth's interpretation of *anhypostasis*, we can see that he leaves himself little choice but to join *anhypostasis* and *enhypostasis* closely together so as to preclude the dominance of the *anhypostasis* that we see in the *Göttingen Dogmatics*. Not only does this coupling give an important ontological foundation to the dialectic of veiling and unveiling, but it also provides a balance to Barth's understanding of the paradox manifested in the human nature of Christ. It is this paradox that Barth continues to work through in his Christology in explaining Jesus Christ as *very God* and *very man*.

Anhypostasis and Enhypostasis

Revelation of Jesus Christ as the "Word Became Flesh" in Barth's Christology

Introduction

ONE OF THE GREAT impediments to grasping hold of Karl Barth's Christology within the larger framework of his theological method is a failure to recognize not only the context, but also the form of his christological argument. This is especially true in the *Church Dogmatics* where Barth engages a wide spectrum of theological and philosophical protagonists in working out his unique (and sometimes mysterious) christological thinking.[1] Therefore, understanding both the context and mode of Barth's argument (dialectical or otherwise), not only brings light to his argument, but also helps guard against the over-characterization of a *grand theme* in an attempt to frame his Christology into a neatly framed paradigm. Karl Barth worked and wrote within specific historical contexts, dictated by the theological, cultural and political questions posed in his day, filtered through his understanding of the Scriptures on one hand, and his consideration of relevant theological/ philosophical talk on the other.[2] Furthermore, one must also consider the

1. George Hunsinger provides helpful insight here. "At the point where most other contemporary theologies resort to the language of experience or the language of reason (whether separately or in conjunction, and however conceived), Barth opts instead for the language of mystery. Nothing is more likely to lead the reader of the Church Dogmatics astray than a nondialectical imagination. One must never fail to ask about the dialectical conceptual counterparts to the position Bath happens to be developing at any particular moment." Hunsinger, *How to Read Karl Barth*, Preface, ix. I would add here that this is especially true with respect to understanding Barth's conception of the ontological reality of Jesus Christ.

2. Timothy Gorringe draws out this point quite well when he states that with respect to Karl Barth, "the great theme of his theology from start to finish, is the reality of God, and faith as response to that reality, is not a prop for the infirm, an opiate for the masses, nor an optional extra in the culture of contentment, but an essential aspect of human liberation, that without human liberation cannot be achieved." Gorringe, *Karl Barth*, Preface, ix.

ongoing (sometimes quite dramatic) development of Barth's theology over the course of his life that emerged amidst the great challenges posed to German social and religious culture during, and after, the First and Second World Wars. Attempts therefore to over-simplify Barth's Christology prove to be a dangerous course, and in this respect we must agree with G. C. Berkouwer that: "The difficulties that meet us in the theology of Barth . . . arise not so much out of his form of expression as out of his *mode* of *thinking*. It is therefore necessary to exercise care in characterizing his theology, lest we fall into the danger of over-simplifying the course of its development."[3]

Nevertheless, while the range and complexity of Barth's theology may preclude the characterization of a single grand theme, we are not left without certain fundamental principles developed in Barth's thinking that help us better understand his Christology within the broader context of his theological method.[4] With his break from liberal theology came Barth's relentless pursuit of a theological method, the impetus of which emerged from God's willing condescension towards humankind expressed through his self-revelation in the Word became flesh.[5] While for Barth the advent of Jesus Christ remains in many respects an ontological mystery, it is not a mystery void of certain clues given to us in Scripture that must be sought out and developed.[6]

With the arrival of the First World War came Barth's disillusionment with the anthropological presupposition that dominated liberal theology, whereupon he turned away from his liberal theological heritage and turned instead towards the Reformed tradition in mapping out a new theological

3. Berkouwer, *Triumph of Grace*, 12–13.

4. For example, we recognize in Karl Barth's theology the significance of the revelation of God in Jesus Christ as the one who bears witness to the triune God and his covenant to reconcile and redeem humanity. Recognizing the dialectic nature of the veiling and unveiling of God's revelation in Jesus Christ is in fact fundamental to understanding Barth's Christology.

5. Garrett Green argues that Barth explicitly rejects any human "point of contact" (*Anknüpfungspunkt*) for revelation. In a reversal of a familiar logical pattern Barth insists that "both the actuality and the possibility" of the revelatory event are grounded in God. In opposition to virtually the entire modern theological establishment, Barth rejects a philosophical or anthropological foundation for theology, Green, *On Religion—The Revelation of God as the Sublimation of Religion*, 13.

6. Barth explains, "The method prescribed for us by Holy Scripture not only assumes that the entelechy of man's I-ness is not divine in nature but, on the contrary, is in contradiction to the divine nature. It also assumes that God is in no way bound to humanity, that His revelation is thus an act of His freedom, contradicting man's contradiction. That is why the language of the prophets and apostles about God's revelation is not a free, selective and decisive treatment of well-found convictions, but—which is something different—witness." Barth, *CD* I/2, 7.

course. Barth first expressed this new theological course in the *Epistle to the Romans*. Yet, even in this turning away from liberal theology Barth did not accept *carte blanche* traditional Reformed theology into his own theological method. Rather, we clearly see over the course of Barth's theological development that while he referred to and made use of traditional Reformed texts,[7] pen was put to paper based upon his own Biblical exegesis and deliberations to express his theological arguments.[8]

With this in view, we approach Barth's Christology, and his appropriation of *anhypostasis* and *enhypostasis* to explain Christ's human nature with the knowledge that the final arbiter in determining Barth's theological argument is anchored first and foremost in his own exegesis of the Scriptural texts.[9] We do ourselves a great disservice (and Barth for that matter) if we are lax in giving due attention to Barth's willing and aggressive biblical exegesis, along with his *openness* to hear what the Scripture says within the context of the passage before him.[10] Certainly, Barth is not bound to any traditional or Reformed interpretation of Scripture, and in fact takes great delight in discovering the Word of God for himself as *contained in the Scriptures* given his exegetical approach, which in many cases provides unanticipated christological discoveries. Berkouwer reminds us that Barth is keenly aware of the priority and necessity of the Scriptures in his theological approach. "Barth is clearly aware of the fact that his theological effort is a human undertaking, but that in this understanding the irresistible and overpowering testimony of the Scriptures propelled him forward on this path of unexpected developments."[11]

7. As a case in point, while Barth was happy to gain acquaintance with (and even accept to some degree) Heinrich Heppe's *Reformed Dogmatics*, he received it subject to his own theological frame of reference and exegesis. In the same vein, while Barth studied and taught on John Calvin's theology, he relied upon his own exegesis of the relevant Scriptural texts when developing a theological motif.

8. Donald Wood argues that Barth was a student and teacher of the Scriptures, and then goes on to say, "Further, I want to suggest, we need to see Barth not only as an astonishingly confident and creative reader of scripture, but as a theologian who thought deeply about what it means to read well the classical texts of the Christian tradition." Wood, *Barth's Theology of Interpretation*, ix.

9. This assumes a post Marburg reading of Barth's theology.

10. In the introduction to his commentary on John 1 Barth describes the work of the biblical expositor: "Conscientious expositors must be as free as possible from such things as religious or non-religious notions, from philosophical or ethical convictions, from personal feelings or reactions, from historical habits of thought, prejudices, and the like. They must have an ear simply for what the text says to them, for the new thing that it seeks to say in face of the totality of their previous subjective knowledge." Barth, *Witness to the Word*, 4.

11. Berkouwer, *Triumph of Grace*, 14.

The Scriptures indeed become foundational in Barth's theology, not only as an impetus marking his move away from liberal to Reformed theology, but more importantly, because he understands that the Scriptures contain the Word of God and attest to the revelation of God through the life of Jesus Christ.[12] Even so, the Scriptures are subordinated to the revelation of the Word of God made manifest in the person of Jesus Christ; because the writing is not primary, but secondary to the object of its attestation.[13] For Barth, the Scripture is the deposit of what was once proclaimed by human lips.[14] Therefore, the Bible is God's Word to the extent that God causes it to be his Word as he speaks through it.[15]

> The Word of Scripture in its very different time and with its very different temporal content as compared with the Word of revelation is now put in its proper position. It is called the Word of the prophets and apostles, and as such, as witness of Christ and in subordination to the Word of Christ, it also speaks the Word of Christ.[16]

Barth's biblical exegesis demands that the Word of God in the Bible must manifest itself by becoming the Word of God—in its revelation to us—through its attestation to the revelation of Jesus Christ. The Bible therefore is not in itself God's past revelation, but that which bears witness to God's past revelation in the form of attestation.[17] Because the Bible attests

12. Barth understands that: "Holy Scripture is the word of men who yearned, waited and hoped for this Immanuel and who finally saw, heard and handled it in Jesus Christ. Holy Scripture declares, attests and proclaims it." Barth, *CD* I/1, 108.

13. Despite Barth's refusal to acknowledge the canon as the infallible Word of God, he nevertheless acknowledges its indispensible nature as that which contains the Word of God. In this respect Barth recognizes that the apostolic succession of the Church must mean that it is guided by the Canon, that is, by the prophetic and apostolic word as the necessary rule of every word that is valid in the Church. See Barth, *CD* I/1, 102.

14. Barth, *CD* I/1, 102.

15. Barth, *CD* II/1, 109.Wolfhart Pannenberg observes that: "The three forms of the Word in Barth are presented in such a way that the claim to communicate God's Word refers back from Christian proclamation to scripture and from scripture to Jesus Christ as the Word of God revealed. Christ alone as the revelation of God is directly God's Word. The Bible and church proclamation are God's Word indirectly and derivatively. They have to become God's Word in specific occasions as witness is borne to Jesus Christ." Pannenberg, *Systematic Theology*, 1:235.

16. Barth, *CD* I/1, 148.

17. Barth, *CD* I/1, 111. Barth understands that the revelation of God in this world is manifested exclusively in the person of Jesus Christ. The Scriptures can only bear witness to that revelation. It is as a witness to the revelation of Christ that the Scriptures derive their authority. See Barth, *CD* I/1, 112. This must be so in view of the human element as the basis of Scripture, which are human attempts to repeat and reproduce

to the revelation of God, to the event of Christ becoming flesh, the exegete must be cautious to guard against possible violence to the text. The exegesis of the Bible therefore should be left open on all sides, not for the sake of free thought, as liberalism would demand, but for the sake of a free Bible.[18] Barth's understanding of this organic relationship between the attestations in Scripture to the revelation of God in Jesus Christ is always marked by event, by God in action, by God's willingness come to us and manifest himself as our only means of knowing him.[19]

> We can never hear Holy Scripture and simply hear words, human words, which we either understand or do not understand but along with which there is for us no corresponding event. But if so, then neither in proclamation nor Holy Scripture has it been the Word of God that we have heard. If it had been the Word of God, not for a moment could we have looked about for God's acts. The Word of God itself would then have been the act. The Word of God does not need to be supplemented by an act. The Word of God is itself the act of God.[20]

This fundamental principle takes on early and vibrant expression in Barth's Christology, and in effect seals his move away from liberal (*anthropologically centered*) theology to a christological (*Christ centered*) method that finds its impetus and forcefulness in the Scriptures, which attest to the revelation of the righteousness of God made manifest in Jesus Christ. Human reason alone, although a legitimate and God endowed attribute, has no capacity in itself to make such a move. For Barth, any thought of doing so is a failure to properly distinguish the divine from the human.

> The reason sees the small and the larger but not the large . . . It sees what is human but not what is divine. We shall hardly be taught this fact by men. One man may speak it to another, to be sure. One man may perhaps provoke another to reflect upon the "righteousness of God." But no man may bring another to

---

this Word of God in human words and thoughts and in specific human situations. See Barth, *CD* I/1, 113.

18. Barth, *CD* I/1, 106.

19. Barth also states that we cannot speak of God. That is, to speak of God means that we speak on the grounds of revelation and faith. "To speak of God would mean to speak that word which can only come from God Himself: the Word, God becomes man . . . Our theological task is to say that *God* becomes *human* and to say it as the Word of *God*, as God would say it." Barth, "The Word of God as the Task of Theology," 185.

20. Barth *CD* I/1, 143.

the peculiar, immediate, penetrating certainty which lies behind the phrase.[21]

While we observe in Barth's theology the undeniable theme of the self-
revelation of the triune God in the person of Jesus Christ, we also observe
this theme amidst its complexities, paradoxes, and nuances.[22] When Barth
speaks of the person of Jesus Christ as self-revelation, he speaks of him as
a creature in the human nature of the man Jesus, which is at once both the
means and limitation of God's self-revelation; a God who reveals himself in
the flesh of Jesus, yet remains hidden in the midst of this revelation. As a
creature, however, this self-revelation of God is God, who reveals in its unity
and entirety the trinitarian identity of God.[23]

Keeping these concepts close at hand, my objective in this chapter is to
consider how Karl Barth develops the revelation of Jesus Christ as the Word
became flesh given his unique appropriation of *anhypostasis* and *enhypostasis* as the ontological foundation of Christ's human nature. I will do so in
four separate, yet, interrelated movements. First, I will assess Barth's theo-
logical/philosophical method in expressing the revelation of God in Jesus
Christ. Second I will examine *Anselm: Fides Quarens Intellectum* and Barth's
argument that Jesus Christ is the true instrument of revelation. Third, I will
investigate the revelatory interrelationship between Barth's appropriation
of *anhypostasis* and *enhypostasis* to express Christ's human nature, and his
development the εγενετο the Word became flesh. Fourth, I will examine
how Barth uses *anhypostasis* and *enhypostasis* dialectically to express the
humanity of Christ in dialogue with Reformed and Lutheran Christology.

Theological/Philosophical Method and the Revelation
of God in Karl Barth's Christology

It is indeed a tenuous path to tread in assessing the role of philosophy in
Karl Barth's Christology,[24] which is unusually marked by the acute nature

21. Barth, "Righteousness of God," 9–10.

22. George Hunsinger rightfully observes in Barth's theology how his work combines genuine unity with irreducible complexity. See Hunsinger, *How to Read Karl
Barth*, 22.

23. Ibid., 79.

24. Barth himself describes the tenuous relationship between theology and philosophy. "For example, is there anything more hopeless than the attempt that has been
made in the last two hundred years with ever-increasing enthusiasm to create a systematic link-up, or synthesis, or even a discriminate relationship, between the realms
of theology and philosophy? Has there been one reputable philosopher who has paid
the least attention to the work which the theologians have attempted in this direction?

of his movement away from liberal theology to the Reformed tradition,[25] but in a way that includes an ongoing dialogue with philosophy.[26] There is, however, little consensus among scholars over the true nature and extent of philosophical influence in Barth's theology. While some argue that Barth completely divorces philosophy from his theology, others identify doctrinal distortions attributed to his over reliance on philosophy.[27] Such polar opposite views indicate a complexity in Barth's theology which raises a fundamental question regarding his understanding of the revelation of God in the flesh of Christ. That is, what is the pre-suppositional nature of Barth's understanding of the human nature of Christ as the mode of God's revelation? In other words, how do we characterize Karl Barth's theological/philosophical method as an expression of the revelation of God in Jesus Christ?[28]

This is quite relevant given a philosophical view of revelation, the impetus of which is based upon human cognition; set against a theological view of revelation, the impetus of which is the movement of God in free

---

Has it not become apparent that the anxiety and uncertainty with which we pursued this course only reminded us that we can pursue this course only with an uneasy conscience? Theology can become noticed by philosophy only after that moment when it no longer seeks to be interesting. Its relation to philosophy can become positive and fruitful only after it resolutely refuses to be itself a philosophy and refuses to demonstrate and base its existence upon a principle with, or alongside of philosophy." Barth, *God in Action*, 42.

25. In speaking of the acute nature of Barth's movement towards Reformed theology I refer primarily to the dramatic change in his theological thinking which finds its impetus in a re-calibrated understanding of the nature of the revelation of God attested to in the Scriptures that is made manifest in Jesus Christ.

26. Kenneth Oakes argues that Barth's break with liberal theology was not as acute as usually portrayed. Rather, Barth's eventual break developed over time not so much out of Barth's disagreement with the epistemology of his teachers, but more over Barth's liberal political views given his involvement with the religious socialists and the worker movements, and dissatisfactions with some of the dualism within Hermann's thought, Oakes, *Karl Barth on Theology* and *Philosophy*, 58.

27. See Oakes, *Karl Barth on Theology* and *Philosophy*, 5–8.

28. G. C. Berkouwer takes a somewhat balanced view of Barth's theological/philosophical method, and suggests that while Barth understands the danger of presupposition (especially philosophical ones), he nonetheless makes relative this danger where he holds that elements of philosophy can be "employed in the service of theological activity . . . On the one hand, it must be fully acknowledged that all manner of presuppositions in a given theology can darken the light of the gospel: on the other hand, it is not legitimate to reconstruct a theology—in this case, Barth's—in light of such presuppositions. In this manner it is possible and legitimate fully to come to an understanding of Barth's theological views, while at the same time fully recognizing that these views hang together intimately with fundamental presuppositions." Berkouwer, *Triumph of Grace*, 19–22.

grace towards humanity (as portrayed by Barth in His Christology).[29] I will address these inquiries by reviewing Barth's theological/philosophical grounding at Marburg specific to the revelation of God; and by examining how Barth's expression of the revelation of God in his Christology (given the back drop of anhypostasis and enhypostasis) shapes his interaction with philosophy.

Theological/Philosophical Revelation and the Marburg School

After two years of study at the University of Bern, Karl Barth was anxious to continue his theological studies at Marburg.[30] However, in view of Fritz Barth's opposition to liberal Marburg theology, and Karl's resistance to his father's preference for Halle or Greifswald, they compromised on Berlin where Adolf von Harnack made the biggest impression on Barth. In Berlin Barth also studied Immanuel Kant's *Critique of Pure Reason,* Friedrich Schleiermacher's *Speeches on Religion to its Cultured Despisers,* and Wilhelm Hermann's *Ethics.*[31]

In April 1907 Barth returned from Berlin and once again enrolled at Bern, but in October (at the insistence of his father) Barth set out for Tübingen.[32] But in the summer semester of 1908 Fritz Barth finally consented to Karl's desire to study at Marburg.[33] It was at Marburg that Barth's

29. Bruce McCormack notes that from the early days of Barth's dialectical theology to the very end, to rightly speak of God one must begin and end with him. This meant beginning with Christology as the self-revelation of God where: "the presence of God in the sphere of human knowing, God's personal act of making Himself an "object" of human knowing in such a way that he remains subject." McCormack, "Why Should Theology be Christocentric?," 64.

30. David Mueller notes in Barth's early theological education that "The most significant event in Barth's intellectual pilgrimage at Bern occurred during the fourth semester, when he encountered both Kant's philosophy and Schleiermacher's theology. This intellectual liberation made Barth anxious to pursue his theological training with Wilhelm Herrmann of Marburg, the leading neo-Kantian theologian of the day." Mueller, *Karl Barth,* 15.

31. See McCormack, *Dialectical Theology,* 37.

32. Fritz Barth insisted upon Karl's move to Tübingen in his last ditch effort to moderate Karl's more liberal bent, Busch, *Karl Barth,* 42–43.

33. In March of 1908 Barth heard Hermann deliver a speech entitled "Gottes Offenbarung an uns" where "Barth would have heard Hermann put forth two characteristic theses of the theologian's later thought: God only becomes knowable inasmuch as God makes Himself known, and the proper response to this revelation is a pious subjection to Jesus Christ. Hermann's first thesis is later expanded into the argument that one can only know God inasmuch as God enlivens and awakens the individual in moral transformation." Oakes, *Karl Barth on Theology* and *Philosophy,* 28.

early philosophical development took a more tangible form through the neo-Kantianism influence of Herman Cohen (1842–1918) and Paul Natorp (1854–1924), through the teaching of Wilhelm Herrmann (1846–1922).[34] Hermann's teaching had the greatest influence on Barth whose concept of revelation was grounded in the themes of life, faith, and experience for the believer in Christ.[35] It was Hermann who provided Barth a thorough understanding of Schleiermacher's religion of experience that Barth wrestled with the rest of his life.[36] Hermann's writings focused on the experience and divine power of *Offenbarung* (revelation), where personal experience is primary over, and separated from dogma. The *Ursprung* (origin) must be recognized as the primary place in religion in the event of revelation, which is just as supernatural as faith.[37]

Revelation in Hermann's thinking exists as a dual structure (a mixture), but a structure that is in fact anthropologically centered, where the human being has a desire to be truthful, but is unable to do so autonomously. This state is met from the theological side when the individual experiences a supernatural power (*Offenbarung*), which creates in the individual a new moral identity. Hermann called this revelatory event *Selbstbehauptung* (self-affirmation). A person who truly desires to be alive self (*das etwas fur sich selbst sein will*) can only draw this power from the hidden resource (*aus dem Verborgenen*) in free self-surrender. We seek God when we long for this reality, and we encounter this reality when God reveals himself to us (*so offenbart sich uns Gott*).[38] The locus of God's revelation emerges from the hidden depths of human *Erlebnis* (experience). God acts in this hidden dimension of an individual life, which is veiled from science, generalities, and objectivities.[39]

Although theological knowledge of revelation was considered valid in its own way at Marburg, it was accepted as being different in kind and

34. Roger A. Johnson states that "Natorp and Cohen are the primary philosophical spokesmen of the movement; Herrmann, as a theologian, appropriates their basic epistemology and philosophy of culture and religion, as this provides the context for his constructive theological work." Johnson, *The Origins of Demythologizing*, 39.

35. After Barth completed his university studies at Marburg in 1908 he stayed on for another year working as an editorial assistant for *Die Christliche Welt* where he became more intimately acquainted with Hermann's "mixture of Kant's critical philosophy and the Schleiermacher of the Speeches, his disdain for both conceptual and historical apologetics within theological work, and his constant emphasis upon the presence of Jesus within the individual." Oakes, *Karl Barth on Theology* and *Philosophy*, 28.

36. See Gorringe, *Karl Barth*, 26.

37. See Fisher, *Revelatory Positivism?*, 144.

38. Ibid., 145.

39. Ibid.

quality from that acquired by philosophy. Hermann agreed with Cohen that knowledge of God had its *Ursprung* in revelation along with its implications for morality. He also agreed with Natorp with respect to the experiential side of revelation. However, Hermann argued against both Cohen and Natorp that an actual divine, life giving power is effective in revelation, which is experienced as it is given by something *jenseits* (beyond) human consciousness. Hermann argued that neo-Kantian *Wissenschaft* (science) could not assess the cognitive claims to the experience and supernatural work of God's revelation in that event. "The active God of revelation, therefore, could not be made into a logical concept (Cohen) nor be reduced to an imminent objectless feeling that accompanies every act of consciousness (Natorp)."[40]

In summary, we observe in Marburg (Hermannian) neo-Kantianism an unwieldy synthesis of anthropological and theological epistemology where the human impetus for attaining knowledge of God becomes a general principle, which in turn condescends to God its willingness to acknowledge the revelation of God.[41] What is important to note here is that Barth's commitment to Herrmann ensures that his early theological thinking bears the marks of centuries of German intellectual life.[42] Interestingly, Bultmann sees in Barth at this early stage of his theological development (as a product of Marburg and a Herrmann disciple) a critical extension of liberal theology. That is, theology was being redeemed out of the deadness of subjectivism into "speech concerning God," who is not subject to our human disposal but one in whom we enter into relationship with as we trust in him in the midst of uncertainty.[43] The problem in Herrmann's thought, however, was not the notion that faith has a unique object; that was the element of truth in his conception.[44] The flaw lay in the complete disjunction between

40. Ibid., 146.

41. Bruce McCormack argues that with the near collapse of the German culture after the First World War came the passing away of a Marburg neo-Kantianism and its scientific grounding. See McCormack, *Dialectical Theology*, 49.

42. Barth's Hermannian education "in which he was formed was not only broadly post-Kantian in distinction between religion and culture, but also dealt with and responded to higher criticism of Scripture, a secularized reading of church history and confessions, and the History of Religious schools . . . there was a strong distinction between (1) the individual's experience of faith and God's love and forgiveness; and (2) either a transcendental or empirical determination of the human subject and its acting, knowing, and being in general. The work of theology falls within the first realm, while the work of psychology, history, and philosophy in the second." Oakes, *Karl Barth on Theology* and *Philosophy*, 27.

43. Hendrikus Berkhof argues here that Bultmann "can see Barth on the very line that runs from Schleiermacher's Speeches directly to Hermann." Berkhof, *Two Hundred Years of Theology*, 165–66.

44. Despite the Schleiermacher and Kantian influence on Hermann's theological/

faith and knowledge. Barth's departure from Hermann would entail an emphatic insistence that God is really and truly known—that *Gotteserkenntnis* (knowledge of God) is possible.[45] After Barth's break with Hermann he would insist that the reality of God always precedes the knowing activity of human beings. Therefore, the reality of God becomes that starting point in divine revelation over against Hermannian idealism, the reality that is made manifest in the advent of Jesus Christ.[46]

After Marburg: Theological/Philosophical Revelation in Karl Barth's Christology

In August 1909 Karl Barth bade farewell to Marburg when he accepted the position of *pasteur suffragant* in Geneva, where he first began writing and preaching sermons to a church congregation. In Geneva Barth takes a rather critical view of the Scriptures, "Calvin's view of the authority of the Bible would be quite wrong for us." He also attacked the Chalcedon definition of Christ as he confessed, "I will gladly concede that if Jesus were like this I would not be interested in him." But, "If Christ begins to live in *us* . . . that is the beginning of Christian faith." Barth's service to the poor, however, had no small impact in awakening him to the realities of ministry work as Barth began to see more clearly how "theology and church could be colonized" and theologians become mouthpieces for ecclesiastical powers.[47] Although he still firmly held to the Hermannian maxims learned at Marburg, Barth began to realize that "the longer I had to preach and to teach, the more the work of academic theology seemed to me to be somewhat alien and mysterious."[48]

Barth left Geneva in 1911 to become pastor in the agricultural and industrial community of Safenwil, Switzerland where his Hermannian orientation toward human consciousness with its cognitive approach in

---

philosophical world, Barth could say, "Although Hermann was surrounded by so much Kant and Schleiermacher, the decisive thing for him was the christocentric impulse, and I learnt that from him." Busch, *Karl Barth*, 45.

45. See McCormack, *Dialectical Theology*, 65.

46. Bruce McCormack argues that Barth rejected Hermann's idealism for a "critical realism." That is, although Barth never fully abandoned idealism "where knowledge of the 'given' was concerned, the knowledge whose subject is God must be initiated by God in view of the limits of human knowledge." McCormack, *Dialectical Theology*, 66–67.

47. See Gorringe, *Karl Barth*, 3.

48. Busch, *Karl Barth*, 57–58.

experiencing the revelation of God begins to change.[49] Practically speaking, Barth learned through the day in and day out rigors of the pastorate that the people of his parish, the ones who struggled with the challenges of everyday life in rural Switzerland, had needs that reached beyond the capacity (and perhaps comprehension) of Marburg academic life.[50] Furthermore, Barth's ministry work in Safenwil (which included no small interest in the working conditions and civil affairs of the people of his church and surrounding community), together with the outbreak of World War I forced upon Barth a critical self-examination of his theology in view of the willingness of his theological forebears to publicly ascent to the German war effort.[51] This self-examination was squarely aimed at Barth's own preaching. The problem that Barth dealt with at this stage of his theological development was not the technical matter of "how do I say it," but the problem of the basic content of preaching; to speak of God based upon the knowledge of God. Barth now begins to reconfigure the beginning presupposition of his preaching based upon the reality that "God is."[52] We also observe that the death of Barth's father in 1912 had a definite impact on his life and certainly gave him pause with respect to his theological direction. Barth himself acknowledges that his rethinking of liberal theology may have been sharpened with the death of his father.[53] In all these events we see the great battle that Barth wages with himself as he begins to work out what it means that God truly and

49. Hendrikus Berkhof rightly observes a gradual shift in Barth's thinking with respect to Hermann where Barth's indictment of human consciousness is extended to trans-individual areas of political and social life such as (capitalism, prostitution, alcoholism, etc.). Moreover, Barth employs the negative conception of "religion" as a means to shield oneself from the righteousness of God. While still consistent with Hermann in understanding God as the fulfiller of human longing in the expression of conscience, Barth now moves away from Hermann in understanding God's opposition to the idolatry of religion. See Berkhof, *Two Hundred Years of Theology*, 183–84.

50. Barth's position in the community led to his significant involvement in socialism and the trade union movement. The class warfare that Barth witnessed in his own parish introduced him to the "real problems of real life." Busch, *Karl Barth*, 69.

51. Of the "ninety-three German intellectuals" who issued a manifesto supporting the war policy of Kaiser Wilhelm II and Chancellor Bethmann-Hollweg were the names Harnack, Herrmann, and Rade. Barth did not know what to make of "the teaching of all my theological masters in Germany. To me they seemed to have been hopelessly compromised by what I regarded as their failure in the face of the ideology of war." Busch, *Karl Barth*, 81.

52. Ibid., 91.

53. Barth states that "The death of my father, which took place in 1912, may have been a contributing factor" to his reappraisal of liberal theology. Barth recalls that one of the last things he heard his father say was, "The main thing is not scholarship, nor learning, nor criticism, but to love the Lord Jesus. We need a living relationship with God, and we must ask the Lord for that." Busch, *Karl Barth*, 68.

freely reveals himself.[54] That is, Barth now takes up the question of the epistemological relationship between the revelation of God and the knowledge of God's revelation to human beings.[55]

In the end, as Barth struggled with how to forge a new theological course, the dominant factor that marked his movement away from Hermannian, neo-Kantian theology to the Reformed understanding of the revelation of God was his turn to, and reliance upon, the Scriptures as the fountain head of theological endeavor.[56] The ground breaking product of this theological/philosophical *re-grounding* came in the form of Barth's exegesis of *Romans*. In many respects Barth's *Römerbrief* (particularly *Romans II*, with which we are primarily concerned) marked a significant transitional period in his theology as he turned to the Bible as the primary source from which to communicate Christian theology.

> Lastly: it may not be irrelevant if I now make it quite clear both to my future friends and to my future opponents in England that, in writing this book, I set out neither to compose a free fantasia upon the theme of religion, nor to evolve a philosophy of it. My sole aim was to interpret Scripture . . . No one can, of course, bring out the meaning of a text (*auslegen*) without at the same time adding something to it (*einlegen*). Moreover, no interpreter is rid of the danger of in fact adding more than he extracts. I neither was nor am free from this danger. And yet I should be altogether misunderstood if my readers refused to credit me with the honesty of, at any rate, *intending* to *ex*-plain

54. Simon Fisher posits that the complicated relationship between philosophy and theology at Marburg, as well as Barth's later reactions to this approach he adopted as a young man is the story about conflict between cognitive styles in "which there were neither victors nor vanquished." see Fisher, *Revelatory Positivism?*, 319–20.

55. Bruce McCormack argues that for Barth knowledge of God is a cognition which is "fulfilled in views and concepts. Views are the images in which we perceive objects as such. Concepts are the counter-images with which we make these images of perception our own by thinking them, i.e., arranging them." However, the human attempt to bring God's revelation to expression in the form of views, concepts, and words is surrounded by an "external limitation" (the hiddenness of God in His self-revelation in Jesus Christ), and "internal limitation" (the intrinsic incapacity of human thought and language to bear adequate witness to God), McCormack, *Orthodox* and *Modern*, 169–170.

56. With respect to Barth's turn to the Scriptures, David Ford states, "In his parish of Safenwil after 1911 Barth was driven to reconsider his liberal theology by finding it inadequate to the demands of preaching, and the attitude of many of his liberal teachers to the First World War confirmed his suspicion of their theology." Two significant influences in this turn was Herrmann Kutter's stimulus to rethink his notion of God, and Barth's decision that biblical exegesis was the basis on which to build his own theology. See Ford, *Barth* and *God's Story*, 18–19.

the text. I must assure them that, in writing this book, I felt myself bound to the actual words of the text, and did not in any way
propose to engage myself in free theologizing.[57]

Barth's turn to the Scriptures, however, did not negate his ongoing dialogue
with philosophy, even as it assumed a new place in relationship to his theology. In fact, Barth's interaction with philosophy remains quite evident as he
admits in the forward to the second edition of *Romans* with respect to the
"closer relationship with Plato and Kant. The writings of my brother Heinrich Barth have led me to recognize the importance of these philosophers.
I have paid more attention to what may be called the writings of Kierkegaard and Dostoevsky that is of importance for the interpretation of the New
Testament."[58] Nevertheless, *Romans* II is first and foremost an exegesis of
Paul's letter to the Romans, which launches in earnest Barth's ardent expression of the revelation of God in Jesus Christ—*as a movement of God's grace.*

> *Even though we have known Christ after the flesh, yet now we
> know him so no longer.* What He was, He is. But what He is un-
> derlies what He was. There is no merging or fusion of God and
> man, no exaltation of humanity to divinity, no overflowing of
> God into human nature. What touches us—and yet does not
> touch us—in Jesus the Christ, is the Kingdom of God who is
> both creator and redeemer. The Kingdom of God has become
> actual, is nigh at hand.[59]

Romans is certainly not lacking in philosophical dialogue that Barth
engages quite aggressively, the theological significance of which continues
to be debated.[60] Yet, even in the face of Barth's expansive interaction with

57. Barth, *Epistle to the Romans*, ix.

58. Ibid., 4. P. H. Brazier argues that any strict definitions of the influence of Kierkegaard in Barth's *Romans* must be seen as relative. "Both Kierkegaard and Dostoevsky provided an illustration of life under the gospel and as such were an aid to Barth
in the interpretation of the New Testament." Moreover, Kierkegaard's influence cannot
be categorically identified in a unique way from other influences on Barth during the
re-writing of the Romans. See Brazier, *Barth* and *Dostoevsky*, 169.

59. Barth, *Epistle to the Romans*, 30.

60. As a case in point William P. Anderson argues that "Theologically and philo-
sophically it is undoubtedly Sören Kierkegaard who had the greatest impact upon
Karl Barth, at least in the early stages of his revolutionary thought. That seems to be
obviously apparent in the indebtedness of his thinking to Kierkegaard's attack upon
all direct communication and easy living, i.e., living comfortably with God." Anderson, *Aspects of the Theology of Karl Barth*, 14. Bruce McCormack, however, argues that
beyond question Kierkegaardian language and concepts play a significant role in *Romans* II. Yet, what does such usage tell us about the degree of Kierkegaard's influence
on Barth? The Kierkegaardian understanding of the paradoxicality of the incarnation

philosophy, we recognize in the driving force of his argument that the revelation of God in Jesus Christ is a knowledge that can only be bestowed upon humanity from above, not simply in the form of a philosophical system.[61] In the well known passage from *Romans* II Barth states that, "If I have a system, it is limited to a recognition of what Kierkegaard has called the "infinite qualitative distinction" between time and eternity, and to my regarding this as possessing negative as well as positive significance." For Barth this simply means that "God is in heaven, and thou art on earth." Understanding this relation between God and humanity was for Barth the "central theme of the Bible and the essence of philosophy."[62] In other words, the idea that human philosophy could in any sense have a role in the supernatural revelation of God was simply inconceivable to Karl Barth.

This "infinite qualitative distinction" finds its clearest expression in the person of Jesus Christ, who manifests the convergence of time and eternity in his appearing, and who in himself distinguishes the revelation of the triune God in contra-distinction to a purported philosophical self-discovery of God.[63] In Christ, the revelation of God reaches down to humanity by piercing the veil of his hiddenness. This is the revelation of God in Christ, which Barth more fully expresses in the *anhypostasis* and *enhypostasis* of Christ's human nature that first emerges in the *Göttingen Dogmatics*. Barth argues: "The content of revelation is God alone, wholly God, God himself. But as God solely and wholly reveals himself, he makes himself known in the three persons of His one essence."[64] Not only is the revelation of God the revelation of his triune essence, but it is strictly grounded in the act of

---

certainly provided Barth with ample ammunition for stressing the incomprehensibility of a revelation which can take place only as a divine possibility and never as a human possibility. However, McCormack concludes that "we overestimate Kierkegaard's importance if we wish to see in him the decisive influence on Barth's thought in this phase." McCormack, *Critically Realistic Dialectic Theology*, 235–236, 240.

61. Eberhard Busch argues that in both editions of Barth's Epistles to the Romans he uses distinctive language that distinguishes God from man ("God is God" and "man is man"). But more than this, the relationship of this God to humanity has to do with God's revelation to humankind in his act of redemption. See Busch, *Karl Barth & the Pietists*, 79.

62. Barth, *Epistle to the Romans*, 10.

63. This theme in Barth's theology (even at this early stage of his Christology) is similarly expressed at Tambach. "A critique of reason is complete only when it issues in applied science; God comes in history only through deeds and evidences; he manifests himself in consciousness only through compelling, revealing, immediately, self-confirming insights and communications—else what is the meaning of all the words about the Word." Barth, *Word of God* and *the Word of Man*, 284.

64. Barth, *Göttingen Dogmatics*, 87.

"His self-revelation"[65] where "God is seen, believed, recognized, and known only in the act of his self-revelation. The human act of seeing, believing, recognizing, and knowing is primarily his work."[66]

Because the content of revelation is God alone, it is not an object of experience as such even though we recognize the instrument or mediator as its form. Barth can therefore say "that even in the humanity of Christ the content of revelation as well as the subject is God alone." This is why understanding the *anhypostasis* of Christ's human nature is so important here because as such, the humanity of Christ becomes this instrument of revelation. "The person of the God-man is exclusively the Word, the Logos of God."[67] Furthermore, because the humanity of Christ (as *enhypostasis*) becomes the mode of God's revelation as the Logos, Barth can deny any natural claim to the revelation of the triune God given that "revelation as God's answer is never and nowhere coincident with the human question represented in the concepts of reason and religion."[68] Although Barth demonstrates an unwillingness to negotiate the knowledge (or knowability) of God as anything other than God's self-revelation, he does not refuse a place to philosophy as a legitimate human endeavor along with all its limitations. Nevertheless, theology and philosophy remain mutually exclusive in their understanding of revelation proper.[69]

> Not that we scorn participating in philosophical work, at least as
> vitally interested dilettantes. Not as though we could promise no
> good from a dialogue of philosophy and theology. But what we
> hear philosophers asking about is the knowability of the thing
> in itself, the absolute, the unconditioned, the origin of things.

65. The theme of God's self revelation manifests itself quite strongly in Barth's early preaching. And it is the self revelation of God in Jesus Christ that for Barth draws the sharp distinction between our life and the life revealed in Christ. "The end consists in that it becomes un-mistakenly clear to us that what *we* are, what *we* overlook, what *we* do, is *not everything*; it is not the *final* thing. Jesus lives! That is finality . . . For it reveals God to us; it places us before *God*; it declares God to us . . . The impossible is possible, the incomprehensible is revealed." Barth, *Come, Holy Spirit*, 67–68.

66. Ibid., 87.

67. In this context Barth defends the *anhypostasis* in view of what he believes to be the Lutheran and Reformed misunderstanding of its true meaning. See Barth, *Göttingen Dogmatics*, 90.

68. Ibid., 95.

69. Barth further states: "The question that dogmatics has to put to preaching would be there even if philosophy could without contradiction accept or proclaim God as an object of possible intellectual or intuitive experience. The doubt that dogmatics would have to raise even were there no critique of pure reason [Kant] rests on the recollection that, according to the definition of preaching, what ministers say about God is suppose to be God's Word. It is what God himself says." Barth, *Göttingen Dogmatics*, 326.

Before we can sit down and talk, we need to agree first whether this is the same as our own theological question as to the knowability of God. On our side such an agreement might come only on the basis of the completion of our own work, and not before. But even when agreement is reached on the fact that the same thing is meant, or on the extent to which it is, the way in which the question of the knowability of this is handled will have to be different in the two disciplines if philosophy is not to become theology or theology philosophy.[70]

In his extensive work on the history of theological (and philosophical) thought in *Protestant Theology in the Nineteenth Century* Barth emphasizes the parallel, yet distinctive roads taken to apprehend the revelation of God; that between the Word of God and the word of man.[71] As a case in point, in his review of Kant, Barth's distinguishes quite emphatically between revelation and rationalism.

We see, then, upon the one hand the inspiration, whose object resides within ourselves, in so far as the idea of humanity and therefore this moral disposition reside within us too; and, upon the other, the 'influence of another, higher spirit.' It is between these two, between the notions of a 'disposition' proclaiming a divine origin on the one hand, and 'revelation' on the other, between the 'supersensory' and the 'supernatural', that the exact border between the things which can be supposed and the things which may not be supposed, runs, in matters concerning the religion of reason. Anyone who speaks of revelation is bursting the religion of reason asunder, for he is bursting asunder 'mere' reason, he is speaking of something which cannot be an object of empirical knowledge. The critical philosophy of religion cannot therefore speak of revelation. This, then, is Kant's 'pure rationalism' in this matter.[72]

---

70. Ibid., 325–26.

71. Barth observes the penchant of philosophical thinking to chart its own authoritative course, "Further, eighteenth-century man began to become conscious of his power for science, and of his power through science. The development of the Renaissance, which had been hindered and reduced for almost one hundred and fifty years through the period of religious wars, now began to make immense strides. Once again man, led by a philosophy, which, was only apparently disunited but was in essentials united, began to be conscious—and more forcibly than before—of a capacity for thinking which was responsible to no other authority than himself." Barth, *Protestant Theology in the Nineteenth Century*, 39.

72. Ibid., 284.

In a similar vein, Barth draws to conclusion his analysis of Hegel's philosophy of religion within the context of revelation and relationship. Barth argues that while Hegel did not dispute the positive and historical nature of revelation and the uniqueness of Christ; Hegel rejected the notion that God confronts humanity in an actual and indissoluble relationship. For Barth, revelation must be understood objectively, as that which comes to us in an outward way. Yet, Barth explains that even as God manifests himself, the philosopher of religion "has already understood him in the preliminaries of this act, and he already has the lever in his hand which he has only to depress to advance from God's act of revealing to the higher level of God being manifest . . . "[73] For Hegel and the philosopher of religion, it is the pure knowing of the human subject, and the knowledge that originally proceeds from this human subject that determines the knowledge of God.

Barth's rejection of human reason as the method to experience the revelation of God in effect forces philosophy into the role of antagonist, which Barth more forcibly expresses in his book on Anselm. Barth's *Anselm* is not simply the continuing development of the revelation/knowledge of God dynamic expressed in the *Göttingen Dogmatics* (which it is), but a clearing away of the philosophical debris that clutters the distinction between the revelation of God as something received from God—by faith—over against the human capacity for obtaining true knowledge of God.[74] Barth notes this distinction in Anselm's thinking: "Strange indeed the contradiction if, against such a background, what he had intended to say about God were something his thinking had created rather than something received."[75] Most

---

73. Barth, *Protestant Theology*, 419.

74. Kenneth Oakes argues that the *Anselm* book does not "represent a great conceptual or theological advance beyond the *Göttingen Dogmatics* and the *Christliche Dogmatik*." Oakes concludes that its real value is Barth's discussion on the topics of the existence of God and role of apologetics. See Oakes, *Karl Barth on Theology* and *Philosophy*, 74. I do not deny the importance of how Barth deals with the existence of God and the resultant impact on apologetics in *Anselm*. However, the point that Oakes misses here is that faith, which must first be present (as a gift of God) is only possible both ontically (which takes precedence) and noetically based upon God's self-communication of himself through his Word. We see therefore in *Anselm* the tangible grounding of faith in the revelation of Christ as the God-man, where the ontological grounding of *anhypostasis* and *enhypostasis* had previously been laid in the *Göttingen Dogmatics*.

75. Barth, *Anselm*, 59. Fisher rightfully observes that a later Barth—after his book about *Anselm* at least—continued to regard revelation as given and theology to be faithful. *Nachdenken* (thought) was in obedience to this divine gift; but then, however, revelation was deemed given in an entirely different way from the earliest writings. Moreover, as far as its contents were concerned, the revelation was primarily revelation of God, as it were "in and for himself," and not therefore a revelation of eternal divine-human relatedness in which two foci are equally indispensable. God *an sich* now enters

important perhaps is that subsequent to Barth's *Anselm* we see a greater emphasis on the revelation God in Jesus Christ made manifest in the reality of his person as God and man (i.e., *anhypostasis* and *enhypostasis*).[76] This God-man is the object of faith—the revelation of God that must precede faith in God, not simply in the existence of God, but in Jesus Christ as the sole means of salvation. This in turn becomes the driving emphasis of Barth's argument in expressing the revelation of God in the *Church Dogmatics*. Faith becomes the line that separates the revelation of God—as attested to in the Scriptures and made manifest through the Word of God in the person of Jesus Christ—from human reason and contemplation about God. Even so, Barth posits that no one can approach the Scripture absent some level of philosophical presupposition, "a personal view of the fundamental nature and relationship of things."[77]

> We have to describe as a philosophy the systematized commonsense with which at first the rationalists of the 18th century thought that they could read and understand the Bible, and later, corrected by Kant, the school of A. Ritschl, which was suppose to be so averse to every type of speculation and metaphysics. It is all very well to renounce the Platonism of the Greek fathers, but if that means that we throw ourselves all the more unconditionally into the arms of the positivists and agnostics of the 19th century, we have no right to look for the mote in the eye of those ancient fathers, as though on their side is a sheer hellenisation of the Gospel, and on ours a sheer honest exegetical sense of facts. There has never yet been an expositor who has allowed only Scripture alone to speak.[78]

This passage is important for two reasons. First, while not denying the primacy of the exposition of Scripture, Barth is candid in his belief that philosophical predisposition cannot be fully expunged in the exegete. Indeed, this relationship between the Scripture and philosophy is one of

---

the theological circle as the sovereign revelation, revealer, and revealedness; what is thereby made manifest is the triune being of God. Such revelation obviously has its 'effects', but these are secondary and do not constitute revelation nor enter the revelatory constellation. To God alone belong the glory and the efficacy of his manifestations. See Fisher, *Revelatory Positivism?*, 319.

76. Hans Urs von Balthasar argues that Barth's great shift in establishing the priority of faith over reason came in his book on *Anselm*, which he more fully develops in the *Church Dogmatics*. Balthasar, *The Theology of Karl Barth*, 137.

77. Barth, *CD* I/2, 728.

78. Ibid., 728.

the more complex areas of Barth's theology.[79] Second, we must not confuse these intricacies in Barth's thinking with his clear delineation between the revelation of God made manifest in Jesus Christ in direct contradistinction to human reason and its endeavor to experience this same revelation.[80] As a case in point Barth strictly distinguishes between revelation and philosophy in the *Doctrine of Creation*, where the covenant of God is revealed—through the creation of God—in the person of Jesus Christ.

> The character of its theme, established in his way, is what distinguishes the Christian doctrine of creation from all the so-called world-views which have emerged or may conceivably emerge in the spheres of mythology, philosophy and science. It differs from all these by the fact that it is based on God's revelation. But this is not merely a formal difference. It is also material. The Christian doctrine of creation does not merely take its rise from another source. It also arises very differently from all such world-views. It not only has a different origin, but has a different object and pursues a different course. The divine activity which is its object can never become the theme of a world-view.[81]

However, even in Barth's concession of the inevitable philosophical presupposition in theology, he still holds firmly to faith in Jesus Christ as the final distinguishing mark between Christian theology and a philosophical system that seeks to understand the revelation of God.[82] Barth can therefore say:

79. It is not surprising that questions remain with respect to the relationship between the Scripture and philosophy in Barth's theology given his understanding of the Word of God *revealed* in the Scriptures. Kenneth Oakes argues that "Barth never settled on an exact and well-defined account of theology and philosophy. In texts separated by only a few years or written at roughly the same time, Barth wrote in a welter of ways about this relationship. He often assembled several arguments or claims within a single work that might appear contradictory, or at least confused, to the more literal-minded. Hence one cannot look at any single text from any one period of Barth's *oeuvre* and assert that his understanding of philosophy and theology have been presented." Oakes, *Karl Barth on Theology* and *Philosophy*, 245.

80. While one can certainly argue the absence of consistent clarity in Barth's theology between the Scripture and philosophy, I would argue that Barth is quite clear in distinguishing the revelation of God made manifest in Jesus Christ in contra-distinction to philosophical reason in obtaining that same revelation. This is indeed a point of clarity in Barth's theology that is undergirded by his appropriation of the *anhypostasis* and *enhypostasis* of Christ's human nature, and explicitly developed in the *Göttingen Dogmatics* and *Church Dogmatics*.

81. Barth, *CD* III/1, 34.

82. Gordon H. Clark calls attention to Barth's rejection of the possibility of knowing God from any universal human capacity, as Schelling and Hegel tried to do. For Barth,

Only rarely did the originators of the great philosophical systems have the will or the courage to make plain the possible compatibility of their thought with Christian faith. And when this was attempted, as in the case of Kant and the older Schelling, it was inevitably to the detriment not only of faith but also of the system of ideas. It cannot be overlooked that the shrewd and ardent attempt of Schleiermacher to adopt to a given point the Christology of the Bible and the Church to his own system of the harmony of opposites, of the finite and infinite, of spirit and nature, can hardly be said to have been successful from the standpoint of this particular philosophical presupposition. Christian faith is an element which, when it is mingled with philosophies, makes itself felt even in the most diluted forms, and that in a way that is disturbing, destructive, and threatening to the very foundations of these philosophies. To the extent that it is faith in God's Word, and is even partially true to itself, it cannot become faith in current world-views, but can only resist them.[83]

More than likely, the full measure of philosophical influence on Barth's theology will remain unresolved given the complexity and breadth of his theological method. Nevertheless, it is my judgment with respect to Barth's development of the revelation of God in Jesus Christ, that first; philosophy plays an important role as a dialogue partner in his inevitable conclusion that true knowledge of God must proceed from God in the revealed Jesus Christ. Therefore, no philosophical system can engender true knowledge of God—*or even attest to it*. Second, the revelation of God is made manifest through the reality of human flesh; that is, flesh assumed by the eternal Logos. Set against human systems of knowledge it does not escape our notice that as *anhypostasis* and *enhypostasis*, the flesh of Christ accomplishes that which is humanly unthinkable. The very Word of God speaks through the reality of human flesh making comprehensible that which cannot be comprehended. This is why the dual model of *anhypostasis* and *enhypostasis* carries such weight in Barth's Christology; because in this ontology is realized both ontically (in its substance) and noetically (by faith in its substance) the revelation of God in the God-man, Jesus Christ.

---

any subjective human experience of the revelation of God must first be derived by an understanding of the Word of God. See Clark, *Karl Barth's Theological Method*, 30–31.

83. Barth, *CD* III/2, 10–11. Trevor Hart observes that for Barth "Christian faith and speech are essentially response and not essentially source. God produces faith and not vice versa. It is concern which lies behind Barth's relentless appeal to the category of revelation and his particular way of interpreting what is involved in revelation." Hart, "Revelation in Karl Barth's Theology," 41.

Anselm: The Grounding of God's Self-Revelation in Karl Barth's Christology

The genesis of Karl Barth's *Anselm: Fides Quarens Intellectum* (1931) came out of a seminar on Anselm's *Cur Deus homo?* in Bonn that Barth hosted in the summer of 1930.[84] A lecture given by Barth's philosopher friend Heinrich Scholz of Münster on the proof of God's existence based upon Anselm's *Proslogion*, produced in Barth a *compelling urge* to deal with Anselm quite differently. That is, Barth wanted to address the problematical Anselm, the Anselm of *Proslogion 2-4*.[85] Barth's intent is to clarify (so to speak) Anselm's theology for both Protestants and Roman Catholics alike as he deals specifically with the knowledge of God, a knowledge which can only be made manifest through God's self-revelation.[86]

Although Barth never had the opportunity to revisit Anselm in the context of the *Proslogion*, he never let go of the abiding epistemological principle (the key, as he describes it), which he developed in this work—that the knowledge of God comes about as the result of faith in God's self-revelation in Jesus Christ.[87] This is the abiding key that flows straight from *Anselm* into Barth's *Church Dogmatics*, the key that Barth attributes to Anselm.[88] Indeed, this grounding of the revelation of God in the person

84. Barth first came across Anselm while in Münster, making explicit reference to him in the prolegomena in his *Christliche Dogmatik*, which in turn brought down upon him accusations of Catholicism and Schleiermacherianism. See Busch, *Karl Barth*, 205. Bruce McCormack notes that "Barth first dealt with Anselm extensively in the summer semester of 1926, in his first seminar on *Cur Deus homo?* (the Bonn seminar was a repetition of the 1926 seminar). The fruit of that earlier study is found in the *Die Christliche Dogmatik*, where Anselm's way of theological knowledge was advocated as a helpful corrective to that of neo-Protestantism." McCormack, *Dialectical Theology*, 423.

85. Barth thought that the only proper way to assess Anselm's proof of the existence of God in the *Proslogion* was to examine it in view of its full context as expressed in the *Proslogion*, 2-4; that is, within the context of his whole theological scheme. See Barth, *Anselm*, preface to the second edition, 11–12.

86. Ibid., preface to the first edition, 7–9.

87. Herbert Hartwell argues that in the *Church Dogmatics* Barth abandoned his previous attempt to use an "existential-philosophical" approach to theology, in favor of the Word of God as the sole source and basis of his theology. He did so because he realized that the knowledge of the absolute truth about God can only be revealed by God himself, who is the truth and source of every other truth revealed to humanity through the Word spoken to humanity—in Jesus Christ—through his Holy Spirit. This can only happen by faith, which is the presupposition of true knowledge. This is the grounding of Barth's theology in concert with Anselm, that faith (*credere*) precedes knowledge (*intelligere*), or stated the other way around; knowledge, by necessity, follows faith (*fides quaerens intellectum*), Hartwell, *The Theology of Karl Barth*, 42–44.

88. Eberhard Busch argues that the delay in Barth's revision of his prolegomena

of Jesus Christ, made manifest through faith in Christ, establishes for Barth the epistemological foundation by which his Christology is marked from this point forward.[89] "Most of them have completely failed to see that in this book on Anselm I am working with a vital key, if not the key, to an understanding of that whole process of thought that has impressed me more and more in my Church Dogmatics as the only one proper to theology."[90]

Barth's book on Anselm was written between *Die Christliche Dogmatik im Entwurf* in 1927 at Münster, and the revised first volume of *Die Kirchliche Dogmatik* in 1932 at Bonn. This is not an insignificant point of historical reference because as Barth himself acknowledges, his work on Anselm solidified his christological thinking with respect to the revelation of God.[91] This in turn confirmed his complete break with any anthropological presupposition in expressing a true Christian doctrine.[92]

> The real document of this farewell is, in truth, not the much-read brochure *Nein!* directed against Brunner in 1934, but rather the book about the evidence for God of Anselm of Canterbury which appeared in 1931. Among all my books I regard this as the one written with the greatest satisfaction . . . The positive factor in the new development was this: in these years I had to learn that Christian doctrine, if is to merit its name and if it is to build up the Christian Church in the world as she must needs be built up, has to be exclusively and conclusively the doctrine of Jesus Christ—of Jesus Christ as the living Word of God spoken to men.[93]

---

was the result of his paying close attention to "following through Anselm's method of thought," resulting in his book on Anselm. It was Barth's preoccupation with Anselm that eventually compelled him to start his dogmatics again from the beginning, which found ultimate expression in the *CD*. Busch, *Karl Barth*, 205–6.

89. Barth, *Anselm*, preface to the second edition, 11–12.

90. Ibid.

91. Berkouwer likewise agrees to the significance of Barth's book on Anselm, which demonstrates a decisive change in Barth's thinking specific to his understanding of the knowledge of God. Berkouwer argues that "'This book, appearing between the Prolegomena of 1927 and the KD from 1932 on, is not an insignificant dogmatic-historical intermezzo. It signifies the Christological concentration taking place in his thought as over against the 'natural' way to the knowledge of God and the way of the analogia entis which in 1932 he called an invention of the antichrist." Berkouwer, *Triumph of Grace*, 42.

92. Barth, *Anselm,* preface to the second edition. Eberhard Busch argues that "This book is a detailed explanation of Anselm's formula *fides quaerens intellectum*, which now became the fundamental model for Barth's theological epistemology." Busch, *Karl Barth*, 206.

93. Barth, *How I Changed My Mind*, 43.

In Barth's *Anselm* we see the convergence of both ontic and noetic reality in the revelation of God in Jesus Christ, where Barth relentlessly drives home Anselm's argument that the presupposition of true knowledge of God flows out of faith in God, who reveals himself through the truth of his Word. Furthermore, we observe conceptually the ontic substance of the *anhypostasis* and *enhypostasis* of Jesus Christ, who as *truly God* and *truly man* is not simply a union of divine and human natures in the God-man, but more forcefully, the Word of God who took to himself the true flesh of humanity as the revelation of the truth of God—made manifest by faith.[94]

Moreover, we observe not only a decisive grounding in Barth's Christology, but also a bridge that leads from his first (and somewhat tentative) appropriation of *anhypostasis* and *enhypostasis* in the *Göttingen Dogmatics*, to his fuller (and clearly more decisive) development of these terms in the *Church Dogmatics*.[95] Said another way, we see in Barth's *Anselm* the weight of his critical thinking take form in expressing the free grace of God and his movement toward humankind in revealing himself as *very God* and *very man* in Jesus Christ. Although Barth does not explicitly use the ontological language of *anhypostasis* and *enhypostasis* to describe the human nature of *very man* in Christ, *he portrays it* in the knowledge of God, derived from the revelation of God, made comprehensible to those in whom he is revealed.[96] Here we recognize the conceptual (but also clear) language of *anhypostasis* and *enhypostasis* expressed in Barth's familiar dialectical language of the veiling and unveiling of God. It is therefore important to take notice of Barth's statement in the *Church Dogmatics* where he explains: "I believe I learned

94. As George Hunsinger observes: "Dialectic was the instrument of Barth's assault against a fundamental premise of liberalism—namely, its insistence on finding the possibility for talking about God in the subjective conditions of religious experience (regardless of how disciplined by "science") or in some related anthropological phenomenon. Not until his breakthrough in studying Anselm, however, would Barth feel that he had adequately come to display the objective logic alien to liberalism but internal to the Christian faith." Hunsinger, *Disruptive Grace*, 333.

95. I speak here of the Barth's emphasis in the *Church Dogmatics* that the human nature of Christ is both *anhypostasis* and *enhypostasis*, which draws out more forcefully the revelation of God through the reality of human flesh. In this way Barth can say that the flesh of Christ has no subsistent reality in its own being, but nevertheless enjoys the reality of humanity in union (and strictly in union) with the Logos.

96. Bruce McCormack argues that there is no revolutionary thought in Barth's *Anselm*. Nevertheless, he takes notice of Barth's interest in forging a new interpretation of Proslogion 2-4. "He was thoroughly convinced that what was offered there was not at all a "proof" in the usual sense of the term. One could not rightly apprehend what "proving" meant to Anselm unless one saw chapters 2-4 of the *Proslogion* in the context of his overall theological programme, that is, the *way* to theological knowledge advocated by Anselm." McCormack, *Dialectical Theology*, 423.

the fundamental attitude to the problem of the knowledge and existence of God which is adopted in this section—indeed in the whole chapter—at the feet of Anselm of Canterbury, and in particular from his proofs of God set out in Prosl. 2–4."[97]

Barth emphasizes that Anselm does not simply set out to develop a *probare* (proof) of God's existence, but rather, the *intelligere* (knowledge) of God's existence from which this proof is derived.[98] It is in this sense that the knowledge of God becomes a matter of priority for Barth to understand Anselm correctly. Therefore, achievement of the knowledge of God issues in the proof of God's existence: "what to prove means is that the validity of certain propositions advocated by Anselm is established over against those who doubt or deny them; that is to say, it means the polemical-apologetic result of *intelligere*."[99]

For Barth, it is the *intellectus fidei* (knowledge that is issued in faith) that concerns Anselm; it is the knowledge that is "desired" by faith. Moreover, the necessary impetus that leads one to this knowledge is the "desire" of faith. In other words, this desire for knowledge is the desire of belief.[100] This essence of faith proves to be essential in Barth's analysis of Anselm. Therefore, it is not merely the "existence" of faith but the "nature" of faith in Anselm's thinking that is the focus of Barth's interest here.[101] It is the *Credo ut intelligam*—"my very faith itself that summons me to knowledge."[102]

Barth draws out of Anselm's argument an important anthropological understanding with respect to faith; that is, faith cannot be exercised apart from something new encountering (or happening) to us, from outside of us. This is a seed being implanted into our very being that produces something

---

97. Barth, *CD* II/1, 4.

98. Regarding Anselm's theology, William Stacey Johnson similarly argues that: "The overarching rubric in Anselm's theology like that of Augustine, of course, was, "I believe in order to understand": *Credo ut intelligam*. Or put slightly differently, faith seeks intelligibility (*fides quaerens intellectum*), meaning that Anselm's theology starts from "belief" and journeys towards consummate 'vision'" see Johnson, *Mystery of God*, 34.

99. Barth, *Anselm*, 14.

100. Barth, *Anselm*, 16–17.

101. Johnson argues that: "This subjective appropriation of the faith is a continuing venture, a task (*Aufgabe*), as Barth puts it, and never a given (*Gegeben*). This is because the affirmations expressed in the Creed (*ration fidei*) do not stand in a simple one-for-one correspondence with the unreachable veracity of the gospel truth itself (*ratio veritatis*)." Johnson, *Mystery of God*, 34.

102. Barth, *Anselm*, 18. John Thompson recognizes the correlation between the *Credo ut intelligam* and the self giving of Jesus Christ, "who imparts the knowledge of himself and there is in *a priori* a denial of any secondary source save that which he employs and uses as a further witness." Thompson, *Christ in Perspective*, 111.

new within us. Furthermore, this seed, which the true believer must receive is the Word of God when it is preached and heard by us, and is received by us through the grace of God bestowed upon us.[103] "Faith comes by hearing and hearing comes by preaching. Faith is related to the "Word of Christ" and is not faith if it is not conceived, that is acknowledged and affirmed by the Word of Christ. And the Word of Christ is identical with the "Word of those who preach Christ"; that means it is legitimately represented by particular human words."[104]

With the necessity of the Word of God in clear view, Barth centers his analysis of *Anselm* given the rule that any legitimate theologoumenon must be measured against the veracity of the Scriptures. The Holy Scripture alone is the plumb line, the criterion for determining what theological development is admissible to the church, and therefore the norm of *intelligere* (understanding). Barth argues that for Anselm the criterion of the Holy Scripture "forms the basic stability of the Credo to which the *credere* and therefore the intelligere refer. While it is the decisive source, it is also the determining norm of the *intelligere*, the *auctoritas veritatis, quam ratio colligit*."[105] And just as the Word of God is the measure of all true theology, so also the Word of God—that which is derived outside human capacity for reason—bestows upon human reason, through faith, the true capacity to seek the knowledge of God.[106] This becomes self evident for Barth who argues that such knowledge must be sought in prayer, all of which flows out of the grace of God. Moreover, that this grace must be sought by prayer implies that "the ultimate and decisive capacity for the *intellectus fidei* does not belong to human reason acting on its own but has always to be bestowed on human reason as surely as *intelligere* is a *voluntaries effectus*."[107] This *intelligere* of God, which can only break in upon the one who seeks it in prayer based solely upon the grace of God as encounter, is made manifest as God condescends to reveal himself in this encounter. This is in fact the

---

103. Barth, *Anselm*, 19.

104. Ibid., 22.

105. Ibid., 33.

106. In explaining Barth's conception of "No Knowledge Without Faith" George Hunsinger explains that: "Everything depends, Barth argued, on whether our rational reflection remains bound to the subject matter of revelation. But this subject matter as such is mysterious and elusive . . . The mystery and miracle of the subject matter find their parallel not only in the conceptual diversity and nonsystematizability of its explication, but also in the miracle and mystery of its mode of rational apperception." Hunsinger, *How to Read Karl Barth*, 53.

107. Barth, *Anselm*, 37.

essence and evidence of God's revelation in this knowledge, as he initiates and moves toward the one to whom he chooses to reveal himself.[108]

> We are already acquainted to some extent with the dialectic in the concept *intelligere*. That there is also an *intelligere esse in re* only *aliquatenus* is not self evident. Even this modified *intellige-re* by which man is enabled to see something of the very face of God, has to be sought in prayer for all the right seeking (it also is grace) would be of no avail if God did not 'show' himself, if the encounter with him were not in fact primarily a movement from his side and if the finding that goes with it, the modified *intelligere*, did not take place.[109]

The knowledge of God that concerns Anselm is solely derived by faith in the one who chooses to reveal himself. Therefore, this knowledge of God, which is incomprehensible based upon human endeavor alone, can never be separated from faith in the one who reveals himself.[110] Barth argues that it is in the recognition and exercise of faith in the incomprehensibility of the object of revelation that by definition precludes any concept of self-actual-ization of this knowledge.[111] This incomprehensibility of the nature of God can only be revealed by God himself through his Word. This is the begotten Word of God, the Word spoken by God to those whom he chooses to reveal himself. Ontologically speaking, Barth makes clear that being consubstan-tial with the Father, this Word is not unlike the Father, but exists as the same substance of the Father, and with the Father. This is the truth of the Father spoken through his Word. This is God moving toward humankind through the revelation of his Word of truth.[112]

---

108. Bruce McCormack identifies as the central point in the *Anselm* book the ques-tion of what it means to "demonstrate rationality" in theology. That is to say, we see in Barth's *Anselm* (particularly reading it in light of *CD* I/1, paragraph 5.4, "The Speech of God as the Mystery of God") an allusion to the dialectic of veiling and unveiling in revelation. Yet, as McCormack affirms, notwithstanding the benefit of *CD* I/1, "it is clear enough that the dialectic of veiling and unveiling is the unspoken—and at a few dramatic points, fully articulated—presupposition of the theological method set forth in the *Anselm* book." McCormack, *Dialectical Theology*, 428–29.

109. Barth, *Anselm*, 38–39.

110. Anselm's faith is based upon the object of faith who indeed assumed a human nature in such a way that the person of God and the person of humanity were one and the same, which can only occur in the case of the one person of God. "For it is incom-prehensible that different persons be one and the same person with one and the same man." Anselm, vol. 3, *The Incarnation of the Word*, 27.

111. Barth, *Anselm*, 39–40.

112. George Hunsinger uses the concept of "no neutrality" in describing the un-derstanding of faith. "The rejection of neutrality was a way not only of doing justice to

> Strictly understood the ratio veritatis is identical with the ratio
> *summae naturae*, that is with the divine Word consubstantial
> with the Father. It is the ratio of God. It is not because it is ratio
> that it has truth but because God, Truth, has it. This Word is
> not divine as word, but because it is begotten of the Father—
> spoken by him.[113]

God's self-revelatory movement toward humankind is presupposed by the ontic necessity of the Word, which fundamentally must precede the noetic necessity. In other words, true knowledge of God is impossible unless the object of that knowledge chooses first (according to his own will) to reveal himself in a way that can be comprehended, and which in turn can be responded to through the exercise of faith.[114] Therefore, true knowledge of the object of faith presupposes recognition of the basis that is peculiar to the object of faith itself.[115] Barth concludes that the "rational" knowledge of the object of faith is derived from the object of faith and not *vice versa*. That is, "the object of faith and its knowledge are ultimately derived from truth—from God and from his will."[116]

---

the subject matter, but also of avoiding the pitfalls of rational orthodoxy (which was typically unable to explain how to integrate the personalist and rationalist dimensions; it was unable to account adequately for the context of personal encounter within which rational reflection in theology was to occur). Neutral understanding was impossible for faith, precisely because faith by definition was self-involving—a living response to a personal encounter with the living God." Hunsinger, *How to Read Karl Barth*, 50.

113. Barth *Anselm*, 45–46.

114. Douglas R. Sharp similarly identifies the ontic/noetic relationship in Barth's *Anselm*. "In the act of knowledge, the ontic always precedes the noetic, and behind the noetic *ratio* of the knowing subject stands the ontic *ratio* of the known object, both of which are bound in the *ratio Dei*, the Word and truth which is God . . . The quest for knowledge consists in the drive within faith to go back across the way already traversed in the movement of conformity from the object of faith to the knowledge of faith, from the ontic *ratio* to the knowing of the noetic *ratio*." Sharp, *The Hermeneutics of Election*, 14.

115. Barth, *Anselm*, 50. Barth expresses this quite clearly in the *Church Dogmatics* where he explains that: "The Word of God becomes knowable by making itself known. The application of what has been said of the problem of knowledge consists in stopping at this statement and not going a single step beyond it . . . If we have understood that the knowability of God's Word is really an inalienable affirmation of faith, but that precisely as such it denotes the miracle of faith, the miracle that we can only recollect and hope for, then as a final necessity we must also understand that man must be set side and God Himself presented as the original subject, as the primary power, as the creator of the possibility of knowledge of God's Word. Christ does not remain outside." Barth, *CD* I/1, 247.

116. Barth, *Anselm*, 52. We see this rational knowledge of revelation motif clearly expressed in Barth's *Church Dogmatics*. "Any reservation, whether against God's Word being actively present in person, or against the active presence of God in person being

Barth notes at the beginning of the *Proslogion* 2 that Anselm defines his name for God as: *aliquid quo nihil cogitari possit*, which Barth paraphrases as "something beyond which nothing greater can be conceived."[117] Barth also observes that Anslem chooses this name as a way to describe God as something "completely independent of whether men in actual fact conceive it or can conceive it."[118] Anslem varied this name slightly to be: *Aliquid quo nihil maius cogitari possit*, which added the emphasis of "nothing more" greater can be thought. For Barth, the point of Anselm's argument was not a "condensed formula" of the doctrine of God, but a genuine description for the name of God with a view to obtaining a true knowledge of God. This is a knowledge which must be presumed by the revelation of God from "the other source;" that is, from God himself. Barth notes here that Anselm's name for God simply demonstrates that there exists between the "Name of God" and the revelation of his existence and nature a "strong and discernible connection."[119] In this context Barth asks: how do we know that God is incomprehensible? Anselm simply answers that just like any knowledge or concept of the nature of God it can only come about by faith. Faith therefore is the prime requisite to any understanding of the nature of God.[120] And so it is by faith that Anselm is able to recognize a name for God . . . "a designation for God which is not totally inadequate, not just a symbol, etc., for the simple reason that it expresses nothing about the nature of God but rather lays down a rule of thought which, if we follow it, enables us to endorse the statement about the nature of God accepted in faith (example, the statement of his incomprehensibility) as our own necessary thoughts."[121]

Barth explains that it is not Anselm's intent to conceive a name for God that reveals him in a way that is incomprehensible (not *in altitudine sua*), but rather, "by conceiving the manner in which he is not to be conceived." That is, God is not to be conceived in a way that anything greater than him

---

here in the flesh in the likeness of man, makes revelation and reconciliation in comprehensible. And *vice versa*, the more definitely the two are seen to be one, the Word of God—flesh, or God Himself in person—the likeness of man, the better is our realisation of what the Bible calls revelation." Barth *CD* I/2, 148.

117. Barth, *Anselm*, 73–74.

118. Ibid., 74.

119. Ibid., 75–76.

120. Gary W. Deddo argues that Barth rejected the traditional Scholastic scheme of asking in order: How do we know God? Does God exist? What is God? Who is God? Barth understands that God's self-revelation of the triune God in the person of Jesus Christ brush these questions aside in view of the biblical witness. The knowledge of God comes about through the triune God's own initiative. See Deddo, *Karl Barth's Theology of Relations*, 18–19.

121. Barth, *Anselm*, 80.

could be imagined or conceivable. This is ruled out by the revelation/faith relationship to Him.[122] Furthermore, the deciding factor with respect to the reality of God's existence and our ability to truly conceive of him is based upon the decisive truth of God himself.[123]

Barth draws Anselm's proof to its critical point by arguing because God is the object of knowledge; the only being whose existence is necessary, and who surrenders himself to knowledge through his own self-revelation—through faith—there is every reason to prove that which is believed by faith.[124] Furthermore, Anslem does this quite literally as he speaks about God by *speaking to God*. Barth in fact understands Anselm's theological inquiry to be undertaken and made through prayer.[125] Therefore, the knowledge that the proof of God seeks to expound and impart is the knowledge that is peculiar to faith in God. This is the knowledge of what is believed, which issues from what is believed. It is a knowledge that must be bestowed upon humanity.[126]

In view of the incomprehensibility of God's nature, Barth uses language familiar to the *Göttingen Dogmatics* with respect to God's *veiling*, which can only be transformed into a *unveiling*, an intelligible comprehension, as it touches us noetically from the outside as a subject made known to us.[127] It is Anselm's faith alone that guides this course of inquiry. Any merit of human reason is buried under the ground of his obedience by faith, which

122. Ibid., 83.

123. Barth, *Anselm*, 97. In the *Church Dogmatics* Barth states that: "Without faith we will definitely remain satisfied with the delimitation which we allotted ourselves. And the lack of seriousness in this delimitation will probably be betrayed in two ways. We shall ascribe to ourselves a capacity for the knowledge of God in opposition to the revelation of God. And we shall, therefore, treat God's revelation as something which stands at our own disposal, instead of perceiving that the capacity to know God is taken away from us by revelation and can be ascribed to us again only by revelation." Barth, *CD* II/1, 184.

124. Barth, *Anselm*, 100. We further see in the *Church Dogmatics* Barth's reference to Anselm as coming closest to the mark in describing the hiddenness of God "on the one hand as the predicate to the glory of God present to man, and on the other in its relationship to the sinful closeness of man against this God present to him." Barth then further expounds, "We thus understand the assertion of the hiddenness of God as the confession of the truth and the effectiveness of the sentence of the judgment which in the revelation of God in Jesus Christ is pronounced upon man and therefore also upon his viewing and conceiving, dispossessing him of his own possibility of realising the knowledge of the God who encounters him, and leaving him only the knowledge of faith granted to him and demanded of him by the grace of God and therefore only the viewing and conceiving of faith." Barth *CD* II/1, 191.

125. Barth, *Anselm*, 150.

126. Ibid., 102.

127. Ibid., 116.

for Anselm is "assent to a decision coming from its object," from the Lord's own communication of himself.[128] Anselm's faith is substantiated through God's revelation of himself, who exists in truth, and as such can in no way be conceived as not existing.[129] Furthermore, Barth argues that Anselm ascribes to his own faith in God the God who wills to reveal himself, not based upon any human merit, but strictly upon the work of God's grace alone.[130]

> God gave Himself as the object of his knowledge and God illumined him that he might know him as object. Apart from this event there is no proof of the existence, that is of the reality of God. But in the power of this event there is a proof which is worthy of gratitude. It is truth that has spoken and not man in search of faith.[131]

We find in the *Church Dogmatics* a direct connection from *Anselm* to Barth's emphasis on the grace of God realized by faith, which emerges out of the cleavage between reason in search of God, and the Word of God that is revealed in a way "intrinsically and independently native to him." In the revelation of God, humanity is encountered by something new, something humankind cannot achieve on its own.[132] Faith confronts humankind from the outside in, and is strictly dependent upon the revelation of God through His Word.[133] "Faith—we could no longer avoid the term at the end of our deliberation on experience in the third sub-section—is the making possible of knowledge of God's Word that takes place in actual knowledge of it."[134] Barth therefore concludes that true faith rests upon the will and work of God as a real event, based upon the proclamation of Christ, which in turn

---

128. Ibid., 151.

129. Ibid., 152.

130. Barth, *Anselm*, 160. I argue that Barth uses Anselm's language to express ontically and noetically the *anhypostasis* and *enhypostasis* of Christ's human nature as the mode of God's self revelation. As Barth explains in the *Church Dogmatics*, "This man Jesus Christ is identical with God because the Word became flesh . . . Therefore He does not only live through God and with God. He is Himself God. Nor is He autonomous and self-existent. His reality, existence and being is wholly and absolutely that of God Himself, the God who acts in His Word. His manhood is only the predicate of His Godhead, or better or more concretely, it is only the predicate, assumed in inconceivable condescension, of the Word acting upon us, The Word who is the Lord." Barth, *CD* I/2, 162.

131. Barth, *Anselm*, 171.

132. Barth, *CD* I/1, 194.

133. Ibid., 213.

134. Ibid., 28.

makes the knowledge of God a reality.[135] As such, the knowledge *of* God and faith *in* God are inexorably intertwined—as the eternal Christ who is the object, power, and measure of the real knowledge of God—which is wholly and concretely an action performed by and experience by humanity.[136] "For faith, He is and remains enclosed in objectivity, in the externality of the Word of God, in Jesus Christ. He must teach man to seek Him and He must show Himself to him in order that he may find Him. But it is by this external object that Christian faith lives."[137]

This Word of God becomes the nexus of revelation and faith expressed in the *Church Dogmatics* which was first grounded in Barth's *Anselm*. Barth can now say more emphatically that the one who exercises faith does not first adopt faith (so as to create it in oneself), but only as it has been granted to him through the Word of God.[138] Ontically, the revelation of God is manifest in its real comprehensiveness through the Word of God, and noetically, received by faith in the object of the Word that has spoken.[139] "But let us come to the point: The basis or root of the doctrine of the Trinity, if it has one and is thus legitimate dogma—and it does have one and is thus legitimate dogma—lies in revelation."[140]

I draw this section to conclusion by arguing the importance of Barth's book on *Anselm* lays not in the fact that it provides revolutionary insights into, or changes to, Barth's theology. But given the backdrop of *anhypostasis* and *enhypostasis*, the veiling and unveiling of God is now grounded both ontically and noetically in Jesus Christ as the revelation of God. Moreover, it is faith in the revealed Christ that engenders the capacity for the true knowledge of God.[141] This sets the stage for Barth's more expansive expression

135. Ibid., 229.

136. Ibid.

137. Ibid., 232.

138. Ibid., 244.

139. Dawn DeVries argues that for Barth, "Faith is secondary—it is a response or a reflex, not a creative or generative human activity." Faith for Barth is a "reflexive" action, which requires a prior presence who is the Lord Jesus Christ. "The fact that faith takes its origin in a relationship that is prior to it and apart from which it could not exist at all means that believing Christians can no longer imagine themselves to be self-determined individuals. In faith, they recognize this for the illusion that it is." DeVries, "Barth on the Object and Act of Faith," 165–166.

140. Barth, *CD* I/1, 311.

141. Stephen Wigley argues that the significance of Barth's study of Anselm lays in the structure of the *Church Dogmatics*, particularly in relationship to how the name of God is revealed to Anselm—in faith and in response to prayer. Wigley further argues that this affects Barth's approach to epistemology and leads to his trinitarian exposition of revelation in the *Doctrine of the Word of God*. See Wigley, *Karl Barth* and *Hans Urs*

of *anhypostasis* and *enhypostasis* in the *Church Dogmatics* as a congruent ontological model of Christ's human nature.

Εγενετο: The Word Became Flesh as *Anhypostasis* and *Enhypostasis* in Karl Barth's Christology

If it were indeed possible to encapsulate Karl Barth's understanding of the revelation of God into a single word, one would not be lax in suggesting: εγενετο; where God's covenant to reconcile humanity to himself finds tangible expression—as a *completed event*—in the person of Jesus Christ.[142] Furthermore, as a completed event, the self-revelation of God must also be viewed as a historical reality.[143] As such, Barth interprets as a matter of theological course any denial of the historicity Jesus Christ to be a rejection of the ontological basis of his being; a being that walked and breathed and lived upon this earth as a *true man*.[144] The reality of Jesus Christ is an objective fact, which in the event of the εγενετο provides Christology with its ontological reference.[145] But how is this reality made manifest ontologically

---

von Balthasar, 139. Although I do not disagree with Wigley in this respect, I would add that this faith, which presupposes Barth's epistemology, finds its center in the event of God's revelation in Jesus Christ where the hiddenness of God is revealed in the humanity of Christ. Barth walks away from his study of Anselm with a deeper understanding of the humanity of Christ in union with the Logos, which I believe greatly contributes to his fuller development of *anhypostasis* and *enhypostasis*.

142. For Barth, the εγενετο, the incarnation of the Word, this *unio hypostatica*, must be understood as a *completed* event, but also as a completed *event*. That is, the New Testament testifies to the reality of Jesus Christ as an accomplished fact, "that in the fullness of time it came true—and it was this that made this time fulfilled time." Barth, *CD* I/2, 165.

143. For Barth, there is no theology without the "immediacy of the eternal omnipresent Word and Spirit of God, in which its *freedom* is based, the freedom of the faith bound to God." This is the mediated presence of revelation. See Barth, "Church and Theology," 286.

144. The reality of Jesus Christ in the flesh was never a question for Barth evidenced by his reading of the Gospel accounts as reliable witnesses to the life of Jesus. But the focus of Barth's attention was the revelation of God in the person of Christ. David Mueller argues that in view of Barth's reading of the Gospels as kerygmatic witness, it is not possible to isolate bits and pieces into a historical reconstruction, separating them from the reality of revelation, and designate them as "the simple gospel." see Mueller, *Foundation of Karl Barth's Doctrine of Reconciliation*, 68.

145. Barth, *CD* I/2, 165. Responding to criticism that Barth's incarnation theology negates the historical Jesus, Anderson asks: Does the sole criteria for discussing the incarnation depend strictly upon the study of the life of an historical phenomenon? Barth does not seem to think so. The position that Barth takes, however, does not abandon the gospel records. On the contrary, Barth emphasizes the Easter message and faith,

in Jesus Christ? Barth's answer centers on the *anhypostasis* and *enhypostasis* of Christ's human nature through which God reveals himself in the flesh of humanity as the very speech of God. It is the event of the Word becoming flesh that this mystery is revealed as a reality.[146] "Understanding the Word of God not as proclamation and Scripture alone but as God's revelation in proclamation and Scripture, we must understand it in its identity with God himself. God's revelation is Jesus Christ, the Son of God."[147] With this in view I will examine the ontological relationship of εγενετο to the *anhypostasis* and *enhypostasis* of Christ's human nature given two separate, but integrated contexts of Barth's Christology: (1) Barth's exegesis of the εγενετο in his lectures on John 1 and, (2) Barth's development of the εγενετο in the *Church Dogmatics*.[148]

Eγενετο in John 1:14

Karl Barth lectured on the gospel of John at Münster in 1925 and 1926, and then at Bonn in 1933.[149] But it is Barth's exegesis of εγενετο, the Word became flesh as expressed in John 1:14 that concern us here. Although Barth does not specifically refer to the *anhypostasis* and *enhypostasis* in his lectures on John 1, we observe in his exegesis of εγενετο a clear synthesis of these concepts where he develops the eternal Word of God as actually "becoming," but a becoming that can only be understood as a paradox. "The paradox is harsh and clear: ho logos egeneto, the Word became, it was there. The concreteness, the contingency, the historical singularity of the eternal, absolute, divine Word is what is stated with this sentence, and to understand

---

and also holds to the position that the Easter message and the passion of our Lord, (i.e., the entire life of Jesus) is the concrete content of the revelation which takes place at Easter. See Anderson, *Aspects of the Theology of Karl Barth*, 124–25.

146. Todd Pokrifka argues that the charge of Barth's *Christocentrism* in reality speaks to Barth's trinitarian theology. To speak of Christ and his incarnation as the center of Scripture presupposes a trinitarian understanding of God because in Jesus Christ is made manifest the revelation of the triune God. See Pokrifka, *Redescribing God*, 185–86.

147. Barth, *CD* I/1, 137.

148. For Barth, the Word became flesh is central to his theology—the reality and life of Christ. Likewise, Charles Hodge clearly affirms that Reformed and true Christianity is not a system of doctrine, nor is it subjectively considered a form of knowledge. "It is a life. It is the life of Christ . . . The effect of the incarnation was to unite the human and divine as one life." Hodge, *Systematic Theology*, 1:174.

149. While at Münster and Bonn, Barth was given the freedom to teach dogmatics and New Testament exegesis out of which his exegetical work on the Gospel of John emerged. See Barth, *Witness to the Word*, ix–x.

John we must take away nothing on either side."[150] Barth's emphasis that the Word became does not point to a coming into being as a creature (although He did in his humanity), but to the paradoxical reality that in the εγενετο the Logos came in the flesh of humanity.[151]

This reality, however, is not simply the Logos assuming humanity, but his assuming the nature of fallen humanity in need of sanctification and redemption. Although Barth acknowledges Christ's becoming includes the assumption of human nature in general (i.e., the assumption of an individual human substance of soul and body), this is not where the emphasis of his argument falls. Rather, Barth's focus is on the "humulis misera ac infirma hominis conditio" to which the eternal Word gave itself. The Logos therefore did not simply assume humanity as originally intended by God before the fall, but humanity that was subject to the corruption of the human image. "But John speaks explicitly of becoming flesh, of assuming the nature of Adam, of the servant form which is proper to human nature under the sign of the fall and in the sphere of darkness, of the fallen and corrupt human nature which needs to be sanctified and redeemed."[152]

Barth argues that this must be so because humanity's salvation depended upon Jesus becoming flesh in our fallen state. Otherwise, his becoming would only heighten our pain. But as it is, he chose to bear the body of our weakness in solidarity with our flesh.[153] As such, I argue that for Barth, in this paradox is embodied the function of *anhypostasis* and *enhypostasis* where the eternal and perfect Logos assumes to himself that which is not like himself, but in so doing he sanctifies it, he takes that which was not real and makes it reality. In other words, by assuming human nature to himself—Jesus Christ makes it true human nature.

Furthermore, it is not simply a matter that the Word became flesh, but "the Word became *flesh* is its revelation."[154] That is, the flesh of humanity becomes the mode of the revelation of God. In this way the *egeneto* is the sign equating the Logos and flesh, an equation that cannot be reversed. The Logos always remains the subject and the flesh the predicate because the Logos remains what he is without this predicate of the flesh.[155] Barth

---

150. Barth, *John* 1, 86.

151. Ibid., 87.

152. Ibid., 88.

153. Ibid., 88–89.

154. Ibid., 90.

155. Ibid., 90. In the *Church Dogmatics* Barth states, "But can or will the Word of God become? Does He not surrender thereby His divinity? Or, if He does not surrender it, what does becoming mean? By what figures of speech or concepts is this becoming of the Word of God to be properly described? "The Word became"—if that is true, and

emphasizes here the superiority of the Word over the flesh in their union, and conceptually expresses the language of *anhypostasis* and *enhypostasis* in the flesh of Christ through the action of the Word. "The *Word* speaks, the *Word* acts, the *Word* reveals, the *Word* redeems. The *Word* is Jesus, the I that will alone speak for long stretches later in the Gospel. Certainly the *incarnate* Word."[156]

Barth further draws out the concept of *anhypostasis* and *enhypostasis* arguing that in the assumption of flesh, the Logos remains the Son of God in every respect in this paradoxical union of two unequal things.[157] The flesh, the instrument of revelation assumed by the Logos as event—*is the Word in action*. This is God in the flesh revealing that which is not flesh. Moreover, it is the flesh that conceals, and it is the Logos himself who is revealed through the flesh.[158] For Barth, that the Word became flesh not only expresses the revelation of God in the flesh of humanity, but it forms the ontological mold into which the *anhypostasis* and *enhypostasis* of Christ's human nature is formed.

Εγενετο in the Church Dogmatics

The revelation of the Triune God made manifest in the flesh of Jesus Christ is a dominant theme expressed by Karl Barth in the *Church Dogmatics*. Negatively stated, the biblical witness to the incarnation of the Word does not mean that the man Jesus of Nazareth, in himself, in his own power, is the revealing Word of God.[159] The humanity of Christ (in his humanness) is not the revelation of God. It is the Logos who is revealed through the humanity

---

true in such a way that a real becoming is thereby expressed without the slightest surrender of the divinity of the Word, its truth is that of a miraculous act, an act of mercy on the part of God." Barth, *CD* I/2, 159.

156. Ibid., 91.

157. Ibid.

158. Ibid., 92. This language is expressed within the context of *anhypostasis* and *enhypostasis* in the *Church Dogmatics*. "As the Word of God becomes flesh He assumes or adopts or incorporates human being into unity with His divine being, so that this human being, as it comes into being, becomes as a human being the being of the Word of God." Barth, *CD* I/2, 160.

159. Eberhard Jüngel argues that Barth's concept of the revelation of God always carries with it the objectivity of his revelation. "According to Barth, we have to speak of God's 'primary objectivity', because in the objectivity of his revelation, in which he lets himself be known to men, *God reveals himself as the Lord* . . . the category of lordship of God expresses the *capacity* for revelation, the *possibility* of revelation which is grounded in the being of God." Jüngel, *God's Being is in Becoming*, 62–63.

of Jesus.[160] Furthermore, Jesus Christ is not simply the revelation of the Logos, but the revelation of the Triune God, where "revelation must indeed be understood as the root or ground of the doctrine of the Trinity."[161] This must be so because the triune God does not act in isolation as the Father, Son, or Spirit but always as one God. Moreover, Barth argues that while God reveals himself given the *attributes* of his triune being, he cannot be "distributed ontologically to Father, Son and Spirit."[162] Barth can therefore say: "The statement that it is the Word or the Son who became man therefore asserts without reserve that in spite of His distinction as Son from the Father and the Holy Spirit, God in His entire divinity became man."[163]

Barth further argues that Jesus Christ reveals in his life and work the triune God—*as a creature*. But he is not only a creature; otherwise, he could not reveal God. If, however, he reveals God despite his creatureliness, he must therefore also be God. In this sense Jesus Christ must be "full and true God without reduction or limitation, without more or less. Any such restriction would not merely weaken His deity; it would deny it." Therefore, as the revelation of his Father, Jesus Christ is equal in deity with His Father.[164]

> This can, of course, be said of the human nature of Christ, of His
> existence as a man in which, according to Scripture, He meets us
> as the Revealer of God and the Reconciler to God. But it cannot
> be said of Him who here assumes human nature, of Him who

160. Barth, *CD* I/1, 323. Bruce McCormack argues (from *CD* II/1, 201 par. 27) "Revelation is, for Barth, a rational event, that is, one that occurs in the realm of human *ratio* through the normal process of human cognition." McCormack explains that God's speech communicates reason with reason and person with person. The divine communication with human reason must be understood as a rational event. And as a rational event, the speech of God's revelation is a trinitarian event. Barth claims that the "Word of God (Jesus Christ, the objective reality and possibility of revelation) is intrinsically verbal—his person is a content-ful reality that is communicable in views, concepts, and words." McCormack, *Orthodox* and *Modern*, 168–169.

161. Barth, *CD* I/1, 332. John Thompson similarly points out: "Barth's view of the Trinity is that one God, Father, Son and Holy Spirit in the divine freedom and love lives a life complete in itself, though this is only known in and through the incarnation." Thompson, *Christ in Perspective*, 21.

162. Barth, *CD* I/1, 362. Barth states that "It is thus legitimate for us to differentiate the three modes of being of the one God on the basis of the revelation which takes place in the sphere and within the limits of human comprehensibility." Barth, *CD* I/1, 372.

163. Barth, *CD* I/2, 33. Barth would also later state that "It is precisely God's *deity*, which rightly understood, includes his *humanity*." In other words, this is a christological statement, Barth, *Humanity of God*, 46. John Thompson observes that consistent with traditional dogmatics (i.e., Heinrich Heppe) Barth posits that while the Son alone in his nature as God became a man, in his union with the Trinity the incarnation is a common work of the Father, Son, and Holy Spirit. See Thompson, *Christ in Perspective*, 22.

164. Barth, *CD* I/1, 406.

exists as man ("for us men" as Nic. Const. says later) but does not allow His being and essence to be exhausted or imprisoned in His humanity, who is also in the full sense *not* man in this humanity, who is the Revealer and Reconciler in His humanity by virtue of that wherein He is not man. He who becomes man here to become the Revealer and the Reconciler is not made. Otherwise revelation and reconciliation would be an event within creation and, since creation is the world of fallen man, they would be a futile event. Because the One who here became man is God, God in this mode of being, therefore, and not otherwise, His humanity is effective as revelation and reconciliation.[165]

For Barth, the revelation of God in the incarnation of the Word directs us to the content of the New Testament that is "solely the name Jesus Christ" in the truth of his "God-manhood."[166] That is, Jesus Christ is expressed by the New Testament witnesses as the revelation of God—the "true God man" and "true man God" as their penultimate word. Their ultimate word, however, is not a synthesis of these terms, but simply the name Jesus Christ.[167] Moreover, when the Word (in union with the Father and Holy Spirit) became humanity, he put on humanity as the covering, the means of his revelation made manifest as both the veiling and unveiling of himself.[168] This is Barth's understanding of the biblical sense of revelation, namely the "veiledness of the Word of God in Him and the breaking through of this veil in virtue of His self-unveiling."[169] This unveiling is in fact the act of God re-

---

165. Barth, *CD* I/1, 430. In this passage Barth alludes to the paradox of *anhypostasis* and *enhypostasis* made manifest in the human nature of Christ as the revealer of God. While the flesh assumed by the Logos is real humanity in its mode of being, it is also not real humanity as the Logos who assumed this flesh. Therefore, as *anhypostasis*, the flesh of Christ has no autonomous existence (having not been created), but is also *enhypostasis*, having been taken up into the eternal Logos through which the flesh assumes real existence.

166. Barth, *CD* I/2, 15.

167. Ibid., 24.

168. Ibid., 35.

169. Barth, *CD* I/2, 56. Barth's trinitarian language of the incarnation echoes that of Herman Bavinck who argues: "The Doctrine of Christ is the central point of the whole system of dogmatics. Here too, pulses the whole of the religious-ethical life of Christianity. Christ, the incarnate Word, is thus the central fact of the entire history of the world. The incarnation has its presupposition and foundation in the trinitarian being of God. The Trinity makes possible the existence of a mediator who himself participates both in the divine and human nature and thus unites God and humanity. The incarnation, however, is the Work of the entire Trinity. Christ was sent by the Father and conceived by the Holy Spirit . . . The Logos, who was with God and by whom all things were made, is the One who became flesh." Bavinck, *Reformed Dogmatics*, 3:235.

vealing himself in the time of the years 1-30, the fulfilled time when revelation becomes history.[170] This is the time of grace, the crisis that breaks into earthly time where the offense of God's revelation confronts humankind in becoming the end of our time and everything that is real in our time.[171] This is the reality of the revelation of God made manifest in the Word, the Son taking upon himself the burden, and in fact becoming flesh.[172] In all of this Barth can state quite emphatically that: "Every statement in the New Testament originates in the fact that the Word was made flesh."[173]

Nevertheless, Barth counters that we cannot fully conceive the Word was made flesh in the fullness of its reality. That the eternal Word of God assumed human nature into *oneness* with himself in becoming "very God and very man" signifies the ultimate mystery of the revelation of God in Jesus Christ.[174] In the εγενετο, in this *oneness* of Jesus Christ as very God and very man is formed the center of reality and mystery in his revelation. However, the objective reality of Christ's advent does not in itself fully reveal ontologically what takes place in the εγενετο.[175] This is the mystery that the church proclaims in the name of Jesus of Nazareth. This is the eternal Logos assuming the flesh of humanity without infringing upon the ontological reality of his being as eternal God in the second person of the Trinity. Moreover, this is an eternal message expressed in time and space of this world both to the patriarchs and prophets of the Old Testament, and more fully realized in the church of the New Testament.

170. Ibid., 58. Thomas F. Torrance almost whimsically asks: Where there is no formal establishment of time with respect to eschatology, must we not go on to form a concept of time in the analogy of the incarnation? "Must we not say with Karl Barth that because the Word has become flesh it has also become time?" Torrance, *Atonement*, 409.

171. Barth, *CD* I/2, 67.

172. Barth, *CD* I/2, 89. Bruce McCormack similarly states in his exposition of *CD* I/2 (especially pages 159–71) that: "When God unites himself to human nature in the incarnation, God does so in such a way that no abrogation, abolition, or alteration of that nature takes place. The human nature is *human* precisely *in* its union with the divine. As such, it remains a veil *even as God unveils himself to human eyewitnesses in* and *through it*—by the testimony of the Holy Spirit to them. Hence the subject of this human life is never given to direct perception. What the disciples apprehend *of themselves* is therefore the humanity of Jesus and it alone." McCormack, *Orthodox and Modern*, 171.

173. Barth, *CD* I/2, 104.

174. Ibid., 124.

175. Barth is careful to not over simplify the ontological mystery of Christ's advent. Bromiley argues that for Barth, the ontological reality of the εγενετο (i.e., the verb made or became) points to the central mystery of the incarnation. See Bromiley, *Introduction to the Theology of Karl Barth*, 25.

> The Christian message declares that in this form, as the Logos incarnatus, He exists in the recollection of the Church, exactly as in this form, as the Logos *incarnandus*, He existed for the patriarchs in the expectation of Israel. To that extent it is the message that the incarnation of the Word is an accomplished event. From this point of view it is the answer to the Pauline-Johannine problem. Is the name of Christ, is Christ the Son of God, really Jesus of Nazareth? Yes, it replies; and so with all its might it must maintain that this and no other is His name, that such He is and not something else.[176]

In view of Barth's emphasis that Jesus of Nazareth is in fact Christ, it is not difficult to appreciate the importance of the ontological grounding provided by the *anhypostasis* and *enhypostasis*, where the reality of the εγενετο carries with it the true mystery of the person of Jesus Christ. In other words, while Jesus Christ is in fact *true man*, this is possible ontologically only as a being *enhypostasis* in union with the Logos, a union from which Jesus (as *true man*) derives his actual subsistence. On the other hand, as *anhypostasis*, the negative (without subsistence) component of Christ's human nature provides a rather unique frame of ontological reference by which the mystery of the εγενετο can only be understood in this christological context.[177] "The miracle of the incarnation, of the unio hypostatica, is seen from this angle when we realize that the Word of God descended from the freedom, majesty and glory of His divinity, that without becoming unlike Himself He assumed His likeness to us, and that now He is to be sought and found of us here, namely, in His human being."[178]

For Barth, the concepts of *anhypostasis* and *enhypostasis* express quite nicely Christ's human nature dialectically in God's veiling and unveiling. This understanding of Christ's human nature explains how Jesus Christ reveals himself to his creation "as one with them," yet remains unchanged as their creator in his divine essence. Taking this concept one step further, Barth understands in this dialectic of veiling and unveiling that Christ must

---

176. Barth, *CD* I/2, 165.

177. Anderson argues that the ontological problem in Barth's concept of the humanity of Christ is the human condition is "expurgated" by the flesh-assumption of the Word so that the subjective is swallowed up in this event of the Word taking human nature upon himself; that is, in the objective. Anderson suggests that true humanity has been removed, becoming purely instrumental in Christ. See Anderson, *Aspects of the Theology of Karl Barth*, 131. Barth of course would respond to this argument with his appropriation of the *anhypostasis* and *anhypostasis* where the flesh of Christ is both real and not real humanity in union with the Logos.

178. Barth, *CD* I/2, 165.

be the revelation of God both ontically and noetically[179] because the knowledge of God made manifest in Christ, his being as humanity alone does not
accomplish true revelation of the triune God. Put another way, if the revelation of Jesus Christ is not realized both ontically and noetically through the
exercise of faith, it is not the revelation of God as the union of very God and
very man.[180] This is the critical lesson that Barth learned from Anselm.

Viewed through the lenses of *anhypostasis* and *enhypostasis* Jesus of
Nazareth is *true humanity* (debunking any docetic claim) who exists in indissoluble union with the Logos. I argue that this assumption of the man
Jesus of Nazareth by the Logos of God is so ingrained in Barth's ontology of
Christ that he has no inherent reason to repeatedly reiterate this principle
(or doctrine as he referred to it) in his Christology. This is especially true
in the *Church Dogmatics*—the principal theological work by which Barth is
judged—where the reality of Jesus Christ as *true humanity* is axiomatic, just
as he remains *true God* in his assumption of flesh.[181] "Every question concerning the Word which is directed away from Jesus of Nazareth, the human
being of Christ, is necessarily and wholly directed away from Himself, the

179. George Hunsinger suggests that Barth understands the human nature of Christ
simply as a (sacramental) sign to the reality of God in Jesus Christ: "What confronts
us directly, therefore, is not the reality but the sacramental sign, not the divine but the
creaturely form of objectivity, not the deity but the humanity of Christ. The distinction
of the creator from the creature has not been renounced ontically, but it has been surrendered, in any direct sense, noetically. That is, the distinction of the creator from the
creature is not visible but concealed by the very different objectivity of the creature."
Hunsinger, *Disruptive Grace*, 80. I would argue here that noetically Barth understands
the human nature of Christ to also reveal his divine essence, but only through the exercise of faith.

180. Hunsinger argues that Barth denies the humanity of Christ as being God. "The
truth of God's identity, as mediated in Jesus Christ, remains hidden in the midst of
revelation, not only (as we have seen) by virtue of its form, but also by virtue of its content. It remains hidden by virtue of its form, because its form is the form of that which
is not God, the creaturely form of Jesus Christ's humanity. It remains hidden by virtue
of its content, on the other hand, because its content is the truth of the inconceivable
content that God's inmost identity is trinitarian." Hunsinger, *Disruptive Grace*, 81. Yet
I would counter that as *anhypostasis* and *enhypostasis*, in the εγενετο, the humanity
of Christ is absolutely assumed by the Logos by virtue of this union. Barth in no way
separates the humanity of Christ from the divinity of Christ. That would be a denial of
his Christology.

181. Anderson argues that while Barth does not seem to be enamoured by the Jesus
of history, one must keep in mind the historical events that helped to shape the thought
of Barth, specifically his perception of the liberal Protestant theology failure to deal
with the limitations of man and the greatness of God. He does not proceed via a Jesus of
history but from the presupposition of the Christological dogma, i.e., from the revelation of God in Jesus Christ. See Anderson, *Aspects of the Theology of Karl Barth*, 124.

Word, and therefore from God Himself, because the Word, and therefore God Himself, does not exist for us apart from the human being of Christ."[182]

While it may be argued that Barth does not explicitly express the humanity of Christ as *true humanity* historically, this does not negate Barth's emphasis of *true humanity* as *anhypostasis* and *enhypostasis*.[183] For Barth, it is the act of creation itself that demonstrates the true humanity of Christ, because absent the will of the Father in begetting the Son of God, as true humanity in the εγενετο, the creation of the first human being in Adam is meaningless. Moreover, it is in Barth's understanding of the union of true God and true humanity that demonstrate his faithfulness not only to Chalcedon, but to Calvin as well. Barth points to Calvin and says:

> Calvin calls Christ prior to His incarnation the eternal Word before all time, begotten of the Father, true God, of one essence, power, and majesty with the Father, and therefore Himself Jehovah, that is, the self-existent one . . . As the incarnate Word Christ is both true God and true Man. The natures remain distinct, but are in mutual communication, so that we can predicate the qualities to each of the other. The Church is redeemed by the blood of God, the Son of Man is in heaven. This is the familiar doctrine of the *idiomata* ("attributes"), and it was the part of the early teaching that Calvin found it necessary to appeal to most.[184]

Furthermore, the very act of God's creation is accomplished with a view to the incarnation, to the Word becoming flesh. This in fact becomes the historical context in which Barth considers the *very man* of Jesus Christ. Being both true God and true humanity, *true* does not only mean that he is humanity as God created him, but that he is this and all we are as well. That is, Jesus of Nazareth is "accessible and knowable to us as a human being, with no special capacities or potentialities, with no admixture of a quality alien to us, with no supernatural endowment such as must make him a totally different being from us." Jesus is real humanity in such a way that he can be the natural brother of any other person.[185] And as our brother, he does the work of God in his oneness with the being of God, as this man.

---

182. Barth, *CD* I/2, 166.

183. Describing the historical development of *anhypostasis* and *enhypostasis* Barth states, "We have seen earlier that what the eternal Word made His own, giving it thereby His own existence, was not a man, but man's nature, man's being, and so not a second existence but a second possibility of existence, to wit, that of a man." Barth, *CD* I/2, 163.

184. Barth, *Theology of John Calvin*, 328.

185. Barth, *CD* III/2, 53.

"It is in this way that He exists as a creature, which cannot be dissolved in its Creator, which cannot itself be or become the Creator, but which has its own reality and worth in face of the Creator, deriving its own righteousness from the Creator."[186]

To the question: how can humanity in its humiliation possibly meet God in his exaltation? Barth responds: only in the union of *true man* in his humiliation and *true God* in his exaltation in the person of Jesus Christ, the God-man, who in his divine essence assumes to himself true human essence. Barth describes this veiling and unveiling of God in Jesus Christ as the two coherent steps inseparably linked, and yet remaining clearly distinct as *very God* and *very man*.

> While the New Testament speaks wholly from the standpoint of Easter and ascension, let us be quite clear that Easter and ascension as such constitute the end and the goal of its witness, to which we are led by a definite way. To begin with, we are set a riddle. From the very start we are also shown that the solution of it is to hand. But it is still a riddle which is followed by the solution. Man in his humiliation, God in His exaltation, or the God-Man in His veiling and also in His unveiling: these constitute two coherent steps, inseparably linked yet also clearly distinct. Some sort of meeting between God and man takes place in the figure of Christ in the New Testament, and in this meeting is the event which is the object of the New Testament witness, *vere Deus vere homo*.[187]

Furthermore, the act of the εγενετο is not limited to the incarnation, but points forward to the crucifixion and resurrection of the God-man, all of which encompass the revelation of God made comprehensible in the person of Jesus Christ as the flesh of God himself (as the shell or form of the Word). These events form an even greater scope encompassing *anhypostasis* and *enhypostasis* as the mystery of the flesh, which exists as a historical reality in testifying to the revelation of the Logos in the humanity of Christ.[188]

> The resurrection of the crucified is important as the revelation of this event, as the triumph of the Word in His human

186. Ibid., 64.

187. Barth, *CD* I/2, 167–68.

188. For Barth, the εγενετο cannot be limited to the event of the birth of Jesus. "The fact that God became Man, that His Word became hearable and we ourselves became reconciled to God, is true because it became true, and because it becomes true before our eyes and ears in the witness of Scripture, in the movement which it attests from non-revelation to revelation, from promise to fulfillment, from the cross to the resurrection." Barth, *CD* I/2, 167.

existence. The Christian message states that the Word became flesh. But it is not enough merely to state this. It tells a story: the story of how this state of affairs came to pass, how it became true that God the Lord took man to Himself by becoming Man. From this point of view the Christian message is the answer to the problem of the Synoptists, whether Jesus of Nazareth is really the Christ, the Son of God. Its answer is Yes, and now it lays all its emphasis on the fact that the sole source of this human being's existence and power is the agency of the Word of God, that in Him the Word of God wills to be taken up and grasped, believed and understood, the Word as the mystery of the flesh, but the flesh as the shell and form of the Word.[189]

Finally, we take notice of the role that faith must play in the revelation of God in Christ Jesus given the backdrop of the εγενετο. It is faith in the God-man that answers the noetic problem of veiling and unveiling in the ontology of Jesus Christ. This is the Logos acting in the flesh of Jesus as the real embodiment of the triune God that can only be revealed by faith in the object of faith; that is, in this God-man. We see here the real thrust of *enhypostasis* and *anhypostasis* in the flesh of Christ, who as God incarnate speaks the very words of faith, which must be received by faith in the one who manifests himself in Jesus.

Faith as it were, discovers that this Man is God. God's personal action as such is its object. Can it be otherwise, seeing the reality of Jesus Christ which is here contemplated is revelation, and revelation is the object of faith, and so knowledge of it is knowledge of faith? The very reason why a distinction is here made between God and man—and obviously the better to understand the unity—is in order that their unity may be seen always as an act of God, and that in this act God Himself may always be seen as the Lord.[190]

We see very clearly here how Barth links the act of God's self-revelation in Jesus Christ—in the unity of God with humanity—to the reality of the εγενετο. Consequently, this personal action of God in becoming humanity must be discovered by faith, and in the object of faith made manifest in union of God and humanity in the person of Jesus Christ.

189. Barth, *CD* I/2, 167–68.
190. Ibid., 168.

Anhypostasis and *Enhypostasis*: Ontology as Dialectic in Karl Barth's Christology

With *anhypostasis* and *enhypostasis* firmly grounded as the ontological foundation to express the human nature of Christ, Barth uses this christological frame of reference to dialectically argue for, and express, the *reality* of Christ's human nature in its union with the Logos. This *anhypostasis* and *enhypostasis* dialectic first emerges (in its formative state) in the *Göttingen Dogmatics* where Barth engages Lutheran and Reformed Christology as his way to distinguish the human nature of Christ in its union with the Logos. Thereafter, this dialectic is more fully developed in the *Church Dogmatics* where Barth argues for a *separate*, rather than a *distinctive* attribute of Christ's human nature in union with the Logos.[191] As we have shown, while both Lutheran and Reformed theology found ontological agreement in Christ's human nature as *anhypostasis* and *enhypostasis*, there remained sharp disagreement over the form in which the Logos became flesh in the incarnation.[192] This ontological variance proves pivotal for Barth as he considers the reality of *very man* in the human nature of Christ as the instrument of God's revelation.

In the *Göttingen Dogmatics* Barth critiques the Lutheran and Reformed controversy over the union of divine and human natures in Christ. "The statement that the human nature has subsistence only by and in the Logos may not be reversed. We may not say that the Logos subsists only in the human nature of Christ."[193] Herein Barth examines the Lutheran and Reformed controversy over the eternal Word of God as *Logos ensarkos* and *Logos asarkos*, also known as the *extra Calvinisticum*, which was rooted in their disagreement over the form of the Logos becoming human nature in

---

191. In the *Church Dogmatics* Barth takes seriously the question: in what sense can the flesh assumed by Christ be understood as separate in the person of the God-man?

192. In adopting the traditional doctrine of the two natures, Luther taught the full unity of the deity and humanity in the person of Jesus Christ, "the full participation of the humanity in the deity and of the deity in the humanity." Furthermore, Luther teaches the "impersonality of the human nature of Christ (an- or *enhypostasis*) given the union of the humanity and the divinity of Christ is one Person. Luther does not agree with the exegetes of the early church who understood Philippians 2:6 f. ("He emptied Himself") as describing an act of the pre-existent Christ at the time of the incarnation; rather he understood it as describing the attitude of the incarnate Christ ". . . He did not give up the 'form of God' and take on 'the form of a servant' once for all at the time of the incarnation; rather the man Jesus possessed the form of God at all times and could have used it and brought it to bear, but at every point he laid it aside and made himself the servant of all rather than their Lord." Althaus, *The Theology of Martin Luther*, 194.

193. Barth, *Göttingen Dogmatics*, 158.

the incarnation.[194] The Lutherans argued that the flesh of Christ is so united to the Logos that wherever the Logos is, there it has the flesh most present with it.[195] Barth contrasts this position with the Reformed who agreed that the whole Logos dwells in the human nature of Christ, but is *not* fully enclosed in, or limited to, the human nature it indwells.[196] Barth identifies the problem indicative to the Lutheran view of the incarnation—that the Logos is understood to be fully enclosed in the flesh of Christ, which in turn logically limits the Logos spatially within the being of the man Jesus Christ. Recognizing this obvious ontological difficulty, the Lutherans also argued that because the flesh of Christ could not be logically separated from the divine Logos in this incarnate union, the freedom from limitation must apply to the flesh as well.[197]

The Reformed rejected the ubiquity of Christ's human nature on the grounds that it denies the reality of *true man* in Christ. That is, if the human nature is not finite, it is by definition not true human nature, which in turn raises a critical question: how then is it possible for the human nature of Christ to be an organ of revelation?[198] The Reformed responded to the Lutherans with their own thesis: "the Logos, while dwelling wholly in the flesh, also remains wholly outside it."[199] Barth argues against the Lutherans given the Reformed principle that ubiquity is strictly an attribute of the divine Logos, and not the man Jesus. He summarizes the Reformed position by explaining that "the Logos so unites the human nature to himself that he

194. Calvin states: "For even if the Word in his immeasurable essence united with the nature of man into one person, we do not imagine that he was confined therein. Here is something marvelous: the Son of God descended from heaven in such a way that, without leaving heaven, he willed to be borne in the virgin's womb, to go about the earth, and to hang upon the cross; yet he continuously filled the world even as he had done from the beginning." Calvin, *Institutes*, 1:481.

195. Barth, *Göttingen Dogmatics*, 158.

196. In expressing the Reformed position with respect to the union of Christ's divine nature with the human nature of Jesus Barth cites Calvin's statement that "we do not imagine that He was confined therein," see Barth, *Göttingen Dogmatics*, 158.

197. Barth, *Göttingen Dogmatics*, 158. Luther adopted and sharpened the doctrine of the *enhypostasis* to read that the human nature of Christ has no hypostasis (separate existence) of its own, but possesses it in the divine nature . . . Luther's idea of the total person in Christ led to the further development of the doctrine of ubiquity—the idea of Christ's exalted human nature as everywhere present. See Lohse, *Martin Luther's Theology*, 229–30.

198. The Lutheran argument for the ubiquity of Christ's human nature hits at the core of Barth's christological method and the expression of Christ's human nature as *anhypostasis* and *enhypostasis*.

199. Barth, *Göttingen Dogmatics*, 159.

totally indwells it and yet is totally transcendent and infinite outside it."[200] Barth then asks: if the two natures in Christ are not separated, does it follow that the humanity is everywhere the deity is? In response Barth agrees with the Reformed position that deity alone is inconceivable and omnipresent because divine nature also exists *outside* the flesh it has assumed. And yet it is no less present in it, being personally with it.[201] Barth clearly favors the Reformed against the Lutherans in the *Göttingen Dogmatics* where he argues for the so called Calvinistic *extra* based upon three main points:

1. This doctrine does not deny the Lutheran concern that God is wholly in his revelation because the Logos in Christ's flesh and the Logos outside Christ's flesh are naturally not two different entities, but remain the same totality.[202]

2. The Lutheran counter doctrine that ties the Logos inseparably to the flesh of Christ leads to the inescapable deduction of the ubiquity of the flesh, which evaporates the true humanity of the Redeemer and thereby eliminates the objective possibility of revelation.[203]

3. The dialectic of "totally in and totally outside" is a valuable safeguard of the mystery where the indirectness of revelation is maintained because the deity is inconceivable. "At one and the same time God is wholly in his revelation and without subtraction a perceptible object, man, and wholly not an object, a man, but the immutable divine subject, not merely as Father and Spirit but also in the medium of revelation itself, in the Mediator, the Son. The Son is both *logos ensarkos* and *logos asarkos*."[204]

Barth draws a clear distinction between the human nature of Christ (as both *anhypostasis* and *enhypostasis*),[205] and the Logos, who reveals himself in this human nature he has assumed. However, because the Logos exists in perfect unity with the Father and the Holy Spirit as a triune God, he cannot limit himself spatially within the human nature that he indwells, nor can the

200. Ibid.

201. Barth, *Göttingen Dogmatics*, 159.

202. Ibid.

203. Ibid., 160.

204. Ibid.

205. As we have shown, Barth did not develop the terms *anhypostasis* and *enhypostasis* as a dual formula in the *Göttingen Dogmatics*. Rather, the emphasis fell on the *anhypostasis* where the human nature of Christ has no subsistent reality aside from its union with the Logos. Barth used *enhypostasis* to affirm the reality of Christ's human nature in its union with the Logos.

human nature be enjoined to the Logos ontologically in his divine incomprehensibility. We see therefore in the unity of the God-man Barth's clear distinction between the subject (the Logos), and the object, (the humanity assumed by Christ) with respect to the *Logos ensarkos* and *Logos asarkos*, while arguing for the *anhypostasis* and *enhypostasis* of Christ's human nature in this union. " . . . the constitution of the God-man does not involve the union of the Logos and a human person but the union of the Logos and the human nature, since the Logos, the Son of God himself, wills to be the person of the God-man."[206]

We note in this passage a concise summary of how Barth understands the union of the Logos with human nature of Jesus Christ in the *Göttingen Dogmatics* where the Logos wills to take to himself a human nature (not a human person) in becoming the God-man. Negatively stated—as *anhypostasis*—this human nature has no subsistent reality strictly in itself. Positively stated—as *enhypostasis*—the human nature of Christ enjoys reality (very man) by virtue of its subsistence in union with the Logos.[207]

In the *Church Dogmatics* Barth once again engages Lutheran and Reformed theology in view of the Calvinistic *extra* with the *anhypostasis* and *enhypostasis* dialectic as the central point of contact. However, in the *Church Dogmatics* we see a clear transition in Barth's thinking as he more deliberately argues the Reformed *extra* in juxtaposition against the Lutheran *solely* concept of the Logos indwelling the human nature of Christ.[208] Consequently, we observe in the *Church Dogmatics* a more evenly balanced argument expressed in Barth's *anhypostasis* and *enhypostasis* dialectic as he works through "the Eutychian leaning of the Lutherans" set against "the Nestorian leaning of the Reformed."[209]

The act of God becoming humanity, this εγενετο, becomes Barth's central thesis in developing the *anhypostasis* and *enhypostasis* dialectic by vetting the point of departure between the Lutherans and Reformed over what it means for God and humanity to be united in Jesus Christ.[210] As

206. Barth, *Göttingen Dogmatics*, 163.

207. It should be noted here that Barth's conception of real subsistence in the human nature of Christ (*enhypostasis*) is always qualified by its *anhypostasis*.

208. Barth, *CD* I/2, 168.

209. Barth, *CD* I/2, 161. For Barth, the use of *anhypostasis* and *enhypostasis* provides an objective measure to judge both Lutheran and Reformed theology in view of their basic agreement with this ontological description of Christ's human nature.

210. Barth acknowledges that the Lutherans and Reformed had the same starting-point, that the unity involved in Jesus Christ is really and originally the unity of the divine Word with the human being assumed by him—the union of two natures. Barth, *CD* I/2, 162.

the mediator between God and humanity Barth rejects Jesus Christ as a third being midway between the divine and human because ontologically he is God and humanity. It is the "and" that conveys this inconceivable act of "becoming" in the incarnation. Moreover, the act of God becoming human is not simply the act of the Logos; but of the Father, the Son, and the Holy Spirit acting in perfect unity as the triune God in becoming flesh through the Son.[211]

> The unity into which the human nature is assumed is this unity with the Word, and only to that extent—because this Word is the eternal Word—the union of the human with the divine nature. But the eternal Word is with the Father and the Holy Spirit the unchangeable God Himself and so incapable of any change or admixture. Unity with Him, the "becoming" of the Word, cannot therefore mean the origination of a third between Word and flesh, but only the assumption of the flesh by the Word.[212]

Presupposing Lutheran and Reformed agreement on Christological essentials (i.e., that divine and human natures are united in Jesus Christ) Barth presses the question of what humanity's *reality* in "God becoming man" means for Lutheran and Reformed theology in view of the *anhypostasis* and *enhypostasis*. He argues that the union of God and humanity's nature in Christ means that this man himself becomes God, but not in a way that is a divinization of humanity. It also means that Jesus is not self-existent because his existence as a human being is wholly that of God who acts in his Word.[213] It is the question of this man's reality in union with the Logos that demands Barth's attention, and in turn his reliance on the *anhypostasis* and *enhyposta-sis* of Christ's human nature in working out his thinking here.[214]

In this context Barth develops the union of the Word and human nature as *anhypostasis* and *enhypostasis*, which he uses ontologically to express

211. Barth, *CD* I/2, 161. Baillie observes that with Barth, the doctrine of the Trinity is not the epilogue to his dogmatics, but the starting point, and indeed broad foundation . . . "Plainly Barth does not regard the doctrine of the Trinity as standing for real distinctions in God, and, moreover, for the *kind* of distinctions on which orthodox belief has always insisted: the three persons are not three parts of God, and yet they are not mere attributes, or shifting aspects, relative to our apprehension, or arbitrarily selected from among others, but are the eternal being of God who has revealed Himself to us in Christ and dwells in us by the Holy Spirit." Baillie, *God was in Christ*, 34–37.

212. Ibid.

213. Ibid., 162.

214. Barth never wavered in his belief in the reality of Jesus Christ as a *true* humanity. The issue he wrestles with is how to express the reality of *true* humanity and *true* God in the person of Christ. Ultimately, even the ontology of *anhypostasis* and *enhypostasis* cannot solve this mystery of the God-man presented in the Scriptures.

that "He exists as Man so far and only so far as He exists as God, i.e., in the mode of existence of the eternal Word of God."[215] Moreover, Barth employs his adoption of *anhypostasis* and *enhypostasis* dialectically to examine the disparity between the Lutheran and Reformed concepts of the reality of Christ's human nature.[216] For Barth, this is the beginning point of the seventeenth century disagreement between Lutheran and Reformed theology over the humanity of Christ. The question was: "What is the meaning of the eternal Word having given His own existence to a man's possibility of existence, to a man's being and nature, and so having given it reality."[217] The material point that concerns Barth is to understand ontologically the reality of Christ's existence as human nature in union with the Logos as—*an instrument of revelation*. While both Lutheran and Reformed theology agreed in principle that Christ's human nature was real, the question that remained unresolved was how this reality is manifested in the human nature of Jesus Christ. In other words, if Christ's human nature exists solely in its assumption of the Logos, how do we distinguish between the Word and human nature in Christ (without positing two persons), while at the same time maintaining the uncompromising unity of the God-man in Jesus Christ? This, in essence, is the question that Barth explores via the *anhypostasis* and *enhypostasis* dialectic.

Presuming that the flesh of Christ exists only so far as it acquires it through the Word, Barth raises the question: how far does such existence—especially in the form of the Word's existence—really belong to the flesh, and whether in such a *sustentatio* God and humanity are really being thought of as one and not perhaps secretly as two?[218] With this in view Barth argues that the Lutheran emphasis on the union the divine and human natures in the εγενετο went beyond the Reformed understanding that the human nature is sustained by the Logos.[219]

> This communis participatio does, in fact, go beyond the Reformed sustentare or even communicare, and anticipates the peculiar Lutheran doctrine of the unity of the natures and of the consequent communicatio idiomatum. But instead of the

215. Barth, *CD* I/2, 163.

216. Ibid.

217. Ibid.

218. Ibid.

219. Paul Althaus observes that: "The contradiction between Luther's understanding of the genus majestaticum (the doctrine that Jesus, according to his human nature, possessed all divine power and attributes at his birth) as the presupposition of Christ's emptying himself within history remains for the most part in contradiction to the genuine picture of the man Jesus." Althaus, *The Theology of Martin Luther*, 197.

one-sided relationship of the εγενετο, instead of the assumptio in which the logos is and continues to be the subject, does this not give us a kind of reciprocal relation between the creator and the creature? Do we not have revealedness instead of revelation, a state instead of an event.[220]

The Lutherans, well aware of the danger in over emphasizing the unity of the divine and human natures—particularly in view of Reformed criticism—were still unable to effectively distinguish between these two natures in Christ. Barth meets this ontological difficulty by arguing that the human nature is united to the Logos according to the doctrine of *anhypostasis* and *enhypostasis*, while at the same time dispelling the argument that appropriation of these terms denies personality to the human nature of Christ (in a Docetic sense). Barth counter-argues that although *negatively*, Christ's flesh has no self-existence, *positively* it possesses real existence in its union with the Word, who becomes God himself in the event of revelation and reconciliation.[221]

> Understood in this its original sense, this particular doctrine, abstruse in appearance only, is particularly well adapted to make it clear that the reality attested by Holy Scripture, Jesus Christ, is the reality of a divine act of Lordship which is unique and singular as compared with all other events, and in this way to characterize it as a reality held up to faith by revelation. It is in virtue of the eternal Word that Jesus Christ exists as a man of flesh and blood in our sphere, as a man like us, as an historical phenomenon. But it is only in virtue of the divine Word that He exists as such. If He existed in a different way, how would He be revelation in the real sense in which revelation is intended in Holy Scripture?[222]

It is clear from this passage that Barth understands *enhypostasis* to be the ontological mode of revelation in the human nature of Christ in congruence with the witness of Scripture. Despite the negative aspect of *anhypostasis*, the strength of *enhypostasis* affirms the reality of Christ's human nature. "Because of this positive aspect, it is well worth making the negation a dogma and giving it the very careful consideration which it received in early Christology."[223] But how should we understand the incarnate Word? What is his form? Given the Lutheran perspective Barth responds that the Word is

220. Barth, *CD* I/2, 164.

221. Ibid.

222. Ibid., 165.

223. Ibid.

found in the little baby in the stable, the one man on the cross. And as such, he is the Word made flesh, the one in who we owe our faith and obedience. This is the decisive point in Barth's understanding of the Word of God who descended from heaven without becoming unlike himself—by assuming to himself—the flesh of real humankind. In this way God himself no longer exists apart from the human being assumed by Christ as Jesus of Nazareth.[224]

Barth argues that the strength of Luther's argument for the unity of the Logos with human nature is grounded in the rejection of any separation of the humanity of Christ from the Logos according to the biblical account. "Moved, and as a rule moved exclusively, by the question of the grace of God, he clutched with both hands, like Anselm of Canterbury and Bernard of Clairvaux before him, at the answer of the Pauline-Johannine Christology, that God's grace was manifested to us really, concretely, and surely in the stable and on the cross, in the human existence of Jesus Christ, that everything was done and completed for us by God Himself in this very human existence and only in it, that our justification was accomplished in His sight and had only to be received in faith."[225] Barth, however, also argues that Lutheran orthodoxy with respect to the humanity of Christ evolved where the *enhypostasis* of Christ's human nature was understood to exist in a reciprocal relationship between the human nature of Christ and the Word. That is, just as Christ's human nature enjoys reality in the Logos as *enhypostasis*; the reversal is also true—the Word enjoys reality strictly through, and in—Christ's humanity.

> This assertion of Luther's was then built up doctrinally by Lutheran orthodoxy in the form of an idea which expressly maintained a perichoresis between the Word of God and the human being of Christ, i.e., a reversal of the statement about the *enhypostasis* of Christ's human nature, to the effect that as the humanity only has reality through and in the Word, so too the Word only has reality through and in the humanity.[226]

As *enhypostasis* attests to the reality of Christ's human nature as the instrument of God's revelation, and *anhypostasis* denies the reality of Christ's humanity apart from the εγενετο, the Lutheran understanding of Christ's human nature existing in a reciprocal relationship with the Logos posed obvious problems for Barth with respect to Christ's human nature as real humanity. "The problems raised by this idea may be plainly reduced to the following questions. Does it take such account of the freedom, majesty and

224. Ibid., 165–66.
225. Ibid., 166.
226. Ibid.

glory of the Word of God that they are in no way merged and submerged in His becoming flesh? And if such account is taken to it, then does the same hold true also of the flesh which He has become?"[227] Barth recognizes that the Lutherans were not blind to the ontological problem they encountered in the *perichoresis*.[228] Practically speaking, they wanted to adhere as much to the *very God* as to the *very man*; that is, they did not want to infringe upon the Word as God in his divinity or upon the flesh of Christ as a creature in his creatureliness. Gerhard argues that although the flesh and the Word are united and always present with each other in their union, the human nature is not exalted as a supernatural or divine nature. Quenstedt qualifies his definition of the union of divine and human natures by arguing that the flesh is not unlimited, and the Word is not restricted, but infinite.[229]

Yet, despite Lutheran qualifications of the *perichoresis,* Barth clearly recognizes the difficulty of this dogma which ventured too far in *blurring* the unity of the Logos with the flesh. For Barth, the Lutheran reversal of the *enhypostasis* of Christ's human nature (i.e., the flesh takes on the unlimited attributes of the Word) cannot stand because with it comes the reversal of revelation. In other words, limiting the Word to a human being—even if it is not intended to assert a spatial limiting appropriate to the flash—results in un-limiting the flesh of Christ, a concept that must be restricted to the Word. Barth argues that in this respect Luther and the Lutherans "ventured too much in their attempt at such a simple reversal of the statement about the *enhypostasis* of the humanity of Christ or at the completion of it by a statement about the "enfleshment" of the Word in the exclusive sense." In the end, the Lutheran adoption of the *enhypostasis* in this sense fails to make a clear statement consistent with the Lutheran affirmation that Jesus Christ is both very God and very man.[230] For Barth, the Word became flesh answers the question posed in the synoptics: is Jesus of Nazareth really the Christ, the Son of God? The answer is an emphatic yes as attested by the *enhypostasis* of Christ's human nature. This is the reality of God's revelation as a completed event in the person of Jesus Christ. This is the

227. Ibid., 166–67.

228. The concept of *perichoresis* first emerged in patristic thinking as a way to describe how the Father and the Son are receptive and permeate each other ("containing" one another) in their relationship to each other as mutually interpenetrative. The noun *perichoresis* was used in a christological way by the patristic Fathers in the sense of "encircle" or "encompass." Gregory of Nazianzus uses *perichoresis* to maintain that the two natures of Christ "reciprocate" into one another, and are alternative. See Prestige, *God in Patristic Thought*, 292–92.

229. See Barth, CD I/2, 167.

230. Ibid.

mystery of the flesh of Christ, flesh that Barth understands to be the "shell and form of the Word."[231]

> Faith, as it were, discovers that this Man is God. God's personal action as such is its object. Can it be otherwise, seeing the reality of Jesus Christ which is here contemplated in revelation, and revelation is the object of faith, and so knowledge of it is knowledge of faith? The very reason why a distinction is made here between God and man—and obviously the better to understand the unity—is in order that their unity may be seen always as an act of God, and that in this act God Himself may always be seen as the Lord.[232]

The Reformed response to the Lutherans emphasized that since the Word is flesh—he also is and continues to be what he is in himself—existing outside (*extra*) the flesh.[233] Barth acknowledges that the Reformed argument of the *extra* was intended to refute the Lutheran concept of *solely*, not as a new innovation, but rather to affirm the continuation of early orthodox Christology. However, Barth also argues that the *Calvinisticum extra* was not a valid argument to support the Reformed concept of "generally of the divine and the creaturely-human in separation." In this way Barth transitions his argument from defending the *extra* as a legitimate understanding of how the Logos becomes humanity (yet existing within and without the flesh of humanity as he argued in the *Göttingen Dogmatics*), to a strict preservation of divine and human natures being separate consistent with Chalcedon. While we may attribute this shift in Barth's thinking to a maturing of his Christology, we also see in this movement a direct link to Barth's fuller development of the duality of *anhypostasis* and *enhypostasis* in the *Church Dogmatics*. That is, the humanity of Christ is derived strictly based upon its assumption by the Logos—and the freedom of the Logos as the second person of the Trinity—to assume to himself the flesh of humanity.

> It is further to be noted that the Reformed position was by no means directed against the positive content of Luther's, not to speak of St. Paul's saying (Col 2:9), but against a negative conclusion derived there-from; and so not against the totus intra carnem but against the numquam et nuspiam extra carnum.[234]

---

231. Ibid., 168.
232. Ibid.
233. Ibid.
234. Ibid., 169.

Barth argues that while they were correct in defending Christ's human nature as *very homo*, the Nestorian error of the Reformed invalidates their understanding of the *extra*. That is, the Reformed understood the *extra* as a *distinctive*, rather than a *separate* attribute of the flesh of Christ. What we see in Barth's thinking here is his refusal to distinguish ontologically between the divine and human natures that are indissolubly united in Jesus Christ. For Barth, the Reformed cut in two (so to speak) the union of divine and human natures by distinguishing them one from the other in a way that negates the *enhypostasis*. As a result, the reality of Jesus Christ as the Logos is separated into two persons.

> When they negated this negation, when they maintained this *extra*, which was only meant as an etiam extra, it could as little occur to the Reformed as to the early doctors to question, in the sense of the Nestorian error, the Chalcedonian unity of the two natures in the person of the Word or, in consequence, the hypostatic union itself. They wished the extra to be regarded, not as *separative*, but as *distinctive*. Along with the *extra* they also asserted the intra with thoroughgoing seriousness. With the Lutherans they asserted a praesentia intima perpetua of the Logos in the flesh, i.e., in the sense of what Luther really meant to assert, an ubiquitas humane naturea in virtue of the operatio gloriosa of the exalted God-Man.[235]

Barth explains that the Reformed simply wanted to maintain the extra; that is, the divinity of the God-man on one hand and his humanity as such on the other. "They did not want the reality of the Logos asarkos abolished or suppressed in the reality of the Logos ensarkos. On the contrary, they wished the Logos asarkos to be regarded equally seriously as the *terminus a quo*, as the Logos ensarkos was regarded as the *terminus ad quam* of the incarnation." The Reformed therefore rejected the reversal of the *enhypostasis*, which seemed to imperil either the divinity or the humanity of Jesus Christ.[236]

With respect to the Reformed insistence upon the Logos asarkos Barth observes their willingness to obscure the unity of the God-man as expressed in the εγενετο. To this point Barth questions if the Reformed static acceptance of the egeneto, together with the ontic relevance of their Christology are in fact preserved in view of the dynamic element in the εγενετο. In the end Barth sees in the Reformed Logos asarkos an obscurity in distinguishing "between the word who assumed flesh and the flesh assumed by the

235. Ibid; *KD* I/2, 185.
236. Ibid., 169–70.

word."[237] Barth further argues that the Reformed asserted—in harmony with Church tradition—that the hypostatic union in Christ is not compromised absent the Lutheran innovation. But as the Lutherans failed to show how far the *vere Deus* is preserved to the same extent as the *very homo* in the *extra*, so too the Reformed failed to show convincingly how far the *extra* does not include the assumption of a twofold Christ, "of a logos ensarkos alongside a logos asarkos, and therefore a dissolution of the unity of the two natures and hypostatic union. In short, it cannot be denied that the Reformed *totus intra et extra* offers at least as many difficulties as the Lutheran *totus intra*." Barth concludes that in either sense (and in view that no synthesis could be reached between the two) each view, when fully developed, raises definite questions against it that are difficult to answer.[238]

> But when we recollect that in the centuries after the Reformation both sides strove genuinely and seriously, but unsuccessfully, in this direction for unification, when, above all, we recollect that there is a riddle in the fact itself, and that even in the New Testament two lines can be discerned in this matter, we will at least be on our guard against thinking of oversimple solutions. Perhaps there can be no resting from the attempt to understand this εγενετο.[239]

In the *Doctrine of Reconciliation* Barth once again takes up the Logos asarkos, but this time with a more critical eye towards his emphasis on the union of divine and human natures in Jesus Christ as reconciler. The material point for Barth is that as reconciler, (i.e., the God-man), the eternal Son must not be understood to exist *in abstracto* (i.e., as λογος ασαρκος). In other words: "The second "person" of the Godhead in Himself as such is not God the reconciler." Because God chose to become humanity according to his gracious will, we do not have to reckon with the Word or the Son of God or any Logos asarkos, other than that Word of God which was made flesh. This is how God chose to reveal himself to us.[240] The problem that Barth struggled to overcome in the λογος ασαρκος was what he described as the "fatal speculation about the being and work of the Logos asarkos, or a God whom we think we can know elsewhere, and whose divine being we can define from elsewhere than in and from contemplation of His presence and activity as the Word made flesh."[241] And yet, Barth concedes that in

237. Ibid., 170.
238. Ibid.
239. Ibid., 170–71.
240. Barth, CD IV/1, 52.
241. Barth states that Calvin himself goes a long way towards "trying to reckon with

this christological mystery "we cannot possibly understand or estimate it if we try to explain it by a self-limitation or de-divinisation of God in the uniting of the Son with the man Jesus. If in Christ—even in the humiliated Christ born in a manger at Bethlehem and crucified on the cross of Golgotha—God is not unchanged and wholly God, then everything we may say about the reconciliation of the world by God in this humiliated One is left hanging in the air."[242]

Barth freely admits to the mystery of the incarnation, the "real divine sonship of the man Jesus" as God the Son who took to himself the flesh of humanity—humanity that was elected and prepared for him, and was clothed with actuality—because he became its actuality.[243]

It is this mystery of the Word became flesh that Barth wrestles with in his analysis of the Logos asarkos through the rubric of the *anhypostasis/ enhypostasis* dynamic of Christ's human nature.[244] Barth concludes that when it comes to describing the incarnation, arguments against the concept of *"anhypostasis* or *enhypostasis"* has no substance because this concept is unavoidable in properly describing this mystery.[245] Although Barth's appropriation of these concepts is not intended to solve the mystery of the union of the Logos with the flesh of humanity, it provides the ontological bearing that Barth uses dialectically to judge the reality of Christ's human nature given Lutheran and Reformed Christology.

---

this 'other' God." For his part, it was Calvin's aim "in that theory to hold to the fact that the Son of God who is wholly this man (totus intra carnum as it was formulated by a later Calvinist) is also wholly God and therefore omnipotent and omnipresent (and to that extent extra carnem, not bound or altered by its limitations)." Barth, *CD* IV/1, 181.

242. Barth, *CD* IV/1, 183.

243. Barth, *CD* IV/2, 49–50.

244. Darren Sumner argues that Barth's solution to the dilemma of the Logos asarkos and ensarkos came in Barth's doctrine of the election of Jesus Christ as the God-man, in whose incarnation affects simultaneously the humiliation and exaltation of Christ. "According to the doctrine of the election of grace as the election of Jesus Christ, of God's self-movement toward humanity, this form is eternal. Rather than the concepts of immanence and economy it is this twofold state, I suggest, that best maps into the life of the Logos as asarkos and ensarkos." Sumner, "The Twofold Life of the Word: Karl Barth's Critical Reception of the Extra Calvinisticum," 55. Ontologically speaking I would add here that Barth would not consider this union absent the *anhypostasis* and *enhypostasis* of Christ's human nature.

245. Barth, *CD* IV/2, 49–50.

Conclusion

We have considered Barth's appropriation of *anhypostasis* and *enhypostasis* (both explicitly and implicitly) as his way to express the revelation of Jesus Christ as the Word became flesh given four separate, but interrelated movements as:

1. Barth's theological/philosophical method in expressing the revelation of Jesus Christ.

2. Barth's argument that Jesus Christ is the true instrument of revelation in *Anselm: Fides Quarens Intellectum*.

3. The revelatory relationship between *anhypostasis* and *enhypostasis*, and the εγενετο in Barth's Christology.

4. Barth's use of *anhypostasis* and *enhypostasis* as a dialectic to express the humanity of Christ in dialogue with Lutheran and Reformed Christology.

Given these interrelated movements, I draw this chapter to a close with the following observations. The influence of philosophy on Karl Barth's theology will no doubt continue to be debated, particularly in view of Barth's distinction between the Word of God revealed in Scripture, and in Christ. Nevertheless, I argue that Barth clearly expresses the revelation of God made manifest in Jesus Christ as the true revelation of God, which is absolutely dependent upon God's movement towards humanity in contra-distinction to revelation attributed to philosophical rationalization or experience. Furthermore, as *anhypostasis* and *enhypostasis*, the reality of the human nature of Christ makes comprehensible that which cannot be comprehended because in this ontology is realized both ontically (in its substance) and noetically (by faith in its substance) the revelation of God in Jesus Christ. It is Barth's appropriation of *anhypostasis* and *enhypostasis*—of God's movement towards humanity in Jesus Christ as the true revelation of God—which provides the ontological grounding for Barth's rejection of philosophy and its claim to the revelation of God.

Written between *Die Christliche Dogmatik im Entwurf* at Münster and the revised first volume of the *Church Dogmatics* at Bonn, the importance of Barth's book on Anselm lays not in a shifting of his theology, but in the fact that now the veiling and unveiling of God is grounded both ontically and noetically in Jesus Christ as the revelation of God. As faith in the revealed Christ alone enables true knowledge of God, the foundation is now firmly established for Barth's more mature expression of *anhypostasis* and *enhypostasis* as the ontological model of Christ's human nature in the *Church Dogmatics*.

For Barth, the εγενετο not only expresses the Word became flesh in Jesus Christ, but it also provides a tangible form to express the *anhypostasis* and *enhypostasis* of Christ's human nature as the Word of God revealed. In the εγενετο exists true humanity—Christ's human nature—which dialectically veils and unveils the revelation of God. Moreover, in becoming true humanity Christ reveals the reality of God in the form of humanity in his birth, his crucifixion, and his resurrection. As such, Barth understands εγενετο not simply (strictly speaking) as the joining of divine and human natures in Christ, but the Logos taking to himself human essence as the revelation of God in Jesus Christ.

Finally, and quite interestingly, Barth uses *anhypostasis* and *enhypostasis* as a dialectic to argue for the reality of Christ's human nature in his dialogue with Lutheran and Reformed Christology. Barth, however, leaves unresolved how to bridge the differences between the Lutherans and Reformed in expressing the humanity of Christ in view of the *logos asarkos* and the mystery of the incarnation. Grounded in the *anhypostasis* and *enhypostasis* of Christ's human nature, Barth allows for a *separate*, but not *distinctive* attribute of the flesh of Christ. In other words, while Barth acknowledges the separateness of the human nature in union with the Logos, he refuses to distinguish ontologically between the divine and human natures which are absolutely united in Jesus Christ.

4

Anhypostasis and Enhypostasis

Coalescence of Christ's Divine and Human Natures in Barth's Christology

Introduction

IN MY VIEW KARL Barth's most obvious point of departure from liberal theology is his insistence that the reality and depth of the sinful human condition by definition precludes any human capacity to initiate, and bring about reconciliation with a Holy God. The incongruity between liberal theology's dependence upon philosophical method to discover the revelation of God, and Barth's absolute reliance upon the grace of God for such revelation is quite obvious here. As such, the foundation of Barth's Christology rests upon the free grace of God manifested in the revelation of Jesus Christ who as the covenant keeper—as very God and very man—initiates and fully accomplishes humanity's reconciliation with God.[1] For Barth, if this foundational truth is misunderstood or compromised, all that follows betrays the truth of the Word of God revealed in the person of Jesus Christ. There can be no compromise here.

Moreover, as the mediator of humanity's reconciliation with God, the eternal Word became flesh by assuming to itself the fullness of human nature in Jesus of Nazareth, which Barth uniquely expresses as both *anhypostasis* and *enhypostasis*. Ontologically speaking, Barth understands in the flesh of Jesus is revealed the eternal Christ both ontically and noetically.[2] Further-

1. For Barth, it is in the freedom of God that he responds to human sin with the divine yes. In other words, God has chosen neither to abandon nor isolate himself from fallen humanity. But rather, he comes to us and reveals himself to us in Jesus Christ as the true covenant partner of God, as true God and true man. "In Jesus Christ there is not isolation of man from God or of God from man. Rather, in Him we encounter the history, the dialogue, in which God and man meet together and are together, the reality of the covenant *mutually* contracted, preserved, and fulfilled by them. Jesus Christ is in His one Person, as true *God,* man's loyal partner, and as true *man,* God's." Barth, *Humanity of God,* 46.

2. Barth's work on *Anselm* grounded his understanding of the revelation of Jesus

more, while the human nature of Christ can (and must) be understood in its *separateness* from the divine nature in union with the Logos, it cannot (and must not) be understood as a being which is *distinct* in this union. Indeed, very God and very man are absolute one. Such is Barth's insistence upon the absolute union of the God-man revealed as Jesus Christ, the true mediator between humanity and God.

I would add here that it is neither possible to accurately understand Barth's ontology of Jesus Christ as true God and true man, nor interpret his application of this ontology to the person of Jesus Christ as the mediator between God and humanity, absent an understanding of *anhypostasis* and *enhypostasis*—as Karl Barth uniquely embraced it. That is, Barth insists that the *enhypostasis* of Christ's human nature must be understood in its relationship to the *anhypostasis* of that same human nature (in their coupling together), from which Barth creates a unique and dynamic view of the humanity of Christ. In this way the *anhypostasis* and *enhypostasis* establishes and grounds the absolute union of very God and very man in Jesus Christ, who embodies and accomplishes reconciliation between humanity and God. To say Jesus of Nazareth is to say very God, and to say the Logos of God is to say very man. For Barth, they must be understood as separate in their essence, but never distinct in this union. They are indeed one.

Furthermore, I argue that in the *Church Dogmatics* Barth's appropriation of *anhypostasis* and *enhypostasis* remains consistent, and in fact serves as the unifying cord that binds together the ontology of Jesus Christ with his role as the mediator of reconciliation—*as the keeper of the covenant*. We find quite enlightening Barth's self assessment of the *Church Dogmatics* after his completion of volume 2 of the Doctrine of Reconciliation. Barth is convinced that he had remained theologically consistent in his *Church Dogmatics* (an answer to claims of a "new Barth"), which he describes as having been developed within the broad lines of Christian tradition. We agree with Barth's self assessment here, and further argue that this theological consistency applies to his expression of the *anhypostasis* and *enhypostasis* as well.

> In the twenty-three years since I started this work I have found myself so held and directed that, as far as I can see, there have so far been no important breaks or contradictions in the presentation; no retractions have been necessary (except in detail); and above all—for all the constant critical freedom which I have had to exercise in this respect—I have always found myself content with the broad lines of Christian tradition. That is how I myself

---

Christ both ontically and noetically, in the exercise of faith, the source of which is strictly based upon the grace of God.

see it, and it is my own view that my contemporaries (and even perhaps successors) ought to speak at least more circumspectly when at this point or that they think they have discovered a "new Barth" or, what is worse, a heresy which has seriously to be confessed as such. Naturally, I do not regard myself as infallible. But there is perhaps more inward and outward continuity in the matter than some hasty observers and rash interjectors can at first sight credit.[3]

That being said, in this section we will examine the interrelated movement from ontology in Barth's understanding of Christ's human nature as *anhypostasis* and *enhypostasis* to his role as the mediator of reconciliation between God and humanity. We will do so by considering five themes of coalescence that Barth uses to uniquely express the indissoluble union of very God and very man as:

1. Jesus Christ: Revelation as Covenant

2. Jesus Christ: The First Adam

3. Jesus Christ: Humiliation and Exaltation in Convergence

4. Jesus Christ: Integration of Person and Work

5. Jesus Christ: Eternal Redeemer

This analysis will focus primarily on the *Church Dogmatics* where Barth expresses these themes of coalescence, which clearly emerge from the *anhypostasis* and *enhypostasis* and often time carry Barth off the beaten track of traditional Reformed theology.

Jesus Christ: Revelation as Covenant

In view of the coalescence of divinity and humanity in Jesus Christ, we begin our analysis with the revelation of Jesus Christ as covenant. This is not done so capriciously, but out of strict necessity given the priority that Barth places in God's covenant with humanity as the impetus for reconciliation with God.[4] Given a Reformed backdrop, Barth embraced the covenant of

---

3. Barth, *CD* IV/2, xi.

4. A. T. B. McGowan argues that Barth "builds the idea of covenant into the central themes of his dogmatic theology." Not only does the covenant relate specifically to the doctrine of election in Barth's theology, but everything is drawn together where God's grace is the basis for the covenant; "election is its outworking, creation prepares the ground, and reconciliation is its fulfillment." see McGowan, "Karl Barth and Covenant Theology," 115.

God as the tangible frame of reference that guarantees the reconciliation of humanity with God. Jesus Christ, the eternal Logos who assumed the same humanity that he had created, becomes the revelation of God as the one true covenant keeper between God and humanity.[5] As such, the reconciliation of humanity with God flows from the fountain of God's covenant which is kept by the one mediator between God and humanity—*the man Christ Jesus.*

> Jesus Christ is indeed God in His movement towards man, or, more exactly, in His movement towards the people represented in the one man Jesus of Nazareth, in His covenant with this people, in His being and activity amongst and towards this people . . . That we know God and have God only in Jesus Christ means that we can know Him and have Him only with the man Jesus of Nazareth and with the people which He represents. Apart from this man and apart from this people God would be a different, an alien God. According to the Christian perception He would not be God at all. According to the Christian perception, the true God is what He is only in this movement, in the movement towards this man, and in Him and through Him towards other men in their unity as His people.[6]

For Barth, the impetus and force of the revelation of God, the movement of God towards his people in the person of Christ[7] is based upon God's covenant with his people.[8] This becomes the launching point from which the mediator sets out to accomplish reconciliation between humanity and

5. Gerald McKenny argues that for Barth it is Jesus Christ, both God himself and God's human partner, who fulfills the covenant. It is God's faithfulness that overcomes the sinful rejection of the covenant by its human partner. In Christ, God is faithful to his own self-determination to be gracious to humanity. And in Christ, humanity answers the question for human self-determination of the elect by Christ's action—as God's human partner—as God's elect. See McKenny, *The Analogy of Grace*, 69.

6. Barth, *CD* II/2, 7.

7. Michael Welker notes that in contra-distinction to Ludwig Feuerbach and his "consciousness of God," (which is nothing more than an "abstract-existential God" of subjectivist faith), Barth points to "a single human person living in the age of the Roman Empire" as the focus of revelation. Welker argues that this revelation of God in the person of Jesus Christ must also be a revelation accomplished by the Spirit of Jesus Christ. "Christology must clarify how the creative God has revealed himself in the power of the divine Spirit in Jesus Christ, in this person and this story." Welker, *God the Revealed*, 51.

8. Barth makes the point that the covenant between God and humanity is the revelation of the man Jesus of Nazareth. "Jesus Christ is indeed God in His movement towards man, or, more exactly, in His movement towards the people represented in the one man Jesus of Nazareth, in His covenant with this people, in His being and activity amongst and towards this people." Barth, *CD* II/2, 7.

God as decreed by God the Father. Stated more precisely, it is the election of Jesus Christ as the covenant keeper who is the one true revelation of God in this covenant.

The Election of Jesus Christ

With the ontology of Christ's human nature being grounded as *anhypostasis* and *enhypostasis* in its union with the Logos, Barth applies this dynamic union of very God and very man to the doctrine of reconciliation. In other words, Barth now answers the question: what does it mean that the humanity of Christ is *anhypostasis* and *enhypostasis* in humanity's reconciliation with God? That being said, there is no place in Barth's Christology where the *anhypostasis* and *enhypostasis* take a higher priority than in the election of Jesus Christ, which without question established Barth as a true christological innovator.[9] We get an early glimpse into Barth's unique approach to the doctrine of election given its placement in the *Church Dogmatics* as part of the Doctrine of God[10] where Barth is clear to express his break from Calvin in his reconstruction of Calvin's doctrine of predestination.[11]

9. We find this to be especially true given Barth's Reformed presupposition (i.e., based on Calvin's writings as his starting point). Fred H. Klooster observes here that Barth's theology in fact sparked a renewed interest in Calvin where the message of the Reformers was valid "in a new form." Klooster, *Calvin's Doctrine of Predestination*, 12. Louis Berkhof states emphatically that the construction of Barth's doctrine of predestination is not even "distantly related" to that of Augustine and Calvin. Berkhof, *Systematic Theology*, 111.

10. See Barth, *CD* II/2, 3. Barth explains that the doctrine of election must be a part of the doctrine of God because originally God's election is not merely of man, but of God himself. As Fred Klooster explains, Calvin did not begin the *Institutes* with the doctrine of predestination, and never placed it at the head of theology. Calvin's final edition of the *Institutes* (1559) did not discuss predestination until the end of book 3, about three-fourths of the way into the work in the midst of his discussion of soteriology. Furthermore, it should be observed that when later Reformed theologians discussed predestination along with the decree of God (and before discussing creation), they have not followed Calvin's final arrangement of materials; see Klooster, *Calvin's Doctrine of Predestination*, 14–15. Calvin himself refers to the election of Christ where: "He is conceived a mortal man of the seed of David. By what virtues will they say that he deserved in the womb itself to be made head of the angels, only-begotten Son of God, etc . . . But if they willfully strive to strip God of his free power to choose or reject, let them at the same time also take away what has been given to Christ." Calvin, *Institutes* 2:933. In this sense Calvin's understanding of the election of Christ is indeed radically different from Barth's.

11. Sung Wook Chung argues that Barth never thoroughly rejected Calvin's theological insights in relation to the doctrine of election without any effort to "retrieve and recapture what he saw as Calvin's legitimate arguments." Moreover, Barth's doctrine of election affirms that theology must begin and end with Jesus Christ who manifests

The work has this peculiarity, that in it I have had to leave the framework of theological tradition to a far greater extent than in the first part of the doctrine of God. I would have preferred to follow Calvin's doctrine of predestination much more closely, instead of departing from it so radically . . . But I could not and cannot do so. As I let the Bible itself speak to me on these matters, as I mediated upon what I seemed to hear, I was driven irresistibly to reconstruction. And now I cannot be anxious to see whether I shall be alone in this work, or whether there will be others who will find enlightenment in the basis and scope suggested.[12]

This reconstruction (as Barth describes it) is centered in God's election of humanity and the election of God himself based upon the eternal union of divinity and humanity in Jesus Christ.[13] For Barth, the emphasis and priority of election is the election of the man Jesus of Nazareth, whose humanity is taken up into and assumed by the eternal Logos where Jesus cannot be understood to exist apart from the Logos because he exists as God himself. This is the way that God moves towards humanity as true God.

That we know God and have God in Jesus Christ means that we can know Him and have Him only with the man Jesus of Nazareth and with the people which He represents. Apart from this man and apart from this people God would be a different, an alien God. According to the Christian perception the true God is what He is only in this movement, in the movement towards this man, and in Him and through Him towards other men in their unity as His people.[14]

God's movement towards humanity in the one man Jesus of Nazareth. It is therefore the covenant relationship between God and the man Jesus of Nazareth, as the Son of Man, that humanity can be included in the election of God enclosed in Jesus Christ. See Chung, *Admiration* and *Challenge*, 205–6.

12. Barth, *CD* II/2, x.

13. Johnson argues that Barth believed the traditional understanding of the doctrine of election needed a "complete overhaul." Barth's reconstruction is summed up in the affirmation that in Jesus Christ God is fundamentally "for" human beings. This divine "for" is comprehensive in its scope. That is, *everyone* is elected to be reconciled with God in Jesus Christ. Whether everyone will fully *realize* her or his election is another matter. If, however, the doctrine of election meant, as it did for Calvin a "double predestination," namely a divine determination of some people for salvation and others for rejection, Barth viewed this as ill-conceived and even hideous. Barth considered God to be a humane God who is committed to humanity. See Johnson, *The Mystery of God*, 58–59.

14. Barth, *CD* II/1, 7.

Barth understands that Jesus of Nazareth exists as true humanity. He is true flesh taken up into the eternal Son of God who manifests God's movement towards humanity as the revelation of God himself. As true man Jesus is the object of God's election of grace, which for Barth constitutes the centerpiece of the gospel.[15] As such, the election of humanity is a direct result of (and that which flows out of) the election of Jesus of Nazareth as the one through whom God elects His people.[16] "Again, God elects that He shall be the covenant God. He does so in order not to be alone in His divine glory, but to let heaven and earth, and between them man, be the witness to His glory . . . He elects the man of Nazareth, that He should be essentially one with Himself in His Son. Through Him and in Him He elects His people, thus electing the whole basis and meaning of all His works."[17]

Barth also understands that the benefit of God's elective grace is directed to humanity in God's movement towards humanity in the man Jesus. "All the joy and the benefit of His whole work as Creator, Redeemer and Reconciler, all the blessings which are divine and therefore real blessings, all the promises of the Gospel which has been declared: all these are grounded and determined in the fact that God is the God of the eternal election of His grace."[18] The love of God towards humanity is made manifest as event through his divine election of Jesus Christ, his only begotten Son, who God sent into the whole world as an expression of his love for the whole world.[19]

But what does it mean that by the grace of God humanity enjoys, and is a participant in, the elective grace of God in the election of Jesus Christ? This is the question Barth wrestles with and brings to conclusion with his rejection of Calvin's doctrine of election.[20] Barth sought out both theo-

15. Barth makes it quite clear that the centerpiece of the gospel resides in the election of Jesus Christ. See Barth, *CD* II/2, 10. Paul Molnar argues that for Barth it is a matter of God's freedom that he determined to be God for us, and lived out that freedom as electing God and electing man in Jesus Christ. As such, this action and power of God is incontrovertible, which Barth understood as "the sum of the gospel," and in fact constitutes the strength of Barth's idea of divine self-determination. See Molnar, "The Trinity, Election, and God's Ontological Freedom," 299.

16. Berkouwer observes that we find in the Scripture a harmony in the election of Christ. The question that we grapple with is whether Christ could and should be called the foundation (origin) of man's election or whether one should say that he is the executor of election. Barth focuses his criticism of the Reformed doctrine of election especially on this point. Barth argues that the Synod of Dort was correct to reject the view of the Remonstrants where Christ was the foundation of election due to the connection the Remonstrants made to grace being offered to all men, making belief or unbelief a deciding factor. See Berkouwer, *Divine Election*, 134.

17. Barth, *CD* II/2, 11.

18. Barth, *CD* II/2, 14.

19. Ibid., 25–26.

20. David Gibson argues that for Barth the continental Reformed efforts to understand the witness of Scripture to divine election struggle over whether Christ be

logically and christologically a different understanding of the relationship between the election of Jesus Christ and those individuals elected by grace "in Christ" through their faith in the God-man.[21] In other words, Barth understands that the eternal decree of God with respect to the election of humanity, as attested to in the Scripture, finds its fulfillment in the man Jesus of Nazareth.[22]

> The election is decisively important for each individual, but it does not follow that it is for the individual a character already imparted to him, immanent in him from the very first. It does not follow that it is bound up with his very existence. It is still the activity of the free love of God. As such, it is intended for every man, and it concerns and determines every man. But it does so without necessitating that he should be elected or rejected immediately and in advance. According to Scripture, the divine election of grace is an activity of God which has a definite goal and limit. Its direct and proper object is not individuals generally, but one individual—and only in Him the people called and united by Him, and only in that people individuals in general in their private relationships with God. It is only in that one man that a human determination corresponds to the divine determining.[23]

For Barth, the solution to the problem of election points to the man Jesus of Nazareth, in who both sides of predestination (i.e., election and reprobation) are fully realized.[24] In other words, God's predetermined election

---

understood in relation to the decree of election as "its foundation, its origin, or merely as its executor?" Barth's exposition of the doctrine of election unfolds against the historical backdrop of a Reformed tradition, which he believes has reduced Christ to the role of election's executor by emphasizing a secret election of the Father. Barth viewed the Reformed doctrine of election as having severed the link between Christ and election, a link which he sought to recover; see Gibson, *Reading the Decree*, 2.

21. See Barth, *The Theology of John Calvin*, 78, 118. In Barth's early thinking with respect to Calvin, he argues that it was needful for Calvin to relentlessly champion the doctrine of "double predestination" as the way to preserve Reformed theology against attacks to its survival. Moreover, in the predestination of God is manifested those who are obedient to God, as recipients of the grace of God, which for Barth is the heart of Calvin's doctrine of predestination.

22. David Gibson further argues: "For all his independent and creative genius, Barth's theology is profoundly catholic, soaked in dialogue and debate with centuries of tradition and modulated and Reformed accent." Gibson, *Reading the Decree*, p. 18.

23. Barth, *CD* II/2, 43–44.

24. Barth explains that both election and reprobation are executed in Jesus Christ. "We can and must say these two things concerning the judgment of God executed in the death of Jesus Christ and the sentence of God revealed in His resurrection, because in both events we are dealing with the execution and revelation of the divine rejection of elected man and the divine election of rejected man. It was in the indissoluble unity

and rejection is not bound up in each individual of humanity; but rather, in one individual, the one in whom individual people are called and united together in him.[25] In this sense only can Barth's thinking with respect to the predestination of humanity be rightly understood. It is the revelation of God in Jesus of Nazareth that the electing God confronts humanity. Moreover, this ontology of Jesus Christ in his election clearly embodies the *anhypostasis* and *enhypostasis* of the humanity assumed by the eternal Son of God, which in turn serves as the foundation and driving impetus of Barth's doctrine of reconciliation.

> In the strict sense only He can be understood and described as "elected" (and "rejected"). All others are so in Him, and not as individuals. It is not right, therefore, to take it as self-evident, as has so frequently been the case, that the doctrine of predestination may be understood and presented as the first and final word of a general anthropology. On the contrary, it is right and necessary to get back from things supposedly self-evident to the true sources, the self-revelation of God and the testimony of Holy Scripture, and to discover the definite form in which the electing God encounters and confronts humanity as a whole, and in which humanity also confronts and encounters the electing God.[26]

The election of God must therefore be God centered (as part of the doctrine of God)[27] rather than anthropologically centered,[28] because for

---

and irreversible sequence of these happenings that the reconciliation of the world with God took place in Jesus Christ." Barth, *CD* IV/1, 515.

25. Barth argues that God's justification of humanity is the free grace of God that marks it off from "the caprice and arbitrariness of a destiny that apportions blindfold its favor and disfavor, which clothes it with majesty and dignity, which gives to the knowledge of faith an infallible certainty—that in the first instance God affirms Himself in this action, that in it He lives His own divine life in His unity as Father, Son, and Holy Spirit. But in it He also maintains Himself as God of man, as the One who has bound Himself to man from all eternity, as the One has elected Himself for man and man for Himself." Barth, *CD* IV/1, 532.

26. Barth, *CD* II/2, 43–44.

27. Barth reasons that "We cannot be too insistent in the recognition and introduction of it as the presupposition of all God's perfect work (as that which is truly and properly perfect in its perfection). It is because of this that we put the doctrine of election—meaning, of course, this decisive word, this mystery of the doctrine of reconciliation, the doctrine of the election which took place in Jesus Christ—at the very beginning, and indeed before the beginning, of what we have to say concerning God's dealings with His creation. It is for this reason that we understand the election as ordination, as God's self-ordaining of Himself. And it is for this reason, then, that we regard the doctrine of election as a constituent part of the doctrine of God." Barth, *CD* II/2, 89.

28. Douglas R. Sharp argues that with the appearance of the doctrine of election in the doctrine of God Barth suggests "that it is not possible to know and speak about God

Barth its nucleus is both the subject and object of election in the person of Jesus Christ.[29] This answers the question how the eternal will of God—in the election of humanity—is revealed and accomplished.[30] Election is indeed the election of God himself, who in the revelation of the Logos became flesh in Jesus of Nazareth.[31] In humanity's reconciliation with God, the true humanity of the Son is the primary content of God's elective grace. This is a "trinitarian happening of the life of God, but which all other divine decisions and actions follow, and to which they are subordinated." This is real history that actually took place in time—in the real humanity of Jesus Christ—and is therefore the execution and revelation of . . . "*the* purpose of the will of God, which is not limited or determined by any other, and therefore by any other happening in the creaturely sphere, but is itself the sum of all divine purposes, and therefore that which limits and determines all other occurrence. For God's eternal election of grace is concretely the election of Jesus Christ."[32]

Barth's convictions here are driven by his own exegesis of Scripture,[33] as well as the ontological fabric of *anhypostasis* and *enhypostasis* realized in

---

without knowing and affirming at the same time that this One is the electing God. Election is in fact the distinctive act by which God is *who* God is." There is therefore an interrelationship between the doctrine of God and the doctrine of election that demands their treatment in intimate proximity to one another. "For Barth, the doctrine of God has dogmatic priority over the doctrine of election, and as such it points to the ontic priority of the subject of the doctrine of God." For Barth, "the *content* of the doctrine of God has ontic priority, while the *content* of the doctrine of election has noetic priority." Sharp, *The Hermeneutics of Election*, 10.

29. With respect to Calvin Barth notes that "We must count it highly in Calvin's favor that methodologically at least he broke with this tradition, treating the doctrine of providence (*Instit.* I, 16-18) in conjunction with that of creation, and the doctrine of predestination (III, 21-24) as the climax of that of the communication of the grace of God manifested and active in Jesus Christ." Barth, *CD* II/2, 46.

30. Loraine Boettner argues that the doctrine of predestination represents the "absolute and unconditional" purpose of God, which is independent of God's creation, and originates solely in the counsel of his will. See Boettner, *The Reformed Doctrine of Predestination*, 13. Barth counters that such thinking wrongly begins as if there is no alternative to the assertion that the doctrine of predestination represents the absolute and unconditional purpose of the divine will, independent of all creation, and solely grounded in God's eternal counsel. See Barth, *CD* II/2, 47. Barth goes on to say that it is necessary to consider predestination given a concept of the deity of God which is true deity because it is "self-determined and self limited." Barth, *CD* II/2, 51.

31. Alister McGrath argues that in Barth's doctrine of election he insists that the concept must not be regarded as a theological abstraction giving testimony to the omnipotence of God. But rather, in the election of Jesus Christ Barth retains the duality of election while altering its traditional meaning (i.e., eternal election or reprobation). See McGrath, *Iustitia Dei*, 401–2.

32. Barth, *CD* IV/2, 31.

33. Sharp suggests that the credibility of Barth's construction [re-construction] of the doctrine of election depends on the exegetical idea that Jesus Christ is himself the

this human nature elected by God from all eternity.[34] In Jesus of Nazareth Barth sees the absolute union of humanity with God the Son, a theological reality that is grounded in the reality of God's election of Jesus Christ.[35] "For finally, of course, the election has to do with the whole of humanity and therefore each individual, although materially it has to do first and exclusively only with the one man, and then with specific members of the people which belongs to Him, which is called by Him and which is gathered around Him; a people which as such is not identical either with the whole of humanity or with an aggregate of individuals."[36]

Fundamentally, Barth understands the election of Jesus Christ to be the consummation of God's revelation to humanity. "Election is that which takes place at the very centre of the divine self-revelation."[37] For Barth, the election of Jesus Christ is the first and decisive part of revelation in which the real presence of God is made manifest in the world as the eternal decree and self-determination of God.[38] With this in view the *anhypostasis* and en-

---

electing God and the elect human. The biblical interpretation that lays this foundation reverses the direction taken by previous constructs of the doctrine. It is this reversal that represents the basis for the Christological orientation of the construction. "Jesus Christ is at the center of the doctrine, not because he is the electing God and the elect human, but because He is the concrete self-revelation of God, and as such he constitutes the only basis on which it is possible to know and say anything at all about the being and activity of God. The exegesis at the basis of this notion is intended to establish the identity of revelation/incarnation and election (or the fact that election constitutes the center of revelation/incarnation), so that it becomes necessary to speak of one of these elements only in terms of, and in direct relation to, the other. The exegesis at this point is meant to demonstrate that revelation/incarnation can be meaningfully grasped only under the rubric of election, and that election cannot be discussed apart from revelation/incarnation. Every component in Barth's doctrine depends ultimately on the exegetical demonstration of the identity of election and Jesus Christ in the biblical witness to God's self-revelation." Sharp, *The Hermeneutics of Election*, 129.

34. Barth states that he must adopt the Reformation thesis, but not without reformulating it. "But we must ground and formulate it in such a way that on both sides it is treated with the seriousness which it deserves. We must do so in such a way that when we utter the name of Jesus Christ we really do speak the first and final word not only about the electing God but also about electing man." Barth, *CD* II/2, 76.

35. For Barth, the doctrine of election cannot be understood as a general abstraction of God's elective will. But rather: "The doctrine of election is rightly grounded when in respect of elected man as well as the electing God it does not deal with a generality or abstraction in God or man, but with the particularity and concretion of the true God and true man. It is rightly grounded when only from that starting-point it goes on to perceive and to understand whatever there is of consequence about God or man in general; from that starting-point alone, and not *vice versa*." Barth, *CD* II/2, 51.

36. Ibid.

37. Barth, *CD* II/2, 59.

38. Ibid., 54. Cornelis Van der Kooi points to the doctrine of election as the center of Barth's theology. "One can consider Barth's doctrine of election as the substantive core of his theology." Van der Kooi argues that if it is true for God as a person in the

hypostasis take on dramatic expression in the election of Jesus Christ who as truly God and truly man embodies both the subject and object of God's elective grace. Understood in this indissoluble and eternal union of divinity with humanity, Barth understands Jesus Christ to be the eternal man elected by God from the beginning as the one who will come and keep the covenant necessary to accomplish humanity's reconciliation with God. In other words, Jesus Christ is the election of God's covenant with humanity.[39]

The Covenant Keeper in Jesus Christ

Karl Barth understands Jesus Christ to be both the subject and object of divine election—established by the eternal will of God—to fulfill the covenant that God made with humanity.[40] Barth sees here a direct connection between the election of God and the covenant of God, which is perfectly accomplished and unified in the person of Jesus Christ. Just as the election of Jesus of Nazareth is the center of the gospel, so too, the fulfillment of the covenant is the central theological event that expresses the grace of God. This marks the covenant partnership between God and humanity made manifest in the revelation of Jesus Christ, together with his election of a people to rule—*as his people*.[41] For Barth, the covenant of God revealed in the Old Testament Scripture is strictly speaking the revelation of God, but revelation that anticipates the revealed covenant keeper.[42] It anticipates the revelation of Jesus Christ in human history.[43]

---

consummate sense to determine himself, and that nothing external to him defines him, then in the concept of election we find the answer to the question: how God determines himself. He elects the man Jesus of Nazareth to be in union with His Son. That is, God has chosen His Son to be in union with this man. Therefore, it is in this life of Jesus that it becomes knowable from whom election proceeds. See Van der Kooi, *As in a Mirror*, 368.

39. Barth, *CD* II/2, 102.

40. Barth argues that the election of God is centered in Jesus Christ. "He is the One in whom God elected man as His man and Himself as the God of man from all eternity. Again, He is the One in whom, in relation to whom, according to whose image, God created the heavens and the earth and man. Again, He is the One in whose person God made the eternal covenant of grace with man. In undertaking to become man and to act as the Representative of all men in His death and passion, what He does is simply the fulfilling of the office which, according to the counsel of God (His own as well as that of the Father), is His own office, the office of the Son from the very beginning, from all eternity." Barth, *CD* IV/1, 364.

41. Barth, *CD* I/1, 318.

42. As *the* keeper of the covenant humanity has to do with one man as God's representative who is the upholder and proclaimer of the covenant. In this sense Jesus Christ is the content and theme of the Old Testament. See Barth, *CD* I/2, 83–84.

43. Barth emphasizes that the Old Testament covenants made with Noah and Abraham, the Deuteronomic covenant, and the covenant at Sinai are historical covenants of promise that point to *the* covenant. In other words the Old Testament covenants await

Moreover, in the covenant between God and humanity—judgment becomes event.[44] This is the Word made flesh fulfilling the covenant of God in his crucifixion on the cross. This is the hiddenness of God who became another in the suffering servant—in the fulfillment of time—in the fulfillment of the covenant.[45] In the person of Jesus Christ, after Bethlehem, Gethsemane, and Golgotha the fullness of Christ's revelation is unmistakable in his resurrection from the dead, which embodies the realization of the covenant and the reconciliation of humanity with God. For Barth, this is not a different stage of reconciliation, but simply a different dimension.[46]

> The occurrence of the resurrection is not a second and further stage, but the manifestation of this second dimension of the Christ event. The resurrection is meant when it says in John 1:14: "We saw his glory." The resurrection is the event of the revelation of the Incarnate, the Humiliated, the Crucified. Wherever He gives Himself to be known as the person He is, He speaks as the risen Christ. The resurrection can give nothing new to Him who is the eternal Word of the Father; but it makes visible what is proper to Him, His glory. It is in the limitation, illumination and verification of this event and not otherwise that the New Testament views the passion of Christ. That is why in the passion it sees so powerfully the hiddenness of God. That is why it speaks so inexorably of the passing of this aeon. That is why it is so naturally aware of the necessity of the sufferings of this time. That is why above all it binds men so strictly and universally under the divine accusation and the divine threat. The power of revelation is the power of God's hiddenness attested by Him in this way.[47]

For Barth, the central theme of the humanity of Christ is the reconciliation of humanity with God realized in the fulfilled covenant. Whereas, the Old Testament covenants reveal the promise of God in the hiddenness of the person of God in the doctrines of creation and the last things; redemption and consummation provides the perimeter surrounding the heart of the matter. That is, the atonement is the center of the covenant fulfilled in Jesus Christ.[48] In Jesus Christ God is humanity, he is "God with us

---

their genuine fulfillment in the revelation of Jesus Christ as the covenant between God and man. See Barth, *CD* I/2, 82.

44. Barth, *CD* I/2, 92.

45. Ibid.

46. Barth, *CD* I/2, 111.

47. Ibid.

48. Barth, *CD* IV/1, 3.

men," which embodies the work of reconciliation in the fulfillment of the covenant between God and humanity. This is the restitution, maintaining, and upholding of fellowship between God and humanity by the removal of its former obstruction which is removed in Jesus Christ in the work of reconciliation. For Barth, this is the fulfillment of the covenant.[49]

Furthermore, Barth understands that this covenant is between God and humanity, a covenant which must be fulfilled by both God and humanity in recognition of their mutual contract. As the servant of God, Jesus Christ stands before God as the representative of all nations and he stands among the nations as the representative of God. Jesus bears the judgments of God as he lives and testifies by the grace of God. Jesus Christ is the elect of Israel, called to be the mediator of the covenant. For Barth, this is important to understand because the eternal Word becomes and is humanity in Jesus Christ. And in this humanity he acts and speaks to reconcile the world to himself. As such, he has bound himself to humanity and all creation because he must restore this broken covenant. Therefore, Christ's atonement acts to fulfill his communion with humanity that he willed and created at the beginning.[50]

Ontologically speaking, the covenant of grace is grounded in the revelation of Jesus Christ, "in the human form and content which God willed to give His Word from all eternity." This is *the* one revelation of God. Therefore, in the revelation of Jesus Christ is the revelation of the covenant, "of the original and basic will of God."[51] This is Jesus of Nazareth taken up into the eternal Word as *anhypostasis* and *enhypostasis*—the embodiment of the eternal Son of God in whose revelation fulfills the covenant of God.[52]

---

49. Barth, *CD* IV/1, 22. John de Gruchy marks an important point here, that Karl Barth's doctrine of reconciliation was firmly grounded in his Christology, which enables him to distinguish and yet affirm an intrinsic relationship between reconciliation with God and sociopolitical liberation. "Just as for Barth there is a very close connection between reconciliation and justification, and between justification and social justice, so he dialectically related the gospel of God's reconciliation to the establishment of a just peace in the world." For Barth, the Christian Church is the "provisional representative" of the sanctification of all humanity, and therefore God's reconciliation of the world to himself. See de Gruchy, "Racism, Reconciliation, and Resistance," 146. As the covenant keeper, Jesus Christ embodies reconciliation not only between God and humanity, but between humanity with itself.

50. Barth, *CD* IV/1, 34–36.

51. Ibid., 45.

52. Kevin Hector argues that for Barth, because God is the *God* of the covenant, he remains free. However, because God is the God of the covenant, God's freedom is freedom for this covenant. In other words, to suggest that God cannot use God's freedom to bind God-self would be to make God a servant to God's freedom. Therefore, rather than starting from an abstract assertion of God's independence, Barth insists that God's

"Therefore if the covenant of grace is the first thing which we have to recognize and say about God and man in their relationship one with another, it is something which we can see only as it makes itself to be seen, only as it fulfills itself—which is what happens in Jesus Christ—and therefore reveals itself as true and actual."[53]

Barth understands reconciliation to be the fulfillment of the covenant[54] realized in the active presence of God in Jesus Christ "under this name and in this form, as distinct from His being in Himself as God and within His activity as creator and Lord of the world."[55] God "maintains and continues" the covenant in a way that accomplishes his eternal will of bringing humanity into covenant with himself.[56] As God's covenant partner Jesus Christ rendered the obedience required by the covenant. As the covenant keeper Christ took to himself the sins of all humanity and suffered the death that humanity was subject to—by offering himself as the necessary sacrifice to vindicate God in relation to humanity. In so doing Jesus Christ chose to suffer the wrath of God in his own body and soul.[57]

Consequently, the covenant fulfilled in Jesus Christ is the only means of reconciliation for humanity with God, which took place in this one who comes to the world "directly or indirectly to every man in Him." In Jesus Christ the world is converted to God, and becomes his friend, no longer an enemy.[58] In Jesus Christ, the covenant that God has faithfully kept—the covenant that humanity has broken—is renewed and restored. "Representing all others in Himself, He is the human partner of God in this new covenant—He in the authenticity, validity and force of His suffering and

---

independence must be seen in light of God's revelation of Christ. God is therefore free from the world in order to be free for the world as God's covenant-partner. See Hector "God's Triunity and Self-Determination," 256.

53. Barth, CD IV/1, 45.

54. In this context Barth uses two passages from Scripture to develop this argument. He gives precedence to John 3:16: "For God so loved the world that he gave his only begotten Son, that whosoever believeth on Him should not perish, but have everlasting life." Barth, CD IV/1, 70. Barth also cites the "parallel saying" of Paul in 2 Cor 5:19: "God was in Christ reconciling the world unto Himself, not imputing their trespasses unto them; and hath committed unto us the word of reconciliation." Barth, CD IV/1, 73.

55. Barth, CD IV/1, 75.

56. Ibid., 79.

57. Ibid., 94–95.

58. Barth is not advocating here a universalistic understanding of redemption, but is emphasizing that the redemption of humanity in this world comes only "in" the covenant keeper Jesus Christ.

dying."[59] It is therefore in and through the covenant fulfilled in Jesus Christ that Barth understands the historical fulfillment of the binding relationship between God and his elect.

> Everything which comes from God takes place "in Jesus Christ," i.e., in the establishment of the covenant which, in the union of His Son with Jesus of Nazareth, God has instituted and maintains and directs between Himself and His people, the people consisting of those who belong to Him, who have become His in this One. The primal history which underlies and is the goal of the whole history of His relationship *ad extra*, with the creation and man in general, is the history of this covenant. The primal history, and with it the covenant, are, then, the attitude and relation in which by virtue of the decision of His free love God wills to be and is God.[60]

In this way Jesus of Nazareth, who is humanity like us in his creatureliness and fleshliness—does not break, but keeps—the covenant of God with His people. His life-action (including his suffering the curse of opposing the covenant of God) is an invasion and conquest of this opposition and tension. He is the "man" who is faithful both to God and therefore also to himself, the "man" who is reconciled with God, true humanity, and in relation to all the rest—*new humanity*. This life-action is executed by God himself in the person of his own Son as Jesus Christ; as humanity who is well-pleasing to God. "He is the total recipient of the grace of God."[61] Barth's adoption of *anhypostasis* and *enhypostasis* fits quite naturally here as the ontological basis to explain Jesus Christ where—God has taken up a human being into union with his being as God—as an act of his divine good pleasure.[62] In this work of reconciling an estranged world with himself, the creator also willed to exist as a creature himself. Barth understands this action as the essence of the covenant. This is the Lord of the covenant who willed to be its human partner and therefore the keeper of the covenant as true humanity in Jesus Christ.[63]

---

59. Barth, *CD* IV/1, 251.

60. Barth, *CD* II/2, 8–9.

61. Barth, *CD* IV/2, 30.

62. Barth, *CD* IV/2, 41–42. Barth alludes here to Jesus Christ taking the form of a bond servant (Phil 2:7), which he views as a parallel to the Word becoming flesh in John 1:14. The point of emphasis lays in the "assumption of flesh" made manifest in Jesus of Nazareth. See Barth, *CD* IV/2, 42.

63. Barth, *CD* IV/2, 43.

Jesus Christ: The First Adam

Karl Barth denied outright the theological legitimacy of any anthropology divorced from the man Jesus of Nazareth, who as true humanity is the true standard by which any anthropology must be judged.[64] For Barth, it is not theologically possible to engage in the study of humanity and ignore the source of its reality—*the man Jesus Christ*. As such, the dynamic of *anhypostasis* and *enhypostasis* becomes quite apparent in Barth's development of the man Jesus of Nazareth as the first Adam; that is, the first and true humanity.[65] This is an important theme in the *Church Dogmatics* developed out of Barth's exegesis of Romans 5:12–21.[66] The recognition that Jesus Christ is truly God and truly man means that the humanity of Christ is not simply *a* true human being, but *the* true human being embodied as Immanuel, as "God with us." Even as Adam was created as the first human being in the Genesis account, the humanity of Christ takes the preeminent place as *the* true human being taken up into union with the eternal Logos. For Barth, Jesus Christ *is* the first Adam.[67]

Karl Barth's hermeneutic can (and often times does) result in an interpretation of Scripture that departs from the Reformed tradition, which he unapologetically identifies as his own. This is certainly evident in the Doctrine of Reconciliation (*CD* IV/1) where Barth develops Jesus Christ as *Lord as Servant* and examines the relationship between Adam and Christ through his exposition of Romans 5:12–21. Barth approaches this text and

64. Henri Blocher argues that for Barth anthropology must be grounded on Christology. Jesus is true humanity, not because our natural essence of humanity reflects his human essence, but because he manifests in his person and event what genuine humanity really is. See Blocher, "Karl Barth's Anthropology," 101–2.

65. Daniel Migliore observes that Barth admitted in his first lectures on dogmatics in 1924 that Reformed theology distinctively emphasizes the sovereignty of God and the "radical difference between God and creation," which must be sounded within the ecumenical church if the witness of Scripture is to be taken seriously. See Migliore, "The Spirit of Reformed Faith and Theology," 352. In other words, Barth approaches humanity as a creature of God that is in dire need of relationship with God, which Barth develops as true humanity found in Jesus Christ.

66. This section also draws heavily upon Barth's essay entitled *Christ* and *Adam: Man* and *Humanity in Romans 5*, wherein Barth further develops his exegesis of Romans 5:12–21.

67. Daniel Price rightly observes Barth's rejection of philosophical existentialism as the premise of theology. For Barth the human being must be considered in the context of his or her relationship to God. It is in Jesus Christ—the self-revelation of God—that a human being is redeemed as a creature of God. Price argues that the idea of a dynamic relationship between human beings and God is one that Calvin began and Barth amplified. However, unlike Calvin, Barth anchors his anthropology in his Christology. See Price, *Karl Barth's Anthropology*, 94–100.

the problem of sin by asking: who is Adam to Paul, and what is relevant for Paul in this humanity and its abstraction in relationship to the will and work of God? In response Barth concurs that according to verse 12 Adam is the man by whom "sin entered into the world, and death by sin; and so death passed upon all men, for that all have sinned." This is how Paul understands Adam as the "exponent of the rule under which all men stand."[68] But how does Paul know this is true? In other words, "where and how has it impressed upon him its truth and validity, the necessary sequence of the one and the many, of all men in disobedience?" Barth argues that according to the text of Romans 5:12–21, in this "first and isolated figure" and in the race he represents, Paul recognizes a different figure, one who also came directly from God not as a creature only, but as the Son of God himself. Yet he was also made in the likeness of sinful men, the one who completely identifies with the humanity he came to make atonement for.[69]

> He, too, was a sinner and debtor, but as the sinless and guilt-less bearer of the sins of others, the sins of all other men. He, too, was the representative of all others. The only difference is that He was not like them. He was not a primus inter pares in a sequence, He represented them as a genuine leader, making atonement by His obedience, covering their disobedience, justifying them before God.[70]

However, rather than arguing based upon the presumed parallel between *Adam* and *Christ* (as usually done), Barth inverts the order and argues based upon the parallel between *Christ* and *Adam*. For Barth, Paul understands that Jesus Christ takes the first place as the original and Adam the second place as "the figure of him that was to come." In Adam we see the negative side of Jesus Christ.[71]

> In the unrighteous man as the head of the old race he saw again the righteous man at the head of the new one. And even the term parallel calls for some explanation. It is not autonomously that the line of Adam and the many who are concluded with him in disobedience runs close to that of Jesus Christ in whose obedience God has willed to have and has had mercy on many and indeed on all. We have only to note how the two are contrasted

---

68. Barth, *CD* IV/1, 512.
69. See Barth, *CD* IV/1, 165.
70. Barth, *CD* IV/1, 512.
71. Ibid., 513.

in vv. 15-17 to see that although they can be compared in form they cannot be compared in substance.[72]

The question at stake for Barth here is: how do we (in view of the testimony of Scripture) define what is true humanity given the creaturely relationship between Jesus Christ and Adam? In other words, in whom is established the true and first humanity? Barth sets out to demonstrate exegetically that the first place rests in the humanity of Christ. Consequently, Adam is understood in a figurative sense as a "rainbow that reflects the radiance of the sun." Adam therefore does not stand against it, but is dependent upon it for existence.[73]

> Is it not clear who and what is the prius and who and what the posterius? Even when we are told in 1 Cor 15:45 that Jesus Christ is the εσχατος Αδαμ, this does not mean that in relation to the first Adam of Gen 3 He is the second, but rather that He is the first and true Adam of which the other is only a type. It is in relation to the last Adam that this first Adam, the unknown of the Genesis story, has for Paul existence and consistence, and that in what is said of him he hears what is true and necessarily of himself and all men.[74]

Barth revisits his exegesis of Romans 5:12–21 in his essay *Christ and Adam—Man and Humanity in Romans 5* (1952) where he argues that the Apostle Paul sees Christ not only as belonging to God and his work, but also as being distinguished from God with respect to his real human nature.[75] Barth argues that Paul puts the man Jesus in his dying and rising

72. Ibid.

73. Ibid. We mark here a clear advance from Barth's exposition of vv.12–21 in *Romans* II where he describes Adam as a type of the coming man Christ (*Romans* II, 164). As a sinner, Adam is "the figure of him that was to come. The shadow to which he stands bears witness to the light of Christ" (*Romans* II, 175). Christ is contrasted with Adam as the goal of our movement in faith, who forces a decision between the two factors. "By doing this, He is not merely the second, but the *last* Adam." Barth's primary concern with respect to vv. 12–21 in *Romans* II is to express the dialectical relationship between the new and the old, between Adam and Christ (*Romans* II, 166). I argue that Barth's subsequent appropriation of *anhypostasis* and *enhypostasis* to describe Christ's human nature played an important role in his re-calibration of Christ as the first Adam, and therefore the revelation of real and genuine human nature.

74. Ibid.

75. David Paul Henry argues that Barth's struggle with the question of "anthropology" forms part of the context in which *Christ and Adam* was written. That is, the hermeneutic of Christ and Adam can be summarized this way: "a genuine understanding of the text is achieved when it is understood from the perspective of faith that focuses on the concrete self-revelation of the Wholly Other God in the person of Jesus Christ." Henry, *Early Development of the Hermeneutic of Karl Barth*, 197, 199.

on one side, and humanity (in the first place—believers) on the other side. Although Paul speaks of Christ as a human individual, the existence of this human individual is not exhausted in his individuality. The very existence of this man manifests the righteous decision of God which potentially includes an indefinite multitude of other individual people who believe in him. These are reconciled with God through this one man—who makes their peace with God through his death—even before they themselves have decided for this peace. When they come to faith in Christ they are simply conforming to the decision already made about them in Christ.[76]

In all of this we see the priority that Barth places on the humanity of Christ in relation to created humanity (including Adam) which conforms with and indeed is based upon the ontological nature of Jesus of Nazareth as *anhypostasis* and *enhypostasis*. That is, the individual human nature assumed by the Son of God is true human nature in such a way that he fully identifies with the humanity he was created in, so much so, that humanity is first in Jesus Christ, not Adam. "He is an individual in such a way that others are not only beside Him and along with Him, but in their most critical decision about their relationship to God, they are also and first of all *in* Him."[77]

Barth further argues that in Romans 5:12–21 the Apostle Paul goes beyond the first half of the chapter by setting the same material in a "wider context." The focus here is that the *special* anthropology of Jesus Christ (i.e., the one human being for all humanity) also constitutes the secret of Adam and is therefore the *norm* of *all* anthropology.[78] In this way Barth draws attention to the *true parallel* that Paul is driving at in this passage. That is, the relationship between Adam and Christ is not expressed in terms of the relationship between Adam and humanity in our "true and original nature," which recognizes in Adam the "fundamental truth of anthropology to which the subsequent relationship between Christ and us would have to fit and adapt itself." Rather, what Barth understands here is that our (human) relationship to Adam is not the primary, but the secondary anthropological truth and ordering principle. In other words, the primary anthropological truth and ordering principle is expressed by that relationship between Christ and humanity. Adam is described as the type of him was to come. The key point for Barth is that humanity's "essential and original nature" is not found in Adam, but in Christ. Adam prefigures Christ, and can only be interpreted in the "light of Christ."[79] Moreover, human existence as constituted by our

---

76. Barth, *Christ and Adam*, 33–34.

77. Ibid., 35.

78. Ibid., 36.

79. Ibid., 39–40.

relationship with Adam as sinners and enemies of God has no independent reality of its own. "It is only an indirect witness to the reality of Jesus Christ and to the original and essential human existence that He inaugurates and reveals. The righteous decision of God has fallen upon men not in Adam but in Christ. But in Christ it has also fallen upon Adam, upon our relationship to him and so upon our unhappy past."[80]

Interestingly, we see also the continuity between the reality of Christ's human nature that can only be enjoyed in union with the hypostasis of the Logos, and true human nature that can only be enjoyed in union with Christ. For Barth, Paul's argument in Romans 5 is not about the formal parallel between two sides in isolation, but set in a context grounded in their material relationship. Therefore, as Barth understands it, the question is not whether Adam is before Christ or Christ is superior to Adam. Paul isn't concerned to argue the two side by side in such a formal relationship, but rather to show that life in Christ helps us to understand life in Adam while making quite clear the material relationship of these two parallel sides. Paul identifies on one side the human nature that is not transformed by sin, which demands our recognition of the great disparity of this human nature with the human nature of the other side. Jesus Christ therefore vouches for the authenticity of Adam, not Adam who vouches for the authenticity of Jesus Christ.[81] Yet even in the great disparity of these two natures, what remains common to them both is that our relationship to Adam is only the type, or likeness of our relationship to Christ. While the same human nature appears in both, "the humanity of Adam is only real and genuine in so far as it reflects and corresponds to the humanity of Christ."[82]

> "The first man is of the earth, earthly, the second man is from heaven." That is how Paul puts it in 1 Cor 15:47. Chris is above, Adam is beneath . . . We are real men in our relationship to Adam, only because Adam is not our head and we are not his members, because above Adam and before Adam is Christ.[83]

The fundamental point for Barth is that real and genuine humanity is the humanity of Christ.[84] The human nature that we share with Adam is

---

80. Ibid., 41.

81. Barth, *Christ and Adam*, 44–45.

82. Ibid., 45–46.

83. Ibid., 46.

84. Pannenberg identifies this concept in Barth's thinking where Jesus is "the prototypal man." Jesus is the one who is completely obedient to God, and completely obedient to his fellow human beings. Moreover, Barth expresses conceptually the clear priority of Jesus's relation to God over his "significance for us." Therefore, the only

preserved as a "provisional copy" of the real humanity that is in Christ. As Adam's heirs, as sinners and enemies of God, we are still in this provisional way humanity whose nature reflects the true human nature of Christ.[85] For Barth, Paul does not look first to Adam to see how he is connected to Christ. Paul looks first to Christ to see how *he* is connected to Adam.[86] The human nature of Christ must therefore come first, and the human nature that we share with Adam comes after. The original relationship between the one and the many is that between the human nature of Christ and the humanity that he created. "Our relationship to Adam depends for its reality on our relationship to Christ." As a result we find the true and essential nature of humanity not in fallen Adam, but in Christ in whom fallen human nature has been cancelled, and what was original has been restored.[87] In light of this relationship we understand that Adam is true humanity only so far as he "reflects and points to the original humanity of Christ."[88] This establishes the relational priority of Christ's human nature that is clearly grounded and made necessary by the ontological reality of *anhypostasis* and *enhypostasis*. This union of human nature taken into the Logos demands such a priority. "Jesus Christ is the secret truth about the essential nature of man, and even sinful man is still essentially related to Him. That is what we have learned from Rom 5:12–21."[89]

Finally and fundamentally, Barth's aim in his exegesis of Romans 5:12–21 is to establish the ontological reality that true humanity is not found in the renewal of fallen nature in Adam, but the renewal of fallen nature in the human nature of Christ.[90]

> What is *Christian* is secretly but fundamentally identical with what is *universally human*. Nothing in true human nature can

---

adequate basis for humanity is precisely in Jesus's relationship to God. See Pannenberg, *Jesus—God and Man*, 198.

85. Barth, *Christ and Adam*, 46–47. Barth argues here that even the perversity of our human nature cannot destroy its formal structure and its provisional copy of the true human nature in Christ.

86. Ibid., 60.

87. Henri Blocher argues that for Barth, "we know nothing of what it really means to be a human being before we look to Jesus Christ, and can tell only on the exclusive basis of what we see in him." Blocher, "Karl Barth's Anthropology," 102.

88. Barth, *Christ and Adam*, 74–75.

89. Ibid., 107–8.

90. Paul T. Nimmo notes that for Barth the paradigm of "true freedom-in-obedience" and "obedience-in-freedom" is revealed in Jesus Christ. As such, being in action of the ethical agent is determined in the being and action of Jesus Christ. See Nimmo, *Being in Action*, 131.

ever be alien or irrelevant to the Christian; nothing in true human nature can ever attack or surpass or annul the objective reality of the Christian's union with Christ . . . So it is Christ that reveals the true human nature. Man's nature in Adam is not, as is usually assumed, his true and original nature; it is only truly human at all in so far as it reflects and corresponds to essential human nature that is found in Christ. True human nature, therefore, can only be understood by Christians who look back to Christ to discover the essential nature of man Vv. 12–21 are revolutionary in their insistence that what is true of Christians must also be true of men. That is a principle that has incalculable significance for all our action and thought. To reject this passage as empty speculation is tantamount to denying that the human nature of Christ is the final revelation of the true nature of man.[91]

Given Barth's understanding of Christ's humanity as *anhypostasis* and *enhypostasis*, his exegesis of Christ as the first Adam is readily apparent. How else can the eternal Logos become humanity other than in the authentic and true form of humankind? The humanity of Adam therefore can only point to, or reflect the true humanity embodied in Jesus Christ.

Jesus Christ: Humiliation and Exaltation in Convergence

While perhaps not as dramatic as his innovative view of God's election of Jesus Christ, Karl Barth clearly forged his own path in expressing the humiliation and exaltation of Jesus Christ as true God with true humanity.[92] Indeed, Barth's self-styled appropriation of *anhypostasis* and *enhypostasis* given the inseparable aspect of this union makes his doctrine of the humiliation and exaltation of Jesus Christ inevitable, and in fact draws into sharper focus the ontological implications of the union of the divine with humanity. In view of the immutable Logos who takes to himself human nature in Jesus of Nazareth, Karl Barth found inconceivable the notion that in Christ can be found—at any point in time—a state of humiliation that is separated from

91. Barth, *Christ and Adam*, 111–12.

92. Anderson argues that: "In Barth, then, the classical doctrine of the two natures and the Reformation concept of the states of humiliation and exaltation have been brought together in a way that marks innovation, for instead of seeing humiliation and exaltation as two successive states, i.e., His state of humiliation followed by His state of exaltation; he sees them as two sides or directions of what took place in Jesus Christ for the reconciliation of man with God. This is His being—humiliation and exaltation—the actuality of Jesus Christ as the very God who humbles Himself and the man who is exalted." Anderson, *Aspects of the Theology of Karl Barth*, 139.

his exaltation.[93] In other words, the entrance of the eternal Logos into this world of time and space could not force upon Christ any change to the glory of his divine being (hidden as it is), which then somehow reverts back to its original state at his ascension.[94] For Barth, this view does grave violence to the inseparable ontology of Jesus Christ as true God and true humanity. Barth argues that everything the New Testament says about Jesus Christ is said in the light of the resurrection and ascension, in the light of this union between the eternal Word and human existence assumed by him which is achieved once for all. As Emmanuel he is "with us always, even unto the end of the world" (Matt 28:20), until we "shall be ever with the Lord" (1 Thess 4:17).[95] But Barth asks how this can be so if the exaltation of Christ also means the laying aside of his lowliness? Does this not infer the reversal of his incarnation? Is not the humiliation of Christ also the revelation of his divine majesty in his lowliness? Is it not the resurrection of the crucified, the triumph of the Word in his actual human existence?[96] The humility of Christ therefore cannot dissipate even at his ascension. For Barth, to speak of Jesus Christ is to speak of the true God who is free to seek and find his own glory. In the freedom of his love he can actually be lowly as well as exalted. Even as the Lord he is for us a servant.[97] "It is in light of the fact of His humiliation that on this first aspect all the predicates of His Godhead, which

93. Berkouwer notes that the distinction between the humiliation and exaltation of Christ is meant to do justice to the testimony of Scripture regarding the historical progress of Christ's life from humiliation to exaltation—through suffering to glory. Moreover, "Humiliation and exaltation do indeed point to that which was present in the historical reality of Christ's life, but it is history which can be understood in its deep and universal meaning only on the basis of the divine program. There is a *unique* connection between humiliation and exaltation." Berkouwer, *The Work of Christ*, 36–37.

94. Molnar argues that Barth's reference to "an assumption of flesh by the Word" implies that what took place in the incarnation was a miracle. That is, in this new and direct act of God in history, the Word "did not cease to be God while truly becoming flesh." There is therefore no hint of a "two-stage Christology in Barth's thought." Molnar, *Incarnation and Resurrection*, 2–3.

95. Barth, *CD* I/2, 165. Johnson identifies Barth's repudiation of static formulae in the so-called *humiliation* and *exaltation* of Jesus Christ. Instead, Barth sees a dynamic direction in Christ's movement towards humanity. That is, the humiliation of God is a downward movement that occurs in Jesus Christ as "the Lord as Servant," which presupposes reconciliation accomplished with the elevation of humanity in Christ. See Johnson, *The Mystery of God*, 102–03.

96. Barth, *CD* I/2, 165.

97. Anderson describes the union of humiliation and exaltation of Christ in Barth's thinking as that which takes place in history. It is both the humbling of the deity in Christ (along with the Father) in becoming humanity, and the exaltation of humanity to the side of God in the fact that God became like humanity. See Anderson, *Aspects of the Theology of Karl Barth*, 139.

is the true Godhead, must be filled out and interpreted." Positively speaking, God is willing and able in the freedom of his love for humanity to humble himself as the true God and distinguish himself from all false Gods.[98]

Barth further argues that to speak of Jesus Christ is also to speak of true humanity, one who is limited, one who suffers; but one who also is exalted by God, who is lifted above his limitation and suffering. Nevertheless, as one with God, he is free humanity. As a creature he is superior to his creatureliness. Although he is bound by sin, he is quite free in relation to it because he is not bound to commit it. As true humanity he is mortal, and has died like we must all die. However, in his dying he is superior to death having been rescued from it, triumphant and alive. In all of this Barth understands Jesus Christ as the true God who humbles himself, and the true humanity who is exalted in his creatureliness above his creatureliness.[99]

Moreover, in his exaltation as humanity Jesus is exalted above us because he is different from us. He is given precedence over us in our common humanity. "As God He was humbled to take our place, and as humanity He is exalted on our behalf. He is set at the side of God in the humanity which is ours." In him are realized true humanity, and our conversion to God.[100] That which is anticipated in him is accomplished and revealed. In Jesus Christ God became like humanity, and humanity has become like God. That is; in him, "God was bound," and in him, the "servant has become a Lord." In Jesus Christ, just as Godhead is humiliated Godhead, to too humanity is exalted humanity.[101]

98. Barth, *CD* IV/1, 130. Warfield similarly recognizes the positive aspect of Christ's willingness to humble himself despite his "subsistence in the form of God." Moreover, Warfield states that though Christ was true humanity, he was much more than humanity according to the teaching of the Apostle Paul. That is, Paul does to not teach that Christ was once God but had become instead man; rather Paul teaches that "though He was God, He had become also man." Warfield, "The Person of Christ," 41.

99. Barth, *CD* IV/1, 131. Berkouwer explains that "Barth's conception of Christ's humiliation and exaltation does not involve two successive "states" of Christ but rather two *sides* or *aspects* or *forms* of what takes place in Jesus Christ in his effecting of reconciliation between God and man. Humiliation and glorification place us before the *double* activity of Christ in his *one* work. This work cannot be distributed "over two different steps or times of His existence," for his whole existence consists precisely in this double form." Berkouwer, *Triumph of Grace*, 133.

100. Anderson argues that for Barth, Jesus Christ—the Word made flesh is primary and everything else, including the gospel accounts of his life and teachings are secondary in relation to him. Barth, however, does not construct an abstract doctrine of Christ, but in a novel and interesting way he seeks to combine the classical doctrine of the two natures and the Reformed doctrine of the two states. "It is precisely in this way that the divinity of Christ is defined, so that it is not an abstract and a priori conception of the divine nature, but, in terms of the dynamic concept of exaltation." Anderson, *Aspects of the Theology of Karl Barth*, 125.

101. Barth, *CD* IV/1, 131. Berkouwer also observes that: "Christ was not *first*

I argue that based upon Barth's understanding of this union—derived from the ontology of *anhypostasis* and *enhypostasis*—he rejects the traditional relationship between the two "natures" of Christ (deity and humanity), and the two "states" of Christ (humiliation and exaltation).[102] But how and to what extent does Barth's understanding of the humiliation and exaltation of Christ diverge from that of traditional Christology? Barth admits that given the witness of Scripture, the humiliation and exaltation of Christ requires a place in dogmatics, but not as traditionally held, which he explains in three separate points. First, in describing what took place in Jesus Christ in reconciling humanity with God, Barth understands that there are two "sides or directions or forms" of the being of Jesus Christ, but not two states. The concepts of humiliation and exaltation in Jesus Christ are forms of action, as the Lord who became servant and the servant who became Lord.[103] Barth explains that he is not describing a being in a particular "form or state," but the "twofold action of Jesus Christ." This is the actuality of his one work that cannot be divided into different stages of his existence, but that which constitutes Christ's existence in this twofold form.[104]

Fundamentally, much like the inseparable but distinctive ontology of Christ's being as very God and very man, and based upon Barth's understanding of the Gospel narratives, Barth does not understand the being of Jesus Christ to exist at any point in time when and where he is not "both humiliated and exalted, already exalted in His humiliation, and humiliated in His exaltation."[105]

---

humiliated and *thereafter* exalted. He is the *one* Jesus Christ "from whom nothing was added in His exaltation." It is evident that in this way Barth *draws the consequences of his view that the being* and *nature of God are revealed in the humiliation*. From this he concludes to the conception that the *glory* of God is to be found precisely in the humiliation. Because Jesus Christ is the self-humiliating God he is at the same time the exalted man. For this reason humiliation and exaltation may not be temporally separated from each other but must be seen together in the one deed of reconciliation." Berkouwer, *Triumph of Grace*, 133.

102. Barth, *CD* IV/1, 132.

103. Ibid., 133. Interestingly, Alister McGrath describes Barth's understanding of theology as an ascending spiral "constructed around the self-expression of God in time, in that Barth's Christology is essentially concerned with the contemporaneity of 'above' and 'below' in the history of the humiliation of Christ on the cross." In this way incarnation and reconciliation are in effect different sides of one movement of God in Jesus Christ. "The diverse aspects and elements of the question of the person and work of Christ are inextricably interwoven, in that God is merely declaring to us what He had consummated in eternity, by a decree which anticipates everything temporal." McGrath, *Making of Modern German Christology*, 134.

104. Barth, *CD* IV/1, 133.

105. Ibid. Anderson notes: "The fact that Jesus Christ is the active subject in this

Where in Paul, for example, is He the Crucified who has not yet risen, or the Risen who has not yet been crucified? Would He be the One whom the New Testament attests as the Mediator between God and man if He were only the one and not the other? And if He is the Mediator, which one of the two can He be alone and without the other? Both aspects force themselves upon us. We have to do with the being of the one and entire Jesus Christ whose humiliation adds nothing. And in this being we have to do with His action, the work and event of the atonement. That is the first reason for this alteration of the traditional dogmatic form.[106]

Second, and this is an important concept in Barth's thinking—especially in view of the *anhypostasis* and *enhypostasis*—Barth argues that the doctrine of the two states of Christ must be interpreted in light of the doctrine of the two natures, and vice versa. "Similarly there can be no autonomous doctrine of the humiliation and exaltation which took place in Jesus Christ, especially without a reference to what took place in Jesus Christ between God as God and man as man."[107] Barth does not deny the two states of the humiliation and exaltation of Jesus Christ, but argues that its reality is grounded in his being.[108] "It is the actuality of the being of Jesus Christ as very God and very man. We cannot, therefore, ascribe to Jesus Christ two natures and then quite independently two states." Barth further argues that we must explain the mutual relationship of the two natures with the two states of Jesus Christ as very God and very man in view of what takes place as the divine work of atonement in his humiliation and exaltation.[109]

---

history, that in Him the humiliated God and the exalted man are one, that He is the God-man, means that He Himself attests to the reconciliation that takes place in this event of humiliation; He is the pledge of it in His existence, its actuality, the truth of it that speaks out, and in this consists His prophetic office and its implications for the anthropological sphere in terms of man's calling, the sending of the community and the hope of the Christian man. It is in Jesus Christ Himself that man's justification, sanctification, and calling is true and actual, and therefore applicable to all men." Anderson, *Aspects of the Theology of Karl Barth*, 140.

106. Ibid.

107. Ibid.

108. Barth fully admits that: "it hardly needs to be demonstrated that in Phil 2:6f and indeed all the New Testament Jesus Christ is regarded in the light of these two aspects and concepts. But if there is, it is not something incidental to His being." Barth, *CD* IV/1, 133.

109. Barth, *CD* IV/1, 133–34. Berkouwer explains that Barth's modification of the doctrine of the "two states of Christ" has its inevitable consequences for the doctrine of the "two natures of Christ." These cannot be understood in isolation, but are inseparably related. "In working out this relationship, Barth wishes to abide by the formulation

Third, to explain the deity and humanity of Jesus Christ on the one hand, and his humiliation and exaltation on the other means that in Jesus Christ, God demonstrates his sovereign freedom in giving himself to the limitation and suffering of the human creature (his humiliation) in becoming a servant.[110] Moreover, in Jesus Christ humanity, without any restriction upon his humanity, in the power of his deity, is freed from limitation and suffering. For Barth, this is not divinised humanity, but humanity set at the side of God—*humanity exalted by God.*[111]

> The humiliation, therefore, is the humiliation of God, the exaltation of man: the humiliation of God to supreme glory, as the activation [Betätigung] and demonstration [Erweis]of His divine being; and the exaltation of man as the work of God's grace which consists in the restoration of his true humanity. Can we really put it this way? We have to put it in this way if we are really speaking of the deity and humanity of Jesus Christ of *His* humiliation and exaltation, of *His* being and *His* work.[112]

But how does the Scripture speak to the humiliation of God in a way that corresponds to Barth's thinking here? Barth turns to the classic hymnal passage in Philippians 2 where Paul speaks of the Son of God "being in the form of God," but emptied himself from enjoying it by taking the form of a bond servant. Barth argues that the κενωσις in fact "consists in a renunciation of His being in the form of God alone." The decisive commentary is given in the text itself. He did not treat His form in the likeness of God (το ειναι ισα θεω) as a robber does his booty."[113] In other words, in his magisterial glory the eternal Son of God was not "bound by his possessions." he was

---

of Chalcedon: vere Deus, vere homo. His concern, however, is not to understand this "vere Deus" abstractly. *In* the humiliation the real deity is made manifest. It is not true that we can first know God's deity (His omnipotence and majesty) and then later come to an understanding of His humiliation. On the contrary, it is exactly *here*, in His humiliation, that the essence of His deity appears: vere Deus. In this humiliation He is also the *vere* homo who is exalted. In this bi-unity the act of reconciliation consists: the humiliation of God and the exaltation of man. According to His deity Jesus Christ did not need and could not receive glorification. He was exalted as man, as the servant who is the Lord. This is an exaltation which did not take place in the resurrection but which was "only made manifest" by it." Berkouwer, *Triumph of Grace*, 133–134.

110. Barth goes on to say that: "God is not proud. In His high majesty He is humble. It is in this high humility that He speaks and acts as the God who reconciles the world to Himself." Barth, *CD* IV/1, 159.

111. Barth, *CD* IV/1, 133–34. Barth describes this as perhaps the greatest objection that the older dogmatics could bring against his thinking here.

112. Barth, *CD* IV/1, 133–34; *KD* IV/1, 147.

113. Barth, *CD* IV/1, 180.

not bound to exist only in the form of God, "different from the creature, from humanity, as the reality which is distinct from God, only to be the eternal Word and not flesh." So that, in addition to his form in the likeness of God he was free to also subject himself to humiliation, and in the κενωσις take the form of a servant being made like humanity—being found in the likeness of humanity. And as God, he could be known only to himself, but unknown as such in the world. This is the hiddenness of his majesty in this alien form. This is God the Son humbling himself in this form in obedience to the Father, even to death on the cross. Moreover, he humbled himself in this way without any alteration of his Godhead. This is his self-emptying.[114] For Barth, this is the reality of the incomparable union of humanity with the Logos as explained by the *anhypostasis* and *enhypostasis* of his humanity.

> He does not consist is ceasing to be Himself as man, but in taking it upon Himself to be Himself in a way quite other than that which corresponds and belongs to His form as God, His being equal with God. He can also go into the far country and be there, with all that that involves. And so He does go into the far country, and is there. According to Phil 2 this means His becoming man, the incarnation.[115]

In my view this clearly demonstrates in Barth's thinking the reality of God's willing humiliation. In Jesus Christ we are confronted with the revelation of a mystery that offends; that for God it is just as natural to be lowly as it is to be exalted. Therefore, when Jesus Christ chooses to enter into and act upon the world he created, and to conceal his form of lordship in the form of a servant in this world, "He is not untrue to Himself but genuinely true to Himself, to the freedom which is that of his love." Even in the form of a servant we have to do with God in his true deity. The humility of his dwelling in Jesus Christ is not alien, but proper to him. "His humility is a *novum mysterium* for us," but for him "this humility is no *novum mysterium*. It is His sovereign grace that He wills to be and is amongst us in humility, our God, God for us." He does not become another God, but in giving himself to us in Jesus Christ he exists and acts as the one he is from all eternity. For Barth, our atonement depends on this reality. The reconciler of the world

---

114. Barth, *CD* IV/1, 180. Warfield sounds a similar theme in the life of Christ: "His life of humiliation, sinking into His terrible death, was therefore not his misfortune, but His achievement as the promised Messiah, by and in whom the Kingdom of God is to be established in the world; it was the work which as Messiah he came to do." It is in Christ's humiliation that Warfield alludes to Christ's self designation as the "Son of Man" taken from Daniel's vision, so that Christ proclaimed himself to be the Messiah he actually was. See Warfield, "Christology and Criticism," 161.

115. Barth, *CD* IV/1, 180.

with God must be God himself in his true Godhead; otherwise, it is a false reconciliation.[116] The freedom in which God can be lowly as well as exalted as the reconciler of the world is not an arbitrary ability, but the action of his holy and righteous freedom in the fulfillment of his own decision, through the obedience of the Son.[117]

> What takes place is the divine fulfillment of a divine decree . . . When we are confronted with this event as the saving event which took place for us, which redeems us, which calls us to faith and penitence, we do not have to do with one of the throws in a game of chance which takes place in the divine being, but with the foundation-rock of a divine decision which is as we find it divinely fulfilled in this saving event and not otherwise. It is therefore worthy of unlimited confidence and only in unlimited confidence can it be appreciated. It can demand obedience because it is not itself an arbitrary decision but a decision of obedience. That is why it is so important to see that this is the character of the self-humiliation of God in Jesus Christ as the presupposition of our reconciliation.[118]

This is God himself—the subject of the act of atonement—in whose presence and action as the reconciler of the world coincide and are indeed identical with the existence of the humiliated, lowly, and obedient man Jesus of Nazareth. As true God identical with humanity, he humbles himself; but he does so without contradicting his divine nature, yet in contradiction to "all human ideas about the divine nature."[119] The giving himself to human existence and suffering is a matter of the humiliation and dishonoring of God himself, but giving without renouncing or losing himself as God. Barth explains that in his humiliation God remains supremely God, and in the death of Jesus he remains supremely alive as he maintains and reveals his

116. Barth, *CD* IV/1, 192–93.

117. Ibid., 194. In his assessment of Barth's understanding of *kenosis* Bruce McCormack explains that for Barth, God does not cease to be God in becoming human. In the person of Jesus Christ kenosis is realized by addition, not subtraction. Nothing proper to deity is left behind when the Son takes on the form of a servant. Kenosis for Barth therefore becomes a positive rather than a negative idea. See McCormack, "Karl Barth's Christology as a Resource for a Reformed Version of Kenoticism," 248.

118. Ibid., 195.

119. Ibid., 199.

deity in the passion of Jesus Christ as his eternal Son.[120] In Christ's passion takes place the redemptive judgment of God on all humanity.[121]

> To fulfill this judgment He took the place of all men, He took their place as sinners. In this passion there is legally reestablished the covenant between God and man, broken by man but kept by God. On that one day of suffering of that One there took place the comprehensive turning in the history of all creation—with all that this involves.[122]

Barth takes notice of two elements in the event of the incarnation as stated in John 1:14. First, he argues that if the accent is put on *flesh* we make a statement about God, and say that without ceasing to be true God in the fullness of his deity, he went into a far country by becoming a human in his second person (or mode of being) as the Son. This is not only the far country of human creatureliness, but also of human corruption and perdition. Second, if the accent is put on *Word* we make a statement about humanity and say that without ceasing to be humanity—who is assumed and accepted in his creatureliness by the Son of God—this Son of Man returned home and his place of true fellowship with God as true humanity.[123] We see here an eloquent application of *anhypostasis* and *enhypostasis* as Barth describes the creatureliness that is accepted by the Son of God into this indissoluble union.

This is the "atonement as it took place in Jesus Christ in the one inclusive event of this going out of the Son of God and coming in of the Son of Man." Barth explains that in the literal and original sense of reconciliation, the word ἀποκαταλλάσσειν (to reconcile) means "to exchange." In this way Barth understands the renewal of the covenant between God and humanity in Jesus Christ to consist in this exchange, "the *exinanitio*, the abasement, of God, and the *exaltatio*, the exaltation of man." It was God who went into the far country, and it was humanity who returns home. This is what took place in the person of Jesus Christ. It is therefore quite obvious at this point to understand Barth's insistence that it is not a matter of two different and successive actions, but "of a single action in which each of the two elements is related to the other and can be known and understood only in this

---

120. Yet, in the act of reconciliation Barth also implies that in virtue of the union of divinity and humanity: "In this suffering and dying of God Himself in His Son, there took place the reconciliation with God, the conversion to Him, of the world which is out of harmony with Him, contradicting and opposing Him." Barth, *CD* IV/1, 250–51.

121. Barth, *CD* IV/1, 246–47.

122. Ibid.

123. Barth, *CD* IV/2, 20–21.

relationship: the going out of God only as it aims at the coming in as man; the coming in of man only as the reach and outworking of the going out of God; and the whole in its original and proper form only as the being and history of the one Jesus Christ."[124]

Barth's argument here powerfully demonstrates his understanding of the absolute union of humanity into divinity through the *anhypostasis* and *enhypostasis* of the human nature which Christ took upon himself in the *kenosis*. "The divine act of humility fulfilled in the Son is the only ground of this happening and being. On this ground the unity achieved in this history has to be described, not as two-sided, but as founded and consisting absolutely and exclusively in Him."[125] Moreover, in this unity—in this convergence of divinity with humanity—Barth understands that there is a specific individual form elected for this purpose. This form, however, is not merely a human, but "the *humanum*, the being and essence, the nature and kind, which is that of all humanity, which characterizes them all as humanity, and distinguishes them from other creatures." In other words, this is "the concrete possibility of the existence of one man in a specific form—a man elected and prepared for this purpose, not by himself, but by God (this is the point of the election and calling of Israel and Mary). But in this form it is that which is human in all men. It is the concrete possibility of the existence of a man which will be like the concrete possibility of the existence of all men and in the realisation of which this man will be our Brother like ourselves."[126]

Furthermore, and quite interestingly so, Barth expands his application of this union of divinity with humanity—conceptualized as *anhypostasis* and *enhypostasis*—to include the union of the *humanum* of all humanity with God in Jesus Christ.

> In Jesus Christ it is not merely one man, but the humanum of all men, which is posited and exalted as such to unity with God. And this is the case just because there has been no changing of God into a man; just because there was and is not creation of a dual existence of God and a man; just because there is only One here, "the Father's Son, by nature God," but this One in our human likeness, in a form of a servant (Phil 2:7), in the likeness of sinful flesh. (Rom 8:3)[127]

124. Ibid., 21.
125. Ibid., 46.
126. Ibid., 48.
127. Ibid., 49.

We note in this context Barth's specific reference to the *anhypostasis* and *enhypostasis* of Christ's human nature which he uses to describe this convergence of the divine Son of God with the "humanum of all men," this assumption of humanity by the eternal Logos. This explains how the eternal Son of God can assume true humanity to himself without doing violence to, or changing in any way, his divine essence while also existing as real humanity. I argue that this particular sense of unity as exemplified in the convergence of humility and exaltation demonstrates the true nexus of Barth's concept of *anhypostasis* and *enhypostasis* expressed in his Christology. Barth explains here that as *anhypostasis* (i.e., *impersonalitas*) Christ exists as humanity because he makes human essence his own by adopting and exalting it into unity with himself. Moreover, this human being also exists as a true humanity, as *enhypostasis*, in this union with the eternal Son of God.[128]

Barth counters the argument against this "theologoumenon" by arguing in Jesus Christ we do not have a human being into whom God has changed himself. But rather we have no less than God himself, who while remaining unchanged unites himself with this human being. Therefore, as the Son of God, he also becomes this human being, which also becomes his existence for all humanity. This is the humility of the Son of God taking to himself a "concrete possibility of human being and essence elected and prepared by Him for this purpose and clothed it with actuality by making Himself its actuality." For Barth, this is the essence of *anhypostasis* and *enhypostasis* for which he can conclude: "the protest against the concept of *anhypostasis* or *enhypostasis* as such is without substance since this concept is quite unavoidable at this point if we are properly to describe the mystery."[129]

Jesus Christ: Integration of Person and Work

For Barth, the absolute union of *very God* and *very man* in the person of Jesus Christ mirrors the absolute union of the *person* and *work* of Jesus Christ as the mediator of reconciliation.[130] At issue here is a refusal in Barth's thinking to distinguish between the event of Jesus Christ as the revelation of God, and the event of Jesus Christ as the mediator of reconciliation. In other words, Jesus Christ exists as the mediator of reconciliation between

128. Ibid.

129. Ibid.

130. Anderson argues that Barth conceives: "The person and work of Christ are seen as a unity which cannot be divided. The being of Jesus Christ is the history of the unity of the living God and the living man, the content of which history is reconciliation." Anderson, *Aspects of the Theology of Karl Barth*, 139.

God and humanity in the sense that in him the reconciliation of God and humanity are event. And in this event "God encounters and is revealed to all humanity as the gracious God and in this event again all humanity are placed under the consequence and outworking of this encounter [Begegnung] and revelation."[131]

Even so, Barth acknowledges the conceptual distinction made between the *person* and *work* of Jesus Christ, and admits that these two titles offer a sense of doctrinal convenience. The question that Barth undertakes to answer is how can Jesus Christ exist in this union of the Logos with true humanity in static isolation from his act or work? Stated the other way around: can Jesus Christ be seen in a work and not be identical with it?[132] Barth responds that the answer to this question must be no.

> In the Fourth Gospel does the Son of God exist in any other way than in the doing of the work given Him by the Father? Does the Jesus of the Synoptics exist in any other way than in His addresses and conversations and miracles, and finally His going up to Jerusalem? Does the New Testament *kyrios* generally ever exist except in the accomplishment and revelation of His ministry and lordship as such?[133]

Moreover, Barth is careful to point out with respect to the being of Jesus Christ that the Council decisions of Nicea, Constantinople, Ephesus, and Chalcedon had a polemic and critical character with a purpose to delimit and clarify a specific question at a specific point in time. That is, these church council decisions should be understood as guidelines for an understanding of the existence and action of Jesus, and not to be used (as they have been used) to construct an "abstract" doctrine of Christ's person.[134] The thrust of Barth's argument here centers on examining the *being* of Jesus Christ as the mediator of humanity's reconciliation with God. Ontologically speaking Barth understands that by definition the eternal Logos takes to himself the form of real humanity as *being in action*. This is the reconciliation

---

131. Barth, *CD* IV/1, 123. Barth further argues that the doctrine of reconciliation has to do "wholly and utterly" with Jesus Christ as the active subject. Therefore, the doctrine of reconciliation must be developed "in the light of definite Christological perceptions and propositions, focusing attention upon Jesus Christ as the beginning and the middle and the end." Barth, *CD* IV/1, 125; *KD* IV/1, 135.

132. Ibid., 127.

133. Ibid.

134. Ibid. In his analysis of Barth's approach to dogmatics, Louis Berkhof observes that while Barth regards the Creeds as worthy of respect, he refused to ascribe to them authority and regard them as rigid tests of orthodoxy, Berkhof, *Systematic Theology*, 63.

of humanity with God by virtue of his advent. His life, passion, death, and resurrection are simply an extension of his revelation of God.[135]

For Barth, if the doctrine of the work of Christ is separated from that of his person, it will inevitably raise the question: cannot this work be attributed to someone other than the divine-human person? In other words, it becomes a doctrinal abstraction of the work of Christ, which ultimately moves toward a form of "Arianism" or "Pelagianism."[136] We observe here the balance made possible by the *anhypostasis* and *enhypostasis* where in the Logos becoming flesh can be found no separation between the being of Jesus Christ and his work. This is the ontological reality of the God-man.

> What is needed in this matter is nothing more or less than the removal of the distinction between the two basic sections of classical Christology, or positively, the restoration of the hyphen which always connects them and makes them one in the New Testament. Not to the detriment of either the one or the other. Not to sacrifice the Eastern interest to the Western. Not to cause the doctrine of the person of Christ to be absorbed and dissolved in that of His work, or *vice versa*. But to give a proper place to them both, and to establish them both securely in that place.[137]

All of this is centered on a proper understanding of the *being* of Jesus Christ—in view of his work of the atonement which Barth emphasizes based upon three christological aspects that merge together and become unified in the "active person of His personal work." The first christological component of the atonement is based upon Jesus Christ as very God. It is

135. Torrance states that Karl Barth employs the *anhypostasis/enhypostasis* and the *hypostatic union* in his Christology based on the inherent union of the being and the act of the incarnate Son of God, which demanded that the doctrines of incarnation and the atonement, and thus Christology and soteriology, must be fully integrated. Because the incarnation means God with us as we actually are, God is with us as one of us, and acting for us in our place. Therefore, it must be understood as atoning reconciliation between God and man at work from the very birth of Jesus, reaching throughout his earthly life and ministry to its consummation in his death and resurrection as one continuous indivisible saving and sanctifying act of God. "Regarded in this way the hypostatic union between the divine and human natures in Jesus Christ is the ontological aspect of atoning reconciliation and atoning reconciliation is the dynamic aspect of hypostatic union, while anhypostasia/enhypostasia serve to disclose the inner logic of God's grace running throughout the whole incarnational self-giving of God in Jesus Christ for us and our salvation. Hypostatic union and reconciliation inhere inseparably in one another and are, so to speak the obverse and reverse of each other. That is the basic position that Barth clearly took up in his Prolegomena to CD II/1, and which he developed throughout the whole of Volume IV." Torrance, *Karl Barth*, 201.

136. Barth, *CD* IV/1, 127–28.

137. Ibid.

God himself who intervenes in the reconciliation of humanity with God in the "cause of the covenant" in becoming human.[138] "He is very God acting for us men, God Himself became man. He is the authentic Revealer of God as Himself God."[139] Barth once again establishes the active work of God who moves towards humanity as the impetus of reconciliation. Although it is the Son of God who becomes flesh in the person of Jesus, he does so in perfect union with God the Father—through the Holy Spirit—in the essence of his being. In Jesus of Nazareth is revealed the glory of the triune God. It is this one who as part of the divine being and event becomes humanity. The very Godhead—that divine being and event—takes part in becoming human.[140]

> This means primarily that it is a matter of the Godhead, the honour and glory and eternity and omnipotence and freedom, the being as Creator and Lord, of the Father, Son and Holy Spirit. Jesus Christ is Himself God as the Son of God the Father and with God the Father the source of the Holy Spirit, united in one essence with the Father by the Holy Spirit. That is how He is God. He is God as He takes part in the event which constitutes the divine being.[141]

138. Barth, *CD* IV/1, 128. Interestingly, Peter S. Oh uses Barth's doctrine of *Communicatio* to argue how Barth defines the union of the divine and human natures in the person of Jesus Christ. First, the *communicatio idiomatum* presumes a "true and full and definitive giving and receiving" on both sides. This definition alone leaves open the possibility for the divinization of humanity and the humanization of deity, and is therefore not plausible to describe the union of divine and human natures in Christ. Second, Barth refers to the *communicatio gratiarum*, which means "the mutual participation of divine and human essence which results from the union of the two in the one Jesus Christ." This is rejected because insufficient weight is given to the human nature. Thirdly, and the most adequate type of *communicatio* is *operationum*, which refers to "operation or action that is geared toward serving and accomplishing its mission." That is, "the hypostatic union of the two natures in the one Jesus Christ is not a synthetic union between the two different types of substance but the common actualization and work between divine action and human action fulfilled and actualized in the one person of Jesus Christ . . . The operationum is qualitatively different in essence from the idiomatum or gratiarum, which insinuate the static and substantial ontology of the Western metaphysical system that was the main folly and cause of both the Sebellian controversies over the trinitarian issue. The communicatio operationum shows why deification of the human nature and humanization of the divine nature are not adequate explications in dealing with the relationship between the two natures . . . The communicatio operationum of relational ontology, unlike idiomatum or gratiarum of substantial ontology, maintains the mutual participation and indwelling without losing its own particularities and furthermore forms an asymmetrical bipolar relational unity in tension. This is the very reason why Barth sees "the existence of Jesus Christ as His being in His act." Oh, *Karl Barth's Trinitarian Theology*, 73–75.

139. Barth, *CD* IV/1, 128.

140. Ibid., 129.

141. Ibid.

The second christological component of the atonement is based upon the fact that in Jesus Christ we have to do with a true human being. As such the reconciliation of the world with God takes place in the person of a true man—who is also true God—as an actual event. He is true humanity in every respect, being made subject to all the limitations of the human condition, yet in a different way than us as our mediator.[142]

> Jesus Christ is man in a different way from what we are. That is why He is our Mediator with God. But He is so in a complete equality of His manhood with ours. To say man is to say creature and sin, and this means limitation and suffering. Both of these have to be said of Jesus Christ. Not, however, according to the standard of general concepts, but only with reference to Him, only in correspondence with His true manhood.[143]

Barth describes the third Christological component of the atonement as that which leads us to the simplest, but also the highest. It is the source of the first two and comprehends them both.[144] For Barth, this is the key component of the union of the person of Jesus Christ with his work of reconciliation, and his willingness to humble himself as the God-man. This is the essence of reconciliation, which is directly connected to and encompassed in the simultaneous humbling of God and exaltation of humanity in Jesus Christ as *anhypostasis* and *enhypostasis*. "As the God who humbles Himself and therefore reconciles man with Himself, and as the man exalted by God and therefore reconciled with Him, as the One who is very God and very man in this concrete sense, Jesus Christ Himself is one. He is the "God-man," that is, the Son of God who as such is this man, this man who as such is the Son of God."[145] This is not a third form of true God and true humanity, but simply their absolute union in the God-man. Barth argues that when the New Testament speaks of Jesus Christ, it speaks to both the one moving from above to below, and the one from below moving up. In this movement there meets very God who becomes very humanity in Jesus of Nazareth.[146]

> Both are necessary. Neither can stand or be understood without the other. A Christ who did not come in the flesh, who was not identical with the Jesus of Nazareth who suffered and died under Pontius Pilot, would not be Christ Jesus—and a Jesus who was

142. Ibid., 130.
143. Ibid., 131.
144. Ibid., 135.
145. Ibid.
146. Ibid.

not the eternal Word of God, and who as man was not raised again from the dead, would not be the Jesus Christ—of the New Testament. The New Testament, it is true, knows nothing of the formulae of later ecclesiastical Christology, which tried to formulate two aspects with conceptual strictness.[147]

For Barth, the New Testament witness is grounded in its object—in the human being of Jesus—who is both messiah and the kyrios in the mystery of his existence. But he can only be known in this way as he reveals it through his Holy Spirit which is attested to by the New Testament in his resurrection from the dead.[148] In turn, the resurrection of Jesus Christ from the dead bears witness to the reality of the God-man made manifest in the flesh. This is the culmination of his work and definitive witness to the reality of Jesus of Nazareth as the Son of God. But as Barth emphasizes here, this revelation can only be made manifest through the Holy Spirit of Christ. "The witness concerns the self-revelation of the Son of God who is identical with this man, not an existing acquaintance with His being and work as such. All such acquaintance with Jesus the Son of God is repudiated. His form as a man is regarded and described rather as the concealing of His true being, and therefore this true being as the Son or Word of God is a hidden being."[149] It is the Holy Spirit of Christ that "lifts the veil" and uncovers the mystery and true identity of Jesus Christ as very God, who is hidden in the flesh of very humanity. Such is the intertwining nature of *anhypostasis* and *enhypostasis* made manifest in this humanity, in the union of the person and work of Jesus Christ.

Jesus Christ: Eternal Redeemer

For Barth, the mystery of the union of true God with true humanity carries with it certain ontological challenges to his Christology, especially in view of his adoption of the *anhypostasis* and *enhypostasis*. On the one hand Barth can readily deny the Lutheran doctrine of the "enfleshment" of the Word in the exclusive sense (i.e., perichoresis) as an obvious denial of the ontological limitation indicative of the reality of Christ's human nature. On the other hand, however, when considering the time/eternity dialectic in view of the absolute union of the divine and human natures, Barth's determination of the *extent* of this absolute union of the God-man is not so simple.

147. Ibid.
148. Ibid., 163.
149. Ibid.

Eternally speaking, the problem that Barth deals with here is the mystery of the father-son relationship; of the eternal Father begetting the eternal Son, and the begetting of Jesus of Nazareth. This becomes an important problem for Barth in view of the *anhypostasis* and *enhypostasis* where Barth understands that the father-son relationship depicted in the Scripture cannot be understood as figurative language. For Barth, in the hidden depths of the essence of the God-head, the father-son relationship is proper and accurate in describing the reality of the Father and the Son in their relation to each other.[150] "The mystery of begetting is originally and properly a divine and not a creaturely mystery. Perhaps one ought even to say that it is *the* divine mystery."[151]

Barth describes the mystery of the Father begetting the Son as that which reaches beyond the creaturely limitations of time and eternity (including the creaturely nature of Jesus of Nazareth), where the unity of very God and very man transcends the disunity of eternity and time. To speak of the eternal Word of God is to speak of Jesus Christ, who as very God and very man conquered time in the atonement.[152] "The first and eternal Word of God, which underlies and precedes the creative will and work as the beginning of all things in God, means in fact Jesus Christ. It is identical with the one who, very God and very man, born and living and acting and suffering and conquering in time, accomplishes the atonement."[153] For Barth, as the Word became flesh the eternal Word invaded time and space and claimed it as his own. Moreover, in every moment of his temporal existence and at every point before or after his temporal existence as true God and true humanity—*Jesus Christ is the same.*[154]

---

150. Barth, *CD* I/1, 432–33.

151. Ibid.

152. Barth, *CD* IV/1, 51.

153. Ibid.

154. Barth, *CD* I/2, 52. Alister McGrath observes that in the *anhypostasis* and *enhypostasis* Barth sees a means of safeguarding the essential unity of Jesus Christ with God. Barth's frequent insistence that God is the subject of Jesus Christ's actions is articulated in terms of the patristic concept of the "carrier" or "bearer." The statement that the Word became flesh does not mean humanity in general, but the carrier of our human essence. Barth affirms that Christ assumed *fallen* human nature (in other words, the Word became "flesh" as well as "man"). Therefore, God performs the actions of Jesus through the human nature which he "carries," this human nature, not being an agent in itself. "Barth emphasizes that God acts *directly*, rather than *indirectly*, in Christ. It is not a question of God acting vicariously through Christ, or delegating Christ to act on his behalf with his authority: Christ is God, and as such God may be said to act when Christ acts." McGrath, *Making of Modern German Christology*, 113–14.

> The Word spoken from eternity raises the time into which it is
> uttered (without dissolving it in time), up into His own eternity
> as now His own time, and gives it part in the existence of God
> which is alone real, self-moved, self-dependent, self-sufficient. It
> is spoken by God, a perfect without peer (not in our time, but in
> God's time created by the Word in the flesh, there is a genuine,
> proper, indissoluble, primal perfect), and for that reason there is
> coming into the world a future without peer for not in our time
> but rather in this God's time created by the Word in the flesh
> there is a genuine, proper, indissoluble, primal future.[155]

Our understanding of Barth's vantage point here (in view of the *an-hypostasis* and *enhypostasis*) must begin with the eternal Logos who is not isolated from the humanity he is elected to assume. "For Jesus Christ—not an empty *Logos*, but Jesus Christ the incarnate Word, the baby born in Bethlehem, the man put to death at Golgotha and raised again in the garden of Joseph of Arimathea, the man whose history this is—is the unity of the two. He is both at one and the same time."[156] As very God and very man Jesus Christ is both the "address of God to man and the claim of God upon man" as the Word of God spoken in his work. This is the work which belongs to him as the eternal Son of God prior to us. "In this He is the pre-existent *Deus pro nobis.*" He is there at the beginning of all things—who as the basis and purpose of the covenant is alone the content of the eternal will of God—which precedes the whole being of humanity and of the world, but with a view toward us. As a fellow human being, as the concrete reality and actuality of the promise and command of God, he is in one person amongst us (in one person), very God and very man.[157]

In virtue of the election of grace and as the keeper of the covenant, the Son is no longer just the eternal Logos. Barth argues that as very God and very man from all eternity: "He is also the very God and very man He will become in time."[158] Barth's allusion to the *anhypostasis* and *enhypostasis* is clearly marked in the *eternal* Jesus Christ as the God-man which is established by God's eternal decree to elect Jesus Christ. Indeed, this is the mystery of the eternal essence of very God and very man, and yet must be so in Barth's thinking where the *anhypostasis* and *enhypostasis* of Christ's human nature provides the ontological grounding for the mystery of his eternal essence.

---

155. Barth, *CD* I/2, 52.
156. Barth, *CD* IV/1, 53.
157. Ibid.
158. Ibid., 66.

> In the divine act of predestination there pre-exists the Jesus Christ who as the Son of the eternal Father and the child of the virgin Mary will become and be the Mediator of the covenant between God and man, the One who accomplishes the act of atonement. He in whom the covenant of grace is fulfilled and revealed in history is also its eternal basis. He who in Scripture is attested to be very God and very man is also the eternal testamentum, the eternal sponsio, the eternal pactum, between God and man.[159]

The reality of very God and very man in Jesus Christ is particularized by his presence in the lowest parts of the earth (Eph 4:9), as he tabernacled in the humanity of Jesus (John 1:14); as he dwelt in this one human being in the fullness of His Godhead (Col 2:9); and as he demonstrates the exercise of his omnipresence. That is, in Jesus Christ is the "perfection in which He has His own place which is superior to all the places created by Him, not excluding but including all other places." As he who created time out of eternity, he can also enter our time of sin and death and be temporal in it, yet without ceasing to be eternal in the time he created.[160]

Ontologically speaking, Barth does not understand the testimony of Scripture to distinguish between the eternal Son and the Son known as Jesus of Nazareth. As a case in point Barth cites Hebrews 1:2f where it says by the Son God created the world; that he is "the brightness of His glory, and the express image of his person," and that he upholds "all things by the word of his power." And then immediately after Barth explains that we are told "when he had by himself purged our sins he sat down on the right hand of the majesty in high," and is "made much better than the angels, as he hath by inheritance obtained a more excellent name than they." Barth concludes that further statements concerning his superiority to the angels would be inexplicable if reference is made only "abstractly" to the eternal Son of God, particularly in view of the supposed need to stand in this exaltation and the inheritance of a more excellent name.[161]

> Indeed, how could the eternal Son of God as such be put (in v. 1) in the same series with the fathers by whom God spoke at sundry times and in divers manners? How could it be said of Him as such that God "hath in these last days spoken unto us" by Him? This is only explicable if, as is expressly emphasized in v. 6, the reference is to the One who is brought into the world

159. Ibid.
160. Barth, *CD* IV/1, 187–88.
161. Barth, *CD* IV/2, 34.

of men, the oikoumenh, and therefore to the One who is both
Son of God and Son of Man. As such He is the One by whom
God made the aeons, and who upholds all things by the Word
of His power.[162]

Perhaps even more to the point is Barth's understanding of the pre-destinarian passages in the New Testament that emphasize the blood—the putting to death of Jesus Christ—which is obviously inexplicable if they refer to a logos asarkos rather than the eternal Son of God and therefore also the Son of Man existing in time. Barth argues from 1 Peter 1:29 that the one who "verily was foreordained before the foundation of the world, but was manifest in these last times," must be the same one of whom it is said to those reading verses 18–19 that they are redeemed with his blood "as of a lamb without blemish and without spot." Furthermore, in Ephesians 1:4; the one that God "hath chosen us in him before the foundation of the world, that we should be holy and without blame before him" is the same one of whom it is said in verse 7 that we have redemption through his blood.[163] Barth also cites Revelation 13:8 where the book of life that is written before the foundation of the world is called the book of the Lamb slain.[164]

However, Barth makes it clear that Jesus Christ is a real human be-ing in a way that distinguishes him from the reality of all other humanity. As a true human being Jesus Christ is also the one who *was Head* before the foundation of the world.[165] He reveals himself to be the presupposition of the being of all humanity, who lays claim to their existence, and whose

162. Ibid.

163. Cunningham examines Barth's development of the eternal being of the God-man in Barth's exegesis of Ephesians 1:4 (and other passages) where the point of emphasis is the extent in which Barth sees the "eternal" unity of the God-man in Jesus Christ. "To defend his contention that the New Testament writers had Jesus Christ, the Word made flesh, in mind and not a logos asarkos, Barth draws attention to the soteriological setting of the New Testament passages linking Christ and creation. Barth believes that the New Testament authors, by clearly identifying the pre-existent Christ with the Redeemer, could not be speaking of the eternal Son as such but rather of Jesus Christ Himself, 'the Mediator, the One who in the eternal sight of God has already taken upon Himself our human nature.'"Cunningham, "Karl Barth's Interpretation and Use of Ephesians 1:4," 27.

164. Barth, *CD* IV/2, 34.

165. Barth's argument that Jesus existed with the Logos (as pre-existent) humanity may be observed as one of the more challenging aspects of his Christology. John Knox states as an axiom that the true humanity of Christ demands that he was not pre-existent in his flesh before his incarnation. See Knox, *Humanity* and *Divinity of Christ*, 93. And yet for Barth, this axiomatic presumption must be reversed. Barth argues if indeed the humanity of Christ was taken up into union with the eternal Logos, how then do we understand the eternal Logos as not existing, from all eternity, as the eternal God-man?

promise for them is valid from the beginning.[166] Again, for Barth this is only possible in the ontological mystery of the Logos becoming real humanity, in whose humanity is taken up into and fully assumed by the Logos in such a way that real humanity becomes eternal God.

> But the inconceivable actually takes place in this man, and is declared and revealed and to be conceived as such. The attempt to interpret it as a mystery cannot on this account be omitted. If it is, the concept of the true humanity of Jesus Christ which is grounded in this mystery will be incomplete. We shall not really know what we are saying when we try to understand and explain the reconciliation of the world with God in relation to reconciled man. Reconciled man is originally the man Jesus. And the man Jesus is originally reconciled man because and as God Himself, without ceasing to be God, willed to be and actually became man as well, this man Jesus. The existence of this man is the work of God in which, without ceasing to be God, He willed to be and became also this man.[167]

Barth's understanding of the eternal Logos becoming real humanity (as *anhypostasis* and *enhypostasis*) also carries with it certain ontological challenges with respect to the humanity of Christ and his presence among his people. The question that Barth wrestles with is: if the revelation of God in Jesus Christ manifests the special presence of God in creation, how then do we understand the eternal presence of the God-man embodied in Jesus Christ?

> If we maintain that the path from the presence with which God is the triune God is present to Himself leads directly and in the first instance to His special presence in creation, we must now take a further step back backwards, making a fresh distinction, and upholding the position that strictly speaking it leads directly and in the first instance, within all the special presences, to His proper presence in Jesus Christ. It is as the One who is present here in this way that He is the God who is specially present

---

166. Barth, *CD* IV/2, 36. Alister McGrath argues that for the later Barth his "Christological concentration" finds its expression not in the history of Jesus of Nazareth in general, or even in the crucifixion or resurrection in particular, but in the preexistent Christ, the Christ before all eternity. It is this divine freedom of revelation (God's freedom to reveal or not reveal himself) that is preserved by the eternal generation of the Son. McGrath concludes that as a result Barth is obliged to assert that Christ is equally present at every stage of redemptive history. See McGrath, *Iustitia Die*, 399–400.

167. Barth, *CD* IV/2, 40.

in Israel and the Church, and as such generally present in the world as a whole and everywhere.[168]

Barth argues that in God's adoption of Israel and the Church, which takes place in Jesus Christ, "there was and is now as then a real presence of God in places on earth." As the presupposition of this adoption, Jesus Christ has a part in the divine Sonship, "*gratia unionis*." As such, Israel and the Church "received [it] from His fullness" and in this way are accepted into him as the children of God "by Him and from Him, and therefore with Him, participating in the real divine presence."[169] In the person of Jesus Christ is not simply the mere presence of God, but God Himself—who as very God and very man—is one whose divinity and humanity are unmixed and at the same time undivided. As Barth explains, it is based upon this union that the adoption of Israel and the Church becomes a reality.[170]

> In the person of His Son, in Jesus Christ, God is not merely present to man as He was and is in Israel and Church, around Him and in Him in the special form of a blessing or injunction, an abasement or an elevation, a declaration or an act in connexion with his work of revelation and reconciliation. But God is Himself this man Jesus Christ, very God and very man, both of them unconfused and unmixed, but also unseparated and undivided, in the one person of this Messiah and Saviour. This is what cannot be said about any other creature, even any prophet or apostle. Jesus Christ alone is very God and very man. And it is on the basis of this unio, but clearly differentiated from it, that there is an adoptio.[171]

For Barth, the reality of coalescence between Christ's divinity and his humanity must be taken seriously and understood for what it is as the revelation of God in the person of Jesus Christ. Although the humanity of Christ is *real* humanity, it is humanity taken up into union with the

168. Barth, *CD* II/1, 484.

169. Ibid., 485.

170. Barth explains that Jesus Christ is "not simply one of the beings—perhaps the highest—which can confess in general or in particular that it lives and moves and has its being in God. On the contrary, in Him dwells the fullness of the Godhead bodily (Col 2:9) . . . And Col 1:9 is even more emphatic . . . Both sentences undoubtedly speak of a bodily and proper dwelling of God in His fullness or completeness . . . And they say of this bodily and proper dwelling of God Himself, which otherwise takes place only beyond heaven and the heaven of heavens, that in Jesus Christ as His dwelling it is present not merely, as elsewhere, as the presupposition of His dwelling in creation, but as itself His dwelling even in creation." Barth, *CD* II/1, 486.

171. Barth, *CD* II/1, 486.

eternal Son of God. As such, this humanity exists beyond the confines of every other human creature.[172] Jesus of Nazareth therefore exists not only as a true human being, but also as true God in the reality of this union, in his participation in the eternal nature of God. Given Barth's grounding of *anhypostasis* and *enhypostasis* in the human nature of Christ, how could it be otherwise? "If we take the reality of the human nature of Christ seriously in its unity with the divine nature, if we free ourselves of all gross or refined Docetism, if we give John 1:14, "and dwelt among us" its full value, there is no room for the old error of God's non-spatiality, and we understand the reality with which scripture can speak of the spatiality of God in the whole width of His revelation (both before and after the epiphany of Christ), and in His ubiquity in the world."[173]

In the end Barth takes seriously the union between divine and human natures in Jesus Christ as an eternal union, which means it cannot be limited by time and space. Moreover, it is based on the reality that the Word dwelt among us as real humanity. Therefore, if this union truly manifests the revelation of God to the world in the flesh of Jesus Christ, the humanity taken up into that union cannot be separated from the divine nature it has been united together with. This must be so for Barth; otherwise there is no real union of divine and human natures in Christ. This is the indissoluble union of divine and human natures undergirded by the *anhypostasis* and *enhypostasis* of Christ's human nature.

Conclusion

It is well recognized that Karl Barth takes a unique and many times innovative approach to Christology that clearly departs from the Reformed tradition. Yet, Barth does not waiver in understanding that he himself is a Reformed theologian. Nevertheless, he argues for the union of the humanity of Christ with the Logos in a way that reformulates the Reformed tradition based upon his own reading of the Scriptures and his appropriation of the *anhypostasis* and *enhypostasis*.

---

172. Barth's unusual position with respect to the human presence of Jesus taken up in the Logos demonstrates his willingness to reformulate the Reformed understanding of the union of very God and very man in Jesus Christ. This in fact becomes axiomatic for Barth based upon his appropriation of the *anhypostasis* and *enhypostasis*. Francis Turretin certainly speaks for the traditional Reformed theology when he argues that it is a radical error to assume that there is a twofold kind of presence with respect to Christ's body. This is contrary to the nature of a true body and cannot be admitted. See Turretin, *Institutes of Elenctic Theology,* 3:509.

173. Barth, *CD* II/1, 486.

As we have shown, Barth's conceptual understanding of the *anhypostasis* and *enhypostasis* is an ontological reality that he clearly applies throughout the doctrine of reconciliation. As such, we see a unifying principle that binds together the person of Jesus Christ as true God and true man with his role as mediator of the covenant in reconciling humanity with God. Furthermore, in Barth's unique appropriation of *anhypostasis* and *enhypostasis* we find a coalescence of divinity with humanity that provides a dynamic flexibility to express Jesus Christ as the mediator of reconciliation. For Barth, because the humanity of Christ is not isolated in his union with the Logos, Jesus of Nazareth not only becomes one with the Logos in the revelation of God, but he assumes the attributes of God in this union. He is the subject and object of divine election, the one in whom both election and reprobation is meted out. He is very God as the Logos in the election of Jesus of Nazareth, and he is very man as Jesus of Nazareth, having been elected as the mediator of the covenant between God and humanity. He is the first Adam, authentic humanity assumed by the Logos for whom the second Adam can only reflect in his fallen state.

As Jesus Christ, he invades time and space having humbled himself as the eternal Son who goes into a far country and returns home as exalted humanity, glorified in his union with very God. As very God and very man his work as the mediator of reconciliation is simply an extension of his being as the God-man. Jesus Christ's work therefore cannot be separated from his being. Jesus Christ must be eternal God in every respect because he is the eternal redeemer. All of these things reflect the coalescence of divinity and humanity in Jesus Christ that Barth clearly develops based upon his own exegesis, and grounded in his unique understanding of the *anhypostasis* and *enhypostasis* of Christ's human nature. That being said, Barth's exegesis of the Scriptures should not be taken lightly because they in fact take the highest priority in his theology—particularly in the *Church Dogmatics*. Barth is very clear to map out and defend his Christology based upon his exegesis of the Scriptures, which he endeavors to understand just as they are written. This certainly holds true for Barth when it comes to his appropriation of *anhypostasis* and *enhypostasis* to explain the human nature of Christ.

5

Barth's Christological Method in View of Chalcedon
Its Nuance and Complexity

Introduction

KARL BARTH'S EXPRESSION OF the humanity of Christ as *anhypostasis* and *enhypostasis* reaches its apex in the Doctrine of Reconciliation (*CD* IV) where he develops Jesus Christ as the servant as Lord.[1] More specifically

1. Barth, *CD* IV/2. While Paul Dafydd Jones agrees that the "*anhypostasis/enhypostasis* formula" marked a "defining moment" in Barth's early theological development, he argues that it is Barth's creative construal of the *communio naturarum, communicatio idiomatum, communicatio gratiarum, communicatio operationum/apotelesmatum*, that represents a highpoint of his mature Christology. For Jones, while Barth's Christology and theological epistemology "took its bearings" from Heppe's *Reformed Dogmatics*, in his mature Christology Barth departs from the "older dogmatics" in favor of his own reflections. Jones understands that the *anhypostasis/enhypostasis* pairing continues to be a "fairly incidental purpose" when it comes to Barth's positive explication of Christ's being and act. "Claims about the standing of Christ's humanity are useful, but less important than descriptions of what the humanity does—namely, participate increasingly in the ontological complex existence in Jesus Christ and play an indispensable role in the event of revelation." Jones, *Humanity of Christ*, 147. I argue against Jones's conclusion that Barth de-emphasizes of the *anhypostasis* and *enhypostasis* in his mature Christology. As we have already demonstrated, the consistent theme throughout the development of the Barth's Christology is the revelation of God in Jesus Christ, which is undergirded by the *anhypostasis* and *enhypostasis* of Christ's human nature (see chapter 3). Furthermore, we have shown how Barth thematically developed the *anhypostasis* and *enhypostasis* in the coalescence of Christ's divinity and humanity in His role as the mediator of reconciliation (see chapter 4). We will further argue in this chapter that it is in fact the *anhypostasis* and *enhypostasis* dynamic which serves as the ontological foundation by which the *hypostatica unio* is actualized in the "doing" of Jesus Christ, and subsequently realized in the *communio naturarum, communicatio idiomatum, communicatio gratiarum*, etc. Moreover, while Barth certainly had many points of variance with traditional Reformed theology, and although he first become acquainted with *anhypostasis* and *enhypostasis* in Heppe's *Reformed Dogmatics*, Barth made this theologoumenon his own in his understanding of the humanity of Christ (as clearly demonstrated in his unique coupling of these terms), which he consistently understood throughout his *Church Dogmatics* as the foundational aspect for understanding the union of divinity and humanity in Christ.

stated; it is in the homecoming of the Son of Man—in Jesus Christ's exaltation as true humanity—where Barth emphasizes Christ's human nature as
anhypostasis and *enhypostasis* in his dialogue with Chalcedon's definition
of the two natures.[2] Having established Barth's thematic expression of these
concepts in the coalescence of divine and human natures in Christ as the
mediator of reconciliation, we now turn to Barth's expression of these concepts as *being in action* with Chalcedon in clear view.[3]

In the Doctrine of Reconciliation Barth first develops the humanity
of Christ as the Lord as servant (*CD* IV/1) in the humiliation of his divine essence, in his Priestly office. Barth now transitions to the exaltation
of the humanity of Christ as the servant as Lord in his Kingly office in close
proximity to the famous Chalcedon two-fold definition of the two natures
as: unconfused, immutable and indivisible, inseparable. This establishes a
critical point in Barth's ontological development of the humanity of Christ
because he now deals specifically with what it means for the human essence
of Christ—as the Son of Man—to be brought into union with his divine
essence. Moreover, Barth considers what it means for the exalted Son of
Man to be brought into union with the Triune God in dialogue with the
Chalcedon definition of the two natures.[4]

Our objective in this chapter is to: 1) evaluate Karl Barth's interpretation of the Chalcedon definition of the two natures in Jesus Christ given the
backdrop of the *anhypostasis* and *enhypostasis* of his human nature; and 2)
examine how Barth uses the concepts of *anhypostasis* and *enhypostasis* in

2. Adam Neder makes the point that considering Barth's most detailed development of the hypostatic union is given in *CD* IV/2, (36–116), it is rather odd that so
little study has been devoted to it. See Neder, "History in Harmony," 148. Neder makes
an important point here particularly in view of the importance that *anhypostasis* and
enhypostasis play in this context.

3. Neder recognizes the importance of speaking of Jesus Christ's history as the
inseparability of being and act, where we see the two-fold movement of divine humiliation and human exaltation. This is critical in understanding Jesus Christ as the mediator of reconciliation between God and man. See Neder, "History in Harmony," 151.

4. Barth takes quite seriously Chalcedon's definition of the two natures of Christ
given the Trinitarian complexity of humanity being brought into union with the Logos.
Michael Welker comments here that the creeds of the ancient church hold true to the
notion that Christ's true humanity must be stressed along with his divinity. This position, however, resulted in some "extremely awkward doctrinal formulations that initially
demanded the articulation of an (ultimately Trinitarian) *self-differentiation within God*
without abandoning the doctrine of the *one* God. The task, namely, to grasp and articu-
late at once both the unity and difference between Jesus Christ's divinity and humanity,
was to be accomplished by what is known as the *doctrine of the two natures*." Barth's
point of departure in his own clarification of the Nicaeno-Constantinopolitanum is
that Christ's divinity cannot be understood as an apotheosis, that is, as the divinization
of an individual human being. See Welker, *God the Revealed.* 263–64.

his critique of the Chalcedon definition of two natures which become the ontological grounding to explain the act of God's revelation of Jesus Christ in the *hypostatica unio*.

How Did Karl Barth Interpret Chalcedon?

As the Council at Chalcedon set out to sharpen the ontological definition of Jesus Christ as very God and very man, it did so in the knowledge that the ontology of the two natures of Christ remains a mystery.[5] In the same vain Barth approaches Chalcedon's definition of the two natures of Christ with the understanding that within this union is embodied a mystery that can only be fully comprehended by God himself. "Primitive Christology . . . did not intend to solve the mystery of revelation and its formula about the two natures of Christ, which was clarified at the Council of Chalcedon in 451. It began and ended with the realisation that this simply was impossible. Its purpose in this formula was not to explain this fact."[6]

Furthermore, Barth argues that Church confessions like Chalcedon are limited with respect to the conclusions they are able to draw because they are responding to a specific point of Church doctrine at a specific point of time. Therefore, they should not be understood as building blocks to construct an abstract doctrine of the person of Christ. "We must not forget that in the doctrinal decisions of Nicea and Constantinople and Ephesus and Chalcedon it was a matter of the being of Jesus Christ as such, these decisions had a polemical and critical character, their purpose being to delimit and clarify at a specific point. They are to be regarded as guiding lines for an understanding of His existence and action, not to be used, as they have been used, as stones for the construction of an abstract doctrine of His 'person.'"[7]

Although Barth judges Chalcedon's definition of two natures to be "factually correct and necessary," he argues that it should not be understood as an absolute and comprehensive statement of the union of two natures in Jesus Christ as testified in the Scriptures. This is an important observation to make because while Barth agrees with the decision at Chalcedon, he argues

5. As a general principle Barth understands the necessity and legitimacy of confessional statements and their expressions of the Christian faith, which were demanded under certain circumstances in response to new questions directed at the ambiguity of older confessions. This is how "the Nicene Creed came to stand alongside the Apostles', the Niceno-Constantinopolitan alongside the Nicene, the Ephesian and Chalcedonian alongside the Niceno-Constantinopolitan." Barth, *CD* I/2, 627.

6. Barth, *CD* I/2, 126.

7. Barth, *CD* IV/1, 127.

that there is more that must be said concerning the union of divinity with humanity in Christ. That is, based upon Barth's understanding of Scripture, the doctrine of the two natures must not be understood as an autonomous one, but in relationship to the divine *action* that takes place in Jesus Christ as the revelation of God.[8]

> And the more exact determination of the relationship between God and man in the famous Chalcedonian definition, which has become normative for all subsequent development in this dogma and dogmatics, is one which in our understanding has shown itself to be factually correct and necessary. But according to our understanding there can be no question of a doctrine of the two natures which is autonomous, a doctrine of Jesus Christ as God and man which is no longer or not yet related to the divine action which has taken place in Him, which does not have this action and man as its subject matter. There is no such doctrine in the New Testament, although we cannot say that the New Testament envisages the being and relationship of God and man in Jesus Christ in any other way than it became conceptually fixed in the doctrine of *the two natures*.[9]

Barth's concern here is not to deny Chalcedon's definition of the two natures, but to more precisely explain what it means to say that Jesus Christ exists in two "natures." For Barth, one of the great mysteries of the incarnation is the fact that divinity condescends to unite itself to humanity despite the antithetical relationship of the one with the other.[10] Therefore, to say that the natures of divinity and humanity are simply joined together in Christ raises the obvious question: what do we mean when we speak of "nature" in this context? Barth addresses this open ended question left by Chalcedon with more precise language to explain the union of divine and human natures in Christ. As we shall see, Barth's concern is to further develop the

8. Barth's conceptual understanding of divinity and humanity in Jesus Christ axiomatically points to the *action* of God in the revelation of Jesus Christ. "Very God and very man. If we consider this basic Christian truth first in the light of "conceived by the Holy Spirit," the truth is clear that the man Jesus Christ has His origin simply in God, that is, He owes His beginning in history to the fact that God in person became man . . . He is God Himself. God is one with Him. His existence begins with God's special action; as a man He is founded in God, He is true God." Barth, *Dogmatics in Outline*, 96–97.

9. Barth, *CD* IV/1, 133.

10. Gustaf Wingren argues that in general Barth does not describe the relationship between God and man as an antithesis in the sense of hostility. That is, while God's revelation itself indicates the differences between God and humanity, it also discloses God's will to come into fellowship with humanity. See Wingren, *Theology in Conflict*, 24–25.

concept of two natures defined at Chalcedon based upon the *hypostatica unio*, which is grounded in his understanding of the *anhypostasis* and *enhypostasis* of Christ's human nature.[11]

> After the conflicts and decisions of the 4th and 5th centuries, the older doctrine and theology of the church came to speak predominantly of the two "natures" of Christ. But this conception was exposed to serious misunderstanding and showed itself to be at least in serious need of interpretation. This does not mean that we have to abandon it. But we have to remember that it is fatally easy to read out of the word "nature" a reference to the generally known or at any rate conceivable disposition of a being, so that by the concept "divine nature" we are led to think of a generally known or knowable essence of deity, and by that of "human nature" of a known or knowable essence of man, the meaning of the humanity of Jesus Christ—for this is our present concern—being thus determined by a general anthropology, a doctrine of man in general and as such.[12]

Given the context of Jesus Christ as the mediator of reconciliation in the homecoming of the Son of Man, Barth approaches the first part of Chalcedon's definition with its intent to guard against the over-emphases of Alexandria.[13] "The first part of the Chalcedonian definition is relevant in this connexion with its safeguarding against the excesses of Alexandrian theology. One and the same Christ, the only-begotten Son and Lord, is to be confessed in two natures [unconfused] and [immutable], and therefore without any idea of commixture of the two or a changing of the one into the other."[14] Barth grants the mystery of this union of genuine divine and human essence, and argues that as *event*, "on the other side of this event and being" it must be equally emphasized that this union of the Son of God with human essence is real and indestructible. In this way Barth approaches Chalcedon through the lenses of the revelation of God in the flesh

11. In explaining Barth's understanding of how the humanity of Christ is the humanity of God, Neder describes Barth's affirmation of *anhypostasis* or impersonalitas of the human nature of Christ. That is, "Jesus Christ exists as a man only as and because the Son of God exists as a man." Neder, "History in Harmony," 158. We note, however, that the emphasis of Neder's argument rests on *anhypostasis* in a disconnected form—separated from its dual formulation with *enhypostasis* as Barth emphasizes in the Doctrine of Reconciliation.

12. Barth, *CD* IV/2, 26.

13. Barth clearly understands the dialectic relationship between the Alexandrian and Antiochian views of the two natures defined at Chalcedon and works through the Chalcedon definition of the two natures with this in mind.

14. Barth, *CD* IV/2, 63.

of Jesus Christ, where Christ's human nature—as the Son of Man—must be understood conceptually as *anhypostasis* and *enhypostasis* in its union with the Son of God.

> The mystery of the incarnation consists in the fact that Jesus Christ is in a real simultaneity of genuine divine and human essence, and that it is on this presupposition that the mutual participation is also genuine. But we must now lay an equally strong emphasis on the other side of this event and being. As it proceeds from the union and unity of the Son of God and human essence, it is also clear that the union of His divine and human essence in that two-sided participation—although it does not become unity—is a real and strict and complete and indestructible union.[15]

But how is this union to be understood in the context of Chalcedon? Barth works to make clear that this union of divine and human essence in Christ is real and penetrates both sides of the equation. In other words, Barth understands that in Jesus Christ as the God-man, the human essence fully participates in the divine essence, and the divine essence fully participates in the essence of humanity. Barth characterizes this as a "radical affirmation" that the divine and human essence is really and completely brought into union in Jesus Christ as the Son of God. Therefore, not only must Chalcedon be interpreted through the revelation of God in Jesus Christ as *event*, but also *event* in the union of this human essence as the Son of Man as it participates in the divine essence.[16]

> There is no element of human essence which is unaffected by, or excluded from, its existence in and with the Son of God, and therefore from union with; and participation in, this divine essence. Similarly, there is no element of His divine essence which the Son of God, existing in human essence, withdraws from union with it and participation in it. We shall have to say what this union and two-sided participation can and cannot mean in

15. Ibid., 64.

16. Otto Weber remarks that for Barth, the revelation of God is reality based upon God's willingness to and freedom to "traverse the boundary between him and us." This is his humiliation towards us. That is, in the mode of the Son's existence "the one God became man." Humanity therefore can be like him as his adopted children in him who is the eternal Son. This is understood within the context of God's revelation as event. Moreover, God's revelation is made known to us in a form that is known to us—as humanity. Revelation is to be spoken of as an utterly free grace occurring in the world in which God, who veils himself, encounters us in a way that we can understand him. See Weber, *Karl Barth's Church Dogmatics*, 42–43.

face of the indissoluble distinction of divine and human essence. For the moment however, we must take the radical affirmation that the divine and human essence are indivisibly united in the one Jesus Christ who is the Son of God.[17]

Barth once again emphasizes that the revelation of God made manifest in Jesus Christ does not simply exist as one person who combines divine and human essence in his being. The emphasis is laid upon the eternal Christ who has taken to himself human essence. "We do not have here a dual, but the one Jesus Christ, who as such is of both divine and human essence, and therefore the one Reconciler, Saviour and Lord. He pre-existed as such in the divine counsel."[18] This is how Jesus Christ was born, lived and died. This is how he appeared in his resurrection. This is how he reigns at the right hand of the Father.[19]

In the second part of the Chalcedon definition Barth describes its safeguards against the excesses of Antioch where he emphasizes the positive meaning of the two natures of Christ are indivisible and inseparable, which affirm that even in their distinctiveness these two natures are totally and definitely united in Jesus Christ. "Jesus Christ, the only-begotten Son of God and our Lord is to be confessed in His two natures [indivisible] and [inseparable], and therefore without any idea of a divisibility of one or the other, or a separability of the one from the other. The positive meaning of the definition on this side was that even in their distinctiveness the divine and human essence were and are united in Jesus Christ, not merely in appearance but in fact, not merely partially but totally, not merely temporarily but definitely."[20]

In this context Barth explains that the reality of the divine essence unites itself to real human essence, which in turn marks the divine humiliation and the exaltation of humanity in their mutual participation in each other. As such, they "cannot be separated for all their distinctiveness." This is the single event and being of Jesus Christ which for Barth clearly speaks to the *anhypostasis* and *enhypostasis* of the Son of Man in union with the Son of God.[21] This is the ontological basis for expressing the mystery of the incarnation.

17. Barth, *CD* IV/2, 64.

18. Ibid.

19. Ibid.

20. Ibid., 65.

21. Ibid.

> If we believe in Jesus Christ, in this One, we do not decide for one element in this history to the obscuring or even exclusion of the other, but we accompany the whole course of the history in its unity and totality. The mystery of the incarnation consists in the fact that the simultaneity of divine and human essence in Jesus Christ is real, and therefore their mutual participation is also real.[22]

Given Karl Barth's interpretation of Chalcedon's definition of the two natures of Jesus Christ we make two observations. First, Barth agreed (at least conceptually) with the Chalcedon language that defined Jesus Christ as one person who exists in two natures, which remain unconfused and immutable, as well as indivisibly and inseparably united in their union. Barth therefore recognizes the intent of Chalcedon to guard against the excesses of both Alexandria and Antioch, which he accepts as accurate and normative for the Church and orthodoxy on the whole. This is especially true in view of the irresolvable mystery of the person of Jesus Christ who exists in this union of God and humanity.

Second, we see in Barth's thinking not simply the being of Jesus Christ as the God-man, but his being as *event* in the union of two natures. That is, in the person of Jesus Christ is made manifest the action of God in his movement toward humanity as an act of free grace. In my view Barth is not seeking to contradict (or even correct) the Chalcedonian language of the two natures. Rather, he seeks a more precise understanding of what it means to say Jesus Christ fully embodies very God and very man in his being. That being said, Barth understands the *anhypostasis* and *enhypostasis* of Christ's human nature to undergird his insistence that the person of Jesus Christ must not be viewed statically in his being as the God-man, but dynamically in the event of God's movement of grace towards humanity.

Barth's Appropriation of *Anhypostasis* and *Enhypostasis* with a View to Chalcedon

Christ's Assumption of Human Nature

The dynamic of *anhypostasis* and *enhypostasis* creates in Barth's Christology an ontological precision that moves beyond the *static* definition of Chalcedon's two natures, where the humanity of Christ exists as a fluid movement of God's revelation in taking human essence to himself in the event of God's

22. Ibid.

reconciliation with humanity.[23] This is the exaltation of humanity in Jesus Christ as the Son of Man—the revelation of God made manifest in Jesus Christ as event. For Barth, the exaltation of humanity in Christ is not contrived humanity, nor humanity that we cannot understand as humanity, but the "human nature" of humanity, which for Barth simply means . . . "that which makes a man man as distinct from God, angel or animal, his specific creatureliness, his *humanitas*."[24]

With Chalcedon's definition of the two natures in the foreground, and the dynamic of *anhypostasis* and *enhypostasis* in the background, Barth explains that the human nature assumed by Christ is the same human nature (even human nature stamped by sin) that is enjoined to all created humanity. This is *real* human nature that the Son of God assumes to himself.[25] This is adamic human nature that is brought into union with the Logos necessary for the mediator of reconciliation. Barth's conceptual language of *anhypostasis* and *enhypostasis* is quite clear and explains how the Logos assumes to himself sinful human nature (*that which is not real*), and makes that hu-

---

23. Hans Vium Mikkelsen suggests that at first glance Barth's Christology appears to be very orthodox in both form and content, and is structured according to Chalcedon's distinction between the two natures of Christ. Mikkelsen further argues, however, that Barth revitalizes this pattern that reformulates Chalcedon in such a radical way that it can no longer be claimed as a Christology that is a "simple" extrapolation of the tradition. See Mikkelsen, *Reconciled Humanity*, 148.

24. Barth, *CD* IV/2, 26. With respect to the elements of reconciliation in Barth's theology, Bruce Marshall identifies three elements of significance for salvation: 1) descriptions of Jesus Christ as a particular person; 2) characteristics of the event of reconciliation that are applied to Jesus; and 3) descriptions of the immediate action and presence of God in the person of Jesus Christ made manifest in the incarnation. Marshall goes on to argue that in describing Jesus as "The Lord as Servant" or "The Servant as Lord" or "The True Witness" Barth is not using identifying descriptions of Jesus Christ. That is, these descriptions still lack the kind of descriptive uniqueness to identify a particular person. See Marshall, *Christology in Conflict*, 121. Barth of course would disagree with this conclusion given the simple fact that the particular person (i.e., humanity) of Jesus Christ cannot be understood, or described, outside its union with the divine Logos in whose particular existence he enjoys as *anhypostasis* and *enhypostasis* in this union.

25. Berkouwer categorizes Barth as an emphatic defender of the impersonal human nature of Christ, and raises the question "whether in the confession of the "vere deus, very homo," and in our theological reflection on it, are we confronted by the doctrine of the 'anhypostasy?'" However, Berkouwer recognizes that Barth understands the human nature of Christ to exist in and through the Word, and concludes that by means of the "anhypostasy" Barth wants to resist the danger of Ebionitism which proceeds from the personality, the apotheosis, of a man who so impressed people that they cry out "He is God." Therefore, according to Barth, the point at issue is not at all a form of Docetism, but is a rejection of an abstract, isolated existence of the man Jesus of Nazareth. See Berkouwer, *The Person of Christ*, 309.

man nature *reality* by virtue of its union with the Son of Man. This certainly points back to Barth's understanding of Jesus Christ as the first Adam, as the genuine human being. This is foundational to Barth's understanding of the christological concept of "*vere Deus* which declares the equality of Jesus Christ with God, but with an explanation of the *vere homo* which declares His equality with us."[26]

> By "human nature," however, we have also to understand the "flesh," human nature as it is determined and stamped by human sin, the corrupt and perverted human nature which stands in eternal jeopardy and has fallen a victim, not only to dying, but to death, to perishing. It is human nature as characterized in this way, adamic human nature, that the Son of God assumed when He became man, and it is as the bearer of this human nature that He was and is the Mediator and Reconciler between God and us. Jesus Christ was and is very man in this twofold sense. The answer is both right and necessary. It is right as a description of the likeness between the humanity of Christ and that of other men. It is necessary as the delimitation which we have to make with this description against every kind of docetic Christology, in which His likeness with us is either crudely or cunningly denied. His humanity is made a mere appearance, and His deity is therefore dissolved into a mere idea, and the atonement made in Him into a philosophical theory or myth. Every sound christological discussion will necessarily start not only with an explanation of the *vere Deus* which declares the equality of Jesus Christ with God, but with an explanation of the *vere homo* which declares His equality with us. And it will always have to keep this at the back of its mind, and take it into the strictest account in the later development of the doctrine.[27]

Barth argues: how can Christ be the true mediator of reconciliation for sinful humanity if he does not himself share in the same sinful flesh? Even so, Barth also argues as Jesus existed in sinful human nature he did not commit any act of sin during his life-time. In this dialectical sense Jesus Christ must be understood as existing both in the likeness of sinful human flesh, and not in the likeness of sinful flesh. "But if we keep to the particular humanity in which Jesus Christ gives Himself to be known, we must first make the formal differentiation that it is characterized by the fact that it is both completely like and yet also completely unlike that of all other men."[28]

26. Barth, *CD* IV/2, 26.

27. Ibid., 25–26.

28. Barth, *CD* IV/2, 27.

Like us as our brother, Jesus is also unlike us in the human nature that he assumes. He is like us in our creaturely form and its determination by sin and death in our opposition to God. This is the form of humanity that has fallen away from God, which exists under the wrath of God as adamic humanity. This is the situation of Christ's humanity—who as the good and genuine creature of God—is the flesh that the Son of God made his own when he became human essence. In this way Christ is very man in this contradiction of human existence. Otherwise, he would not be like we are in this totality, and he could not be our Lord and savior as our head.[29]

> But the fact that He is not only *a* true man, but *the* true man [der wahre Mensch], is not exhausted by His likeness with all other men. He is not only completely like us, but completely unlike us—and it is only when we add this complementary truth that we realise the full meaning of the *vere homo* as it applies to Him. But the unlikeness consists in what must necessarily become, and has become, of "human nature" when He assumed it in likeness with us, of flesh when it became His. It relates to the particularity of the history which took place when He became man, and still takes place as He, the Son of God, is man.[30]

Barth understands Jesus to be like us as our brother in a dialectic relationship with us. He is totally different from us by the fact that in the history of his human existence there also took place an "exaltation of the humanity which as His and ours is the same."[31] Barth goes on to explain that while Jesus Christ shares our human essence, he does so on a higher level, which dialectically means that while his humanity is like ours, it is also not like ours.[32] "It means the history of the placing of the humanity common to Him and us on a higher level, on which it becomes and is completely unlike ours even in its complete likeness—distinct from ours, not only in degree but in principle, not only quantitatively but qualitatively,

---

29. Ibid.

30. Ibid; *KD* IV/2, 28.

31. Ibid., 28.

32. Dietrich Bonhoeffer sounds a very similar chord with Barth here with respect to Jesus Christ as the new humanity. "Jesus Christ *pro me* is pioneer, head and firstborn of the brethren who follow him. This pro me is thus related to the historicity of Jesus . . . Jesus Christ is for his brethren by standing in their place. Christ stands for his new humanity before God. But if that is the case, he is the new humanity. Because he acts as the new humanity, it is in him and he is in it. Because the new humanity is in him, God is gracious towards it in him." Bonhoeffer, *Christ the Center*, 48–49.

He confronts us in this unlikeness because and as He is the Son of God and man as such, like us as such."[33]

But Barth goes further. He explains that as the Son of God—the divine subject humiliated himself in becoming humanity. And in the same action—this humanity was exalted as the Son of Man in this indissoluble union.[34] "As this divine subject which became a man—humiliating Himself as such—He exists in a history which cannot be that of any other man. What else can the Son of God who humbled Himself as man become and be but the Son of Man who is not divinised but exalted [erhöhte] to the side of God? What else can the Lord who became a servant become and be but the servant who became a Lord? This is the secret of the humanity of Jesus Christ which has no parallel at all in ours. This is the basis and power of the atonement made in Him on this side—as it is seen below from man."[35] Barth emphasizes here that the divine being of Jesus Christ, the Lord as servant who exists as *homoousia* with the Father, was sent by the Father to this world of humanity. And he took to himself the lowliness of humanity in his obedience to the Father as Jesus of Nazareth. Ontologically speaking (and in view to the Chalcedon definition of *homoousia*), Jesus Christ manifests both the humiliation of deity as the Son of God, and the exaltation of humanity as the Son of Man, without distinction in time or event.[36] As we have already shown, this marked the distinction of Jesus Christ as the mediator of reconciliation—the keeper of God's covenant as very God and very man. This in turn prepared the way for developing the correlation between the humanity of Christ with the Chalcedon definition of the two natures based upon the ontology of *anhypostasis* and *enhypostasis*.

33. Barth, *CD* IV/2, 28.

34. Barth emphasizes that as the Son of Man, this exaltation of humanity is made manifest in Jesus Christ. Barth can now clearly emphasize the exaltation of the humanity of Christ based upon the coalescence of humility and exaltation revealed in Jesus Christ as the mediator of reconciliation.

35. Barth, *CD* IV/2, 28; *KD* IV/2, 29.

36. Karl Barth understood the exaltation of humanity to also apply very personally to believers in Christ. In his well known sermons entitled *Deliverance to the Captives*, which were primarily preached at the prison at Basel, Barth does not hesitate to express the "freedom" enjoyed by those who experience the reality of the promise of Christ: "Nevertheless I am continually [with thee]." Barth encourages his listeners "Do you realize that the Bible is a *book of freedom*, and that divine worship is a *celebration of freedom*?" . . . This is what happens to us when we leave behind the "with myself" and break through to the conviction: "nevertheless I am continually *with thee*. What kind of a 'thou' is this? Is it a man? Yes indeed, someone with a human face, a human body, human hands and a human language. One whose heart bears sorrows—not simply his own, but the sorrows of the whole world. One who takes our sin and our misery upon himself and away from us." Karl Barth, *Deliverance to the Captives*, 16–17.

He is in our lowliness what He is in His majesty (and what He can be also in our lowliness because His majesty is also lowliness). He is as man, as the man who is obedient in humility, Jesus of Nazareth, what He is as God (and what He can be also as man because He is it as God in this mode of divine being). That is the true deity of Jesus Christ, obedient in humility, in its unity and equality, its *homoousia*, with the deity of the One who sent Him and to whom He is obedient.[37]

Barth now addresses the ontological implications of what it means for the eternal Logos to assume to himself the nature of humanity. That is, as the incarnate Logos in whose existence as the Son of God became the existence of humanity, we do not have "two existing side by side or even within one another." Rather, Barth insists that there is only one God the Son. There is no one and nothing that exists either alongside or in him.[38] This is the dialectical union of divine essence and human essence in the Son of God.

But this one exists, not only in His divine, but also in human being and essence, in our nature and kind. He exists, not only like the Father and the Holy Ghost as God, but in fulfillment of that act of humility also as man [im Vollzug jener Demutstat auch als Mensch], one man, this man. The Son of God becomes and is as men become and are. He exists, not only inconceivably as God, but also conceivably as a man; not only above the world, but also in the world, and of the world; not only in a heavenly and invisible, but in an earthly and visible form. He becomes and is, He exists—we cannot avoid this statement; to do so would be the worst kind of Docetism—and objective actuality.[39]

It is the actualized union of divinity and humanity that occupies Barth's thinking here. In view of the "older dogmatics" Barth notes that the *unio hypostatica* was also referred to as the *unio personalis* or *immediata*, and played a key role in the classical doctrine of the incarnation in all the great

---

37. Barth, *CD* IV/1, 204. Barth argues that the "older dogmatics" understood that the Son of God "really condescended to us and became like us, one of us, and took our place to do for us what only God could do for us, by assuming our "human nature," by existing in it and therefore as a man like ourselves, by dying and rising again, so that, placed as one of us at the right hand of God the Father. He became and is and will be to all eternity the Mediator between God and us men. By the "human nature" in which He who is very God is also very man we have to understand the same historical life as our own, the same creaturely mode of existence as an individually distinct unity of soul and body in a fixed time between birth and death, in the same orientation to God and fellowman." Barth, *CD* IV/2, 25.

38. Ibid., 50.

39. Barth, *CD* IV/2, 50; *KD* IV/2, 53.

confessions. Moreover, Barth takes notice here of the *communio naturarum*, the communion of the divine and human essence in Jesus Christ without change and admixture, and without cleavage and separation. But it is the *unio hypostatica* that takes precedence in Barth's thinking with a clear view towards the *anhypostasis* and *enhypostasis* of Christ's human nature, which remains the ontological grounding for such a union. At bottom, Barth is concerned with the union "made by God in the hypostasis (the mode of existence)" of the Son of God and the man Jesus of Nazareth.[40]

> But however we may understand and expound these points in detail, they all rest on the "hypostatic" union, i.e., the union made by God in the hypostasis (the mode of existence) of the Son. They all rest on the direct unity of existence of the Son of God and the man Jesus of Nazareth. And this is produced by the fact that in Himself this One raises up to actuality, and maintains in actuality, the possibility of a form of human being and existence present in the existence of the one elect Israel and the one elect Mary. He does this by causing His own divine existence to be the existence of the man Jesus.[41]

Therefore, with respect to an understanding of the *unio immediata* (i.e., *unio hypostatica*), which includes a *communio naturarum*, Barth argues that such an expression of this union "does not remove or alter either the divine essence of the Logos or the human essence existing by Him and in Him." This is the centrality of the divine-human actuality in Jesus Christ.[42] Barth distinguishes the *unio hypostatica* from all other unifications and unions, and must therefore be understood in its utter uniqueness; that is, it is *sui generis*, which can only be understood in terms of itself.[43] As such, Barth notes that this union of divine essence with human essence cannot be understood as an analogy to the triune union of the Father, Son and Holy Spirit in the one essence of God.[44] This is an important distinction because the union of divinity and humanity in Jesus Christ is not a *unio coessentialis* that consists in a twofold existence of the same being.[45] This must be true

40. Ibid., 51.

41. Ibid.

42. Ibid.

43. Barth makes specific reference to Heinrich Heppe's *Reformed Dogmatics*, from which he develops the unio hypostatica in this context, but with the caveat that "I am not slavishly bound to it in detail." Barth, *CD* IV/2, 52.

44. See Benjamin Leslie on the objectivity of God and human subjectivity in Barth's Trinitarian theology, Leslie, *Trinitarian Hermeneutics*, 228.

45. See Colin Gunton on Barth's understanding of the transcendence of God. Gunton, "The triune God and the freedom of the creature," 48.

because the divine essence is superior to the human essence that it assumes to itself in Jesus Christ. "It is the unity of the one existence [Einheit der einen Existenz] of the Son of God with the human being and essence which does not exist without Him. Above all, although the Son is equal with God the Father and God the Holy Ghost, He is not of equal being and essence with the humanity assumed by Him."[46]

This is the foundational point for Barth in understanding the union of divine and human essence in Jesus Christ; that the "divine humanity of Jesus Christ is not a relationship between two equal or even similar partners." This is a union based upon the mercy of God demonstrated by his inconceivable condescension in turning towards the antithetical character of humanity by becoming real humanity in Jesus of Nazareth.[47] Moreover, because this union of divinity and humanity is not one of a *unio essentialis* (as Barth clearly defends in the *Calvinistic Extra*), Barth goes so far as to ask whether the incarnation of God in Jesus Christ is not in fact surpassed by his ongoing providential care which he never relinquishes. "Is it really anything more than one event within the general *concursus divinus*?"[48] Barth's answer is that as *enhypostasis*, the humanity of Christ is sharply differentiated from the divinity of Jesus Christ through which God maintains and rules the world in virtue of his creative action as God. He therefore maintains his own existence in relation to the world, and the world in relation to God.[49] "It is one thing that God is present in and with everything that is and occurs, that in Him we live and move and have our being (Acts 17:28), but it is quite another that He Himself became and is man. Even this union and unity cannot therefore be compared or exchanged with the *unio personalis* in Jesus Christ."[50]

For Barth, the union of divinity and humanity must not be understood as an analogy—as in the union of two people that presupposes two self-existent beings. Such an analogy is impossible because the union of the Logos with humanity is also defined as *anhypostasis*.[51] As the one who is both creator and Lord of heaven and earth, the Son of God adds to his divine existence human existence with the expressed purpose to bridge the antitheses between God and humanity as the mediator between God

---

46. Barth, *CD* IV/2, 52; *KD* IV/2, 56.

47. Ibid. See Robert Jensen on Barth and the Triune God's free choice in the incarnate Son. See Jenson, *Systematic Theology*, 1:140.

48. Barth, *CD* III/3, 49.

49. Barth, *CD* IV/2, 52–53.

50. Ibid.

51. Ibid.

and humanity.[52] This is the movement of God in the Word becoming flesh—in the *egeneto*. This is the event of his movement towards humanity through his union with humanity in Jesus of Nazareth as *anhypostasis* and *enhypostasis*,[53] where fallen (and false) human essence—which could only point to true and real human essence—now becomes true and real human essence as the Son of Man.[54]

Barth draws a careful distinction here between the unity of God with humanity in Jesus Christ in correspondence with the *unio mystica*; that is, the presence of grace where God gives himself to each individual, or assumes

---

52. Ibid., 54.

53. Graham Ward recognizes Barth's innovation of the "dual formula," and the important theological consequences of this formulation, and argues that for Barth, Jesus Christ is described primarily as a *unio personalis sive hypostica* and only secondarily as a *unio naturarum* (*CD* I/2:162). Ward identifies here a hierarchy of descriptions—primary and secondary—that allows not only for the positive teaching of the *enhypostasis* but also for the negative teaching of the *anhypostasis*. Ward argues that *anhypostasis* safeguards two theological axioms for Barth: "first, the utter uniqueness of this unity and, second, the lack of a point of contact between God and human beings in creation." Therefore, *anhypostasis* accords emphasis to a *unio personalis sive hypostica* rather than a unio naturarum. Ward suggests that *anhypostasis* withdraws the Godhead deep into its own mystery; whereas, *enhypostasis* speaks of an indwelling human being in Christ similar to the reality that all things exist in and through Christ. This dual formula and the distinction between primary and secondary aspects is important for Barth because *enhypostasis* negates any suggestion of a *communis participatio*, which Barth sees as the Lutheran error in Christology. As such, "does not this give us a kind of reciprocal relation between Creator and creature?" (*CD* I/2:164). Ward argues that there is a wide range of distinctions to be made between "reciprocity" and "relation" (i.e., relation between Creator and creatures without that being reciprocal (understood as symmetrical). Ward concludes that Barth's "inability to think through an asymmetrical relation that would bind more closely a unio personalis sive hypostica with a unio naturarum—Barth's modern and uncritical construal of "nature"—forestalls such an exploration. As such the work of Christ cannot be characterized in terms of the ordinary human operations of the world—in politics, economics, social and cultural milieu, his friends, his family, his enemies, his admirers. Christ becomes the perfect expression of Cartesian subjectivity: autonomous, self-determining, self-defining, the atomized subject of a number of distinct properties or predicates; as Barth himself puts it, the 'espistemological principle.'" (*CD* IV/1:21) Ward, *Christ and Culture*, 9–12. Despite Ward's argument against Barth's denial of distinctions to be made between "reciprocity" and "relation," I argue that Barth would certainly not characterize the humanity of Christ as not a being of ordinary human operations of the world.

54. Barth states that: "Redemption through righteousness has not only happened; because it has happened, it has also become manifest and effective. God's work was also God's Word. In acting, God also spoke. But God's Word is a creative Word which bears fruit. And its first fruit is that it finds witnesses, a witnessing people . . . In this people who can understand their existence only in the Word of God, redemption through righteousness becomes provisionally and relatively but most effectively an event and recognizable as such." Barth, *Heidelberg Catechism for Today*, 51.

the individual into unity with himself as part of the Christian experience and relationship. Barth understands that such a correspondence actually inverts the relationship between the Christian and Christ. Therefore, the believer's relationship to Christ is not a repetition of the being of God in Jesus Christ that corresponds to our knowing the being of God in Jesus Christ.[55] Such thinking may suggest that the relationship between the *unio hypostatica* and the *unio mystica* may be reversed, where the unio mystica may be understood as the basic phenomenon and the unio hypostatica in Jesus as the secondary.[56]

Barth argues that "Paul himself did not say that God lives in me, but Christ." The Christian therefore does not claim the fullness of the union of God for his own experience, but that "other," the mediator, Jesus Christ, in whom it has taken place for him. This understanding differentiates the giver and gift of grace from the Christian as the recipient and its outworking in the Christian's life. Barth's argument draws to conclusion a material insight that he describes as having decisive importance. "The fact that the existence of God became and is also in His Son the existence of a man—the unio hypostatica as the basic form of the Christ-event—seems to dispense with formal analogies altogether, according to the general drift of our discussion."[57]

In effect Barth shifts the Chalcedon argument of the *unio hypostatica* from one of strict *being* to one of *being* and *event* made manifest in the revelation of God in Jesus Christ. As being and event the incarnation of Jesus Christ by definition supersedes all earthly analogies in his direct revelation of God. In other words, there is no earthly relational analogy that corresponds to the *anhypostasis* and *enhypostasis* of the human nature that Christ assumes to himself in the event of his revelation.

> It was obvious that in Jesus Christ we have to do with an event
> and being [Geschehen und Sein] which, as the direct revelation
> of God, not only speaks for itself, but speaks also for its own
> uniqueness, i.e., for the fact that it is analogous only to itself

---

55. Barth argues against Donald Baillie (*God was in Christ*) and Baillie's attempt to formulate a new interpretation of the Chalcedonian definition. With respect to Gal 2:20 "Nevertheless I live; yet not I, but Christ lives in me" Barth understands Baillie to argue that it is not merely a statement about the being of the apostle or Christian, but it "offers a *schema* for the knowledge of Jesus Christ Himself." Barth argues that this is not a new discovery, but is in fact the secret *via regia* of all Neo-Protestant Christology, except that "it is not always pressed forward from this point to the Chalcedonian definition." Taken to its logical conclusion Barth suggests that Baillie's argument moves to interpret Christ in light of the Christian rather than the Christian in the light of Christ. See Barth, *CD* IV/2, 55–57.

56. Barth, *CD* IV/2, 55–56.

57. Barth, *CD* IV/2, 57.

and can be understood only in terms of itself . . . But we cannot really know Jesus Christ without realising from the very outset the futility of this search for analogies, and the inadequacy of all analogies to His own becoming and being.[58]

Furthermore, Christ is the head of his church which manifests the form of his earthly body.[59] And as his church, this people exist as Christ's "earthly-historical" form of existence.[60] Although there is no earthly analogy for these concepts, Barth draws upon a heavenly/earthly analogy of the church and its union to Christ. That is, Barth employs the ontology of *anhypostasis* and *enhypostasis* to express the relationship of the church (in human essence) to that of its head (in divine essence). In this relationship the church does not exist independently from its head, nor is it of the same essence as its head, but it exists in virtue of its union with its head—in the *existence* of Christ.[61] It is in the *anhypostasis* and *enhypostasis* relationship of the church with its head; in Christ, which in fact determines the reality of his church.[62]

> It is of human essence—for the Church is not of divine essence like its Head. But it does not exist in independence of Him. It is not itself the Head, nor does it become such. But it exists (ανυποστατος and ενυποστατος) in and in virtue of His existence.[63]

58. Barth, *CD* IV/2, 58; *KD* IV/2, 62.

59. Barth takes quite seriously the relationship between Jesus Christ and his church. That is, in his humanity Jesus Christ became indissolubly united to his church as its head and source of being. For Barth, one could not speak of the Christian Church and not understand and describe it as "the living congregation of the living Lord Jesus Christ." Barth, "The Church: The Living Congregation of the Living Lord Jesus Christ," 61.

60. Barth, *CD* IV/2, 59.

61. Michael Welker argues that for Barth, the church is joined to Christ through his work of reconciliation through the power of the Holy Spirit. In other words, God awakens and gathers the church to himself by the power of the Holy Spirit, which is realized in its union with Christ. See Welker, "Karl Barths und Dietrich Bonhoeffer Beiträge zur zukünftigen Ekklesiologie," 120–137.

62. Alister McGrath argues that the life, work, and doctrine of the church are totally dependent upon this presupposition: it is through Christ that she proclaims that true and authentic reconciliation with God as a present reality for those within the Church. "The Christian faith and the Christian church alike stand or fall with the authenticity of the proclamation that God has established a new relationship between Himself and sinful man, and the life of faith stands or falls with the knowledge of the present actuality of this relationship." McGrath, "Justification and Christology," 46.

63. Barth, CD IV/2, 59.

It is the antithesis of the heavenly and the earthly—united together in Jesus Christ—which emerges as the fundamental principle for Barth in the context of Chalcedon.[64] The material point is that divine essence alone is the subject in the event of this union. "It is apparent at once that divine and human cannot be united as the essence of the one and the same subject." For Barth, regardless of how we may define divine and human essence, we do violence to either one or the other if we do not define them with a clear distinction—even antithesis. This must be true despite Barth's regard for the "original divine reference of human essence." Therefore, when we say that in the being of Jesus Christ exist the union of divine and human essence, we speak of the union of that which, by definition, cannot be united.[65]

Therefore, in the union of divinity and humanity in Jesus Christ is actualized the assumption of human essence by the Son of God while maintaining his own divine essence. This means that Jesus Christ exists as the Son of God while also participating in human essence, and he exists as the Son of Man while also participating in the divine essence of the Son of God. On both sides there is a genuine and true participation. And as such, Barth can say that the divine essence of the Son of God "gives to the human essence of Jesus of Nazareth a part in His own divine essence as the eternal Son" who remains co-equal with the Father and the Holy Spirit in the God-head.[66] This is the grace of God made manifest in Jesus of Nazareth—in the *anhypostasis* and *enhypostasis* of human essence, which is exalted through its union with divine essence in the event of Jesus Christ. In the act of God the Son, God brings into union divinity and humanity in his being as very God and very man. Barth emphasizes that in Jesus Christ is not simply found a unity, but a union of two-sided participation in the *communio naturarum*.[67]

> In the one Subject Jesus Christ divine and human essence is united, but it is not one and the same. This would presuppose one of three things: that God had ceased to be God and changed Himself into a man; that man had ceased to be man and become God (if anything, an even more dreadful thought); or (worst of all) that there had been formed of divine and human essence a third and middle thing, neither God not man.[68]

64. As Michael Welker notes, Barth's theological grounding is based upon the *movement* of God's revelation and the foundation of faith's orientation. Because God is in heaven, we are to expect God's action, God's engagement in the reality of our lives "from above, straight down from above." Welker, Creation and Reality, 34.

65. Barth, *CD* IV/2, 61.

66. Ibid., 62.

67. Ibid., 63.

68. Ibid.

Barth argues that according to the witness of Scripture, the actuality of Jesus Christ is realized as both God and humanity together in a true and genuine union. This is a union without destruction of either the one or the other—as the reconciler and mediator between God and humanity—as the one who restores and fulfills the covenant instituted by God with his human creation.[69] As the mediator of the covenant, however, the human essence of Christ is not to be understood as the subject here. The human essence is not an individual possibility which has existence and became; that has actuality in and by itself. How, then, could it be the subject?[70] Nor can divine nature—divine essence—Godhead as such, be considered as the subject of atonement and incarnation because he exists in and with the existence of the Father, Son and Holy Spirit as the common predicate of the triune subject in its modes of existence. Moreover, it is only in the modes of his being that he can be known and expressed in relation to himself. This one God, who exists in the modes of Father, Son and Holy Spirit, is the divine subject who carries and determines divine essence, and not conversely. Barth argues that in John 1:14 we are not told that the Godhead, the divine nature, became flesh, but the divine Logos becomes flesh. He is the subject in and with his divine essence who exists and is actual God the Son.[71]

> That is why it says that He, the Son, the Word became flesh. It is only as this happens in the act of this Subject, that there takes place this union of divine and human essence. And all that we have seen concerning this union—the two-sided participation of the divine and human essence, the genuineness of both even in the conjunction, but also the reality of the union as such—in short the whole doctrine of the two natures in the strict sense depends on this primary and proper union and unity as it is described in John 1:14.[72]

It is in this sense that Barth rejects the notion that the person of Jesus Christ is constituted in two natures defined as divine and human. For Barth, the "doctrine of the two natures" cannot stand on its own as a true statement. "Its whole secret is the secret of John 1:14—the central saying by which it is described. Whatever we may have to say about the union of the two natures can only be a commentary on this central saying. Neither of the two natures counts as such, because neither exists and is actual as such. Only the Son of God counts, He who adds human essence to His

69. Ibid.
70. Barth, CD IV/2, 65.
71. Ibid., 65–66.
72. Ibid.

divine essence thus giving it existence and uniting both in Himself. In Him, and Him alone, they were and are united."[73] For Barth, the emphasis of the incarnation must fall conceptually on the divine subject as the Son of God, which gives precedence to the doctrine of the *hypostatica unio* over the *communio naturarum*. However, the question must be raised: is Barth using a minimalist view of the *hypostatical unio* with a contradictory view towards Chalcedon when expressing Jesus Christ as the union of very God and very man, rather one person with two natures?[74] I argue that Barth is not expressing the union of the divine Logos with humanity in a way that contradicts the Chalcedon definition, and certainly not with a minimalist view towards Chalcedon. What we see here in Barth is his emphatic defense of the incarnation that must be understood in light of the revelation of God in Jesus Christ—*as event*. This defines in a nutshell the essence of how Barth understands the revelation of Jesus Christ who in his being not only reveals the Godhead, but acts on behalf of the Godhead.[75] As the Son of God he is the divine subject who moves towards humanity by taking true humanity to himself; humanity that is—and must be—*anhypostasis* and *enhypostasis*. Although he remains unchanged in his divine essence in union with the Father and the Holy Spirit, the Logos has brought human essence into union with himself. The divine Son of God is always the subject of this union, and the human essence that he assumed to himself is always the object of this union. And it is the *anhypostasis* and *enhypostasis* of Christ's humanity that serve to regulate and keep separate the divine essence from human essence, while at the same time maintaining their indissoluble union. This is how Barth understands the *hypostatica unio*.

---

73. Barth understands the Godhead as such to be meaningless unless understood in terms of its modus of existence as Father, Son and Holy Spirit. With respect to the human nature of Christ, it too becomes meaningless absent its union with the divine essence in the Logos. The significance of the *anhypostasis* and *enhypostasis* is quite evident here. As expressed in John 1:14, it is the Son of God who is the subject in uniting humanity to himself, a humanity that only enjoys reality as the object of this union in the Logos.

74. This is the conclusion drawn by Paul Dafydd Jones.

75. Jones argues that while Barth accepts the importance of Chalcedon with respect to its defense of Christ's divinity, he shows little interest in one of its key conceptual elements, the concept of nature (physis) used to explain Christ as being fully divine and fully human. Instead, he adopts what Jones describes as a "decidedly minimalist alternative;" that is, Christ as *vere Deus vere homo*. Jones recognizes in this "alternative" an indication of Barth's interest in developing a Christological course "beyond Chalcedon" that is based upon the biblical narratives and a highly actualized ontology. See Jones, *Humanity of Christ*, 7.

Chalcedon: In Dialogue with Lutheran
and Reformed Christology

In this context Barth further considers the Chalcedon definition of the two natures of Jesus Christ as *hypostatica unio*—grounded in the *anhypostasis* and *enhypostasis*—in dialogue with Lutheran and Reformed Christology.[76] With respect to Lutheran orthodox *Christology*, Barth argues that their main interest was not so much the central question of the mystery of the hypostatic union, but the resultant (and secondary) mystery of the *communio naturarum* and its consequences; that is, the relationship between Christ's divine and human essence in their mutual participation. As such, the Lutherans were primarily concerned with the mutual participation enclosed in the union of two natures with particular interest in the communication of properties between the divine and human natures. The main concern for the Lutherans was that "the divine triumph over the distinction and antithesis between God and humanity took place directly, and is a fact, in the humanity of Jesus Christ." They emphasized that we cannot experience and know the Godhead as such directly, who can only be experienced and known in the humanity of Jesus Christ.[77] For the Lutherans, the *unio hypostatica* was only a preparatory point that leads to the attainment of the true end—the *communio naturarum*. Furthermore, the person observable in the humanity brought into union with divinity is also the principle in the event of the hypostatic union.[78]

> And obviously there was a desire to maintain the ασυγχυτως and ατρεπτως of Chalcedon, and therefore the genuineness and integrity of the two natures, just as in the Lutheran Eucharistic doctrine the bread did not cease to be bread as it was identical with the body of Christ. Yet this emphasis in Lutheran theology does not fall on this differentiating proviso, on the ασυγχυτως and ατρεπτως, but on the αδιαιρετως and αχωριστως of Chalcedon, on the arctissima et intima περιχωρησις and ενδυασις of the two natures (Quenstedt), on the equations which result from it, as that the Son of God, and therefore God in His divine essence, is this man, the Son of Mary, and above all, conversely,

76. We note here that similar to his dialogue with Lutheran and Reformed orthodoxy with respect to the *Calvinistic Extra* (that is, the essence of divine nature in union with human nature), Barth engages Lutheran and Reformed Christology once again in view of Chalcedon and the essence of human nature in union with the divine nature in Jesus Christ.

77. Barth, *CD* IV/2, 66.

78. Ibid., 67.

that this man the Son of Mary, is the Son of God, and therefore
God in His essence.[79]

Barth further argues that in practice the Lutherans may make statements
about the humanity of Christ that describe the divine only, and not the human essence, which demonstrates their concern for the *communio naturarum*. Moreover, while the Lutherans rejected the Monophysite heresy of
Eutyches which was rejected at Chalcedon, in Barth's view they strongly
rejected Nestorius as they "appropriated the concern of the Alexandrian
theology as purified at Chalcedon."[80]

   In contrast, Barth argues that given the context of Chalcedon the Reformed did not have the same interest in the presence of the divinity in
the humanity of Christ as the Lutherans. Although the Reformed did not
deny the *communio naturarum*, their emphasis was laid upon the fact that
the Word became flesh. In contradistinction to the Lutherans, however, the
Reformed emphasized that the Word became flesh based upon the *unio hypostatica* as the meaning and basis of the *communio naturarum*. The Son of
God is understood as the subject of the incarnation, as the one who creates
and maintains the *communio naturarum* by virtue of his "act of equating
divine and human essence, and not so much upon the consequent equation." For the Reformed, statements about the humanity of Christ must correspond to his existence in divine essence, rather than the human essence he
assumes into unity with his eternal existence.[81]

> And it is obvious that, while they did not question, but sol-
> emnly affirmed the Chalcedonian αδιαιρετως [indivisible]
> and αχωριστως [inseparably], they necessarily took a greater
> interest in the ασυγχυτως [without confusion] and ατρεπτως
> [unchangeable], in the opposition to Eutyches and therefore
> the distinction between the two natures, in their distinctiveness
> even in union, and especially in the continuing distinctiveness
> of the divine essence of the Logos, but consequently in that of
> the human essence united with it as well.[82]

   For the Reformed the emphasis of the incarnation rests upon the sovereignty of the Son of God as the subject, who acts in the free grace God by
taking to himself the flesh of humanity, which is not merged or dissolved in
the humanity that he assumed. Moreover, this one who exists in divine and

79. Ibid.
80. Ibid.
81. Ibid., 67–68.
82. Ibid., 68.

human essence is not to be understood as a neutral *thing*; that is, as a "human essence illuminated and impregnated by divinity." Given the Chalcedon distinction of the two natures, the Reformed looked with a caustic eye to the Lutherans and what they perceived to be the threat of the divinization of the humanity of Christ. Given the backdrop of Chalcedon, the Reformed sought to defend the concern of the School of Antioch without dividing up Jesus Christ into a Son of God and Son of Man.[83]

> They had no desire to seek or see or grasp the overcoming of the opposition between God and man, and therefore the reconciliation of the world with God, elsewhere but in the humanity assumed by God, and therefore in the man Jesus of Nazareth. But to see and grasp it in Him, they tried to direct their true attention to the One who overcame in the overcoming, and to the act of His overcoming—to Jesus of Nazareth as the Christ, the eternal Son of God, and to the act of God which took place and is a fact in Him.[84]

It is in this sense that Barth claims for himself a similar orientation as the Reformed towards the Chalcedon definition of the union of two natures in Jesus Christ. Barth, however, allows himself a caveat in the Lutheran sense with respect to their interest in the *communio naturarum*[85] when he states: "we do not fail to appreciate the attraction of the particular Lutheran interest in the *communio naturarum*, nor do we wish to ignore the concern which underlies it. It is only that the preference ought to be given to the Reformed concern, and the Lutheran taken up afterwards in so far as it shows itself to be justified."[86]

Barth draws to conclusion his historical analysis of Lutheran and Reformed Christology in view of Chalcedon's definition of the two natures with the summary statement that: "as the Son of God became and is man, as He caused His existence to become that of a man, as He united divine and human essence in Himself, He exalted human essence into Himself, and as very God became very man."[87] This is Barth's understanding of the *Christ-event* in history where God himself "became and was and is and will be very man in His Son Jesus of Nazareth, the Son of Man." But the emphasis of this Christ-event—of this homecoming of the Son of Man in this history—is the exaltation of human essence by the fact that "God Himself lent it His

83. Ibid., 68–69.
84. Ibid.
85. Ibid., 69.
86. Ibid.
87. Ibid.

own existence in His Son thus uniting it with His own divine essence."[88] Moreover, this exaltation of human essence is common to all humanity. For Barth, Jesus of Nazareth is humanity as we are; he is our brother.[89]

> But He was and is our first-born Brother. As a man like all men, He was and is the Head of all men. As He became a servant for us, He became our Lord. For in Him, in this man, we have to do with the exaltation of the essence common to all men. In virtue of the fact that He is the Son of God, and therefore of divine and human essence, He is the Son of Man, the true man. Completely like us as a man, He is completely unlike us as the true man. In the essence common to us all, as a man like ourselves, He is completely different. This is His exaltation.[90]

The Mutual Participation of Divinity and Humanity

But how does Barth understand conceptually this union of divine and human essence that is accomplished by the Son of God in his incarnation? How does this mutual participation of divine and human essence take place in and with this union? First, Barth argues that this is not a rigid union like "like two planks lashed or glued together . . . as if each retained its separate identity in this union and the two remained alien in a neutral proximity." But rather, the Son of God—acting as the divine subject—unites in this action each of the two natures without the alteration of their being in this union.[91] "By and in Him the divine acquires a determination of the human,

---

88. John Macken identifies a correspondence in Jesus Christ between the humility of the Son of God and the exaltation of the Son of Man. In this way correspondence not only allows the mutual determination and convergence of Christology and anthropology, but also demonstrates an antithetical parallelism where polar opposites may reflect one another and therefore establish and maintain radical distinctions. Macken explains that this is how Barth sharply distinguishes the humanity of Christ from his divinity (see Macken, *Autonomy Theme in the Church Dogmatics*, 60–61). I would add that we clearly see in Jesus Christ a correspondence, a convergence of humiliation and exaltation that is ontologically accomplished as the human essence of Jesus is taken into union with the eternal Logos as *anhypostasis* and *enhypostasis*. This is always the frame of ontological reference for Barth in this union of divine and human natures.

89. Barth, *CD* IV/2, 69.

90. Ibid. We also note here Barth's clear allusion to Romans 5, and his understanding of Jesus Christ as the first Adam, as true humanity taken up into Jesus Christ.

91. Ibid., 70. Jones marks what I believe is consistently demonstrated in Barth's *Church Dogmatics*, that Barth's interpretation of the New Testament plays a pivotal role in his mature Christology. Jones argues that to fully appreciate Barth's actualistic understanding of the union of divinity and humanity in Christ as the "Word becoming

and the human a determination from the divine. The Son of God takes and has a part in the human essence assumed by Him by giving this a part in His divine essence. And the human essence assumed by Him takes and has a part in His divine by receiving this from Him."[92]

Stated more precisely, Barth argues that this mutual participation of divinity and humanity must be understood as the Son of God who acts in this event.[93] In other words, while his divine essence (shared with the Father and Holy Spirit) and his human essence (*per assumptionem*) are of course real, they can only act as he exists in them.[94]

> He Himself grasps and has and maintains the leadership in what His divine essence is and means for His human, and His human for His divine, in their mutual participation [ihrer beiderseitigen Teilnahme]. He is the norm and limit and criterion in this happening. He is, of course, the One who is of divine essence and assumes human, the Son of God and also the Son of Man. But it is He Himself and not an it, either divine or human. If we keep this clearly before us, it is apparent that the mutual participation of the divine and human essence as it takes place in and by Him does so in a twofold differentiation.[95]

---

flesh" one must "reckon with Barth's exegetical claims." It is the Scriptures that affects and shapes Barth's description of Christ's person and work. See Jones, "Heart of the Matter," 173.

92. Barth, *CD* IV/2, 70.

93. Bruce McCormack clearly points out that for Barth, what God is and what he can do is learned through the "following-after" of his movement into history. That is, what it means to be human must be learned from the history of the man in who human nature is restored into what God intended it to be. In the incarnation of Jesus Christ is made manifest in time the eternal being-in-act. Therefore, the second person of the trinity did not "become" the "Logos as human" at the point of the incarnation. The second person of the trinity (eternally speaking) already has a name, which is Jesus Christ. McCormack argues that in this understanding Barth does not depart from the Chalcedon formula, but has reinterpreted the significance of its central categories in terms of a "historicized" ontology; that is, understanding God's being as a being-in-act. See McCormack, "Ontological Presupposition," 360.

94. Barth, *CD* IV/2, 70. Eberhard Jüngel refers to Barth's understanding of Jesus as the royal man, as the one human being through which God's intention for humankind can be conceived. Furthermore, his royalty does not exclude, but includes all humankind reflected in him. Moreover, Jüngel argues that humanity is the implicit subject of Barth's Christology because it is a reflection of every human being. "Christology is the carefully considered foundation of anthropology in Barth's characteristically christological thought." Jüngel, *Karl Barth*, 128.

95. Barth, *CD* IV/2, 70; *KD* IV/2, 76.

Barth, however, is careful to distinguish this mutual participation of divinity and humanity in Jesus Christ between the 1) participation of Christ's divine essence in his human essence from 2) the participation of his human essence in the divine. That is, Christ's divine essence is that which is originally proper to him; whereas Christ's human essence is adopted by him, and assumed by his divine essence.[96] Their mutual determination therefore remains distinct because: "The determination of His divine essence is *to* His human, and the determination of His human essence *from* His divine. He gives the human essence a part of His divine, and the human essence receives this part in the divine from Him."[97] For Barth *mutual* cannot be understood to mean *interchangeable*. In other words, the relationship between the two natures is not reversible because each has its own role. In this context Barth emphasizes this union is a real history that takes place from "above to below and also from below to above." However, it takes place from above to below first—and only then from below to above—where the coalescence of the self-humiliated Son of God is also the exaltation of humanity. And yet, in this coalescence of humility and exaltation, we see Christ as the subject of this history. For Barth, this is true not simply because the divine and human essence in Christ are different by definition, but because they have a different character in their mutual relationship.

Moreover, when the Son of God becomes humanity he assumes human essence to his own divine essence in becoming Jesus of Nazareth—the Son of Man.[98] "Jesus, the Son of David and Mary, was and is of divine essence as the Son of God, very God, God by nature. The Son of God exists as Jesus exists, and Jesus exists as the Son of God exists. As very man Jesus Himself is the Son of God and therefore of divine essence, God by nature."[99] Barth marks this differentiation in relation to the mutual participation of divine and human essence. That is, the human essence that is assumed by the Son of God, the human essence that Christ unites with his divine essence "became and is divine essence."[100] This human essence, however, is not divinized in this union. "Jesus Christ became and is the Son of Man only because and as the Son of God took human essence and gave it existence

---

96. Ibid., 70–71.

97. Ibid., 71.

98. Ibid., 70–71. Paul Molnar argues that in the incarnation Barth preferred to speak of an assumption of the flesh by the Word of God because it implied that what took place in the incarnation was a direct act of God in history. That is, the Word remained the Word and did not cease to be God while truly becoming flesh. See Molnar, *Incarnation & Resurrection*, 2.

99. Ibid., 71.

100. Ibid.

and actuality in and by Himself. There was and is, therefore, no Son of Man who, conversely, has assumed divine essence in His human essence and thus become the Son of God."[101]

Barth further clarifies that the two elements in this history—the humiliation of Christ as the Son of God and his exaltation as the Son of Man—are not to be understood as a simple correspondence. Although the humiliation of the Son of God means that he became humanity, his exaltation as the Son of Man does not mean that he became God. Barth asks: how could Christ become what he already was from all eternity as the Son of God, and that which he did not cease to be as the Son of Man? He is one and the same as Son of God and Son of Man. However, this does not mean that Christ did not become true humanity or that he became humanity and then ceased to be humanity—exchanging his humanity for, or changing it into divine essence. Otherwise, he did not actually accomplish his humiliation as the Son of God, which would bring into question how he could be the reconciler and mediator. Therefore, the exaltation of the Son of Man who was also the Son of God is not to be understood as the divinization of his human essence in correspondence to his becoming humanity.[102]

> The human essence of the Son of God will always be human essence, although united with His divine essence, and therefore exalted in and by Him, set at the side of the Father, brought into perfect fellowship with Him, filled and directed by the Holy Spirit, and in full harmony with the divine essence common to the Father, Son and Holy Spirit. It will be the humanity of *God*.[103]

This is how Barth understands the twofold differentiation of divine and human essence and their mutual participation in Jesus Christ. The divine essence of the Son of God is wholly that which gives, and the human essence of the Son of Man is that which is exalted to existence and actuality only in and by him.[104] This is the quintessential essence of Barth's understanding of the *anhypostasis* and *enhypostasis* in the human nature of Christ. We cannot look at the two natures of Christ as though they simply existed side by side; that is, a Son of God who is not Son of Man, and a Son of Man who is not the Son of God. We cannot speak of Jesus Christ in words that refer exclusively to his divine or exclusively to his human

101. Ibid.
102. Ibid., 72.
103. Ibid.
104. Ibid.

essence. In the one Jesus Christ belongs everything that is divine essence and everything that is human essence.[105]

Within the enclosure of the hypostatic union, it is the divine nature that illumines and penetrates the human essence so that all the attributes of the divine nature of Jesus Christ may be ascribed to his human nature. Barth makes it clear, however, that this does not involve a destruction or alteration of the human nature. Yet, it does mean that "this nature experiences the additional development (beyond its humanity) of acquiring and having as such all the marks of divinity, of participating directly in the majesty of God, of enjoying in its creatureliness every perfection of the uncreated essence of God."[106] True salvation therefore is realized in Jesus Christ in so far as this takes place and is actualized in him. That is, in his human nature the God-head can directly reveal itself as a new and divine "element of life" that has entered the world of humanity. It is this entrance of divine essence into the world of humanity that directly accomplishes its reconciliation with God in this new and eternal life.[107]

The Exaltation of the Son of Man

In the *communicatio gratiae*—in the mutual participation of divine and human nature that results from the union of the two in Jesus Christ—Barth understands that the basic concept of the one Son of God and Son of Man (the hypostatic union) is not an empty one, but points to the fullness of this union of two natures *in the event of a movement to human essence*. Yet this movement has a twofold character. On the one hand there is God himself as the acting subject in his mode of existence as the Son of God, who is of the one divine essence with the Father and the Holy Spirit. On the other hand there is human essence, which receives the Son of God's existence and actuality. The results of this act of God is that the Son of God also now exists in his being as the Son of Man.[108] As such, what takes place is primarily a determi-

105. Ibid., 74.

106. Ibid., 77.

107. Ibid. This is the consistent theology of Karl Barth that finds its source in the Scripture, and is confessed by Reformed Creeds that "God reveals Himself to man in Jesus Christ" in whom the people of God have a head. He is the Lord Jesus Christ, God and man (God and sinful man) united as one. See Barth, *Knowledge of God and the Service of God*, 57–59.

108. It is the Son of Man who lived in the history of this world that substantiates the revelation of God in time, in his act of reconciliation. As John Webster notes, Barth's most extended treatment of the Christological construal of history is Barth's presentation of Christ's person and work in the Doctrine of Reconciliation. For Barth, this history is "the most actual thing, the sum and substance of God's time with us and for time for God." Webster, "Barth's Christology," 33.

nation of divine essence, not its alteration. This is in fact the election of Jesus Christ.[109] "God does not first elect and determine man but Himself. In His eternal counsel, and then in its execution in time, He determines to address Himself to man, and to do so in such a way that He Himself becomes man. God elects and determines Himself to be the God of man."[110]

Barth understands that the Christ of the Scripture remains immutable in his divine essence, even as he humiliates himself as the Son of Man in his election and determination to exist in divine and human essence in the one Son of God and Son of Man. This is how Christ addresses and directs his divine essence to his human essence.[111] In effect, human essence also becomes the essence of God as he assumes and adopts it in Jesus Christ. In this way the divine essence of Jesus Christ condescends towards human essence with an "open-handed generosity." Even in Jesus Christ it is not itself human essence. But in Jesus Christ it is not without it, but absolutely with it.[112] Moreover, Christ exercises grace by "becoming the Son of Man as the Son of God, and therefore in the strictest, total union of His nature with ours." This is accomplished in the power of his divine nature, which is addressed to human nature in acquiring *this* form. This explains why the participation of the two unions in Jesus Christ is only one-sided—*that of the human in the divine*. Indeed, the first instance is that of the divine in the human where it has its "ultimate depth and unshakable solidity" as a participation of the human in the divine. This is God who bound himself to humanity and must come first because it is the presupposition of the other.[113]

Based therefore upon the presupposition that God has bound himself to humanity in acquiring the form of humanity, Barth asks what does it mean for Christ in the human sphere that "all the fullness of the Godhead dwells in Him bodily."[114] In general terms, Barth answers that it is human essence as determined by the electing grace of God. But, it is also human essence that is confronted by the divine essence in that God willed to be and became humanity as well as God. That is, without becoming divine, the humanity of Christ is an essence that exists in and with God, being adopted, sanctified, and ruled by him. In other words, this is the "exaltation which comes to human essence in the one Jesus Christ."[115]

109. Barth, *CD* IV/2, 84.

110. Ibid.

111. Ibid., 85.

112. Ibid., 87.

113. Ibid.

114. Ibid.

115. Ibid., 88.

For Barth, this exaltation of human essence is expressed in the language of *communicatio idiomatum*, which is more deeply expressed in the *communio naturarum*, but even more deeply expressed in the *unio hypostatica*, on this side of the *communicatio gratiarum*. In this ontological progression we see the precedence that the *unio hypostatica* takes in view of the *anhypostasis* and *enhypostasis* of Christ's human nature. This is the movement of God's grace towards humanity; his willing condescension in the union of divine essence with human essence in Christ. This is the total and exclusive determination of the human nature of Christ by the grace of God. It is the exaltation of Jesus Christ as the Son of Man that follows the humiliation of Christ as the Son of God, which is fulfilled in it.[116] As such, the human essence of Christ as the exalted Son of Man is the same humanity as ours. As the exalted Son of Man—as our head—he remains our brother as the first-born among many brothers. Therefore, the human essence he becomes as the recipient of God's electing grace is not altered in any way. On the contrary, as the recipient of the electing grace of God, the human essence of Christ is affirmed in its exaltation as the true essence of humanity.[117]

> It is genuinely human in the deepest sense to live by the electing grace of God addressed to men. This is how Jesus Christ lives as the Son of Man. In this He is the Mediator between God and us men in the power of His identity with the Son of God and therefore in the power of His divinity. How can it be otherwise? How can this fail to be the supreme thing that may be said of His human essence, and therefore that which also distinguishes Him from all other men?[118]

Barth understands that grace is divine giving and human receiving. It is therefore the grace of God that was actually received by Jesus Christ as the Son of Man, who as the Son of God becomes the determination of his human essence. Furthermore, not only does this one exist as humanity (as does all humanity for their own existence), but this is particularly true for the Son of Man because although he exists as a creature (and therefore because God exists), but also because he exists as God exists.[119] "His existence

116. Ibid.

117. Ibid., 89.

118. Ibid.

119. Ibid., 90. John Webster offers a simple but enlightening insight. Above all, Barth distances himself from apologetic investigation of the *possibility* of Christian dogmatics by referring to some general realm of human piety or some theory of knowledge or ontology. He rejects anything in the way of an extra-theological argument in favor of

as man is identical with the existence of God in His Son. God in His Son becomes man, existing not only as God, but also as man, as this One, as the Son of Man, Jesus of Nazareth. This existence of God as the man Jesus Christ is the particular grace of His origin addressed to human essence in Him."[120]

As the Son of Man his origin and determination is determined by the grace of God alone. The Son of Man is not an abstraction—he is not of himself—but derives entirely from his own divine origin.[121] In all of this Barth makes it clear that the Son of Man finds his ontological bearings as *anhypostasis* and *enhypostasis* in union with the divine nature of Christ.

> In all this we are again describing the *enhypostasis* or *anhypostasis* of the human nature of Jesus Christ. We may well say that this is the sum and root of all grace addressed to Him. Whatever else has still to be said may be traced back to the fact, and depends upon it, that the One who is Jesus Christ is present in human nature is the Son of God, that the Son is present as this man is present, and that this man is none other than the Son. We can and should state this as follows. It is only as the Son of God that Jesus Christ also exists as man, but He does actually exist in this way. As a man, of this human essence, He can be known even by those who do not know Him as the Son of God.[122]

It is the duality of *anhypostasis* and *enhypostasis* that regulates the humanity of Christ by first affirming his humanity as the same humanity as us (yet without committing sin), and secondly by guarding against the divinization of his human essence. "The Son of Man is not deified by the fact that

---

theology. Barth's response to apologetics is not simply a denial of generally available knowledge of God upon which the revelation of Christ is built. Barth is concerned to refute the principle that knowledge can be found in an ontology or anthropology as the basic science of human possibilities. Underlying all this is Barth's theological realism of the ontological supremacy of God in his self-revelation. See Webster, *Barth's Ethics of Reconciliation*, 23–26. Graham Ward argues that for Barth, the Christian community must embrace the "reality and truth of the grace of God addressed to the world in Jesus Christ" (CD IV/3, 704). That is, the Christian community is enjoined to speak to the world the reality of Jesus Christ on one hand, recognizing that he is not a concept that humanity can think out for itself—the problem of antithesis (CD IV/3, 706), but on the other hand, understand that we speak and think like poor heathen no matter how earnestly we imagine that we think or speak of it (the grace of God addressed to the world in Jesus Christ) (CD IV/3, 707). Therefore, with the knowledge of the diastasis for which there is no "real synthesis" the fallible Christian community, as the witness to a better hope, testifies to the word and truth of God—"a new thing in relation to that contradiction" (CD IV/3, 708). Ward, "Possibility for Christian Apologetics," 57.

120. Barth, *CD* IV/2, 90.

121. Ibid., 91.

122. Ibid.

He is also and primarily the Son of God." Moreover, Jesus Christ does not become a fourth mode of being in the Trinity. Rather, he assumes humanity in its full being, just as he enjoys full being as eternal God. "Godhead surrounds this man like a garment, and fills Him as the train of Yahweh filled the temple in Is. 6. This is the determination of His human essence."[123] This is the grace of God—revealed in the action of God—through the being of the Son of Man. "This is a history which in the living Jesus Christ is played out between His human being as the Son of Man and His divine being as he Son of God which He is also and primarily; a history between the Father, and also between the Holy Ghost and Son, who as such is also the Son of Man. How else, then, can this determination of His human essence take place and be seen and understood except as an event?"[124]

Barth further explains that a proper understanding of the *active character* of the existence of Jesus Christ in his unity as "Son of God and Son of Man" recognizes that there is no alteration of his humanity in this union. As the Son of God, Christ fully participates in the unconditional affirmation of the Father and the Holy Ghost (John 3:34), which distinguishes him both qualitatively and quantitatively from all other human beings.[125] The Son of God becomes a guest in this world where he dwells in the flesh of humanity as the eternal Word, and reveals his glory in the exaltation of human essence.[126] "But it is not self-evident that He is adopted for it. This is not something which is in and of itself. He is a creaturely, human and even sinful essence. It is flesh with all the weakness of flesh. It is the electing grace of God—and this is its exaltation from this standpoint—which makes it adapted for this purpose."[127]

---

123. Ibid., 94. Paul Metzger argues that not only did Barth's employment of the *anhypostasis* and *enhypostasis* model set aside the time-eternity dialectic, but it would provide him with categories needed to solve the dilemma of their strict opposition in their dialectic relationship. This establishes the basis for Barth to develop a truly incarnational model of Christology, one that would enable him to "set forth a positive yet dialectical conception of the engagement of God and humanity, and Christ and culture." Metzger, *Word of Christ*, 39.

124. Ibid.

125. Barth, *CD* IV/2, 94–95.

126. Ibid., 96. David Lauber touches on this theme; that in the humanity of Christ, Jesus participates in "the human situation in a form of solidarity." This includes the fallen state of humanity as sinners and as enemies of God. Although Christ committed no sin, he participates in the sin of humanity by taking the place of humanity. Furthermore, it is the uniqueness of Jesus Christ's life and passion that accomplishes the redemptive action wherein we are embraced in Christ's existence. See Lauber, *Barth on the Descent into Hell*, 29.

127. Ibid.

Barth argues that as the human essence of the Son of God, Jesus of Nazareth is empowered by the New Testament concept of the *exousia*, which is imparted to him and exercised by him. Because he is the Son of God, the Son of Man has freedom and is empowered to act by the electing grace of God.[128] Yet, as Barth insists, there is no reason to question the pure humanity of Jesus Christ in relation to this empowering of his human essence.[129]

> It is to Him and not this organ, to His human essence as such, that there is given "all power in heaven and in earth" (Matt 28:18). It does not possess, but it mediates and attests the divine power and authority. It bears and serves it. It is adapted in its function for what the incarnate Word, the Son of God and Son of Man, wills to do, and does actually do, for and to the world as He exists in it, in the human sphere. It is not, therefore, itself a divinely powerful and authoritative essence in which Jesus Christ, very God and very man, the divine Subject existing and acting in the world, makes use of His divine power and authority.[130]

In Jesus of Nazareth is revealed absolute divine power and authority. Omnipotence and divinity, however, are not imputed to the human essence of this man in whose existence and action identify him as true humanity together with the action of true God. The event of this action is the grace of God that comes to human essence. In this event, in its *pure creatureliness* the human essence acquires divine *exousia*; that is, divine power and authority. In the occurrence of this event, in the weakness and particularity of Jesus Christ in his human essence belongs the divine universality. This is the life of Jesus Christ who lives in both divine and human essence. Moreover, in this event the human essence of Jesus Christ acquires divine power and authority to conquer death.[131] Barth explains what Jesus Christ does as the Son of God in virtue of his divine essence, and what he does as the Son of Man in his human essence as *common actualization*, which he does in conjunction and the strictest relationship of the one with the other.[132]

> The divine expresses and reveals itself wholly in the sphere of the human, and the human serves and attests the divine. It is not merely that the goal is the same. The movement to it is also the same. It is determined by two different factors. But it is along the same road. At no point does the difference mean separation.

128. Ibid.
129. Ibid., 98.
130. Ibid.
131. Ibid., 99.
132. Ibid., 115.

Nor are abstractions possible to the one who knows Jesus Christ. There is no place for a dualistic thinking which divides the divine and the human, but only for a historical, which at every point, in and with the humiliation and exaltation of the one Son of God and Son of Man, in and with His being as servant and Lord, is ready to accompany the event of the union of His divine and human essence.[133]

In the divine movement of God that unites divine essence with human essence is found the one will of Jesus Christ. In this man—in the power of Jesus Christ—is the power of the omnipotent God. In the human death and passion of Jesus Christ is found the final depth and self-humiliation of God as he secretly entered and traversed in this world, which ended publicly in the *extremity of misery* prepared for him by God. Yet the glory of Jesus Christ is the exaltation of humanity to God. In the obedience of his human life is his triumph in his work of atonement, which is publicly revealed in his coronation having been resurrected from the dead.[134]

> In the work of the one Jesus Christ everything is at one and the same time, but distinctly, both divine and human. It is this in such a way that it never becomes indistinguishable. Where Jesus Christ is really known, there is no place for a monistic thinking which confuses or reverses the divine and the human. Again, there can be only a historical thinking, for which each factor has its own distinctive character. The divine and the human work together. But even in their common working they are not interchangeable. The divine is still above and the human below. Their relationship is one of genuine action.[135]

We observe here the structural union between God and humanity in Jesus Christ where the divine and the human work together, but are not interchangeable. As *anhypostasis* and *enhypostasis* the human nature has no

133. Ibid.

134. Ibid., 116. I greatly appreciate John Webster's comments with respect to Karl Barth's language of Christ's reconciliation as being a present and real work. That is, throughout the doctrine of reconciliation Barth quietly argues against theological existentialism. For Barth, "questions of the 'realty' and 'meaning' of Jesus are a function of Jesus' presence and activity, not of the historicity of the person of faith." Barth rejected the liberal theological notion that Christological language needs to be supplemented by descriptions of "cognitive, interpretive, or experiential acts." Rather, Barth believed that our knowledge of Jesus Christ is ingrained within his reality as the "risen, ascended, and self-communicative one." More than any other modern theologian Barth shakes himself free from the presupposition that Jesus is past. See Webster, *Barth's Moral Theology*, 128.

135. Barth, *CD* IV/2, 116.

capacity to act upon the Logos. Therefore, the divine Logos must act upon the human nature of Christ in this union. This is the movement of God from above towards humanity in the person of Jesus of Nazareth, which is realized in genuine and historical action.

Conclusion

We start by saying that Karl Barth's thoughtfulness and energetic thinking in his development of the exaltation of the Son of Man is a great theological achievement. It not only provides unique insight into the ontological character of the humanity of Christ, but it also brings to a great theological crescendo Barth's expression of the *anhypostasis* and *enhypostasis* of Christ's human nature. In this context Barth does not shy away from a critique of the Chalcedon definition of the two natures of Christ, and he does so through the ontological lenses of the *anhypostasis* and *enhypostasis*. While Barth recognizes the Chalcedon language to successfully safeguard against the extremes of Alexandria and Antioch, he pursues a path beyond Chalcedon, not as a contradiction, but as a more precise way to understand what it means to say Jesus Christ fully embodies very God and very man in his being. Grounded in the *anhypostasis* and *enhypostasis*, Barth expresses the person of Jesus Christ, not in the static being of very God and very man—but dynamically—in the event of God's movement of grace towards humanity.

But Barth's greatest achievement in this context is his expression of the dynamic of the Son of Man who is brought into union with the Son of God through the revelation of Jesus of Nazareth. Barth uses the backdrop of *anhypostasis* and *enhypostasis* to express the *hypostatic unio* as the ontological grounding for the union of divinity with humanity. Moreover, and interestingly so, Barth also uses *anhypostasis* and *enhypostasis* to express how the body of the church is brought into union with its head, Jesus Christ, to enjoy real subsistence in this union. Barth draws here a heavenly/earthly analogy of the church and its union to Christ. In this way the church of Christ manifests the form of Christ's earthly body (human essence), which does not exist independently from its head. Therefore, its union with Christ as its head (divine essence) determines the real existence of the church, which in Barth's thinking is quite naturally expressed as *anhypostasis* and *enhypostasis*.

6

Beyond Chalcedon

The Significance of Anhypostasis and Enhypostasis in Karl Barth's Christology

Introduction

THUS FAR WE HAVE distinguished between the historical protestant under-standing of *anhypostasis* and *enhypostasis* as autonomous concepts, and Karl Barth's provocative appropriation of these terms as an ontological formula to explain the human nature of Christ in union with the Logos. We have explored Barth's interpretative construal of these concepts as first expressed in the *Göttingen Dogmatics* and then more fully developed in the *Church Dogmatics*. We have considered Barth's development of *anhypostasis* and *enhypostasis* given the political, social, and theological events that emerged during the early to mid-twentieth century and how such events factored in shaping Barth's development of these concepts. We have also analyzed Barth's development of the Word become flesh in Jesus of Nazareth, which flows out of the coalescence of Christ's divine and human natures given the backdrop of the *anhypostasis* and *enhypostasis* formulation. Moreover, we have evaluated how Barth works out his understanding of these concepts within the context of Chalcedon's *static* definition of the union of divine and human natures in Christ, from which Barth transitions to an *active* defini-tion of the union of these two natures.

Given these crucial factors that helped shape Barth's unique adop-tion of *anhypostasis* and *enhypostasis*, we are now able draw out more precisely the *significance* of these concepts as an ontological formulation in Barth's Christology, particularly in view of his understanding of the dynamic union of the eternal Christ with humanity. That is, we are now able to peer more deeply into Barth's understanding of the *Logos in action*, the eternal Word who freely takes to himself the flesh of humanity made manifest in Jesus of Nazareth. But more than this, we can now see more clearly into Barth's development of this movement of the Logos towards humanity to accomplish—in a very tangible form—the ontological union of Jesus Christ with humanity. For Barth, in the *objective* sense, this is a union of Christ with all humanity by virtue of his becoming true humanity. But in another more *subjective* sense, it is Christ's particular union with his church, his community of saints, given the backdrop of God's reconciliation with humanity. Therefore, in view of Barth's Christology that emerges out of his formulation of *anhypostasis* and *enhypostasis*, we now focus our attention on the dynamic relationship between the ontological union of divine and human natures in Christ, and Christ's ontological relationship with his church. As we shall see, one ontological relationship cannot be properly understood without the other.

For Barth, the ontological reality of Jesus Christ's union with his church finds its center in the royal man. And it's as the royal man that the ontological relationship between the human and divine essence in Christ strikes its true mark; that is, in Christ's relationship with his church. As the royal man the eternal Son of God willingly became a human being in all its frailty and humiliation who in turn exalted this humanity in union with his divine essence in the active and overpowering movement in the Word became flesh. With this in view we now push forward our understanding of how Barth's appropriation of *anhypostasis* and *enhypostasis* takes on a tangible Christological/anthropological form in the reconciliation of humanity with God in Jesus Christ—*as the royal man*. We do so in four related aspects of the revelation and being of the royal man. First, we will see how the revelation of the royal man marks the coming of the Kingdom of God in whom the Word of God is spoken, and in whom all humanity is brought into union with him. Second, we will examine the ontological relationship of Jesus Christ as the royal man with his community of believers as h*is church*. Third, we will consider how Barth determines that true humanity can only be understood in the humanity of the royal man. Finally, we will explore Barth's solution to the paradox of Christ's humiliation and exaltation through his development of true sanctification accomplished in the royal man.

The Coming of the Royal Man

As we have shown, Karl Barth rejects any notion that the humiliation and exaltation of Jesus Christ can be separated in time, but are in fact simultaneous events as mediator between God and humanity.[1] Just as the Son of God is humiliated by taking to himself the flesh of humanity, so also the Son of Man—as true humanity—is exalted in this union with the Son of

---

1. Refer to the section in chapter 4, Jesus Christ: Humiliation and Exaltation in Convergence.

God. It is this *true humanity* that Barth develops as the royal man in part II of *The Doctrine of Reconciliation*. I argue that this marks the seminal point of Barth's Christology. It is as the royal man (and in the royal man) that the reconciliation of sinful humanity with a holy God reaches its conclusive movement in the revelation of God as the Word became flesh. This is crucial to understand in Barth's Christology for a number of reasons.

First, it is as the royal man that Barth's ontology of the human nature of Christ comes to light in its brightest form where we see the theological *significance* and *impact* of Barth's unique formulation of the *anhypostasis* and *enhypostasis* emerge with forcefulness. Second, Barth lays down firm theological ground (much in the Reformed tradition) in explaining the problem of sin and its alienation from God. It is in the royal man that true humanity comes upon the scene in Jesus of Nazareth, who by his very presence negates the negation of sin and humanity's alienation from God. And yet, Barth parts ways with Reformed thinking with respect to his understanding of the ontological union that Jesus Christ shares with all humanity as the royal man, as well as his rejection (once again) of the Reformed doctrine of divine election.[2] Third, out of Barth's development of the royal man comes his fuller development of the mode by which the ontological relationship between Christ and His community comes to fruition—*through the power of the Holy Spirit of Christ*. In other words, it is *this* ontological relationship that determines the subjective relationship between Jesus Christ and his people as his church. Fourth, it is in the resurrection of the royal man where Jesus Christ—as true humanity—is fully revealed as true God.

The royal man reveals what it means that Jesus Christ came upon the scene in this world of sinful humanity as the Word became flesh. And it is as

2. With respect to Barth's understanding of Jesus Christ's union with humanity, Adam Neder cites Barth's statement that: "The ontological determination [ontologische Bestimmung] of humanity is grounded in the fact that one man among all others is the man Jesus." Barth, *CD* III/2, 132; *KD* III/2, 158. Neder observes in Barth's thinking here the "irreducible fact of human nature," that Jesus Christ is a human being. Therefore, his fulfillment of the covenant of grace establishes the context within which all human beings exist, which is fundamentally determined by the relationship of lordship and obedience embodied by Jesus Christ. "Thus election, covenant, Christology, anthropology, history, participation, and ontology are all inextricably linked. The essence of human life is to be drawn into the covenant, to exist within the sphere of this relationship. Jesus Christ is himself the relationship of the transcendent Lord and the perfectly obedient servant. The occurrence of this relationship constitutes his history. Therefore, human life is life "in him," life in the history of this relationship." Neder, *Participation in Christ*, 31. As Neder points out, the importance of the ontological relationship between Jesus Christ and humanity in Barth's Christology is unmistakable. We further note here that this ontological relationship in Barth's Christology is grounded in his unique formulation of *anhypostasis* and *enhypostasis*, which provides the necessary basis to determine the reality of this union.

the royal man—true humanity as the Son of Man exalted in its union with the eternal Son of God—that the *anhypostasis* and *enhypostasis* of Christ's human nature find its fullest expression. This is the unrelenting movement of the eternal Son of God who comes to us—who invades the kingdom of this world with the Kingdom of God—and speaks the Word of God in the form of a human being. In this section we will examine this movement in three simultaneous but distinct modes as: 1) The Coming of the Kingdom of God in the Royal Man, 2) The Word of God Spoken Through the Royal Man, and 3) The Union of God with Humanity in the Royal Man.[3]

The Coming of the Kingdom of God in the Royal Man

For Barth, the statement that the Word became flesh marks the invasion of the Kingdom of God into this world of sinful humanity. In other words, God demonstrates his mercy towards humanity in the man Jesus Christ who brings with him the Kingdom of God *as one of us*. And as one of us he looks upon us, and exists with us in the dreadful state of our human condition where he "was on earth as God is in heaven."[4] This coming of the Kingdom of God in the royal man penetrates the veneer of sinful humanity through Christ's proclamation of his Kingdom and the great blessing to humanity that comes with it.[5] This marks an important point in Barth's Christology where the Kingdom of God in Christ emerges "as the basic Word in His proclamation of the Kingdom of God."[6] It is the being of Jesus who brings with him the Kingdom of God, who in himself explains the being and the blessing of humanity. Barth explains that the blessing Jesus pronounces upon human beings "is indeed a matter of their own being." But it is a being born out of the fact that their own being is lighted up (beleuchtet) in a new and different way by the Kingdom of God brought near to them in Jesus

3. As we shall see, Barth distinguishes between the ontological union of Jesus Christ with all humanity and the particular/subjective ontological relationship that Jesus enjoys with his church.

4. Barth, *CD* IV/2, 184.

5. Helmut Gollwitzer observes that the doctrine of the Trinity which Barth developed in the prolegomena of the *Church Dogmatics* is fully developed in the doctrine of reconciliation. In other words, the humanity of God is not God's arbitrary action, but God's self-revelation. That is, "God's being is in becoming" is realized in the "becoming of his kingdom" in Jesus Christ and the emergence of his church. See Gollwitzer, "Kingdom of God and Socialism in the Theology of Karl Barth," 87.

6. Barth, *CD* IV/2, 188. Barth emphasizes here that in the Gospels (particularly the sermons in Matthew and Luke) Jesus strictly uses the word μακαριος in pronouncing the beatitudes.

Christ.[7] Barth's point here is that the being of Jesus as the Kingdom of God come into this world not only brings with him blessing to humanity, but he also explains and interprets the being of humanity, and as such determines and characterises the very essence of human being. In this way our own being is directly related to the Kingdom of God in Jesus Christ.[8] "It is evident that even where the emphasis falls on faith and the hearing and keeping of the Word of God it is primarily a question of the impress made on a man's action, its determination or characterisation."[9]

It is through this movement and ordering of the Kingdom of God that the blessings of the Gospel are realized and enjoyed by human beings. These are μακάριοι (blessed) based upon hearing and seeing something outside themselves. Barth soundly rejects any notion that humanity (in its own being) embodies something excellent (i.e., faith, mercy, etc.) or is able to practice excellence in itself (i.e., peacemaking, unselfishness, etc.). Rather, Jesus declares these people to be μακάριοι, not because they are in themselves, in a vacuum (leeren), something excellent and therefore practice that same excellence, but because with their eyes and ears they see and hear *in Christ* the Kingdom of God (Matt 13:16).[10] In the revelation of Jesus Christ the Kingdom of God confronts humanity in its state of misery with the intent to renew it from its vulnerability and suffering. It is therefore quite clear for Barth why Jesus—as the eternal Word of God—must reveal himself as a sufferer. He is in fact the supreme human sufferer who exists in solidarity with all human beings, who shines the light of the Kingdom of God on this human life, on "the old man." At the same time the blessing that Jesus bestows upon these sufferers in their lives of misery and vulnerability is the Kingdom of God that has come near to them. Therefore, when Jesus declares that the poor are blessed, he makes a *synthetic* rather than an *analytic* statement. In other words, this blessing is the movement from above to that below which typifies the Word of God in action. This is Jesus giving himself as the royal man who brings with him the Kingdom of God and the promise of eternal blessing in his Kingdom.[11] In this way his proclamation and action are one

7. Barth, *CD* IV/2, 189; *KD* IV/2, 210.

8. Within the context of the Kingdom of God, Berkouwer states that Barth clearly emphasizes in his theology the *triumphant* reality of Christianity and the freedom that we enjoy from anxiety and fear. In other words, with the coming of Christ came the elimination of any "competition between Christ and the principalities, between God and the devil." For Barth, all of this underscores the actuality of the triumph of Christ. See Berkouwer, *Triumph of Grace*, 355.

9. Barth, *CD* IV/2, 189.

10. Barth, *CD* IV/2, 189–90; *KD* IV/2, 210.

11. Barth, *CD* IV/2, 191.

in the same, which is realized in the "present (if hidden) impartation of full salvation, total life and perfect joy" because the salvation and joy which now appears in the midst of misery and suffering is resolved in Jesus.[12]

> This man does not only speak. He accomplishes what He says. He makes actual what He declares to be true. He tells in and with the beatitudes that to-day, hear and now, He is for those whom He addresses in this way; that He is their σωτήρ, the One who shows them His powerful mercy, the One who gives them all that is His by giving them Himself . . . And in the fact that He does it he is the royal man, the supreme and most proper image of the invisible God.[13]

The life of the royal man must therefore be understood as historical because "His life *was* His act." Barth argues that this is how the New Testament community looked back on this history. They made no distinction between the person and work of Jesus. They looked upon his completed work as the work of his person and his person as the subject of his work. In this reality is captured historically a dynamic understanding of Jesus in his life act—his coming for the sake of his community. "The totality of His being in its scope for them and the whole world was identical with the totality of His activity."[14]

The historical significance of the royal man, however, is not limited to the human beings he confronts. He came also to confront the nothingness—the evil—that imprisons and takes possession of human creatures. Barth observes the martial like movement of the royal man in his exorcisms, who binds the strong man, so that he may enter into and spoil the strong man's house. Jesus moves toward the root of evil as the stronger man who takes up the battle for humanity. This in fact defines the distinctive warfare of the Kingdom of God where the royal man comes upon the strong man of this world and forces him to yield.[15] In this same sense Jesus moves to action as an offensive militant in *raising people from the dead* as the declaration of his will—as a manifestation of the character of his Kingdom. However, while these are military acts, they are also acts of mercy. Barth argues that according to the Scriptures, the actions of Jesus focus on the reality of human misery, *rather than the cause* of human misery.[16] This is important for

---

12. Ibid., 192.

13. Ibid.

14. Ibid., 193.

15. Barth, *CD* IV/2, 230.

16. Barth, *CD* IV/2, 232.

Barth because the coming of Christ clearly demonstrates the impact of his Kingdom upon all humanity in their state of misery.

With this in view Barth argues that the Reformation, as well as most of Protestant theology before and after the Reformation (following Luther and Calvin), missed this aspect of the gospel—this power to liberate humanity from evil and death. The result was that Protestant orthodoxy became blind to this dimension of the Gospel in the New Testament; that is, its power "as a message of mercifully omnipotent and unconditionally complete liberation from φθορα, death and wrong as the power of evil."[17] For Barth, historical Protestant theology (influenced by Augustine) focused on the problem of repentance rather than its pre-supposition—the Kingdom of God—the grace of God in the revelation of Christ. This focus on repentance emerged out of an anthropological oriented theology that Barth interprets as a moralistic perspective that de-emphasizes the question of humanity itself.[18] Barth concludes that this rather sullen approach of Protestant theology fails to recognize the deprivation of its own doctrine of justification and sanctification by ignoring its radiance, the character of the self-revelation of God in the Son of Man.[19] Barth's paradigm of *anhypostasis* and *anhypostasis* is quite impressive here as the humanity of Christ—which has been raised up into union with the Logos of God—reveals the power and reality of the Kingdom in a historical context. For Barth, it is the obvious movement of God in the revealed Kingdom of God that must take priority and carry the weight of theological orientation. This is the self-revelation of God that emerges from the miracles of Jesus as the freedom of grace made manifest in him.[20]

Barth marks an important connection between the actions of Jesus and the faith of those to whom and among whom they occur. This is important for Barth because the distinctive nature of this connection cannot be ignored if we are to genuinely understand the nature or direction of the

---

17. Ibid., 233.

18. Ibid., 232–33.

19. While we do not argue against Barth's emphasis on the power of the gospel to liberate humanity from evil and death, we wonder at Barth's broad brush view of the Reformation's understanding of this theological point. Berkouwer observes in Barth's theology not so much an over-emphasis of God's grace offered in the gospel, but a de-emphasis on the power of evil (including demonic evil) that Barth neglects subsequent to the coming of the Kingdom of God in Jesus Christ. In other words, sin remains a problem that cannot be ignored, which the Reformers took seriously in their understanding of the antithesis between sin and grace. See Berkouwer, *Triumph of Grace*, 380–381.

20. Barth, *CD* IV/2, 233. Barth concedes that we can at least learn from the Reformers what free grace might be, and therefore learn and perhaps recognise its radical nature revealed in the miracles of Jesus.

miracles of Jesus.[21] Barth emphasizes here that it is not so much the quantity (i.e., faith as a mustard seed) of this faith, but its quality. It is the genuine nature of faith, the kind of faith in which Jesus charges his disciples to preach the Kingdom of God that has drawn near in word and deed.[22] Barth argues that according to the Gospels Jesus acted in an expectation to find this faith—even as a grain of mustard seed—where he would in fact meet with it.[23] We see for example true faith in "Jesus as the King," which Jesus Christ comes to meet with in response to the two blind men who cried out "Jesus, Son of David, have mercy on us," because they recognized "by faith" that Jesus of Nazareth actually is the King of Israel.[24]

Barth further observes in the Gospels the relationship between the characteristic action of those who suffered and the faithful God of Israel who fulfills his promise—in a tangible sense—by working a miracle on their behalf. Barth interprets this as their relationship to Jesus as their deliverer, in whom "the hope of Israel has found its fulfillment." Barth speaks here of the ontological relationship between Jesus and his people even before they exercise faith in him as their healer and Lord. In other words, Barth argues that human beings believe in Christ based upon their relationship with him *as a matter of being*. Therefore, the fact that these who suffered also believed means that they were already in this ontological relationship with Christ—which is primarily a matter of being—and only secondarily a matter of the mind or will. That said, the critical point for Barth is that Jesus recognized them. He found them before they knew him because they already belonged to him as their deliverer. They in turn responded with their own recognition of him as their savior. For Barth, the climax of these miracle passages is the

21. Barth observes in the New Testament and the coming of the Kingdom of God in Jesus Christ an important connection between the actions of Jesus and the faith of those to whom and among whom they occur.

22. Barth emphasizes here that Jesus means this particular faith when he reproves his disciples after he calmed the storm by asking: "Why are ye so fearful? How is it that ye have no faith?" (Mark 4:40). We see this also when Jesus encourages the synagogue ruler: "Be not afraid, only believe" (Mark 5:36). Even more dramatically we see this when Jesus asks the two blind men: "Believe ye that I am able to do this?" and after they reply that they do, he says to them: "According to your faith be it unto you" (Matt 9:28f), and so on. Barth notes here that excepting one occurrence, (Luke 7:50), this faith stands in relation to the working of a miracle. Moreover, in almost every instance this faith is clearly brought into direct connexion with the actual event of the miracle, which appears to be insignificant in appearance and usually is the subject of inquiry or definite demand. However, this is a faith that for all its appearance of insignificance is endued with a specific nature in which there is a prospect of a miracle occurring. See Barth, *CD* IV/2, 233–34.

23. Barth, *CD* IV/2, 234.

24. Ibid., 235.

freedom these people exercised by throwing themselves and their physical need at the feet of Jesus, and therefore (in his person) at the feet of the faithful God of Israel.[25]

> They had the freedom to recognize and confess and claim Him as the One who could save them totally and therefore in this affliction, thus healing them physically, making them whole, restoring to them a normal life, rescuing them from the threatening power of death. He was under no compulsion to do this. But He could do it.[26]

To sum up, Barth argues that Jesus Christ came to the people of Israel in the absolute free grace of God to be present with them *in his being* as their Savior. As the royal man, he brought with him the Kingdom of God as an expression of his pity for them in their belonging to him as sufferers. And for some, because they understood themselves to be his as sufferers, they had the freedom to throw themselves at his feet and call out to him for help. Barth explains that "they had the freedom to trust Jesus for this overflow of his mercy, to be absolutely certain in the power of his free grace that he could also do this."[27] The freedom of this confidence was grounded in their faith, the faith to which Jesus called them to himself, faith that he missed in some and found in others. Barth argues that the distinctive feature of this faith in the New Testament miracles of Jesus was the faith *in Jesus himself*, and therefore in God as the faithful and merciful God in his covenant with Israel. This faith was confidence in his power, the power of the Kingdom of God that the royal man brought with him in a real and concrete way.[28] This was genuine faith based upon the fact that the royal man *already* called them his own in virtue of the fact that their being had been brought into relationship with his being. In other words, this is the ontological reality of the royal man in relationship with his people, the outworking of which derives from the *anhypostasis* and *enhypostasis* relationship between Christ and his Church.[29]

25. Ibid.

26. Ibid., 236.

27. Barth, *CD* IV/2, 236.

28. Ibid.

29. Refer to the section, "The Ontological Relationship of Jesus Christ with His People," later in this chapter for a more thorough treatment of this point. We note here that Barth draws upon the concept of *anhypostasis* and *enhypostasis* to express the ontological relationship of the church (human essence) to that of Christ (divine essence). In other words, the church has no existence independent from its head, but exists by virtue of its union in his existence. The church therefore exists as *anhypostasis* and *enhypostasis* in its union with Christ.

The Word of God Spoken Through the Royal Man

The significance of the Word of God spoken in Jesus Christ cannot be over-emphasized in Barth's understanding of the union of *Word* and *act*—in the Word became flesh.[30] As Barth sees it, "a very concrete aspect of His life-act is to be found in the fact that He spoke concretely." This is crucial for Barth because Christ's self-impartation through the Word of God that he spoke was a *human Word* that was spoken and received as a "supremely particular and distinctive Word;" that is, as his own Word.[31] "No human word, even if it is spoken with God's commission and in God's service, can as such speak in this way or say or accomplish such things. God's direct presence is needed for this. God Himself must come and speak."[32]

The synthesis of *anhypostasis* and *enhypostasis* clearly emerges as the mode of declaring the Word of God. This is God speaking his own Word through the humanity he has brought into union with himself, a Word that cannot be coordinated or compared with any human word. In this Word *God speaks*. In the existence of the royal man is God himself—in person—who speaks this Word. This context sheds some helpful light into Barth's understanding that "Jesus is the one and only Word of God."[33] Barth can therefore argue that the power of Christ's human Word burst through any perceived translation barriers of the first century community because it was his own Word, of the one who arose again from the dead and lives evermore. This is the "royal Word of the royal man concerning the royal dominion of God."[34]

30. Trevor Hart suggests that Barth's entire theological project could be described as a "theology of proclamation." That is, Barth's theology is predicated on the assumption that "the only legitimate starting point for truly *theological* activity, is the claim made by faith that God has spoken, that he has proclaimed His Word to humankind, that he has revealed himself." Hart characterizes Barth's understanding of this divine speaking as the "enhumanization of God's own Word as the man Jesus of Nazareth." Hart, *Regarding Karl Barth*, 28.

31. Barth, *CD* IV/2, 194.

32. Barth, *CD* IV/3.1, 98.

33. Ibid.

34. Barth, *CD* IV/2, 195. In relation to the Old Testament Barth explains that the New Testament community was confronted with the new Word of Jesus as the Christ in his coming and existing in history. This was the Word of his life and action in harmony with his Word as it had already been spoken and received in the national history of Israel. Therefore, the New Testament Word of Jesus was the fulfillment of the Old. He is the one Prophet of the covenant in its two-fold form as first concealed and then revealed. Barth, *CD* IV/3.1, 70–71.

For as it heard Him speak, it saw the surrounding world, the
nations and their orders and disorders, the whole cosmos, confronted and addressed by Him. It heard His Word as the Word
of reconciliation intended for the world and directed to it. And
so, when it heard Him speak this Word, it knew at once to whom
it was spoken and what it had itself to do when it heard it—to go
and proclaim to the world what He had proclaimed to it. That is
how matters stand with His Word as a human Word.[35]

Although the speech of Jesus is described in the Scripture by the verb
διδασκειν (as teaching), Barth argues that there is no real differentiation in
Christ's speech between ευαγγελιον (the gospel) or διδαχη (teaching). Barth
understands in the strict sense that everything Jesus says is both ευαγγελιον
and διδαχη where the use of these parallel descriptions serve to draw out for
the readers or hearers the rich nature of the Word of Christ. Moreover, there
is a significance in these words that exceeds the Greek concept of teaching
where Jesus speaks with a definite background reference to the Law and
Prophets of the Old Testament. As such, the teaching of Christ (διδαχη)
takes place in the context of the *explicatio* and *applicatio* of these texts, the
aim of which points to his climactic call for repentance, where the διδασκειν
transitions into ευαγγελιζεσθαι or καρυσσειν: "The time is fulfilled, and the
Kingdom of God is at hand" (Mark 1:15). Barth explains that this is how
Jesus expounded and applied the Old Testament, which prompts his cry out
for repentance as the climax of his doctrine. It was not simply a matter of the
honorable teaching of the Old Testament given in the past, but it is also the
book of the present and the future.[36]

This undergirds how Jesus understood his being and teaching, a
teaching that was not simply speech in the "here and now," or speech as one
moment of time. No, Jesus understood himself as fulfilled *kairos*. In other
words, the *moment* that is the Word of Jesus is the event that every past or
future word or event moves, in relationship to the revelation of its actual
scope. Jesus taught at the crucial point of this *kairos*, which was unlike any
teaching before him due to the historical fact that he was there, the one
who in himself came not to destroy the law and the prophets, but to fulfill
them.[37] Therefore, the teaching of Jesus to the μαθητησ was not simply the
sum of abstract truths and demands, but the διδαχη of the Christian church
that took place in his name that is born witness to in the acts of his apostles

---

35. Barth, *CD* IV/2, 195.
36. Ibid., 198–99.
37. Ibid., 200.

and other believers.[38] "It was thus their διδασκειν of the λογος του θεου (Acts 18:11). There is an unmistakable convergence of the term with that of ευαγγελιζεσθαι, καρυσσειν and even καταγγελειν, etc."[39]

Barth argues that in the true sense διδαχη is specifically the exegetical substance of the apostolic preaching of Christ in the community and thereafter by the community to the world. In turn, because the apostolic διδασκειν is itself the preaching of Christ, it takes on the character of the call to repentance (Acts 5:31), which is already proper to it as the διδασκειν of Jesus himself.[40] It is in this context that Barth describes New Testament speech as *kerygma*, which looks backwards to a conclusive event as well as forwards to the revelation of this conclusive event. More succinctly, Barth describes it as a "conclusive or definitive speech in all its forms." It means decision. Born out of the coming of the Kingdom of God in Jesus Christ, it moves swiftly toward its own revelation. This is *preaching* in the New Testament, the proclamation of the coming of the kingdom, "the fulfillment of the lordship of God on earth." This marks the concrete institution of the Lord's rule in direct contrast to all human institutions and kingdoms. It delivers the final blow to all human kingdoms with the "complete and irrevocable seizure of power by God as a historical reality among men." *Kerygma* is distinguished from the Old Testament exodus or the covenant with Abraham or at Sinai, which as great promises in the history of Israel find their center and fulfillment in this event that can now be "proclaimed."[41]

> "Many prophets and righteous men have desired to see these things which ye see, and have not seen them; and to hear these things which ye hear, and have not heard them" (Matt 13:17). This inability to see and hear is the limit of the Old Testament speech. And conversely, the new thing in the κηρυσσειν of the New Testament is that it starts from this seeing and hearing. Incidentally, of course, it is this that differentiates it positively from all other κηρυσσειν, whether moralistic or sacramentalistic.[42]

---

38. Ibid., 201. Barth also understands that by definition the teaching or Word of Jesus is a manifestation of his grace given to us as the light of life. This grace was not mute but spoke through the Word of Christ as "self-disclosure and self-impartation" as the prophetic Word of God. Grace therefore means that God expresses himself before humanity, by declaring himself as the truth in his existence. This is the free grace of God given to humanity through the free Word of God. See Barth, *CD* IV/3.1, 81–82.

39. Barth, *CD* IV/2, 201.

40. Ibid.

41. Ibid., 204.

42. Ibid.

For Barth, the New Testament *kerygma* is realized in the same event that is proclaimed in it.[43] This is where Jesus speaks strictly of himself as the one who comes and who brings with his coming everything that is to come. That is, Jesus does not speak of an assumption of power which has not yet taken place or will take place in some other way. Jesus speaks of that which is accomplished in his coming.[44] Therefore, this power is realized when Jesus speaks because his proclamation becomes actuality the moment he speaks it. For example, Barth argues that we see this actuality when Jesus proclaims freedom from the debt and slavery that has ensnared humanity. When Jesus says to the lame man in Mark 2:5, "Son, thy sins be forgiven thee;" the sins of this lame man are in fact forgiven. When he says to the same lame man in Mark 2:11, "I say unto thee, Arise, and take up thy bed, and go thy way into thy house," the σοι λεγω is decisive: "He arose, took up his bed, and went forth before them all."[45] In this we see the indissoluble union of speech and act in Jesus where the speech of Jesus is also his conclusive Messianic act. There is no act of Jesus which is not the definite Word of his proclamation.[46] "But it is only in this one case, in relation to the κηρυσσειν of Jesus Himself, that we can maintain the coincidence, or identity, in which the κηρυσσειν of the kingdom of God is itself the kingdom of God, and therefore unconditional, absolute κηρυσσει, the Word which is also the content of the Word."[47]

Barth argues that all other genuine κηρυσσειν in the New Testament only points to the κηρυσσειν of Jesus made manifest in his life-act as redeemer. Therefore, all New Testament proclamation derives from the κηρυσσειν of Jesus. Consequently, the *kerygma* of the apostolic and Christian community become participants in that which is proper to it (the *kerygma* of Jesus), characterized as a definitive action in which the Word is identical with its

43. Pannenberg observes that Barth drew special attention to the link between the first sermon of Jesus (Luke 4:17f.) and Isa 61:1f (*CD* IV/2, 197f.) in the sense of fulfilling the salvation proclaimed there in the person of Christ. Pannenberg argues that it wasn't important to Barth that in both the Isaianic messenger of peace and in Jesus that there is a distinction between the breaking in of God's rule and the person of the messenger (Barth does not refer to Isa 52:7). Barth in fact stated that there is no distinction between God's lordship and the person of Jesus (*CD*, IV/2, 198). Pannenberg concludes that while this may be true christologically with respect to the relationship between the eternal Son with the Father, it does not apply to the preaching of Jesus. "Barth ignored the self-distinction of Jesus from the Father that is the inalienable condition of his deity and his identity with the kingdom of his Father. See Pannenberg, *Systematic Theology*, 2:457–58.

44. Barth, *CD* IV/2, 204.

45. Ibid., 205.

46. Ibid. Barth understands that the Evangelists, underlying tradition, and John's Gospel also leave inseparable Jesus as the *Word itself* who also proclaims the *Word*.

47. Barth, *CD* IV/2, 205.

content. Barth further argues that by its participation in the proclamation of Jesus, this *kerygma* becomes something more than ordinary speech, and is in fact more than the supreme Word of the Old Testament proclamation. Congruent with Christian saving faith found only in Jesus Christ, Christian *kerygma* is greater than any other human speech because it focuses strictly as *kerygma* about Jesus Christ himself.[48] Barth states that Jesus clearly demonstrates this truth when he proclaims, "For all the prophets and the law prophesied until John. And if ye will receive it, this is Elias, which was for to come" (Matt 11:13f). Barth further states that while Jesus is "still outside," he is "really inside" (noch draußen, schon drinnen). And to the extent that he is inside, he must be called the first whose speech is described in the Gospel story as κηρυσσειν (as seen in Matthew's Gospel) where Jesus himself proclaimed the Kingdom of God was at hand (Matt 3:2).[49]

Therefore, the κηρυσσειν that Jesus speaks is the promise of the Old Testament which is realized in the present, "the time is fulfilled." For Barth, the Evangelists see the κηρυσσειν of Jesus to be the promise of the Old Testament which passes over into this proclamation (the κηρυσσειν of fulfillment), which anticipates and assumes the character of proclamation in its fulfillment.[50] Therefore, in his becoming humanity it is the κηρυσσειν of Jesus himself—his self-proclamation—which forms the content of the κηρυσσειν of those who came before and after him.[51] Barth emphasizes this point citing the Apostle Paul in Romans 16:25 where he says "my gospel" is the *kerygma* of Jesus Christ. In other words, the gospel which is proclaimed by Jesus Christ is the proclamation of him, of himself. Therefore, there is no place for Christian preaching that claims for itself any imminent power as a self-sufficient *kerygma* and self-operative hypostasis that is the προτον and the εσχατον. True Christian preaching points beyond itself as it bears witness to the reality and the history of Jesus Christ.[52]

The speech of Jesus is his life-act, wholly his Word and wholly his activity *as* his Word. Barth cites the Gospels as proof that it is not merely a Word

---

48. Ibid., *CD* IV/2, 204–5.

49. Barth, *CD* IV/2, 206; *KD* IV/2, 229. Barth also cites Matt 11:2f where he explains that it is obvious Matthew did not think this formula (that recurs in the first account of the kerygma of Jesus Himself in Matt 4:17), carried the exact same significance when spoken by John as when it was spoken by Jesus. But since Matthew cited both he obviously did not think that it meant two completely different things. See Barth, *CD* IV/2, 206.

50. Ibid.

51. Barth cites the Apostle Paul, "We preach not ourselves, but Christ Jesus the Lord; and ourselves (we regard as) your servants for Jesus' sake" (2 Cor 4:5). Barth, *CD* IV/2, 208.

52. Ibid., 209.

of Jesus, but a spiritual event that accomplishes a corresponding change in the physical sphere and visible circumstances of the world around.[53] His word is an action that is spoken in fulfilled time by the one who fulfills it. It is no longer strictly a promise, but is itself that which is promised. It is a definite Word framed in the form of a definite plan. In other words, the Word of Christ is his preaching of the Gospel—his proclamation—in this complete and cosmic form.[54] "It is always the revelation of the decision which has been made in the fact of His human existence among other men, and therefore in and with His speaking to and with them. It is always an activity in this distinctive sense."[55]

This explains how the miracles of Jesus become the "cosmic actualizations of His *kerygma*, and are performed in this context to summon men to faith." That is, the miracles of Jesus should not be understood as independent events, but events that render a twofold service to faith and the call to faith. Barth sees here an indissoluble connection of proclamation, miracle, and faith. The miracles of Jesus therefore do not take place in a vacuum, but as the actualization of the Word of Jesus as his call to repentance and faith. Moreover, Barth notes that the Jesus of the Gospels refused to work miracles as a way to manipulate people to believe who had otherwise rejected his preaching.[56] The miracles of Jesus are never arbitrary but have to do with the presence and action of God as a new thing that comes upon humanity. The miracles of Jesus are something new that comes from the outside in, which could never enter the heart of humanity as experience or an idea. They are the antithesis of that which torments and destroys humanity and demonstrate that he does not will the distress, shame, and ultimate destruction of humanity, but their salvation. For Barth, this is clearly connected with the coming of the kingdom of Christ and his seizure of power on the earth. This is the power of his revelation, of his speaking and acting in his own cause in direct contradiction and opposition to the power of destruction.[57] "That is why the activity of the Son of Man, as an actualisation of His Word and

---

53. Ibid.

54. Ibid., 210.

55. Ibid.

56. Barth notes in this context that "independent" miracles, which take place and are recounted and claim attention outside this context of preaching and faith, are miracles of a very different type. Barth also notes in the Gospel accounts that apart from a few healings Jesus "could not will to" work miracles in his own city (Mark 6:5). See Barth, *CD* IV/2, 217–18.

57. Barth, *CD* IV/2, 225–26.

commentary on it, necessarily has the crucial and decisive form of liberation, redemption, restoration, normalization . . . "[58]

In essence, Barth understands that as the royal man the activity of Christ is first and foremost the Gospel in action where he saves the life and being of humanity not only for the sake of humanity but for the sake of God's glory. Barth argues that this must be so because the glory of God is in fact threatened by the destruction of humanity.[59] At bottom, it is Jesus alone who in his words and deeds can infallibly lead any human being to faith in himself. Therefore, the faith that is awakened by the totality of his life-act is faith in him, in the "One who had sent Him and was in Him, in God's free grace."[60]

> Even the Word of Jesus is an incomprehensible act. It has the dimension of miracle. It has the character of an act of divine mercy and power. That is why the two blind men in Matt 9:27f (as distinct from the man born blind in John 9:1f), and many others in the New Testament, do not derive their faith from a miracle which they have already experienced, but go forward to the miracle which they are to experience with hands which seem to be empty.[61]

Barth labored to emphasize the reality of the Word of God spoken through the royal man is a human word, a word spoken by the Word became flesh in Jesus of Nazareth. We mark here Barth's development of the critical connection between the exaltation of humanity in the royal man through whom the Word of God is spoken by this true man—in his indissoluble union with true God. Moreover, Barth's development of the royal man's union with the Godhead and humanity quite forcibly demonstrates the influential dynamic of the *anhypostasis* and *enhypostasis* where Jesus Christ proclaims the gospel, the *kerygma,* which he alone can reveal. It is the true hearing of the Word of Jesus that belongs to this dimension of faith in the one who—in the mercy and power of God—can also (if he so chooses) work miracles that are worked in the indissoluble union with his *kerygma.*[62]

58. Ibid.
59. Ibid.
60. Barth, *CD* IV/2, 239.
61. Ibid.
62. Ibid.

The Union of God with Humanity in the Royal Man

Karl Barth takes quite seriously the ontology of the royal man in relationship to *all* humanity; that is, the union of all humanity in Jesus Christ.[63] I argue, however, that this unity should not to be interpreted as universalism resulting in the justification and sanctification of all humanity in Christ.[64] But it does speak to Barth's understanding of an ontological reality that Jesus shares with all humanity whether they believe in him as Messiah or not.[65]

63. Timothy Gorringe rightly argues that Karl Barth's anthropology is grounded in Christology where Christ being human has ontological implications for all other human beings. The crucial point here is that all human beings are creatures whom this man is like (despite his unlikeness), and in whose "sphere and fellowship and history this one man also existed in likeness with them." Gorringe notes in Barth's anthropology that he was responding to the pessimistic view of what it meant to be human, which emerged from nineteenth and twentieth century thinking (i.e., Fichte, Nietzsche, Jaspers, Sartre, and Darwinianism). See Gorringe, *Against Hegemony*, 197–98.

64. Bruce McCormack posits that more than likely Barth's actualistic ontology would be taken more seriously if not for the fact that the "exaltation" of human "nature" in the history of Jesus of Nazareth is grounded in the election of all human beings in him. "It is because all are in Him by virtue of election that He can constitute, through His lived obedience, human being as such." McCormack, "So That He May Be Merciful to All," 227–28. McCormack argues that this shift in Barth's doctrine of election first developed in *Romans* stabilizes the swinging pendulum of election and reprobation in Jesus Christ, and as a result "inclines Barth even more surely in the direction of 'universalism.'" McCormack, however, goes on to argue that while Barth drew back from the conclusion of universalism, he left open the "opening up and enlargement of the circle of election." That is, Barth leaves room for the divine freedom. "What is at stake in Barth's rejection of an *apokatastasis panton* is ultimately his understanding of the *reality* of Jesus Christ. Jesus Christ is not only the One who has come (in the incarnation); He is also the One who comes (in the power of the eschatological Spirit) and the One who will come (in His visible return)." That is, until the return of Christ in His glory, even the very best Christology (together with the doctrine of election from which it finds its root) can only be a witness to the reality that Christ is. Therefore, it cannot provide an exhaustively true account of this reality. McCormack concludes that at the end of the day, Barth's position on universalism mirrors von Balthasar's; that is, it is something for which we ought to hope and pray for, but not something we can teach, McCormack and Anderson, *Karl Barth* and *American Evangelicalism*, 247–48.

65. We observe two points with respect to Barth's understanding of this ontological union that Jesus Christ shares with all humanity. First, the *anhypostasis* and *enhypostasis* of Christ's human nature, which has been exalted in union with the Logos is human nature that corresponds with all humanity. Otherwise, the royal man would not be true humanity in his existence. Secondly, Barth's doctrine of election demands this ontological union. For Barth, the fact that God's election of humanity was fulfilled in Christ alone carries with it the weight of Jesus Christ's solidarity with all humanity. Berkouwer argues that Barth's understanding of *God's universal election* in Christ runs the danger of minimizing the relevance and history of the kerygma. This in effect "casts a shadow" of unbelief in one's own election, "the *dangerous* shadow of not believing in God's election which has already made the life that is lived in Christ danger-less

Based upon his reading of the Gospel texts Barth argues that even those who perpetrated evil action against Jesus did not altogether cancel out how they responded to him. That is, people always came together "spontaneously" wherever Jesus went as they heard him "gladly," even rejoicing "for all the glorious things that were done by him (Luke 13:17); being startled and glorifying God (Matt 9:8) when they saw that he spoke with authority and not as the scribes (Matt 21:26)." Barth rejects any sense of irony in these accounts and concludes that it must be accepted that although these people did not believe in a way to become his disciples, they themselves were "brought into a very real union with Jesus by the fact that he was moved with compassion when he saw them."[66]

In this context Barth seizes upon the reality of the true humanity of Jesus of Nazareth experienced in the depths of human suffering. Seeing the misery of humanity around him, Jesus took their grief "into His heart, into Himself" as the good shepherd. Barth explains that the tragedy of those who encountered Jesus, but did not believe in him was their inability to recognize their own misery for what it was. They simply suffered in it. They did not recognize the one who came to take away their misery by taking it upon himself. Despite being moved by his presence, his words, and his acts, they sunk back into their own indifference. Yet their failure to see their own misery and suffering did not alter this fact of their existence, neither did it affect the great gap in their existence from the existence of the royal man. Moreover, it did not alter the fact that Jesus Christ had come and was present with them to fill this gap, to be their head, their σωτηρ; the true shepherd who came not for his benefit, but he for theirs. In this way the royal man's compassion reflected the compassion of God who in the humanity of Jesus of Nazareth conclusively proves his fidelity to humanity.[67]

Barth insists that failure to see the royal man for who he really was did not alter in any way the true and deep solidarity between Jesus and this people. To think otherwise is to miss the reality and impact of Jesus in this world as being and action made manifest in his visitation with humanity.[68] Therefore, the compassion of Jesus Christ demonstrated in his being and action extends to and encompasses the multitudes that he came to be among.

---

because of *God's* decision. Barth's attempt to remove this shadow by qualifying unbelief as on "ontological impossibility"—in view of the triumph—does not *eliminate* the problem but *accentuates* it." Berkouwer, *Triumph of Grace*, 364.

66. Barth, *CD* IV/2, 185.

67. Ibid., 187.

68. Ibid.

The great joy which was to be for all people was already an objective event. And it is this fact as such which is the concern of the gospel records. As they saw it, it is only by this fact as such that the question of faith was raised—the question which the community in which these records had their origin found to be answered by the work of the Holy Spirit.[69]

The royal man moved upon the earth in response to human misery and suffering. He approaches human beings in their misery and calls them (and causes them) to live as a delivered creature. Humanity can therefore "rise up and walk, again see and hear and speak," having been delivered from torment and embarrassment.[70] For Barth, it is in this encounter that the being of Jesus Christ normalizes the existence of all human beings. "He can be a man again—a whole man in this elemental sense. His existence as a creature in the natural cosmos is normalised. We must not ignore or expunge the phrase—as a creature in the natural cosmos. It is as such that he is radically blessed by the miracles of Jesus."[71]

Barth concludes that if the humanity of Christ is to be taken seriously according to the witness of the New Testament, it must be understood in the context all humanity, not simply the community of Christians. In other words, the fact that the Word became flesh means that the royal man became a human being for all humanity where his very existence unites all humanity with God by virtue of his exaltation of humanity in Jesus. The being and action of Jesus Christ makes this fact unavoidable if we are to accept the witness of New Testament. While Barth acknowledges that evil afflicts all humanity and therefore brings with it a sense of punishment for their sin, he counters that the miracle stories clearly demonstrate that Jesus heals human beings, making them whole and bringing them back to life in the elemental sense, delivering these human beings from death.[72] In his

69. Ibid.

70. Barth, *CD* IV/2, 221–22.

71. Ibid., 222.

72. Barth qualifies this point. He notes that there is only one story, the healing of the paralytic in Mark 2:1f where there is a prior reference to the sin of the one who is healed. Even so, while there is no demand for repentance, the sin is forgiven in view of the faith of those who brought him to Jesus. Using the same free initiative Jesus later says to the man, "Arise, and take up thy bed, and go thy way into thine house" (v. 11). Barth explains that the obvious point of this story is to establish the connection between the miracles of Jesus and His proclamation. "With the same free power with which the Son of Man later tells the paralytic to rise and walk He first forgives him his sins. And He does the second in order that "ye may know" that He has the power to do the first." Barth also points out that only in the story of the healing of the sick man at the pool of Bethesda do we have a subsequent reference to the sin of the one who is

coming, the royal man brings with him the reality of the Kingdom of God, which bursts upon creation in Jesus of Nazareth. His coming constitutes a dynamic union between God and humanity as the eternal Son of God in becoming the flesh of humanity. In so doing he invades the misery of this world by proclaiming the eternal Word of God—as God—but through a man having exalted humanity out of its false existence into the reality of its true being in its union with Jesus.

Understanding Anthropology in a Christological Context

As we have shown, Barth argues that Jesus of Nazareth lived and moved upon this earth as the first Adam, not the second.[73] As the royal man, Jesus embodies true humanity as God originally mandated in creation.[74] In this section we will further develop Barth's anthropological understanding of human existence and the reality of human existence as determined by the humanity of Christ. With this in mind, the question that Barth deals with is: what is the meaning (or power) of Jesus Christ's existence as the Son of God who became the Son of Man (in our anthropological sphere), as the reconciler of humanity with God?[75]

---

healed: "Behold, thou art made whole: sin no more, lest a worse thing come unto thee" (John 5:14). Therefore, the point of the story is found in the sovereign removal of this man's sickness. Moreover, Barth argues that there is no mention of sin in the rest of the stories. In the truest sense it is not their transgressions that are imputed to them by Jesus (2 Cor 5:19), but only that they are poor and tragic and suffering creatures. Barth, *CD* IV/2, 223–24.

73. Refer to chapter 4, "Jesus Christ: The First Adam."

74. Henri Blocher posits that Barth's argument for the eternal pre-existence of the man Jesus issues from the "christological concentration" from which the Church Dogmatics was born. This provides Barth the necessary flexibility to move back and forth from a "lighter view (pre-existent in God's design, that is fore-ordained, not yet really existing)" to a "heavier one (really pre-existent, as a matter of being)," understood as the man Jesus and His role as the genuine basis of creation. Blocher goes on to argue that we speak of Jesus Christ as the Agent of creation (which he was as the Logos *before* he took on human flesh) together with the name Jesus Christ; the underlying truth that emerges is the identity of the subject (the second Person of the Trinity) and the human nature of Christ as *anhypostasis* and *enhypostasis*. See Blocher, "Karl Barth's Anthropology," 104–11.

75. Marc Cortez notes that the advent of twentieth century brought with it a rise (a surge) of interest in theological anthropology born out of a number of factors. The growing interest in the human person, a "turn toward the self" evidenced by modern philosophy and art, the proliferation of scientific disciplines devoted to understanding the human person, and the human atrocities wrought by World War I and II raised serious questions about the nature of being human. Theological reflection upon these

Barth describes this power of Jesus Christ's existence as "the direction of the Son." This is the direction given to humanity in the divine power and authority of Christ, who as the eternal Son of God is also the Son of Man. So that—as the true and royal man—Jesus is Lord in our own anthropological sphere.[76] This is the power of his existence and work in his royal office as the one who became a servant for us so that he may also become our Lord. Moreover, this is the pre-supposition for Barth's development of Part II in the *Doctrine of Reconciliation* where he further asks: what is the power of the existence of the man Jesus Christ for all humanity? To what extent is there a way from him to us as our Lord? How can his past, present, and future being reach and affect us as the act of divine power? Barth frames his response to these questions around the being of Jesus Christ as the Son of Man and his being with us, where his action is his *action for us*.[77]

> Whatever we may have to say later about the sloth and sancti-
> fication of man, and the edification of the Church, and love, is
> wholly included and enclosed already in the being and action of
> the Son of Man, and at bottom it can be understood and repre-
> sented only as a development and explanation of it.[78]

Barth points here to what is not "wholly self-evident;" the reality of human beings realized by the existence of the Son of Man and being recipients of the direction of the Son, the "ones to whom He is already on the way as the Resurrected." It is our knowledge of his being as the royal man among us and his actions for us that corresponds to knowledge of ourselves—the knowledge that we are in fact his. The question, however, that Barth further addresses here is how can this be said of us? How is this possible in the anthropological sphere, the sphere of the unreconciled world that exists in contradiction and oppositions to God?[79]

---

events made significant contributions to the growth of theological anthropology. Karl Barth's response to these questions of human being found its foundation in the being of Jesus Christ. Cortez goes on to argue (from Barth's perspective) that theological anthropology should therefore "begin its understanding of the human person by looking first to see how Jesus Christ manifests true humanity." Cortez, *Theological Anthropology*, 5–6.

76. David Congdon notes that in Barth's response to liberal theological anthropology, Barth suggested a "theanthropology;" that which makes theology evangelical. That is, in Barth's approach to locate the existence of humanity in the corresponding existence of Jesus Christ, he aims to be truly existential among the existentialists. See Congdon, "Theology as Theanthropology," 31–32.

77. Barth, *CD* IV/2, 264–65.

78. Ibid., 265.

79. Barth, *CD* IV/2, 266.

Barth responds that our knowledge of Jesus Christ includes the knowledge that we are indeed his own. That is, "Where there is this knowledge, it also includes man's knowledge of himself." However, Barth rejects the notion that this is simply an abstraction of human capacity in general. Rather, this is a realm, a reality strictly realized for those who are claimed by Christ as his own. The issue that Barth deals with here is: how is this realm realized? In other words, how are we able to come to a serious and transforming realization of this enclosing and controlling of our anthropological sphere by the royal man, and achieve this knowledge of ourselves as we confess ourselves to be Christians? For Barth, the key to this knowledge is not losing sight of the power and lordship of the Son of Man that reaches and affects the whole anthropological sphere. This is true for each individual—not simply as an offer and possibility—but as a reality and event where this sphere of influence is actually determinative for all human existence. Barth emphasizes here that the significance of the royal man's existence and his relationship to the existence of all humanity is not just potential, but actual. Jesus lives as one of us, as our brother. And as our brother his power and lordship sets us in a freedom that is interchangeable, which must be exclusively used and lived out in its uniqueness. The question is whether or not we know and use this freedom in the life that we live.[80]

With this in view Barth emphasizes that the royal man—who exists in his power and lordship—must remain the center of our attention. In other words, Christ must not simply become the content of a christological statement leading to the develop of a separate statement where Christ is no longer the subject. If this happens, we (humanity) begin to emerge at a certain distance from him as beings in relationship to Christ, but also beings with our own independent existence.[81] Barth takes quite seriously the fact that the anthropological sphere is genuinely dominated by the Son of Man as its Lord. Therefore, the knowledge of ourselves must be included and enclosed in the knowledge of Jesus. Consequently, our self-evaluation can only take place before him.[82]

80. Ibid., 267.

81. We note here a clear delineation of the *anhypostasis* and *enhypostasis* dynamic, which Barth applies to Christ's relationship with his church. Barth describes the ontological relationship between Christ (as the heavenly Head) with the church (as the form of his body) in an "earthly-historical" form of existence. In this relationship Barth understands that the church "is not itself the Head, nor does it become such. But it exists (ανυποστατος and ενυποστατος) in and in virtue of His existence." Barth, *CD* IV/2, 59.

82. Barth, *CD* IV/2, 268. Wolf Krötke argues that for Barth, human endeavor to understand humanity means that if we want to know ourselves as human beings, the first place to look is not ourselves. That is, to *establish theologically* what constitutes

> As the One who is with us and for us He decides what we can
> and should and must become and be in Him and through Him
> and with Him. He in whom the old is already past and the new
> has already come draws the sharp line between the two which
> we have now to know and observe. It is only as we look at Him,
> therefore, that we can know and observe this line.[83]

Barth frames this crucial argument around the incarnation of the Son
of God in view of its eternal foundation and revelation. This is the homecoming of the Son of Man and his exaltation to fellowship with God, which
establishes his lordship over all things as the *communicatio idiomatum et
gratiarum et operationum*. In the isolated history of this one man—in this
communication between divine and human being and activity in this one—
is the reconciliation of man with God through God's own incarnation. This
is his unique history. However, it is not a private history, but a representative
and therefore public history. The history of Jesus Christ marks the place of
all other humanity in the accomplishment of their atonement—the history
of their head in which they all participate. His history must therefore be understood as world history in its truest form because it embodies our history
as well.[84] That God was in Christ reconciling the world to himself includes
each one of us. In this way, the essence of our humanity has been elevated
and exalted—*in Jesus of Nazareth*. Yet, even as our genuine brother who
exists in perfect likeness with us, he remains unique and unlike us as the
royal man. For Barth, this explains our union with God that takes place in
the unique existence of Jesus Christ (before we are in any position to accept
or reject it) because we *were* taken up into fellowship with God. This is a

---

the character of humanity requires our observation of the concrete human person
to whom God bound himself and entered into human history. Krötke observes that
Barth's principle of theological anthropology is especially provocative today because it
does not at first glance appear to demonstrate a connection with what we already generally know about the human being, which creates the danger that all such statements
of theological anthropology end up hanging in isolated space, becoming incomprehensible outside of theological discourse. Yet, as Barth responded to liberal theology
(Rudolf Bultmann in particular) in the *Church Dogmatics*, he was not concerned with
questioning the structural openness of the human being as God's creature. This in fact
is one of the fundamental assertions of his anthropology. To be human means to stand
in relation to God ontologically. See Krötke, "The humanity of the human person in
Karl Barth's anthropology," 159–60.

83. Barth, *CD* IV/2, 268.

84. Timothy J. Gorringe argues that for Barth there is no secular history in the strict
sense. That is, history as a whole is the record of both the providence of God and the
"confusion of human beings," where the gospel of Christ is being proclaimed to the
world. The act of God in Christ is a clear decision for the new human being and the
form of the world based upon his reality. See Gorringe, *Against Hegemony*, 258.

fellowship for which we were ordained, but had been broken. Nevertheless, we are taken up into this fellowship in him, the one.[85]

This fellowship is an objective reality because the Christmas message speaks of what is objectively real for all humanity in Jesus Christ. Barth emphasizes that we are what we are in *Him,* in his fellowship with God. This means that we share God's good pleasure in him, in his obedience to God, and in his movement towards God. We of course have no standing in this fellowship or make this obedient movement toward God apart from him or without him in some abstract and subjective self-awareness. However, there is no question of our not being in Jesus Christ as the elected and revealed Lord, whom as the head of all humanity represents us and our own obedience in him. This is how true humanity begins and ends with the humanity of Jesus Christ through what he was done on our behalf. Therefore, no human being turns to God in obedience who does not also participate in Jesus Christ in this turning, and in this being raised and exalted with him to true humanity. "Jesus lives, and I with Him."[86]

Ontologically, because our existence is taken up into his (as *anhypostasis* and *enhypostasis*), we are claimed as those who are already directed and obedient to God in him, as those who are already born again and converted, as those who are already Christians. This embodies the peace that we enjoy with God in Christ, which flows out of our justification. Barth explains that as those who share the same humanity with Jesus in him as our head and representative, we are indeed righteous and acceptable and pleasing to God even as we are. Being in and with him as our brother, and having been forgiven of our sins for his sake, we are accepted as the children of God where Jesus Christ is also our sanctification.[87] This means that being of like humanity with him as our Lord and Head, we are claimed by him as those who are regenerate and converted, as those who have engaged in turning to God as Christians.[88]

The basis of our Christianity therefore rests in the exaltation of the Son of Man with the Son of God, which anticipates our exaltation as brothers of this one. This is the root of human sanctification. This is the life and love of the Christian community and becomes a key point of reference for Barth as he points to the New Testament witnesses who could not speak of the one who made himself known to them without also speaking of

85. Barth, *CD* IV/2, 269–70.

86. Ibid., 270–71.

87. Refer to chapter 6, "The Sanctification of Humanity in Jesus Christ," where this is more fully developed.

88. Barth, *CD* IV/2, 273.

themselves. Their testimony about Jesus spoke of his sovereignty over them and over those to whom they spoke their word and witness. Barth stresses this point in his understanding that the testimony of the New Testament witnesses is an *ontological statement* about their own being in him.[89] "It is an ontological declaration about their own being under His sovereignty, as those who were righteous and holy before God in Him, as those who belong to God's covenant which in Him was kept and fulfilled from the human side as well as the divine."[90]

Moreover, Barth argues that the New Testament witnesses looked beyond the ignorance and unbelief of the humanity around them in this ontological declaration about them and every human being like them. That is, in the distinctive essence of Jesus Christ we see that while he exists as the one he alone is, he is not alone. Jesus Christ is the "royal Representative, the Lord and head of many."[91] In this ontological connection between the man Jesus Christ on the one side and all humanity on the other side—and between *active* Christians on the one side and *prospective* Christians on the other—is found the basis for the New Testament gathering and upbuilding of the community. Therefore, those who know him are depicted as a community strictly grounded in the royal man, a community of Christians that is sent out to the world based upon their being in Jesus Christ, in whom he entrusts this task of mission to the world.[92] All of this is based upon the fact that Jesus Christ would not be who he is if he had no community, and if this community did not have a missionary character. For Barth, this ontological connection between Jesus and his community is the legal basis of the *kerygma* that forms the Christian community, and with which the community is charged. Furthermore, this ontological connection forms the basis of the reality that the *kerygma* "does not indicate possibilities but declares actualities." The fundamental principle that Barth emphasizes here

89. Ibid., 274–75.

90. Barth, *CD* IV/2, 275.

91. Ibid.

92. Timothy Gorringe observes that Barth develops his anthropology with a view to the pessimistic view of what it means to be human that emerged during and after the Second World War. Gorringe argues that Barth's anthropology is a vindication of creation grounded in Christology. Although there is not any direct knowledge of human nature from the human being Christ (having been derived by the Holy Spirit), his human nature has ontological implications for all other human beings because they are creatures like Jesus in all his unlikeness. That is, "in the person of this One we are confronted by the divine Other." Therefore, to be human means to be with God by virtue of our listening to God. See Gorringe, *Against Hegemony*, 197–99.

is that when we say Jesus Christ in the New Testament sense we make an ontological declaration about other human beings as well.[93]

> But the anchor of the soul is that "the forerunner is for us (προδρομος υπερ ημων) entered, even Jesus," so that He is there in their place, Himself being the second "immutable thing" which is before them, as the Word of God is the first from which they come. They hope, therefore, as they stand both behind and before in an ontological connexion. On both sides the declaration that Jesus is our confidence is sure and not unsure because it has an immutable foundation.[94]

Barth argues that as Christians we exist in Jesus Christ because we have heard him as he has been proclaimed to us. This ontological connection becomes a reality for us in him alone because—*we really are in him*. From our being in him issues all that we will and do. Consequently, our being in Christ is an indestructible being. Barth cites the Apostle Paul and his development of this reality in the closing section of Romans 8.[95]

> Jesus Christ who died and rose again, and ascended back to heaven is there at the right hand of God and intercedes for us (εντυγχανει υπερ ημων, v. 34). God foreknew them (προεγνω) even before they came into being, before the world was. He predestined (προωρισεω) those whom He foreknew to be conformed (συμμορφοι) to the image of His Son. And it is according to this foreknowledge and predestination that He has acted for them in time. He called them to the place where they belonged on the basis of His eternal election—to use the phrase of 1 Peter 2:9, "out of darkness into his marvelous light" (εκαλεσεν). And as those whom He called He justified them (εδικαιωσεν)—without

93. Barth argues that similar ontological declarations are found in the *Heidelberg Catechism* and Church hymns. See Barth, *CD* IV/2, 275. To further bolster his point Barth draws upon Hebrews 6:17–20 to explain this ontological connection between Jesus Christ and his community of Christians. Citing this passage Barth speaks of "two immutable things" (πραγματα αμεταθετα) as Christians take refuge by laying hold of the hope set before them have a "strong consolation" (ισχυρα παρακλησις), because it is not possible for God who has called them by His promise to deceive them. This first promise is established by the character of the promise itself in the Word of God. The second is based upon the fact that those who trust in his Word have the hope set before them for which they reach out "an anchor of the soul, both sure and steadfast, and which entereth into that within the veil." Therefore, even though they still exist in this life, they already exist in the life beyond as they live in this hope and its fulfillment that is before them. See Barth, *CD* IV/2, 275–76.

94. Barth, *CD* IV/2, 275–76.

95. Ibid., 276–78.

any cooperation on their part, and therefore unconditionally. And as those who are generally justified by Him He glorified them with a heavenly glory (εδοξασεν).[96]

This is the being given to Christians with Christ in heaven, which at every point (even the last; vv. 29–30), speaks of an event. This is God acting on behalf of Christians who can only come as those who are already foreknown and predestined and called and justified and even glorified. They are these people because of this intersection of the eternal and temporal will of God as it moves to action in the royal man. Christ intercedes for them as these people, as God himself, because he is not against them, but for them (v. 31). This is not only the condition—but the basis of their being—which makes it an indestructible being. This is the reality of God's free grace for them and not against them, God's disposition toward them and their being brought about by Christ, and therefore by God himself.[97]

> "He that spared not his own Son, but delivered him up freely for us all, how shall he not with him also freely give us all things" (τα παντα χαρισεται, v. 32)? "Who can say anything to these things?" (v. 31). Who can accuse or condemn the elect of God, or effectively question or contradict their being as His saints? (v. 33). God is always there first as their δικαιων (v. 33), for Christ is there (v. 34). Their being as God's saints could only be imperiled or destroyed by a breaking or snapping (χωριζειν) of the connexion between Christ and them and therefore between God and them. But how can this be possible? Who or what has the right or power for this χωριζειν? "Who shall separate us from the love of Christ?"—the love in which none has taken up himself into this ontological relationship but in which He has assumed them all into it.[98]

It is important to note here that in explaining our being in Christ, Barth clearly argues against any mystical notion of our own ability to look away from and beyond ourselves, or transcend our own being in a purely formal negation. Any effort to do this results in our looking into an empty beyond, which brings us back around to looking at ourselves again. The point that must not be lost in Barth's thinking is that we cannot lose ourselves, but neither can we find ourselves in an effort to lose ourselves in this way. That is, we remain the stuff of the old humanity "within the frontier which we see

96. Ibid., 278.
97. Ibid.
98. Ibid.

from within." Therefore, the only way we can look beyond ourselves is to look at an object that irresistibly draws our attention.[99]

Barth describes this irresistible draw as hearing this superior and genuine *Yes* where the unavoidable *No* remains valid and effective. It is only when we look away from and beyond ourselves, as we see something confronting us as *a someone*, and in this *someone*—we see ourselves. Therefore in him, in this other, we are "summoned and irresistibly impelled to seek and find ourselves." This alone is the knowledge, the liberation which humanity is given and shown its true frontier. However, this does not become a reality simply by being cut loose from ourselves. Even in this new reality we still have the old human being "behind and below us" even as we have Jesus Christ "before and above us." It is in him that we ourselves as the new humanity—elevated and exalted to fellowship with God—enjoy the certainty of our exaltation which is "inviolable, impregnably and indestructibly certain." This is how Barth understands Paul in the closing verses of Romans 8—that we cannot be separated from the love of God.[100]

We sum up by recognizing Barth's uncompromising insistence that as the first Adam, Jesus of Nazareth—the royal man—embodies true humanity in our own anthropological sphere as God intended. It is the being of the Son of Man, as the royal man, who comes to humanity and exalts humanity in his union with the Son of God. This marks a significant point of Barth's Christology as an expression of the *anhypostasis* and *enhypostasis* formulation where the being and action of the royal man accomplishes the reconciliation of humanity with God. That is, our knowledge of him as his own (those who are actually affected by his existence), includes the knowledge of ourselves. This is not a self-obtained knowledge, but a knowledge that is realized in the existence of the royal man, through his relationship with humanity in this anthropological sphere. As the royal man, he dominates the anthropological sphere as its Lord, who in his history was reconciling the world to himself in the essence of our humanity. It is in our union with God, being taken up into his existence in the unique and historical existence of the royal man that establishes our ability to accept or reject true fellowship with God in this union. Moreover, and quite significantly so, this ontological connection between Jesus and his community is the legal basis for the *kerygma*, which establishes and charges this community as his people.

---

99. Cf. *CD* IV/2, 284.
100. Ibid., 285.

The Ontological Relationship of Jesus Christ with His People

The Basis of this Union

An important and quite unique strength in Karl Barth's *Doctrine of Reconciliation* is the significance he assigns to the ontological relationship between Jesus Christ and his community of believers. Having argued for the royal man's *objective* union with all humanity, Barth now presses this ontological concept forward by arguing for God's *subjective* union with his church in the royal man.[101] In other words, Barth now deals head-on with the grounding, the reality of *being* Christians in Jesus Christ. This marks an important point in Barth's development of the royal man's ontological relationship with his people, which comes about through the work of the Holy Spirit to accomplish this union as an ontological reality. Barth marks here the crucial distinction for Christians who find peace with God in Jesus Christ apart from those who do not, which corresponds to the Apostle Paul's understanding that being a Christian is grounded in the being of Jesus Christ as their impregnable surety. Consequently, the Christian is compelled to state as their confession "Jesus lives," which includes their confession "and I with Him." For Barth, the confession of the Christian community is an expression of their faith in the being of Jesus Christ as the realization of the divine decision made for all human beings.[102] That is, it is the community of Christians who *experience* the reality of their participation in the exaltation of Jesus Christ.[103]

The undergirding principle for Barth is that "there is no Jesus existing exclusively for Himself, and there is no sinful man who is not affected and determined with and by His existence." That being the case Barth argues that Christian proclamation in the New Testament clearly sees these two oriented together, which magnifies the antithesis between the being of Jesus over against sinful humanity. In turn, this serves to magnify even more the decision of God made about sinful humanity in Jesus, and therefore the

---

101. We use *objective* union here to describe Karl Barth's understanding of the ontological union that Jesus Christ enjoys with all humanity by virtue of his exaltation of humanity as the royal man; whereas the *subjective* union applies specifically to the community of Christ.

102. Cornelis van de Kooi provides good insight here that Barth focuses on the active verb sense of election. Barth is concerned with the God's electing and willing where the emphasis lies on the acting, the movement of God. Therefore, human knowledge of God is strictly the result of this acting and willing of God that becomes knowable in the history and person of Jesus Christ. See van der Kooi, *As in a Mirror*, 375.

103. Barth, *CD* IV/2, 280.

"ontological connexion between the two." Therefore, the important connection between the being of the man Jesus and other human beings is its
ontological character.[104] "But the matter itself, as well as the New Testament
school in which we have to consider it, forces us to take these statements
seriously, i.e., both the statements and also this connexion, as statements
about a being of the man Jesus, and therefore a being of other men (our own
being), as statements of an ontological character."[105]

For Barth, the being of the royal man establishes his ontological connection with other human beings through the *anhypostasis* and *enhypostasis* relationship where Barth argues that the New Testament compels us
to understand the connection between the man Jesus and all other human
beings in ontological and therefore dynamic terms. That is, on the one side,
the royal man in all his majesty and uniqueness is grounded in the fact that
he is the eternal Son of the eternal Father, and therefore exists as both God
and humanity. On the other side are mere human beings, but human beings
who exist under this Lord and therefore belong to him. These are ordered
in relation to the royal man; who abide in him and with him, and have
been exalted into the royal man's fellowship with God. They have been ar-
rested and turned from their own evil way becoming obedient to God as his
saints—true covenant partners with God in him.[106]

This helps to explain the anthropological axiom in Barth's thinking.
In other words, the only way for us to truly know ourselves is to know
ourselves in Christ, which can only be attained outside ourselves in this
other, this one who is in fact different from us. Therefore, while God himself
becomes real humanity, it will always be another, a concrete antithesis from
us.[107] Hence, to know ourselves in Christ is not a matter of beginning with
us first and then looking to Christ as a way to complete ourselves in our
knowledge of him. No; Barth's concern here has first to do with the being
of Jesus Christ and our being *in* him.[108] It is the love of Jesus Christ that
penetrates his hiddenness and therefore the hiddenness of our being in him.
Jesus not only causes himself to be seen, but he also causes us to be seen in
him. This defines the ontological binding between the community of Christ
and its Lord. Consequently, we are enabled to see his lordship and kingdom
and ourselves as his own possession that dwell in his Kingdom, all of which
confirms the fact that both he and we are hidden. "And if in His love and

104. Ibid., 281.
105. Ibid.
106. Ibid., 282.
107. Ibid., 283.
108. Ibid.

revelation we can see Him and ourselves in Him, and love Him in return, we are merely seeing and loving that which is concealed, and in so doing necessarily confirming both His and our own concealment. The exception proves the rule."[109]

But our ability to see what is hidden and therefore to know Jesus Christ and ourselves in him first demands a penetration and removal of that which hides. Barth describes this as an event; an exception and not a state. This does not mean, however, that Jesus Christ is now at our disposal where only a little openness and readiness on our part is enough to know him and ourselves in him, being brought into a true covenant-partnership with God. Barth explains that his fellowship with us—and ours with him—cannot be received and valued in this "cheap and easy" way. The exalted reality of our reconciliation taken place in Christ, our eternal salvation, and the peace we enjoy with God as attested to in the Scriptures rejects any thinking along these lines. According to the Bible, God is not accessible and at our disposal in this way.[110] "For we are speaking of the one who is high and lifted up, and of the majesty of our being in Him and with Him. There can be no question of any such accessibility."[111]

Barth explains that this concealment rests on the reality of his being as the royal man, as our Lord, Representative, and Savior. It rests on the mystery of his cross, the mystery of his exaltation and our exaltation in him, and therefore our humiliation. As such, the mystery of atonement and salvation that has taken place is directed to us (his community) in the man Jesus of Nazareth, where this concealment belongs inalienably and centrally to Jesus and in him to us.[112] For Barth, this is the ontological reality of the community of Christ existing (being) in Christ, but a being that exists in mystery and concealment. Once again we mark here the clear and important influence of the *anhypostasis* and *enhypostasis* relational dynamic. That is, the concealment of Jesus Christ—which is enclosed in his human nature in its union with the Logos—also extends to his community of saints whom enjoy the ontological reality of his being by virtue of their union with him. "He would not be the One He is for us, nor we those that are in Him, if not in this concealment. The point at issue is how we can ever see and know our being in Jesus Christ, and therefore ourselves as those who are established in Him, as those who are no longer away from God but towards Him, as regenerate

109. Ibid., 286.
110. Barth, *CD* IV/2, 287–88.
111. Ibid.
112. Ibid., 296.

and converted, the saints of God, Christians. There can be no question as to the being of Jesus Christ, and therefore our being in Him."[113]

Barth emphasizes that the basis of our being in Christ derives from God's eternal love for us, a love expressed independently from our cooperation or reciprocation. What God requires from humanity—and the critical point at issue for Barth here—is a change in its way of thinking that corresponds to a redirected will and attitude. This is a reoriented attitude and determination of our existence which comes to us. And in relation to that love, and in response to it, we love him in return. Barth argues that we must do this because the being of Jesus Christ and our being in him are irrefutably grounded in itself. Given this ontological orientation, his being and ours in him cannot fail to correspond to the Christian orientation and determination of our existence.[114] "But how is this possible except in relation to this being? How is it possible except in an awareness of it, i.e., as its reality acquires for us the character of truth, i.e., as we see and know and understand it. Reality which does not become truth for us obviously cannot affect us, however supreme may be its ontological dignity."[115]

The reality of this love between Jesus Christ and his people (and our being in him) corresponds to our recognition of this relationship. However, Barth raises the question: how can the unknown become a known reality for his people? In other words, how can we perceive Jesus Christ and our being in him? What must happen for this to be so? Barth answers that we must look to the reality of the crucified Jesus Christ as our King, Lord, and substitute. In the crucified Christ alone are we able to have peace with God. Therefore, we must first look to the reality of the crucified Christ before we can look at the exalted Jesus as the King and our Lord, and therefore ourselves as his possession. In other words, we must first look to that which is concealed.[116] Barth asks here: "What does it really mean to see the Crucified: the Servant who was and is the Lord; the Humiliated who was and is the Exalted; the King of Gethsemane and Golgotha? What is truth if the real Jesus is the One who was rejected and condemned and executed, and the whole reality of our being is enclosed in this One who was put to death?"[117]

Barth emphasizes that Jesus Christ did something for us which we could not do for ourselves. The New Testament clearly bears witness to the fact that we have no capacity to act on our own behalf. Consequently,

113. Barth, *CD* IV/2, 296.
114. Ibid., 296–97.
115. Ibid.
116. Ibid., 297.
117. Ibid.

there is no alternative. Our perception of the objective reality that is the revelation of Jesus Christ must be an event that comes to us, apart from us—from the other side. Otherwise it would not come at all. Moreover, it is not enough to simply say this is truth. Barth argues that the Scriptures tell us more than that. This reality and its truth, the being of Jesus Christ and our being in him—concealed in his crucifixion—are power.[118] The New Testament explains this power by the fact that the crucified Jesus Christ has risen from the dead.

> But in the present context this means that He discloses Himself to us with the same will and power and in the same act as He closes Himself off from us. We have to hear the two sides of the message in their irreversible sequence, the first as the first (which has always been heard too), and the second as the second. He is the Crucified who as such closes Himself off from us, and He is the Resurrected who as such discloses Himself to us.[119]

In his resurrection from the dead Jesus Christ declares his majesty and distinctive sovereignty as a human being, as the royal man. Barth explains that according to the New Testament, the whole of Jesus Christ's life and death is both humiliation and exaltation. But it is his resurrection from the dead that reveals him as the one who is exalted in his lowliness.[120] The light of this self-revelation in the majesty of the royal man is the content of the New Testament gospel, which stands or falls on the proclamation of his name. The gospel therefore cannot be interpreted as the doctrine of human religion or morality, nor can it be relatively understood as human understanding explicated as human faith. It is the Christian community calling upon Jesus and the salvation achieved in him as the one who lives as an ontological reality. It is achieved in him as the truth, as the crucified and majestic royal man on the basis of his self-declaration to us, which serves to disclose us to ourselves. This is so because he does not exist without us. Jesus Christ is the first-born brother of all humanity as its head and representative.[121] Barth paints here a vivid picture of Christ's humanity, which is exalted as the royal man, in whom the community of Christians are exalted with him based upon their union with him—their being in him. The *anhypostasis* and *enhypostasis* dynamic between Christ and his church speak quite forcefully here.

---

118. Ibid., 298.
119. Ibid., 298–99.
120. Ibid., 299.
121. Barth, *CD* IV/2, 299–300.

He Himself is only as *we* also are elected and called to Him
. . . He reveals the fact that we set up in Him. Nor is all this
abstract. Not for a single moment is it isolated from Him. It is
concrete and supremely real in and with His self-revelation, His
resurrection, His life from the dead. It has its sure foundation
in our union with Him (quite apart from our recognition and
response). Thus in and with the being of Jesus Christ as the
new man our new being is not merely concealed but brought to
light—not, of course, as we discover it in Him, but as He Himself reveals it to us in Him.[122]

Jesus Christ emerged from his concealment through his self-revelation. He declared himself in his resurrection from the dead. Barth argues
that the problem for humanity is refusing to take seriously the cross as the
crown of the human life of Jesus. It is the cross that demonstrates the reality of God's self-humiliation in his Son, to which the Son of Man willingly
submitted himself to endure. Only in the cross do we see the completeness of the divine and human will along with the divine and human act, the
perfection in which Jesus Christ suffered (as our representative) the death
that humanity had merited when he died in our place.[123] Barth argues that
the power of Christ's resurrection speaks for itself. It opens our very being
for the new and exalted man, the being we actually are in him. In Christ
we are awakened to the fact that we are *actually there*. For Barth, these are
the changes that must take place before we can begin to be Christians.[124]
Stated the other way around, a Christian understands and confesses that
he or she is a Christian strictly as a result of this power, which is the basis
of this being. Therefore, achieving this faith comes only as a witness to this
great power, which moves to open humanity for Jesus Christ and their own
being in him. It is a miraculous work.[125] "Unless we define this more closely

---

122. Ibid., 300.

123. Barth, *CD* IV/2, 301. We note here Barth's reliance upon the New Testament
as the beginning point for this argument, which Barth uses in a very distinctive way to
explain what is addressed to us and summons us, applies what it says to us, and therefore claims us with respect to it. The New Testament bears witness to the person Jesus
Christ as the "whole nexus and history and reality and truth bound up in this name."
Moreover, this witness is addressed to individual human beings who can acquire this
information by receiving the witness, having already been claimed in anticipation as
those to whom it concerns. Therefore, the objective content of truth in the reality of
Jesus Christ includes our own reality. This presses in upon us from its *objectivity* to our
subjectivity in this correspondence. See Barth, *CD* IV/2, 303.

124. Ibid., 307.

125. Ibid., 309.

it might seem to be no more than a purely formal and to that extent empty and therefore equivocal description of this power and its mystery."[126]

Barth explains in more precise language that the power of the resurrection of Jesus Christ is known by the fact that it "snatches" humanity upwards. This upward movement, however, is not to be understood in the abstract as some form of inward spiritual life. Rather, it is a distinct matter of a person's life in its totality, of a person as the soul of their own body and therefore of their outward life with all its distinctive elements and functions in relation to other cosmic creatures. This is the actuality of the exalted man Jesus from whom the power of this life derives. He is exalted in the totality of his soul and body, just as he is humiliated in the totality of his outer and inner life. He reveals himself in the flesh and blood of his being. The power that proceeds from his resurrection, and he himself as the resurrection, enriches and nourishes the whole of a human person (spiritual and material). It is this power that preserves the human being as a whole.[127] For Barth, this reality answers the question how it is possible and actual for a human being to become a Christian. It is derived from the resurrection of Jesus Christ in the sovereign operative power of revelation—the transition from him to us—of his communication with us. This is a power that reveals and makes known to us our own election as it takes place in him, of the transition from him to us, of his communication with us.

All of this is summed up in the fact that Christ's humiliation as the Son of God and his exaltation as the Son of Man occurred for us in the deliverance and establishment of our own being, in receiving our new determination in Christ. This is the operative power necessary for us to become Christians.[128] This is the power of the Holy Spirit, which marks the center of Barth's understanding of the ontological union of Jesus Christ with his community. I argue that this ontological union clearly corresponds to the *anhypostasis* and *enhypostasis* formulation that has become so important in Barth's Christology. And it is from this central point—this point of convergence—that Barth can now further develop the ontological union between Jesus Christ and his community in three interrelated ways that I define as: 1) the role of the Holy Spirit, 2) the historical reality of the Holy Spirit, and 3) the Holy Spirit as the solution to the paradox of Christ's humiliation and exaltation.

---

126. Ibid.
127. Barth, *CD* IV/2, 316–17.
128. Ibid., 318.

The Role of the Holy Spirit

One enduring criticism of Karl Barth is the paucity of a fully developed pneumatology in his *Church Dogmatics*.[129] One, however, cannot help but muse on the possibilities of a more robust pneumatology if Barth had been able to draw the *Church Dogmatics* to closure with his inclusion of the doctrine of redemption. We of course will never know. Nevertheless, we recognize in Barth's development of the exaltation of the Son of Man the decisive confluence of the Holy Spirit in the exaltation of the man Jesus of Nazareth as the royal man. This is important to note in our present context because Barth understands that the true union of humanity with God is an ontological relationship that begins and ends with the Jesus Christ through the power of his Holy Spirit.[130] Barth argues that the New Testament presupposes the power and operation of the Holy Spirit in its presence and action, which enables human beings in their natural limitations to become witnesses of Jesus Christ. Having been awakened by the Holy Spirit these same human beings can now see Jesus Christ and themselves in him. It is in the light of this knowledge—as determined by the Holy Spirit—that they are able to think and will in a new way. This is the Holy Spirit creating the fellowship between brothers and sisters in Jesus Christ as one people—*as his people* and *his community*. Moreover, it is the Holy Spirit who directs the *kerygma* of Christ's community and sets them apart from other human beings in this world. The Holy Spirit forms and directs them as his witnesses.

129. In his comparison of the work of the Spirit in the theologies of B. B. Warfield and Karl Barth, Daniel Migliore notes that while Warfield is criticized for concentrating all of his thinking about the Spirit on the work of Scriptural inspiration, Karl Barth is criticized for leaving all too undeveloped his doctrine of the person and work of the Spirit in his *Church Dogmatics*. Migliore, however, strikes the mark by taking notice of the "especially rich passages" in *CD* IV/2 where Barth develops the theme of the Spirit and its active role in the whole course of the life, ministry, death and resurrection of Jesus Christ. Citing *CD* IV/2, 324 where Barth states that God gives Jesus the Spirit without limit as the wholly sanctified man, Migliore argues that this passage demonstrates a clear invitation to an explicit and strong pneumatological dimension of Christology that can complement (not replace) the classical Logos Christology. However incompletely developed in Barth, this Christology of the Spirit-filled, Spirit-driven, and Spirit-empowered Jesus looks every bit like an genuine theological novum. See Migliore, "*Veni Creator Spiritus*," 168–71.

130. We note here that Barth carries his development of the work of the Holy Spirit forward in *CD* IV/3.1 given the context of the Word of Jesus Christ as the Prophet of God. Barth argues that reconciliation in itself is both real and true, which is proven in the enlightening work of the Holy Spirit in his "disclosure, declaration and impartation." Barth concludes here that "This is the basis of certainty and clarity when it is a matter of the knowledge of Jesus Christ and His work through the work of the Holy Spirit," Barth, *CD* IV/3.1, 11.

He calls them to action and in so doing directs and controls their activities, giving to them the power to execute that which he directs.[131]

Given this context I argue that Barth addresses head on the presupposition that the Holy Spirit alone—as the Alpha and Omega—is the principle and power of the Christian life. Barth explains it as the correctness of our being and action that marks our entrance into his sphere of existence and activity. It is the power of the Holy Spirit itself that ensures his communion (his bearing witness) with our spirit as his children.[132] "We know Him in fact as the power whose mystery and character we have discussed, as the exclusive and sovereign Creator, Founder, Ruler and Fashioner of all individual and collective Christian being and essence."[133]

With this in view Barth argues that there is no such thing as a *non-pneumatic* Christian.[134] Rather it is axiomatic for the Christian community to exist as a pneumatic body because the Holy Spirit separates Christians by taking them aside and placing them under his own power (unter seine Gewalt und Ordnung gebracht).[135] In this way Christians experience the "washing of regeneration" which consists in "the renewing of the Holy Ghost" (Titus 3:5). This is the newness in which they now live and should be addressed as recipients of unction from the holy one (1 John 2:20). As such, Christians are the ones who are led by the Spirit (Rom 8:14). They are counted as happy because the spirit of God and his glory rests upon them (1 Pet 4:14).

> They have the spirit as απαρχη (Rom 8:23), as αρραβων (2 Cor 1:22, 5:5), as σφραγισ (2 Cor 1:22; Eph 1:14), and therefore as promise (Luke 24:49). There is then no limit to the confidence, the axiomatic certainty and joy, with which the community, and in the community all Christians, may believe and love and hope and pray and think and speak and act. "The Holy Ghost is a witness to us" (Heb 10:15). Where he is, there is liberty (2 Cor 3:17). This is the secret of the confidence with which they exist as the community and as Christians.[136]

---

131. Barth, *CD* IV/2, 319.

132. Ibid., 320.

133. Ibid.

134. Suzanne McDonald argues that Barth is clear that the distinction between the elect and "apparently rejected" is determined by the presence or absence of the gift of the Holy Spirit by which the community of Christians is enabled to know and live in accordance with the reality of its election, and with the knowledge that the only true rejected one is the Son. See McDonald, "Evangelical Questioning of Election in Barth," 260.

135. Barth, *CD* IV/2, 321; *KD* IV/2, 359.

136. Barth, *CD* IV/2, 322.

In speaking of the Holy Spirit Barth raises a crucial question when he asks: why is it that he is the Holy Spirit by definition? Why is it that Christians are continually summoned and enabled to depend upon his authority and power with unassailable confidence? Barth responds that the answer is "staggering in its simplicity." He is the Holy Spirit with a holiness ordered by its uniqueness for which there are no analogies, because he is no other than the presence and action of Jesus Christ himself. This is Jesus Christ who in the power of his revelation—made manifest in the power of his resurrection—will continue his work from this point forward. It is this Spirit—the Spirit of Jesus Christ—who is the power of the revelation of the royal man. It is he who makes one a Christian. For this reason and based on this fact, he is the Holy Spirit.[137]

This principle underscores Barth's understanding of what the New Testament says about the Spirit as a clear and direct line from Jesus Christ himself to his community of Christians. This Spirit is the Spirit of Jesus Christ (Phil 1:19; Rom 8:9), the Spirit of the Son whom the Father has sent forth into our hearts (Gal 4:6). The emphasis here is that he is *his* Spirit in whose power and operation he exists and acts as he does. He is αγιον (holy) because he is κυριον (Lord). He became and is and will be Jesus of Nazareth wholly by the power of the Spirit. Therefore, Jesus does not need to receive him because he came into being as "He became the one who receives and bears and brings Him."[138] Barth's argument bears directly upon Jesus as a man, but not a man who was subsequently gifted and pierced by the Spirit like other human beings (i.e., the prophets before him or the his disciples after him or ourselves as Christians). Jesus of Nazareth has the Spirit from the very beginning. He is the Word who became flesh (John 1:14), and therefore a true man like us in his humanity; but not like us because as a man he was not conceived of the flesh, but of the Spirit (John 3:6).[139]

> But because as a man He was not conceived of the flesh, but of the Spirit (John 3:6), He at once became spirit in the flesh; a man who in the lowliness of the flesh, as from the very first He was on the way to His abasement in death, lives also from the very first by the Spirit, Himself creating and giving life by the Spirit.[140]

The royal man is taken up into union with the eternal Logos through the power of the Holy Spirit and exists as real humanity, but not humanity

137. Ibid., 323.
138. Ibid., 324.
139. Ibid.
140. Ibid.

like us. He is the man of divine good pleasure who fulfills the righteousness of God in achieving its goal. Barth notes here that in subjecting himself to John's baptism of repentance as an act of solidarity with the whole people, Jesus is concealed in an incognito as this man. And as such he will fulfill this sign of baptism in even greater concealment in his death on the cross. Yet in this concealment the fullness of the Spirit is given to him without limit so that his being as the flesh of humanity directly corresponds to his being as Spirit.[141] Barth argues that all these things point to Christ's desire, his will not to live alone in this life, but to live in fellowship with other participants. The humanity of Christ involves his humiliation and exaltation, his death and resurrection, which are reflected (not repeated), and in the lives of those who exist in direct correspondence to his life. This is made a reality as Jesus Christ gives his Spirit—the Holy Spirit—to the people of his church, doing so as the crucified and risen, "as the power of His death revealed in His resurrection."[142] This Spirit is given to the community of individual Christians as the great παρακλητοσ, who is the mediator and advocate and spokesman of Jesus Christ on behalf of his own people. The Spirit of Christ speaks about him and for him as his representative (and his cause) with the intent to help his people understand it as their cause in making it their own. The Spirit of Christ is therefore recognized and confessed as the one he is,

141. Ibid. Barth notes from John's Gospel the Baptist's saying that "I saw the Spirit ... abide upon him" (John 1:32), and according to the Baptist's later witness (John 3:34) that God does not give the Spirit to the one whom he has sent as he gave him to the prophets and then to apostles and the community and Christians. Moreover, in Rom 1:3f Paul describes Christ's two-fold historical descent where he is the Son of God as a man (κατα σαρκα) derived from David and his seed, but who also at the same time is powerfully marked off (ορισθεις εν δυναμει) from from all other human beings as the Son of God (κατα πνευμας αγιωσυνης) by the Spirit who sanctified him as the Son of David as real humanity. In this way he came from the place from which no other human being has ever come (εζ αναστασεως νεκρων). According to the hymn in 1 Tim 3:16, he was revealed in the flesh. Barth argues that this is the radical sense in which the Holy Spirit is the Spirit of Jesus himself. That is, as the Son of God, Jesus is also spiritual humanity. And as such, he moves along the way that leads to the cross that is revealed when he is raised from the dead, which is decisive in this context. "The Spirit is holy as the power in which the man Jesus is present and alive even after death as the One who was crucified for the world's salvation, and in which He continually acts as the man He became and was and is, as the One who was crucified in the flesh." Barth, CD IV/2, 325.

142. Barth, CD IV/2, 325–26. Barth argues that when Jesus says to His disciples, "Receive ye the Holy Spirit" it is he himself who does this, but he does so on the far side of that frontier. He is the one who has crossed it, who in his death fulfilled both his humiliation and exaltation, and in his resurrection proved himself to be the "holy servant" (Acts 4:27f) and therefore the Lord. He is the one who is crowned in his death and revealed as the King in his resurrection and who achieves his presence and action in the existence of other human beings. Therefore, they have the Spirit sent from him as the Holy Spirit. See Barth, CD IV/2, 325–26.

who is met with obedience in the truth of his revelation, which cannot be hidden under a bushel but must be set upon the candlestick to light all that are in the house (Matt 5:14f.).[143] "He will be the αλλος παρακλητοσ (John 14:16) to the extent that His work will begin on the far side of the dying and rising again of the man Jesus, consisting in, and deriving from, the self-revelation of this man in His fulfillment."[144]

Barth understands that Christ's promise of the Spirit is a living promise because he himself (who was raised again from the dead) lives within it, making himself present in it. This is the place of the Spirit as his mediator, advocate and representative. He can therefore say "I will not leave you comfortless: I will come to you" (John 14:18).[145] In this way the presence and action of the Holy Spirit fulfills the promise of his coming *in time* before his final revelation at the end of time. Moreover, he proves himself to be the Spirit of Christ who lived among humanity by fulfilling and revealing the life of Jesus in his death and resurrection, as the object of the Christian community, by impressing it upon them and thereby revealing it to them as the decisive factor in their own human existence. This is the power of the Holy Spirit to reveal the joyous light and liberation; the peace and life in Christ.[146] This is the dynamic and integrated movement of Jesus Christ in his humanity together with his Holy Spirit in the community of Christians. Moreover, it is the acceptance of Jesus Christ as the one who came in the flesh that makes one a Christian—acceptance of which is made possible only in the Holy Spirit.[147] With this in view Barth also explains that it is not possible to know which comes first; the outpouring of the Holy Spirit of Christ in the Christian's life as their acceptance of Jesus as Lord, or their free acceptance of themselves as those who belong to him and therefore

143. Ibid., 327.

144. Ibid.

145. Ibid.

146. Barth, *CD* IV/2, 327. We note here that Barth understands this power and work of the Spirit of Christ not in an elect/reprobate sense, but in the Christian/non-Christian sense. It is by this knowledge that the Christian is marked off from the nations and transitions to its mission to the nations. This knowledge of the Christian creates a division, "not into the good and bad, the elect and reprobate, the saved and lost, but into Christians and non-Christians." Barth adds that division must be made continually so that each new day we are asked if we are Christians or non-Christians. As such, in each new day we must cease to be non-Christians and begin to be Christians, which requires the Holy Spirit for this purpose. With respect to this division Barth cites 1 Cor 12:3: "No man speaking by the Spirit of God says: αναθεμα Ιησουσ (which is only a sharpened form of the confession of those who think that they can be neutral in relation to Him): and no man can say: κυριοσ Ιησουσ but by the Holy Ghost." Barth, *CD* IV/2, 327–28.

147. Ibid., 328.

share his prerogatives. Barth expresses here the natural (or supernatural) state of being that becomes a reality for the community of believers who are brought into union with Christ. In either case it is the love of God that is directed to them in Christ (Rom 8:29).[148]

Finally, we note that Barth argues for this work of the Holy Spirit based upon New Testament language where the holiness and power of the Holy Spirit derives from the Spirit of Jesus Christ, and is therefore his self-revelation. It is this disclosure to other human beings and his fellowship and unity with them that speaks to the mystery of Christ's majesty in the lowliness of his death, and our ability to understand it.[149] The Holy Spirit therefore is holy because it is the self-expression of the man Jesus in his turning toward us and our conversion in turning toward him. His disclosure for us and our disclosure for him comes to us in this two-fold sense as a new thing in earthly history. This is the alteration of human life and nature in the creation and existence of the Christian community. I argue that for Barth this reflects the two-fold dynamic of the *anhypostasis* and *enhypostasis* formulation that uniquely expresses the ontological reality of the church and its union in Christ. And as such, it is the revelation of the triune God in the humanity of Christ through the power of his Holy Spirit. For Barth, this is the only answer that can be given to understanding the mystery of Christ's majesty.[150]

The Historical Reality of the Holy Spirit

It is through the life, the death, and the resurrection from the dead of Jesus Christ that flows the outpouring of the Spirit as the self-impartation of Christ to his people. This reality answers the historical problem raised

---

148. Ibid., 329.

149. Ibid., 331.

150. Barth explains that this is the only answer. In the being Jesus Christ as the Holy one is the "sum of particularity, and in His work the sum of particular operation." Barth argues that this is the supreme and all-embracing aspect of the New Testament understanding of the holiness of the Holy Spirit; that is, the Spirit of Jesus Christ. It is the name and the man Jesus Christ that legitimizes the power and operation of the Holy Spirit as his Spirit who comes from him as the Spirit of his revelation. In this sense, however, Barth argues that the New Testament does not describe the Holy Spirit exclusively as the Spirit of Jesus Christ. In a considerable number of passages it calls him the Spirit of God, or of the Lord, or of the Father, often linking the origin of his being and coming not only with the name of Jesus Christ, but also exclusively with these other names. Yet in these combinations is constituted the same basic schema where writers such as Paul and John exercise the freedom to use the name of God or the Father as well as Jesus Christ regarding the nature and origin of the Spirit. Barth, *CD* IV/2, 332–33.

by Barth.[151] And it is the historical action and presence of the Holy Spirit in this self-imparting that accomplishes God's will on earth by actualizing the existence of his people. Barth argues that the will of God is in fact the background of earthly history; the second and higher dimension of his being and operation that must be kept in mind as we think and speak of the Holy Spirit and his work. Stated another way, it is the Holy Spirit of the eternal God that actualizes or drives the central history of humanity and determines its continuance in time. Every other form of world history can only exist as an accompaniment, so that from God's perspective we have to do with this totality in dealing with the unity between the man Jesus and other human beings born out of the being and operation of the Holy Spirit.[152] For Barth, it is in view of the distinctive character and reach of this history that we must understand the new dimension that is opened up. That is, God himself is present and active in it. This is important to understand as this history is marked off from all other histories because God Himself is at work in it . . . "in its origin, in the existence of the crucified and risen man Jesus, the royal man; in its goal, in the existence of the Christian community and individual Christians; and in the transition or mediation from the one to the other, in the power and operation of the Holy Ghost.[153]

It is the power and operation of the Holy Spirit in the royal man that mediates a transition of history from simply world history to the rise of the Christian community in the world. This helps to explain the being of the royal man and his history in revealing the work of God in all the decisive factors of this history. Moreover, this specific history must be distinguished from the presence and activity of God throughout all of human history as the Lord of all history. Barth argues that this is not a matter of understanding an obscure metaphysics but our understanding of the reality of history in this world and the part that humanity has in it.[154] Consequently, the historical setting of Jesus Christ can only be rightly understood in the illumination of its own light. Barth develops this historical setting by describing three decisive factors. The first and controlling factor is the existence of the man Jesus who in his coming makes this whole history possible and actual. This is a divine work that is also accomplished as a human work in the sphere of

---

151. Barth, *CD* IV/2, 333. The point that Barth drives at here is the outpouring of the Spirit, which is the effect of Jesus Christ's resurrection, of his life, of his conquest of death, and therefore the occurrence of his self-impartation ("Because I live, ye shall live also," John 14:19) answers the historical problem of the communication and union of Christ with his church.

152. Barth, *CD* IV/2, 334.

153. Ibid., 335.

154. Ibid.

His limited existence.[155] "As God does not will to exist, to be God, merely for Himself alone, but in the world, in the midst of men and for them, this man exists as the origin which includes the execution and the goal of all that God wills to do, and has done, and still does among men and for them."[156]

The second factor (which Barth describes as the third factor in order), is the goal of history; that is, the existence of the community of Christians. These are found by God when they are found in the man Jesus of Nazareth as their head. They find themselves in him as their origin where God achieves his own end in their existence.[157] The third factor links together the first and second as the power of this transition in the downward movement from Christ to his community of saints. This is evidenced in God's will to be here on earth, not just in Heaven, where God not only exalts this one man but also causes many others to share in his exaltation. This third (and middle factor) of history is that God reveals himself as the one who is with Jesus, and therefore with all Christians, having exalted them in Jesus. Barth explains that it is when we see "clearly and forcibly" within history these three equal moments we understand the movement of God—not simply intellectually—but "existentially" as our own history.[158] Therefore, to know God in this history is to know ourselves as well. This is important to understand for Barth because there can be no "complete" correspondences to the Trinity of God apart from God's own being and life within the creaturely world.[159]

> Even the history with which we are now concerned cannot be described in this way. Only one of its three factors coincides with the one of the three modes of being (or "persons") of God, although in this case the coincidence is quite unequivocal, the third and middle factor, the divine power of the transition from Christ to Christendom, being identical with God in the mode of being of the Holy Spirit.[160]

Barth describes this as the center, and must be considered if we are to recognize the light of the triune God that shines throughout this history. However, we cannot say that the existence of the man Jesus at the beginning of this history is materially identical with God the Father, nor is the existence of Christendom at its end materially identical with God the Son.

155. Ibid., 336–37.
156. Ibid.
157. Ibid.. 337.
158. Ibid.
159. Ibid., 338.
160. Ibid., 338–39.

Instead Barth points to the "formal" character of the first factor, that it is the origin of the whole history, the origin which already anticipates and includes within itself the goal.[161]

> . . . just as God the Father has to be called the *fons et origo totius Deitatis* in the trinitarian being and life of God. And we can point only to the formal character of the second factor—that it is the goal of this history which corresponds and refers back to its origin, just as in God Himself the Son is the One who is eternally loved by the Father and who eternally loves Him in return, so that He is Deus de Deo, lumen de lumine . . . consubstantialis Patri . . . [162]

In this history God himself is present and active as the triune God. But he is only recognizable at the place beyond the formal similarity between this history and the triune being of God; that is, the place where we find the Holy Spirit.[163] As the Holy Spirit, he is not only the divine power mediating between Christ and Christians, but also the mode of being (of the one God) that unites the Father and the Son. In this way the Holy Spirit more and more forces himself upon us as the true theme of this history—*our history*.[164] Barth then turns to the question of the actual operation of the Holy Spirit as the endowed power enabling those to become what they had not been before—witnesses of the great acts of God—that take place in Jesus Christ. In other words, the question is: what kind of intervention is this really? Barth responds that this is the intervention of the triune God where in the mystery of his being and work in our earthly history is found the expression of who God is in himself. This is expressed concretely as God the Father and the Son in their fellowship, unity, and love of the Holy Spirit, who is himself the Spirit of the Father and the Son; who as the one, is one in himself in these three modes of being.[165] "This is why it takes place with

---

161. Ibid., 339.

162. Ibid.

163. John L. Drury marks in par. 64.4 (The Direction of the Son) that even though the Holy Spirit is named after the Son, the Holy Spirit emerges as the true theme of this section. Drury argues that the centrality of the Spirit in 64.4 is a direct result of the emphasis on the true humanity of Christ in *CD* IV/1, where the true human essence of the Son requires the Spirit's empowerment. Therefore, the only way for the humanity of Christ to give us divine direction is through the activity of the Holy Spirit. See Drury, *The Resurrected God*, 73.

164. Barth, *CD* IV/2, 339.

165. Ibid., 341.

such sovereign freedom, and cannot in any sense be controlled for us. This is why it can properly be known only in an act of worship."[166]

For Barth, the mystery of the triune God is a mystery that we stand before objectively because God himself lives in what takes place between the man Jesus and human beings as we become Christians. Therefore, his life is not alien to us.[167] However, there also exists in the realm of human history the problem of historical interaction between Jesus of Nazareth and other human beings, a problem of confrontation given the distance between them. Jesus is the royal man and we are not. However, (and this is the critical point to grasp in Barth's thinking here) Jesus becomes the royal man not for himself, but for us because he desires to be with us. Therefore, his very existence as the royal man anticipates our existence with him. Yet the problem remains. How can Jesus be true and the other (his community) also become true? This is a spiritual problem that the intervention of the Holy Spirit alone can solve. Moreover, this is not a problem of human history, but of divine being, the problem of God's own being which is solved by the personal intervention of his Holy Spirit. Therefore, God, in solving the problem of personal intervention, solves our problem as well.[168]

For Barth, all of this reflects the triune God as a God of action where the being of God the Father and God the Son with the Holy Spirit (who is the Spirit of both) and whose eternal procession they are both actively united. Therefore, this is a history exclusively realized in the life and being of God, a history between the Father and the Son that culminates in the fact that God is also *Spiritus Sanctus Dominus vivificans, qui ex Patre Filioque procedit.* Moreover, this movement of the Father and Son in history is not determined based upon divine necessity as if they are being held as two prisoners. "They are not two mutually conditioning factors in reciprocal operation. As the common source of the Spirit, who Himself is also God, they are the Lord of this occurrence." Barth explains that the life of the Triune God is a life that is free because its life is Spirit, which is the basis of God's whole will and action "even *ad extra*, as the living act which He directs to us. It is the basis of His *decretum et opus ad extra*, of the relationship which He has determined and established with a reality which is distinct from Himself and endowed by Him with its own very different and creaturely being."[169]

---

166. Ibid.

167. Barth describes the active unity of the Father and the Son in the Holy Spirit given that like the Father and the Son, as the Spirit of the Father and the Son, is the one true God, *qui ex Patre Filioque procedit, qui cum Patre et Filio simul adoratur et conglorificatur.* See Barth, *CD* IV/2, 342.

168. Ibid., 342–43.

169. Barth, *CD* IV/2, 345.

It is therefore the freedom of the Triune God that determines the election of humanity in covenant with himself—a covenant where the Son become humanity—in order to fulfill it on behalf of humanity. For Barth, this is the covenant of creation that in effect conquers the opposition and contradiction of humanity necessary to save it from destruction. This is God's atonement of humanity with its final goal aimed at the redemption of humanity to eternal life with himself.[170] Moreover, it is the Spirit of the man Jesus Christ that proceeds from him, attests him, and unites other human beings with him. Barth is careful here to explain that the Spirit of the Son of God is not different from the Spirit of the Father, but the Spirit in whom both the Father and the Son—who are eternally distinct—are also eternally united. This is the Spirit of God the creator, reconciler, and redeemer of his creation, who elects humanity and causes this humanity to be free. In so doing God joins himself with humanity in a faithfulness that is no less free.[171]

For Barth, the mystery of Jesus Christ as the Son of Man emerges from the reality of his being as the eternal Son of God. He is himself God, but God who also exists as the Son of Man whose Spirit proceeds from him, and attests him, and unites other human beings with him. This is the Spirit of God acting and revealing himself in this world in human history. This is the history between Jesus and humanity which corresponds to the self-revelation of God expressed through the *anhypostasis* and *enhypostasis* dynamic embodied in Christ's relationship with his church. This relationship seals the reality and truth of God's faithfulness to us—in his faithfulness to himself.[172]

The Solution to the Paradox of Christ's Humiliation and Exaltation

We approach this section with Barth's self-reflection that all he has said thus far about Jesus as the reconciler of the world and our relationship with him as Christians has been spoken in riddles, but not riddles of his own making. Rather, this riddle emerges out of Jesus Christ as our Lord who is also a servant. In his crucifixion Christ is also the life-giver. In his end Christ is also the beginning for humanity; in his concealment he is also revealed. This is the riddle of the lowly state of Jesus who is exalted as the true and royal man. Therefore, to understand Jesus Christ in his royal humanity depends on our facing the severity of this antithesis and keeping it before us. This is crucial for Barth who argues that all Christian errors can be traced back to the

170. Ibid.
171. Ibid., 347.
172. Ibid., 347–48.

effacement of this antithesis either on one side or the other. Yet "paradox" cannot (and must not) be the final word in relation to Jesus Christ. There-fore, to properly address and overcome this riddle (this paradox) posed in the person of Jesus Christ, the question of the Holy Spirit (concretely the Spirit of Jesus Christ) must be addressed as the basis and necessity of the antithesis found in it. Barth addresses his solution to this riddle from two different standpoints: first, from the Son of God as the humiliation of the ex-alted; and secondly, from the Son of Man as the exaltation of the humiliated. Given these two standpoints Barth argues that "we have to see the fact and the extent that the Spirit of Jesus Christ (by which the latter is self-attested both as humiliated and exalted) is the Holy Spirit, who as such has power and authority over us."[173]

Jesus Christ's existence as the royal man corresponds to his divine Son-ship and his sovereign uniqueness as the one who proclaims and brings with him the Kingdom of God. Barth explains that despite his divine and human light, Jesus is wrapped in the deepest concealment as the divine judge who was himself judged. As the living God and only true living human being, Jesus was crucified and destroyed where he entered into the darkness of death. This is the antithesis in Jesus Christ's existence where the Holy Spirit intervenes and is at work between Jesus and human beings as the Spirit of Jesus Christ.[174] This is the "self-activation and self-revelation" of the living Jesus Christ that we can believe and confess in the face of this antithesis. But Barth raises the question: "how far" does the Spirit of Jesus Christ lead the community of Christians in their conversion, in this revelation as the Spirit of reality? In other words, to what extent is he the Spirit of truth in his own most proper work? Barth responds that as the Spirit of truth he is none other than the living God, the Triune God who is "present and revealed and active." He is the Spirit of the Father and the Son.[175] "If He instructs us concerning the necessity of that antithesis in the existence of Jesus Christ, and all that this means for our existence, He also instructs us concerning the overcoming of this antithesis, which means that He leads us to the basis of this matter and sets us on it."[176]

This instruction (belehrt) of the Holy Spirit is foundational in Barth's understanding of the cross where the royal man is crowned as he attests to the grace of God in the convergence of his lowliness and his exaltation. It is at the cross where the Son of God bears witness to the life of God himself in

173. Ibid., 348.
174. Ibid., 349.
175. Ibid., 350.
176. Ibid.

his human life, who as the royal man is crowned in this place of shame. But it is the Holy Spirit of God—as the Spirit of Jesus Christ himself—which is the power of the witness of the Son of God in his human life and declared in his resurrection from the dead. He is the Spirit of truth who reveals the life of the man Jesus as the life of the Son with the Father. He reveals and solves the antithesis that dominates this life, the antithesis that is overcome by the will of God in Jesus Christ.[177]

The exaltation of Jesus Christ explains the Christian community that emerges from his resurrection.[178] This community says yes to this royal man and the glory of the Son of God revealed in his human majesty. This is the exaltation of the Christian's life as it has taken place in him.[179] For Barth, the riddle of Jesus Christ's life is that the humiliation of the Son of God actually reveals the exaltation of the Son of Man, and our own exaltation in him as our brother and head.[180] This is so because in his humiliation Jesus Christ acted and revealed himself as the true Son of God, and he became and remains humanity as the Son of God. From all eternity he is decreed by God as the elect man, exalted in all the lowliness of his humanity, and revealed in his resurrection and ascension as true humanity who lives in eternal fellowship with God at the right hand of the Father. Barth asks: how could it be otherwise when Jesus is the man who in all his humanity exists only as the Son of God? Even so, in his exaltation Jesus Christ does not cease to be true humanity. If he were not still true humanity he would not be our brother, nor properly represent us, nor bear away our rejection according to His election. But he has in fact become humanity as the Son of God. He has become the royal man who represents us to God.[181] "The majesty of the Son of God is the mystery, the basis, of the exaltation of the Son of Man; of the fact that the man Jesus of Nazareth is called and is the Lord. Therefore "Jesus is Victor" is simply a confession of the majesty of the incarnate Son of God."[182]

Barth argues that the riddle of Jesus Christ's existence is resolved in the revelation of God's glory where in the mystery of his existence both humiliation and exaltation are true. All of the differences between the two are true and actual as they united in the one free love which is God himself. In his mercy the Father decreed the cross of Golgotha and determined the

---

177. Ibid., 252; *KD* IV/2, 391.
178. Ibid., 353.
179. Ibid., 254.
180. Ibid., 355.
181. Ibid., 358.
182. Ibid.

humiliation of his Son for the sake of humanity; that is, for humanity's exaltation in the humanity of Christ. Transcending the agony of the cross, Jesus Christ wholly takes to himself in the majesty of his humiliation a groaning creature and exalts this humanity in him, investing it with the reflection of his own glory as well as that of the Father.[183] In his being Jesus Christ unites the merciful act of the Father with the majestic act of the Son; two acts in the one incontestable living act of God.[184]

> It does not attest a No alongside a Yes. It does not attest a Yes that may revert to a No. It attests a No which is spoken for the sake of the ensuing Yes, and which is powerful and necessary and unforgettable in this order. And it attests Yes which is a valid and definite Yes—a Yes and Amen (2 Cor 1:20)—as it comes from this No. Its witness does not, therefore, destroy the fact that is so puzzling, but transcends it by causing the work and wisdom of God to be known in it.[185]

This witness (Zeugnis) is the Holy Spirit of Jesus who is the Spirit of the Son as well as the Spirit of the Father. As the Spirit of God he is the Spirit of truth who lights up the life of the man Jesus as the life of the Son with the Father, and the Father with the Son. Barth emphasizes that the Holy Spirit is not merely the gift of the Father and the Son, but he is God himself with the Father and the Son. He is the giver and the source of truth, the "*Creator Spiritus*: the Creator of all knowledge of the truth, of all walking and life in it. He is the Paraclete who really guides the community in all truth."[186] He is the Spirit of God himself, who is the power and lordship of the man Jesus. For Barth, the work of the Holy Spirit explains the transition from Jesus to us and our participation in the exaltation in the Son of God as true humanity.[187] The Holy Spirit therefore empowers our participation in Jesus Christ (this transition from himself to us) as exalted and true humanity.[188] Therefore, given that the Holy Spirit is the power and Lordship of the man Jesus, and because as Jesus of Nazareth he is the Son of God, we can soberly and precisely state how the operation of the Holy Spirit gives direction in this real and dynamic sense. In other words, to receive and have the Holy

183. Ibid.
184. Ibid.
185. Ibid., 358–59.
186. Ibid., 359; *KD* IV/2, 401.
187. Ibid., 360.
188. Ibid., 361.

Spirit is simply to receive and have direction, which is the determining factor for those who are Christians.[189]

This is the key point for Barth, that the direction of Christ's Holy Spirit as the Son of God explains the transition from Jesus to us.[190] This means that a definite place is fixed by the Holy Spirit as an imperative—a supreme and definite summons. This work of the Holy Spirit alarms and unsettles, but it also directs us to the grace of God in our existence to freedom and peace. It brings humanity back to its own beginning and being.[191] The direction of the Holy Spirit warns and corrects.[192] It enables the acceptance as our reconciliation with God and exaltation as it has taken place in Jesus Christ for us.[193] The direction of the Holy Spirit leads us in the face of the choices that confront us, enabling us to ask God what he wills us to do. Barth argues that the Holy Spirit actually reveals, imparts, and writes on our heart and conscience the will of God applicable to the moment at hand.[194]

The reality of the Holy Spirit is therefore concretely the Spirit of Jesus who instructs the Christian as part of the Christian community. This is the power and Lordship of the living man Jesus who as the true Son of God summons human beings to respond in their responsibility as true human beings.[195] Understood in its basic essence, Barth's argues that the Holy Spirit positively wills and effects in his awakening and calling a human existence that deserves to be called a life because it is lived in the light of the royal man. This human being becomes attentive and moves to him having received the Holy Spirit, recognizing and acknowledging that Jesus died and has been raised form the dead for this human being. Not only does Jesus live for this person, but he is also the owner and bearer, the representative and Lord of this person's life who has been exalted in the exaltation of Jesus to a living fellowship with God as a new creature (2 Cor 5:17).[196]

As we consider Karl Barth's development of Christ's union with his church we are drawn to its ontological grounding. Whereas Barth explicitly defines this union as *anhypostasis* and *enhypostasis* in the context of the homecoming of the Son of Man, Barth now develops the dynamic of this

189. Ibid., 362.
190. Ibid.
191. Barth, *CD* IV/2, 364–65.
192. Ibid., 367.
193. Ibid., 369.
194. Ibid., 372.
195. Ibid., 373–74.
196. Ibid., 375.

relationship between the royal man and his church.[197] In essence, Barth now deals with the royal man and the decisive work of his Holy Spirit (his direction) to accomplish his ontological union with his church. For Barth, it is the direction of the Holy Spirit that achieves the actual union of the royal man with his church. And in this union we see the *anhypostasis* and *enhypostasis* dynamic expressed as the Holy Spirit of the royal man, which not only enables this union, but in doing so transitions Christians from their being as false humanity to true humanity actualized as beings in Christ.

Faith and Salvation

Karl Barth never wavers in expressing the reality of Jesus Christ in his being as the revelation of God in a two-sided movement—from above and below. One side of this revelation is the action of God revealed in his movement towards humanity in the humiliation of the Son of God. The other side is the action of God revealed in the exaltation of the Son of Man as the royal man. And it's in the royal man—in his exaltation—that God unites the community of saints with himself. Out of this humiliation and exaltation of Jesus Christ emerges the reality of the church that the Son of God came to claim for himself in his self-revelation. However, this revelation of Jesus Christ demands a human response of faith leading to salvation.[198] I argue that for Barth faith and salvation of the community of saints can only be properly understood in the context of the royal man's ontological relationship with his church. The reality that the Word became flesh is not restricted to a fixed point in time, but encompasses the continuum of Jesus Christ's dynamic movement

197. Barth argues that this community is the form of Jesus Christ's body (with Christ as its heavenly head), which exists as Christ's earthly-historical form of existence. The Church therefore is of human essence, but it does not exist independent from its head. "It is not itself the Head, nor does it become such. But it exists (ανυποστατοσ and ενυποστατοσ) in and in virtue of His existence. It lives because and as He lives, and elected and awakened and called and gathered as a people by Him." Barth, *CD* IV/2, 59.

198. Dawn DeVries argues that for Barth faith is not "a creative or generative human activity." It must be understood as a response or reflex to something outside itself, a separate origin or root. The root is of course the presence of the living Lord Jesus Christ. Because faith takes its origin from a relationship that is prior to and apart from it, believing Christians can no longer imagine themselves as self-determined individuals. Moreover, as the object of faith, Jesus Christ actually imposes himself (*sich aufdrängt*) on human beings requiring the response of faith. DeVries goes on to site Barth in *KD* IV/1, 835 that for those who recognize Jesus Christ by faith, "unbelief has become an objective, real and ontological impossibility and faith has become an objective, real and ontological necessity for all and for each person." DeVries concludes that for Barth faith is not a meritorious work, but in keeping with the Reformed doctrine of incapacity, it is a human transformation realized in Christ. See DeVries, "Does Faith Save?," 165–67.

toward humanity as he summons and joins the community of Christians to himself.[199] As we have shown, Barth argues that the eternal Son of God takes to himself true humanity in the Son of Man as Jesus of Nazareth. And while his humanity veils the majesty of his divinity, Jesus Christ is not left without a witness. It is in fact the Holy Spirit (the Spirit of Jesus Christ himself), which awakens human beings to his summons. And it is this summons that speaks to the ontological relationship of Jesus Christ to the Christian community that is realized in its faith and salvation.

Scripturally speaking, Barth argues that the real presupposition to the blind man's faith in Jesus (John 9) was the Son of Man's power to give this blind man sight as he experienced it. In other words, the door to this man's faith could not be opened from the outside (by the blind man himself), but only from the inside by Jesus as he made himself known to this blind man as the Son of Man. However, Jesus did not simply open the blind man's physical eyes, but more importantly—the eyes of his faith—which occurred with irresistible power as this blind man was awakened and called to faith by Jesus himself. "He was hurled into that *proskynesis* as though he had been struck by lightning." Barth emphasizes that all the elements were necessary for this to happen . . . "the factual, objective, ontological relationship between Jesus and Himself; in this relationship the miracle of free grace in its overflow; the physical encounter with Jesus as the actualisation of this relationship; and again, and supremely, the decisive fact that Jesus Himself spoke of Himself, that of Himself He gave Himself to be known by him through His Word, that as the object of His faith, which He was already, He made Himself also the Creator of his faith."[200]

For Barth, the remarkable lesson of John 9:1 is the defining point for humanity is the same point where Jesus sees a blind man as he passed by. This is the moment that humanity starts (i.e., of the miracle of Jesus and therefore Jesus himself—and therefore God) to which we see humanity moving in Matthew 9:27.[201] It is the crying out to Jesus for mercy where faith is not simply the root, but the fruit of human encounter with Jesus. For Barth, faith is qualified in this twofold sense; (1) humanity turning to Jesus and his power, (2) based upon the reality that Jesus has turned to us in his power. Given Barth's understanding of the New Testament language

199. There is perhaps no clearer demonstration of the significance that *anhypostasis* and *enhypostasis* bring to bear on Barth's Christology than his understanding of the union that Jesus Christ enjoys with his church as an ontological reality and necessity.

200. Barth, *CD* IV/2, 237–38.

201. Barth refers here to the two blind men who followed after and cried out to Jesus for mercy, who were subsequently healed by Jesus based upon their faith in Him (Matt 9:27).

he argues that faith in miracles has nothing to do with the "monstrosity" of believing in the possibility of all kinds of miracles or omnipotence.[202] The miracles of the New Testament testify to the power of Jesus Christ turning to human beings with the expressed intent of turning these human beings to him evidenced by their faith in him.

Barth further argues that there is a way which leads "from faith to miracle" when we consider what is really meant by the formula: "Thy faith hath saved thee." That is, the function assigned to faith taken from the passage in John 9 is decisive for understanding similar passages where sufferers are asked to believe in relation to acts of power for which they ask, or simply need. Nevertheless, Barth emphasizes in these situations that there is no *partial cooperation* of a human being in the occurrence of the miracle which comes about. The original σεσωκεν σε ("hath saved thee") does not simply refer to a part of the process, but to the whole. Therefore, the idea of saving or being saved is an action in which there is a Savior and a person being saved, which leaves no room for cooperation between the two. But Barth raises the question, how can using the formula: "Thy faith hath saved thee" be understood where humanity's *faith* can be called *the Savior*?[203] "The obvious difficulty is sharply brought out by the puzzling relationship between the two other sayings of Jesus. For in Mark 10:27 we read: 'With God all things are possible,' but in Mark 9:23: 'All things are possible to Him that believeth.'"[204]

Barth explains that this problem begins to give way when we consider that in the miracle stories and throughout the New Testament, faith is described *secondarily* as an act or disposition of humanity. The decisive thing is the action of faith in humanity, which proceeds from a primary thing that awakens and calls a human being to it. In the New Testament sense the word *faith* not only describes the believing activity of humanity, but the presupposition of this human activity that does not belong to the mental sphere but to the sphere of reality. More specifically, Barth describes it as the "factual, objective, ontological standing" of humanity; not all humanity, but certain human beings "in a concrete relationship with Jesus Christ and the God who is active and revealed in Him."[205]

Therefore, the individual who exercises faith in Christ does so because there already exists this ontological (i.e., concrete) relationship with Jesus Christ. Barth explains that this is the status of all who believe, which Paul

---

202. Barth, *CD* IV/2, 237–38.

203. Ibid., 240.

204. Ibid.

205. Ibid., 240–41.

describes as being "in Christ." This means that Christians belong to him, having been set at his side. This marks a crucial point in Barth's thinking as he argues that only in virtue of this ontological relationship between the royal man and these particular human beings are they able to believe *in him*.[206]

> The act or work of their faith derives from their being, just as a shoot does from a root. Who can say where the root ends and the shoot begins. What is a shoot if it no longer grows from the root (as on a tree-trunk which has been cut down)? Is not the only sure distinction between the two the fact that the one is visible and the other is not? Those who believe in the New Testament sense do so, as their own free act, because they have the freedom to do so from the One in whom they believe. And in the exercise of this freedom they reach back to that which is before their faith and independent of it. They cling to Jesus, to the God active and revealed in Him. And they are sustained by this ontological reality both behind and before.[207]

Barth argues from the Scripture that this ontological reality is evidenced by the sayings of Jesus in the New Testament where the human action of faith simply represents the transition from this origin (in Jesus) to this goal; from the free election of humanity in Christ to humanity's free calling. Reduced to its most essential terms, Barth describes the human action of faith simply as "from Jesus to Jesus."[208]

> When we look to the place from and to which faith goes we see in truth and clarity that it is indeed "the substance of things hoped for, the evidence of things not seen"; that it really does justify the sinner; that it really does save the sufferer and through him other sufferers; that nothing is in fact impossible to it; that the way from faith to miracle is indeed open and can be traversed.[209]

It is therefore faith in Jesus Christ that actually saves human beings. The inner delimitation of what is promised is self-evident because the reference is not to the human action of faith, but to human action only in relation to its origin and goal. For Barth, we cannot attribute to this faith any human capacity or desire. Rather, it ascribes to the *true force* in which Jesus himself acted, which is the force of the kingdom of God that

206. Ibid., 241.
207. Ibid.
208. Ibid., 241–42.
209. Ibid., 242.

has drawn near in him.[210] "The way from faith to miracle would close at once—indeed, it would never be open—if the power of faith were desired and claimed as a power in which man had the capacity to do just as his desire or fancy led him."[211]

Barth concludes that it is the grace of God who grants to human beings the freedom of faith, which enables the believer in Christ to rightly do these things. Given that this origin is also its goal, faith operates contiguously with the free grace of God and as such may be called its "anthropological counterpart."[212] But this counterpart to the grace of God as true humanity can only claim this reality by virtue of its union in the royal man, a union that becomes reality through the living action of the God-man and his Holy Spirit. For Barth, this is the very nature of the union of human beings in the royal man, which is directly connected to his union with the Logos as *anhypostasis* and *enhypostasis*.

The Passion and Cross of Christ

For Barth, the royal man comes to the cross in his unique historical being and relationship to God. All that has transpired before in the life of Jesus leads him here because it is the cross that forms the christological center of God's reconciliation with humanity in "the Son of God who became the Son of Man." The cross describes the existence and activity of Jesus of Nazareth; it controls and determines this whole. Christ came to this world to suffer and die as an offender against divine and human law. He agreed to do so of his own free will with the knowledge that it would lead to his end—to his being led away into this darkness. This is the story of the Gospels and the New Testament that attests to the risen and exalted man, Jesus of Nazareth, whose story is the story of his passion.[213]

Barth argues that the Gospels state outright the problem of Christ's impending death is the "problem of all problems," of his existence and relationship to God in his life's work. This becomes obvious at his end where Jesus faces a true and final darkness that even he could not see through directly, a darkness he traversed like a tunnel.[214] For Barth, Christ's passion is connected to what precedes, forming a single whole. It fulfills all that came before it where the name of God is revealed and sanctified conclusively in

210. Ibid.
211. Ibid.
212. Ibid., 242–43.
213. Barth, *CD* IV/2, 249–50.
214. Ibid., 250–51.

Jesus in whom his will is done on earth as it is in heaven. His passion brings the Kingdom of God to earth in a form and with a power that as a man he can only give a terrified, but determined assent. It is here, in his passion, where Jesus Christ exists conclusively as the one he is—as the Son of God who is also the Son of Man. For Barth, the secret of Golgotha is that in its deepest darkness Jesus entered into the glory of his unity with the Father. Even in his abandonment Jesus Christ is directly loved by the Father. This is not a new secret, but the secret of the whole, a secret that is revealed in the resurrection of Jesus.[215] Therefore, on the cross, in his passion, Jesus Christ was proclaimed to be King according to the will of the Father and himself as the Son. It was therefore right and necessary that he proclaimed as his final word (as given in Mark and Matthew) τετέλεσται in his declaration that everything has now been completed.[216] "It was in this way, in this absolute fulfillment, that He now bowed His head, not before men, or death, but before the Father whose commission He had executed to the letter. It was in this way that He gave up the ghost (19:28f)."[217]

Barth further argues that the 1st century Christian community clearly thought in Pauline terms; that is, it was not the resurrection, but the death of Jesus that they found *in nuce* the redemptive act and actuality of his existence. They heard the "Yes" pronounced in Jesus to humanity together with the corresponding "Yes" to sin, death and Satan. The cross therefore had positive meaning as a decisive redemptive turning point for them and for all humanity.[218] It was his life that led the way to this turning point and to

215. Ibid., 252.

216. Ibid., 256.

217. Ibid.

218. Wolfhart Pannenberg argues that for Paul the starting point of reconciliation lies in the atoning death of Jesus Christ where the judgment on sin in the death of the Son is the basis of "the possibility of reconciliation." Although the expiatory effect of Christ's death is not just an objectively closed event, it becomes fruitful for individuals only as their own deaths are linked to Christ's death. Pannenberg maintains that the idea of reconciliation explains and clarifies the need for receiving and appropriating the expiation grounded in the death of Jesus. Whereas reconciliation offered by the one side must be accepted by the other side, so the expiation grounded in Christ's vicarious death must be appropriated by confession, baptism, and faith on the part of each individual. Otherwise, neither vicarious expiation nor reconciliation can be represented as a concluded event in the death of Christ (Rom 5:10). Both cases require an inclusive statement. But the inclusive sense of representation has an expiatory function. There must be repetition in the process of propagating the gospel by apostolic proclamation and appropriation through faith, confession, and baptism. In Paul, Christ was linked to others precisely by the vicarious suffering of death as the punishment for sin. However, the thought of inclusive representation might also lead to a violating of the independence as persons of those that are represented. Inclusive representation can similarly result in the notion that Jesus Christ alone is man before God, that he has so taken our

his death on the cross that confirmed his existence and relationship to the Father together with all that he said and did.[219] With this understanding of Christ's death in view, Barth cites Christ's statement to the Baptist that "it becometh us to fulfill all righteousness" (Matt 3:15). That is, Christ's insistence that he be granted the baptism of repentance as one in the crowd demonstrates his own solidarity with them as he anticipates God's imminent judgment.[220]

Properly understood, the passion of the Son of Man includes the work of Pilate and the Gentiles—but only secondarily. Barth states here: "For by delivering Jesus to him, Israel unwittingly accomplishes—"they know not what they do" (Luke 23:34)—His handing over to humanity outside Israel where the Messiah of Israel becomes the Savior of the world."[221]

---

place and acted and suffered in our favor that we can add to what he has done nothing of our own. This means the replacement and suppression of those in whose place the Son of God came. Pannenberg states that this tendency in the thought of inclusive representation did not seem to be problematic to Karl Barth, which becomes clear in Barth's statement that "in Jesus Christ, God removed not merely sins but "their very root, the man who commits them" (CD, IV/1, 77)." Pannenberg raises the question if Christian theology can really say in the event of the death of Jesus Christ—in his own person—"has made an end of us as sinners and therefore of sin itself (p. 253)?" Paul says that sin dies only with the death of sinners and that this has already happened for believers due to the linking of their death to the death of Jesus (Rom 7:4). However, Pannenberg argues that by ascribing to the event of Christ's death what Paul describes as baptism, Barth has raised the question if the final result is not the total disappearance of our independent humanity. Pannenberg concludes that Barth's concentration of the concept of reconciliation on the death of Jesus Christ as a closed event of the past (see n. 52) has fateful consequences. Because he does not think of the event as open to a process of reception, the result is that he can view the judgment on sin in the death of Christ as comprehensive and definitive only if in this event God "has delivered up us sinners and sin itself to destruction . . . removed us sinners and sin, negated us, canceled us out" (p. 253). Pannenberg, *Systematic Theology*, 2:428–32.

219. Barth, *CD* IV/2, 257–58.

220. Ibid., 258.

221. Barth alludes here to the betrayal of Judas (and in his person the elect tribe of Judah to which Christ himself belonged), and of Judah (the Jews as they are summarily called in John's gospel) as the called people of Israel. Historically speaking, this is not the main theatre of world history, but the vineyard of the Lord. In it we find Israel represented by its ecclesiastical and theological leaders, but also by its *vox populi*, that rejects and condemns Jesus and then delivers him over to the Gentiles for judgment. Barth emphasizes that it was this delivering up by Israel, in their rejection and condemnation to death of Jesus Christ, which brings to conclusion the history of Jesus as he gave himself up, and was given up by God. We also see here the primitive empires of the world in its Roman or Hellenistic forms confronting the Kingdom of God strengthened by its divine calling and election, and therefore its supreme dominion. So in Jerusalem, as humanity decided for humanity over God, the Son of Man engaged in battle as he freely chose for himself that which was laid on him by the divine determination of his

In stark contrast to Israel's rejection of Jesus and its desire for his destruction, Barth draws our attention to John 12:26 where Christ states: "where He is, there shall also the servant be."[222] Barth marks here the relationship that the community of Christians has with Jesus is not a matter of morality (trying to do the things he does), but a matter of being, of ontology. This is vitally true for Christians in their fellowship with Christ, in their state of affliction and suffering. To follow Jesus involves those who are elected, called, and therefore free to follow Jesus and deny themselves, to give themselves in total service to him. Concretely, this means that each follower of Jesus must take up their own cross, which in a sense denies fear, hatred, or trying to escape the affliction that falls on Jesus. The true follower of Christ fully embraces the cross by taking it up and carrying it. This of course is not the cross of Christ, which has been carried once and for all. This is not a repetition of his suffering and death.[223] "But it is a matter of each Christian carrying his own individual cross, suffering his own affliction, bearing the definite limitation of death which in one form or another falls on his own existence, and therefore going after Christ as the man he is, following "in his steps" (1 Pet 2:21)."[224]

The central point for Barth is that the regeneration and conversion of humanity takes place on the cross of Jesus Christ. Jesus comes to his crucifixion as Lord and King of all humanity who exercises his sovereignty and inaugurates his kingdom as a historical reality. This is consistent with the New Testament, which does not portray the cross of the royal man in a negative light because it is in fact his coronation.[225] Moreover, the cross is the dominating characteristic of the Son of Man's royal office. It is the goal of his existence and anticipates the new beginning of humanity in this world. Christ's death is the complete fulfillment of his humiliation as a human being—as God himself became one with us in his Son. It is also the exaltation

---

life. It is here that the unholy *must* of Israel also points to the destruction of Jesus on the cross. See Barth, *CD* IV/2, 260–62.

222. Barth draws out here the relational union that the disciples of Jesus have with their Master where "The disciple is not above his master, nor the servant above his lord . . . If they have called the master of the house Beelzebub, how much more shall they call them of his household?" (Matt 10:24f.). Barth goes on to explain that if the disciples were ashamed of Jesus and his words then he would be ashamed of them (Mark 8:38) when they tried to escape the inevitable outcome. They would also drink the cup that he drinks, and be baptized with the baptism that he is baptized with (Mark 10:39). See Barth, *CD* IV/2, 264.

223. Barth, *CD* IV/2, 264.

224. Ibid.

225. Barth, *CD* IV/2, 291–92.

of humanity as true humanity. Therefore, Barth concludes that: "The secret of the cross is simply the secret of the incarnation in all its fullness."[226]

The cross is the crown of life for Jesus because in his crucifixion he genuinely took to himself the situation of humanity as it stands before the judgment of God, making it God's judgment in his person. As a result he radically transformed it and truly demonstrated himself to be our brother in his acceptance of this outcome of his life from the beginning.[227] In his humiliation the judgment of God falls on him—in our place. But this is also his exaltation, which he shared with those in whom he shares his brotherhood. The death of Christ therefore makes human beings who are in themselves unholy to be saints of God. The cross becomes his crown of life because in his crucifixion, as our brother, the royal man accomplished our liberation from our old humanity to a new one.[228]

The cross is also where Jesus stands in the place of humanity, the place marked for the death of humanity having fallen victim to it. Death is the end of all human life. It makes relative and overshadows all that was previously attained and therefore becomes the abasement of everything that came before.[229] Barth draws this together by explaining that the light of Christ's resurrection was the light of his cross. This was the light that his witnesses saw and understood as his whole life and proclaimed it as the life which is given to the whole world. It is this orientation to his death where he is exalted in tandem with his humiliation that clearly sets his life apart from all other human life because it is the act of God.[230]

As we reflect upon Barth's theological achievement in this section we are compelled to consider the being of Jesus Christ as our mediator of reconciliation with God and what this really means in Barth's thinking. That is, as our mediator, Jesus not only represents us to God but He does so as one of us, uniting us with himself in his being. The human nature of Christ therefore establishes the point of contact, the point of union, between a Holy God and

226. Barth draws this together quite nicely with reference to what he has already established as the humiliation and exaltation of Jesus Christ being one and the same event. "What we have called the way of the Son of Man into a far country and the homecoming of the Son of Man, and what older dogmatics called the *exinanitio* and *exaltatio* of Jesus Christ, are one and the same event at the cross . . . The Word was really made real flesh. It was really God who really reconciled the world to Himself—in the One who was true God, omnipotent in the depth of His mercy, and also (in His death and passion) true man, allowing free rein to this omnipotent mercy of God." Barth, *CD* IV/2, 292–93.

227. Ibid., 293.

228. Ibid., 294.

229. Ibid.

230. Ibid., 294–95.

sinful humanity. This is an ontological contact, a simultaneous union of the royal man with the Father and with humanity, which uniquely expresses the fullness and significance of how the *anhypostasis* and *enhypostasis* of Christ's human nature accomplished the reconciliation of humanity with God.

The Sanctification of Humanity in Jesus Christ

I argue that Karl Barth's expression of the royal man reaches its theological climax in his development of human sanctification. This is the culmination of Jesus Christ's relationship to his community of saints embodied (both figuratively and quite literally) in their sanctification. Everything about the royal man points to this event where the sanctification of Christ's church is realized in its union and exaltation with Jesus Christ. In this event Barth deals with the question of Christ's concealment as the royal man, but a concealment that does not absolutely negate our perception of Jesus Christ, and us in him. Moreover, Barth makes it quite clear that we cannot know Jesus Christ and ourselves in him without the knowledge that we are sinners, a knowledge that does not darken our perception of him despite the distortion caused by our sin. Therefore, Christ's concealment from us cannot simply be explained by the existence of human sin. For Barth, because Jesus Christ is our true representative, our *being in him* is our justification and therefore the forgiveness of our sins, even that of our cognition. But even more than that, our union in Christ is our sanctification together with the knowledge of the renewal of our life—and therefore of our cognition. We must reckon with the fact that if Christ's concealment from us were simply a question of our own sin, God made provision for us in the royal man to counteract its effects, which in turn removes this concealment.[231] The answer to the problem of Christ's concealment therefore comes about as an alteration of our being—*it is an ontological event.*

This alteration comes about as our being is taken up into the being of the royal man, into his exaltation as the Son of Man in union with the Son of God. The crowning achievement—this movement—is the royal man's exaltation of human essence out of the depths of sin and death into his own being. Therefore, his exaltation sanctifies not only his own human being, but also the human beings that comprise his community—*in him.* This is the act of God's reconciliation with humanity (in the royal man) that Barth works out in a series of movements to demonstrate the ontological reality of Christ's humanity as it is taken up into the Logos together with his church. Given this backdrop, we will consider Barth's development of

231. Barth, *CD* IV/2, 288.

the royal man's action on behalf of his church to accomplish this work of sanctification, as the change of being (this alternation), necessary to accomplish this ontological union. It in we see the being and movement of the royal man as he confronts human sinfulness, sloth, and misery, which in turn brings about the justification and sanctification of the saints in their awakening to conversion. This is an ontological movement that I argue finds its impetus and thrust in the *anhypostasis* and *enhypostasis* dynamic of Christ's human nature.

Human Sin in the Light of the Royal Man

For Barth, the alteration of our being in becoming the community of Christ can only be rightly understood given the condition of human sinfulness prior to this alteration. That is, sinful humanity wills and commits sin, and is determined and hardened by it. However, sinful humanity is sanctified by the existence of the man Jesus and the direction which he gives.[232] The royal man comes to us and deals with the reality of our sinfulness in the act of his Lordship, in the light of his overcoming sin. "It is in view of the lordship of the Son of Man, in the power of His direction, and therefore in the knowledge of Jesus Christ by the Holy Spirit that we may know sin and the man of sin." Barth explains that this is important to understand because humanity is corrupt even in the self-awareness of its corruption because it cannot see beyond this inner conflict, a conflict enclosed within a purely relative compass. Therefore, we never really see ourselves as beings of sin. And as a result we cannot turn to a true knowledge of our corruption, but only turn away from it.[233] "God and His revelation and faith are all needed if He is to realise the accusation and judgment and condemnation under which he stands, and the transgression and ensuing need in which he exists."[234]

Barth deals with the inability to see ourselves as sinful beings by expressing the central theme of his Christology: "But the Word made flesh, the grace of God encountering man, his salvation, the Gospel, is Jesus Christ." In the existence of Jesus Christ as the Son of God and the Son of Man, as the light which reveals the sin of humanity to itself, human beings are able to see and confess ourselves as sinners. Christian knowledge is therefore a genuine knowledge of sin (Sündenerkenntnis), revelation, and faith, which is the knowledge of Jesus Christ. As the Son of Man his true humanity is fulfilled in his death and revealed in his resurrection. Christ's exaltation as

232. Barth, *CD* IV/2, 378.
233. Ibid., 379.
234. Ibid.

the royal man explains his identity as the Son of God who lives and rules in full communion and conformity with God the Father.[235]

As the royal man Jesus lives the life of new humanity brought about by the death of old humanity suffered by him. This is the rising of true humanity in his existence and death through the destruction of false and perverted humanity. In this way the royal man conquers enslaved humanity through his life in the Spirit—as he willed to be like us—by becoming one of us. This is the action of God's mercy bestowed upon old and perverted humanity enslaved in this flesh, but flesh still embodied as a *good creature*[236] that he elects and loves.[237] Barth explains that it is the mercy of God which reveals the shame and un-holiness of humanity in this correspondence, this living encounter with Jesus Christ. Barth draws out here the consequence of our encounter with a holy God as our shame becomes obvious in the face the of the true God's distinction from all false idols. This distinction is made not only in and for himself, but also in his encounter with us as Emmanuel: "God with us," as very man as well as very God in Jesus Christ.[238] "But none of us is confronted with God Himself, or shamed by Him, in the existence of another man. This takes place only, but genuinely, in the existence of the true man in Jesus, the Son of God."[239]

The Christian's confrontation with the being of Jesus reveals their shame given their knowledge of the truth. The Christian is therefore freed (or indeed forced) to recognize their shamefulness by the direction of Jesus Christ in his Holy Spirit. This is not a dead or formless awareness, but awareness in the light of the Son of Man.[240] Moreover, the resurrection of the Son of Man reveals that he died in our place the death of old humanity, the humanity of sin. Jesus of Nazareth is the new man who lives in our place as the Holy One of God, in whom the Christian is exalted as the saint of God. Barth emphasizes that there is neither continuity nor harmony between the

---

235. Barth, *CD* IV/2, 381; *KD* IV/2, 427.

236. In a clear departure from traditional Reformed doctrine, Barth rejects the characterization of human sin, the evil act of a human being, as something that takes place automatically from within as a function of creaturely nature. Barth takes the counter-view that sin is "a new and responsible work, and it is in contradiction to his nature, so that when he does it he is a stranger to himself." Barth argues that even in committing sin, a human being does not "cease to be in the hand of God, and to be the man who was not created evil but good." Barth, *CD* IV/2, 393.

237. Barth, *CD* IV/2, 384.

238. Ibid., 385–86.

239. Ibid.

240. Ibid., 388.

death of the old man and the life of this new man.[241] In his action the eternal Son of God acted against sin. And in so doing he suffered in our place the death of the old humanity, the human being of sin as none other than God himself as the Son of Man.

This is God's response to this enemy that has disturbed the peace of created reality, which is antithetical to him. Moreover, this response is not a distant one, but one made in its midst. Although this enemy, this evil work, did not in any way affect God's own life and being, God must respond to it as something absolutely intolerable. Barth explains it as an infinite and absolute evil that cannot be countered merely by rearranging the world. Nor can it be destroyed through the mediation of a mere creature because no creature alone is capable of removing this evil. By necessity God himself came down and gave himself. He sacrificed himself in order to free humanity from this evil and introduce a reconciled world in this royal man. Barth argues that the absurd notion of this reality demonstrates the absurdity of sin and how serious it actually is; because in this way God himself is affected and harmed by it.[242]

The Sloth and Misery of Humanity

Barth now turns to the material question dealt with in this section: "What is sin as seen from the standpoint of the new man introduced in Jesus Christ?" In other words, what is the action of old humanity that is overcome in the death of Jesus Christ? Or, what is the character of this human being revealed in Jesus Christ's resurrection "in the light of the divine direction which falls on him from the source?" Barth describes this character of old humanity as its sloth, its "sluggishness, indolence, slowness or inertia." This is evil inaction that characterizes human sin, which is forbidden and held as reprehensible by God. Barth describes this as a "heroic, Promethean form of sin," which comes to light as the pride of humanity and is the root cause of the fall of humanity. It is this human sin that is directly confronted by Christ, the Son of God, who humbled himself by becoming flesh. In Christ's counter-movement toward humanity, sin is unmasked by the divine condescension revealed in him.[243] Therefore, God's reconciling grace is not merely justifying grace, but also wholly "sanctifying and awakening and establishing grace." This means that sin is not simply the heroic form of pride, but also the "unheroic and trivial

241. Ibid., 399.
242. Barth, CD IV/2, 401–02.
243. Ibid., 403.

form of sloth." As such, sin takes the form of evil inaction as well as evil action. Not only is rash arrogance forbidden, but so is slowness and failure as well. For Barth, this is the spectrum of human sin that Jesus confronts in his exaltation of humanity where he exalts the sinner out of the sinfulness of pride and sloth, and the unity and reciprocity which exists between the two.[244] Humanity therefore stands in great need of both humiliation and exaltation in relation to the totality of its life and action.[245]

More specifically, Barth argues that sloth is the human refusal to be illuminated by the existence and nature of God. Instead, it chooses to reject him, to be without God in this world. "The slothful man, who is of course identical with the proud, begins where the other leaves off, i.e., by saying in his heart: 'There is no God.'"[246] This is why our brother, Jesus of Nazareth, is a stranger in this world whose existence among us is an intolerable demand because the God who is this God is not acceptable. In a sense this describes the "rigid front" that sinful humanity presents to Jesus, this visible resistance to his presence in the form of human sloth. Barth describes this sin as the rejection of the outstretched hand of God and the refusal of his grace, as one who neglects his or her own calling and therefore is untrue to his or her own cause. Instead, this human being exchanges its true reality for a false reality, living as a mere shadow of itself that Barth contrasts to the person of Jesus Christ, the true brother of humanity given to us by God. Therefore, it is in the being of Jesus Christ that any human being is able to find its own true realty, its "own humanity as it is loved and elected and created and preserved by his God in the person of this One."[247]

This is how Karl Barth's adoption of the *anhypostasis* and *enhypostasis* dynamic of Jesus Christ encompasses the humanity of Christians whose beings are taken up into the being of the royal man. This is the ontological grounding of a human being who becomes its true self in Christ. Viewed the other way around, a human being who refuses the man Jesus (and therefore its own God) also refuses its true self and own reality becoming lost in its attempt to assert itself. Barth argues that this is the great paradox centered in the sin of slothfulness. In the end, a slothful human being becomes only a shadow of its true self. Barth describes this as humanity in contradiction, as one who contradicts God and therefore themselves. In the end, humanity would be lost in this self-contradiction if not confronted by the man Jesus on whom he or she stumbles and falls when brought face

244. Ibid.
245. Barth, *CD* IV/2, 404.
246. Ibid., 405.
247. Ibid., 408.

to face with the superior contradiction of God. The will of God, however, is that this slothful human being should not perish.[248] It is the "Yes" of God that makes the limited time of humanity a time that is filled by God's dealings with humanity through his calling and blessing. This human relationship to God defines the meaning of every human history where knowledge of God presupposes human knowledge of its historicity, as a being in time and in the limits of time.[249]

However, the movement to the knowledge of God—the ability of humanity to see itself in the reality of the royal man and in relationship with him—can only be realized through the direction of his Spirit. For Barth, this is the receiving of his Holy Spirit, which means to receive his direction and accept his summons. It is to see oneself in Jesus Christ as the one who is elected, created, and determined for existence in this humanity.[250] This power of the Holy Spirit is strange and alien to us. It is stronger than us and moves with a sense of finality from its origin to a definite end.[251]

The direction of the Holy Spirit reveals the reality of the royal man as he confronts us in our slothfulness; he who exists as the true and normal form of human nature and lives the authentic human life according to the Spirit in the flesh. "This means concretely that He lives wholly to God and His fellow-man." His life is "one long exaltation, purification, sanctification, and dedication of the flesh." His life manifests the genuine flesh of human nature in contradistinction to the only flesh we know as natural human beings in its abnormal form, in its decomposition. The life of Jesus therefore acts to normalize human nature, humanity that has come to itself and encounters us in Jesus, who is at peace with himself as the soul of his body. He lives in the unity intended for humanity in the relationship of body and soul, which God ordained to exist in conformity with our nature. Jesus wholly exists as body and soul, and as such is wholly himself, the soul of its body in its free control and the body of its soul in its free service. Jesus is humanity as we are, but he is more than we are because in his royal freedom he exists in a freedom that is originally his own. Therefore, Jesus enjoys

248. Barth, CD IV/2, 408–07.

249. Barth, CD IV/2, 422–23.

250. Barth, CD IV/2, 433. Adam Neder notes in addition to the justification and sanctification that occurs in the conversion and reconciliation of humanity, a third aspect in Barth's thinking is described as vocation. Neder describes vocation as the telos of justification and sanctification where Barth understands that the being of humanity in Christ is not restricted to possession and action, but also a being in expectation. Therefore, new humanity in Christ is teleologically directed as an eschatological being where Jesus Christ is the promise of humanity's future. See Neder, Participation in Christ, 54.

251. Barth, CD IV/2, 436.

life in himself that he fashions and normalizes, where God's "valid and effective" direction meets us in Christ. In other words, he is a human being who is like us and us confronts us with the truth of our nature; the sanctity and dignity of humanity. This is the glory of human life.[252] "If, therefore, we receive His Spirit, we know ourselves in Him as those who are elected and created and determined for existence in the truth of his human nature, for an authentically human life."[253]

Barth concludes that the vileness of human dissipation is an undeniable fact. But this form of human being is not nothing, but something. "It is a real disposition of the human will and its decisions and achievements." This humanity manifests itself as the unwillingness to know God and its willingness to be without and against its fellow human beings. This is a willingness to live in the disorder and degeneration of its own nature, refusing to make use of the freedom to be a whole human being, which is in fact addressed and given to humanity in the direction of Jesus and the sanctifying movement that derives from him.[254] "Our general definition of the sin of man in the form of sloth—that he lets himself fall—is particularly applicable to this aspect of it."[255]

For Barth, human sin is the decision to act or not to act, the perversion of the human will that precedes all the aberrations that take on concrete form. This is the dissipation of humanity rooted in its disobedience to God. It is humanity's unbelief and enmity against the grace of God directed to humanity. It is the transgression of God's law. "The transgression as such is the law which all his thoughts and words and works will more or less obviously follow."[256] Sin is transgression at work in the human being who wills what should not be willed and refuses to do what should be done. This is the fact of our being. For Barth, to think otherwise is an illusion.[257]

> The power of human dissipation, like that of human stupidity and inhumanity, is so great because man himself is no less dissipated than stupid and inhuman. It is from this source, form within ourselves, that our sloth draws its inexhaustible strength in this form too. That which is born of the flesh, and thought and said and chosen and done in the flesh, can only be flesh,

252. Barth, *CD* IV/2, 452.
253. Ibid.
254. Ibid., 453.
255. Ibid.
256. Ibid., 454.
257. Ibid., 455.

and cannot overcome the flesh, even though it may have the character of a most serious and sharp contrast.[258]

The reality of this human dissipation contrasts sharply to the humanity that God took to himself, exalting this humanity in the man Jesus into fellowship with his own divine life. Barth marks here God's knowledge of us as exalted humanity when he addresses his mercy to us in Jesus Christ where the light of Christ's humanity reveals the sickness of our sinful being in the flesh.[259] As the royal man, Jesus exercised his royal freedom by giving up his life to God and humanity. He in fact allowed his life to be taken from him by humanity, discontented humanity that denies its finitude and destroys its peace with God and its fellow human beings, and does nothing but harm itself.[260] For Barth, this is slothful humanity that God has in mind, humanity who refuses to act and rejects the grace offered by God. It is this humanity whose reconciliation with God and its own sanctification is at issue when the name of Jesus is proclaimed.[261]

Consequently, the slothfulness of humanity reaches its natural outcome in its own misery. This is the exile of humanity, the sum of woe created by human stupidity, inhumanity and discontent. This is the far country that the Son of God came into, the one from which he returns home as the Son of Man; not in isolation from us, but as our head and representative who brings us with him. He came into this far country in the light of his being, revealing our false existence in exile and misery, who responded as though the true God had come to us in vain, as though he had not taken us up with him (which in truth he has) and sharing his royal freedom with us. For Barth, this is the character of human misery that chooses its own life below in opposition to the divine life above.[262] This is the human being who remains below where it does not belong, but where it irrevocably has its place as long as its corrupt will is not broken by the direction of Jesus Christ. This is the human sin of sloth.[263] It is the sloth and misery of humanity that stands opposed to the reality of the Son of God who descends to our misery, and the Son of Man who ascends to God's glory. Nevertheless, the royal man—who exists in the midst of human slothfulness—becomes its victor in

---

258. Ibid.

259. Ibid., 464.

260. Ibid., 467.

261. Barth, *CD* IV/2, 478.

262. Barth, *CD* IV/2, 483.

263. As Barth explains, what he describes as the fall of humanity from the standpoint of its sin as pride is what the older dogmatics called in its totality the *status corruptionis*, which Barth refers to as the misery of humanity. See Barth, *CD* IV/2, 484.

his crucifixion as our head and representative. This is the revelation of his resurrection, "the issue of His direction, the outpouring of the Holy Spirit on all flesh." However, Barth argues that even in its misery humanity does not belong to the devil or itself, but to God. While the "Yes" of divine grace is terribly concealed in the "No" of divine judgment, it is still spoken by God to this humanity.[264]

> Jesus lives as very man, and therefore as the very God who humbled Himself to man, who came to him in his misery, who took his misery to Himself. Thus even in his misery man lives as the man for whom Jesus lives. To omit this qualification of man's misery is necessarily to deny Jesus Christ as the Lord who became a servant and the servant who became Lord, and therefore to blaspheme God.[265]

Barth argues that whether or not one raises an objection to human misery based upon a deficient experience of it, its objective reality remains. Moreover, no human being but Jesus alone has ever known the true depth and breadth, the true essence and darkness of human misery. The misery we experience is only the shadow of his cross touching us.[266] The critical point for Barth here is that our understanding of the bondage of the will must always be understood christologically. It cannot be proved empirically or by *a priori* reflections. It is a statement of faith. It is also a theological statement that correlates to the freedom that Jesus Christ has won for us and granted to us in himself. However, Barth reiterates that it is not a decision for determinism.[267] Rather, it describes the perversion of

264. Ibid., 484.

265. Ibid., 485. Barth notes here the he is not yet dealing with death. In this context humanity still exists and lives, and has not yet been reached by the final event that comes upon humanity from this source . . . "just as in the pictures of the headlong plunge of the damned the jaws of hell are only opened and eternal fire is only waiting for them. The misery of man is "only" his being in this plunge into them. It is "only" his being in the movement towards death." Barth, *CD* IV/2, 487.

266. Ibid., 487. Barth notes: "(1) that the good which remains to man as a sinner is not merely a "relic" but the totality of his God-given nature and its determination, and (2) that in the same totality he exists in the history of the perversion of this good into evil, and is caught up in the movement from above to below. His total being in this movement is his *miseria* which has its limit only in the *misericordia Dei*." Barth, *CD* IV/2, 489.

267. Barth argues that this is not a statement for determinism . . . "the fact that this is not clear in Luther's *De servo arbitrio* is the objection that we are forced to raise against this well known work and also against the ideas of Zwingli and Calvin. It can take up into itself both determinism and indeterminism to the extent that they are to be understood as the hypotheses of an empiricist or *a priori* philosophy. It necessarily excludes both to the extent that they set themselves up, on this or that foundation, as

the human being that results from its sloth in relationship with God. Barth clearly rejects the idea that humanity (even in its state of slothfulness) cannot will and decide because it lacks the will to do so. If this was so, humanity would cease to exist as human being, becoming instead a part of a mechanized movement from without.[268]

> This would involve the transformation of man into another and non-human being—an idea which we have exerted ourselves to repudiate from the very outset in this world context. But the freedom of man does not really consist—except in the imagination of the invincibly ignorant—in the fact that, like Hercules at the cross-roads, he can will and decide. Nor does the bondage of his will consist in the fact that he is not able to do this.[269]

Barth explains that while humanity chooses the path it has entered, it is not a choice made as true humanity because it has turned aside from this genuine possibility. All its choices having yielded to corruption can only act corruptly. The starting place therefore is the repudiation of its freedom. "He cannot, therefore, do that which corresponds to his freedom." Instead humanity must do that which it could not do in the exercise of it. This is the bondage of the human will, which most bitterly characterizes human misery.[270] The liberation of humanity that Jesus brings is its new birth and conversion as it has taken place in him. This is the freedom that humanity has and exercises in Christ as a new creation, which is free from committing sin. Instead it is free for faith in and obedience to Christ. In Christ humanity enjoys genuine freedom, οντως ελευθερος (John 8:36), which Barth identifies as the sanctification of humanity that serves to limit its former bondage. Nevertheless, the tension between the freedom of sanctified humanity in Jesus and its solidarity with all humanity in the flesh still remains.[271]

---

metaphysical dogmas." Barth, *CD* IV/2, 493.

268. Barth, *CD* IV/2, 493–94. Barth continues that sinful humanity has rejected its freedom to be genuinely human citing John 8:34, "Whosoever committeth sin is the servant of sin." For Barth, this biblical formulation describes the whole doctrine of the bondage of the will. "*Non potest non peccare* is what we have to say of the sinful, slothful man." Human sin therefore excludes human freedom, just as its freedom excludes its sin. There can be no middle ground because for slothful human beings there is only the first alternative. "He has not ceased to be a man. He wills. He is a Hercules, the arbiter of what he does. Be he does what he does in the corruption of his will. He does not, therefore, do it *libero* but *servo arbitrio*." Barth, *CD* IV/2, 495.

269. Ibid., 494.

270. Ibid., 495–96.

271. Ibid., 496.

He is the one who is limited by this limitation, and as such the one who needs sanctification, liberation. To the extent that he is this, he is not free, and everything that we have said about the bondage of the human will applies in all seriousness to him too. To the extent that he is in the flesh and not in the spirit he is "dead in sins" (Col 2:13; Eph 2:1). He is not just half-dead, or apparently dead. He is a corpse awaiting the resurrection . . . [272]

In the end, Karl Barth takes quite seriously the reality of sin which dominates the human condition and the misery that accompanies it. This is the human condition—the old humanity—which is clearly revealed by the new humanity introduced in Jesus Christ. Barth explains this sin as sloth. It is old humanity's evil inaction characterized by its own pride and willingness to reject God, to be without God in this world. This is human sin that the Son of Man confronts having humbled himself in becoming flesh and unmasking this sin in his revelation of God, bringing with it God's reconciling grace characterized as both justifying and sanctifying grace. Jesus is indeed a stranger in this world whose very existence brings with it an intolerable demand upon sinful humanity, humanity that has exchanged true reality for a false realty of existence. Therefore, only in the being of Jesus Christ can any human being realize its true being. For Barth, the ontological grounding of sanctified humanity in the royal man is striking, particularly in view of its emergence out of the *anhypostasis* and *enhypostasis* dynamic where humanity becomes its true self in union with the royal man. However, this ontological reality can only be accomplished through the direction of the royal man in receiving his Holy Spirit. It is in this direction, this summons, that the Holy Spirit reveals the reality of the royal man as he confronts us in our slothfulness. In other words, as a human being like us (yet without sin), Jesus confronts us with the truth of our nature, its sanctity and dignity. This is the glory of human life. This is the freedom that Jesus Christ was won for us and granted to us in himself. As a result, the bondage of the will and the freedom from this bondage in our sanctification must be always understood christologically.

The Royal Man and Human Sanctification

Having addressed the state of sinful humanity in its sloth and misery, Barth now transitions to the royal man and the sanctification he accomplishes for his community in their union together. For Barth, the term *sanctification* constitutes the scope of part two in the doctrine of reconciliation (*CD*

272. Ibid.

IV/2) realized in the exaltation of humanity. That is, sanctification is the other half of the movement of Jesus Christ in the humiliation of God as our justification. As such, in Christ's movement toward humanity, not only is humanity justified in the humiliation of the Son of God, but it is also sanctified in the Son of Man's exaltation in this indissoluble union. Barth explains that "in the fact that as He turns to man in defiance of his sin He also, in defiance of his sin, turns man to Himself." This is humanity's new existence as a faithful covenant-partner who is well-pleasing and blessed by him. "'I will be your God' is the justification of man. "Ye shall be my people" is his sanctification."[273] Barth explains that sanctification (*sanctificatio*) can also be described by the less common biblical terms as "regeneration (*regeneratio*) or renewal (*renovatio*), or by that of conversion (*conversio*), or by that of penitence (*poenitentia*) which plays so important a role in both the Old and New Testaments, or comprehensively by that of discipleship which is so outstanding especially in the synoptic gospels.[274]

However, Barth argues that the term sanctification must be kept in the foreground because it includes the idea of the "saint," which focuses our attention on *the being* and *action of God*. This is important to understand in Barth's thinking because it keeps before us that which is normative for understanding these other terms. Moreover, sanctification is decisive in the fact that God is the active subject not only in our reconciliation generally, but also in the conversion of humanity to himself. "Like His turning to man, and man's justification, this is His work, His *facere*. But it is now seen and understood, not as his *iustificare*, but as his *sanctificare*."[275]

Barth considers here the full spectrum of the doctrine of reconciliation in "clarifying" the mutual relationship between justification as its first part and sanctification as its second part.[276] In doing so, he works out the ontological reality of the *anhypostasis* and *enhypostasis* of Christ's human nature in direct relationship to his community of saints. To this end Barth argues that with sanctification we are not dealing with a second divine action that takes place simultaneously with it, or precedes it, or follows it

273. Ibid., 496.

274. Ibid., 500.

275. Ibid.

276. Ibid., 501. Adam Neder argues that for Barth reconciliation is the fulfillment of the covenant in Jesus Christ. It is the "accomplishment and revelation of the three-fold conversion (Umkehrung) of sinful humanity to God, the displacement of the old humanity and the establishment of the new humanity in him." Reconciliation comes about as the event of the justification, sanctification, and calling of humanity in Jesus Christ, which together constitute the being of humanity in him. See Neder, *Participation in Christ*, 51.

in time. Rather, God's action in reconciling the world to himself in Jesus Christ is a unitary action, which consists of different "moments" with a different bearing. Therefore, God's one action accomplishes both the justification and sanctification of humanity because it is both the condescension of God and the exaltation of humanity in Jesus Christ. Both are accomplished together. This is the movement of God from above to below in justification and from below to above in sanctification in the one historical being of Jesus Christ as true Son of God and true Son of Man. This is the grace of God expressed in one totality of his reconciling action through the one whole and undivided Jesus Christ.[277]

Therefore, to speak of justification and sanctification is to speak of two different aspects (two moments) of one salvation event. Consistent with Chalcedon, Barth explains that the existence of Jesus Christ as true God and true humanity in one person does not mean that true deity and true humanity are one and the same, or that one is interchangeable with the other. Yet, the reality of Jesus Christ as the Son of God who humbled himself in becoming humanity, and the Son of Man who was exalted to fellowship with the Logos—*is one.* Because Christ's humiliation and exaltation are not identical, and given the christological ασυγχυτως and ατρεπτως of Chalcedon, Barth explains that we can easily deduce the same is true of justification and sanctification. As the two moments in the one act of reconciliation accomplished in Jesus Christ, they are neither identical nor interchangeable concepts.[278] "Justification is not sanctification and does not merge into it. Sanctification is not justification and does not merge into it. Thus, although the two belong indissolubly together, the one cannot be explained by the other."[279]

Moreover, Barth argues that since justification and sanctification are only two moments and aspects of one and the same action, they belong inseparably together. Therefore, one must not ignore the mutual relationship of the two, and in turn purport a God who works in isolation, suggesting a "cheap grace." Barth argues that to separate justification and sanctification is to separate the one actuality of Jesus Christ and the Holy Spirit, which serves to isolate the self-humiliating Son of God on the one side, and of the exalted Son of Man on the other. Barth concludes that if we accept the αχωριστωσ and αδιαιρετως of Chalcedonian Christology, justification and sanctification must be distinguished, but not divided or separated.[280] Because the two

---

277. Barth, *CD* IV/2, 502.
278. Ibid., 503.
279. Ibid.
280. Ibid., 505.

are inseparable, the doctrine of justification must be described as the way from death to life in which *God* goes with him. Moreover, the doctrine of sanctification must demonstrate that God is already with *humanity* in his reconciliation of the world with himself in Jesus Christ. In all of this Barth marks a clear coalescence between the union of Christ's humiliation and exaltation with the justification and sanctification of His Church. Barth also argues that Calvin saw and expressed this point with particular clarity.

> There is hardly a passage in which we have any doubt whether the reference is to justifying or sanctifying grace, and yet he everywhere brings out the mutual relationship of the two moments and aspects. His primary statement, and starting-point is as follows: . . . There is thus no justification without sanctification . . . We cannot, therefore, glory in God without *eo ipso*—and this is for Calvin the basic act of penitence and the new life—renouncing all self-glorifying and thus beginning to live to God's glory. (13, 2)[281]

In this context Barth addresses the question of an *ordo* (*salutis*) with respect to the relationship of justification and sanctification. That is, Barth deals with the question of a superiority and subordination in the one event of grace and salvation. Barth reckons that in the temporal state there is no such order because justification and sanctification take place simultaneously in Jesus Christ as true God and true man, as the humiliated and the exalted. Yet Barth also argues that this does not set aside the question of their order; not in a temporal sense, but in a sense of substance. Although Barth admits that this order cannot be easily established, he argues that justification must be understood as first and basic, and to that extent the superior moment and aspect of the one event of salvation. Sanctification is the second and derivative, and therefore inferior given the condescension of God as the eternal Word who in assuming our flesh exalted it in the existence of the royal man.[282]

However, Barth also argues that this is not the end of the matter because the existence of the royal man answers the question of obedience; that is, the summoning and preparing of humanity for the service of God, which is of great importance in the Bible. Sanctification therefore cannot simply be subordinated to justifying grace in view of this whole event, but must be taken into account given its meaning and purpose. Barth's point here is that while sanctification is the second in execution (*executione posterius*), it is in fact the first in intention (*intentione prius*). In other words,

281. Ibid., 505–6.
282. Ibid., 507.

the answer to the question: what is it that God wills and effects in the reconciliation of humanity with himself, is found in the incarnation of the
Word of God where he wills and affects the existence of the royal man
and his lordship over all his brethren, and the whole world.[283] In view of
his humiliation in the judgment that he took upon himself for us, and the
justification of humanity that he accomplished for us, Jesus Christ wills
and affects the existence of a "loyal and courageous people of this King
in covenant with Himself, and therefore the sanctification of man." Barth
therefore concludes that with respect to the relationship between justification and sanctification; teleologically, sanctification is in fact superior to
justification. This is the divine order of the divine will and action revealed
in Jesus Christ. But in no way does it cancel out the priority of justification.
"Might it not be that in this—in this particular function and respect—the
Prius is also the *Posterius* and vice versa? This would mean that both answers have to be given with the same seriousness in view of the distinctive
truth in both—intersecting but not cancelling one another."[284]

For Barth, the objective of sanctification is *at the very least* the transformation of humanity from breaking—to keeping—the covenant that
God has made with us from all eternity. Sanctified humanity therefore is
awakened and empowered by the action of a holy God in becoming a saint
of God. Therefore, the sanctification of humanity that has taken place in
Jesus Christ *is* in fact our sanctification. This also means that sanctification
is originally and properly the sanctification of Jesus of Nazareth.[285]

> For it was in the existence of this One, in Jesus Christ, that it
> really came about, and is and will be, that God Himself became
> man, that the Son of God became also the Son of Man, in or-
> der to accomplish in His own person the conversion of man to
> Himself, his exaltation from the depth of His transgression and
> consequent misery, his liberation from his unholy being for ser-
> vice in the covenant, and therefore his sanctification.[286]

This sanctification takes place in the history of the man Jesus of Nazareth who is sanctified by God as the acting subject in the royal authority

283. Ibid., 508.

284. Ibid.

285. Barth, *CD* IV/2, 514. Barth cites 1 Corinthians 1:30 in arguing that Jesus Christ
not only becomes our justification, but our sanctification as well. Barth notes: "As E.
Gaugler rightly observes (op. cit., p. 76), this saying expresses in the shortest possible
compass the truth that even sanctification has to be thought of in terms of the history
of salvation." Barth, *CD* IV/2, 515.

286. Ibid.

given to him by God.[287] As such, not only did Jesus take our place and act for us as the Son of God in our justification—as the Son of Man—he also became our sanctification by sanctifying himself. Therefore, Christ's humiliation to death in our justification, and our exaltation to fellowship with God in this corresponding counter-movement of our sanctification, constitutes God's own act of free grace addressed to us in Jesus Christ. In and with the sanctification of Jesus Christ is achieved our sanctification as participants in him grounded in the "efficacy and revelation of the grace of Jesus Christ."[288] For Barth, this is the clear teaching of the New Testament where Jesus says "And for their sakes (υπερ αυτων) I sanctify myself, that they also might be truly sanctified" (John 17:19). Barth argues that the Apostle Paul makes the same argument in his letter to the Church in Corinth where he says: "But ye are washed, but ye are sanctified, but ye are justified in the name of the Lord Jesus, and by the Spirit of our God" (1 Cor 6:11).[289] Barth concludes that this is the eternal decree and will of God.[290] This is the height from which God's decision about our sanctification was resolved and corresponds to the depth that Jesus Christ became humanity and acted on our behalf as our Lord and head in our conversion to God. The meaning and content of the history of the royal man is therefore crowned in his death at Calvary where from all eternity the will of God is fulfilled by him on the earth in time. Barth argues that this is why Paul can say, "The temple of God is holy, which temple ye are" (1 Cor 3:17). That is why those gathered into the community must be called saints because they are sanctified and therefore "saints in Jesus Christ" (1 Cor 1:2; Phil 1:1). They are saints in and with the one who originally and alone is the Holy One.[291]

Moreover, the sanctification accomplished in the royal man is effective and authoritative for all humanity, not merely for the saints of God. That

---

287. Barth cites John 10:36 where Jesus calls himself the one "whom the Father hath sanctified." However, being humanity as the Son of God, Jesus can equally say, "I sanctify myself" (John 17:19). In addition, Barth argues that according to Heb 10:29 it is he himself in the first instance who is sanctified by his blood as the blood of the covenant. Moreover, Jesus addresses God as Holy Father (John 17:11) and he prays, "Sanctify (thou) them through thy truth" (John 17:17). Yet he is the fulfillment of this request as the Son of the Father. See Barth, CD IV/2, 515.

288. Ibid., 516.

289. Ibid., 517.

290. Barth cites 2 Thess 2:13, where Paul thanks God that he "hath from the beginning (απ αρχης) chosen you to salvation through sanctification of the Spirit and belief of the truth;" and Eph 1:4, which begins the great opening hymn with, "According as he hath chosen us in him before the foundation of the world, that we should be holy and without blame before him in love." Barth, CD IV/2, 517.

291. Ibid., 517–18.

is, the participation of the saints in the sanctity of Jesus Christ is not the conclusion of a private arrangement between him and them, but his cause as the King of all humanity. For Barth, the sanctification of humanity must be understood in the context of God's creation where he attests to his Lordship of all humanity in their sanctification as the counterpart to justification.[292] This clearly draws together the coalescence of (1) the humility and exaltation of Jesus Christ with (2) the justification and sanctification that Jesus Christ accomplishes for his church—all of which is decisive in view of the *anhypostasis* and *enhypostasis* dynamic of Christ's human nature. That is, the fact that the Word became flesh must be understood in the context of all humanity whom Jesus Christ has joined to himself. Barth adds that in all its particularity the sanctification of humanity speaks to the universal action of God, the purpose of which is the reconciliation of the world, and not merely this group of individuals in the world.

> As it creates the fact of the existence of these men, this people, within the world, their sanctification attests the great decision of God which in Jesus Christ has been made not only concerning them but concerning all the men of every time and place. This takes away from the particular existence of these men any appearance of the accidental. It gives it the stamp of supreme necessity and obligation. It removes its declaration and expression from the atmosphere of the pride of religious self-seeking and self-sufficiency. It sets it in the larger sphere of the creation of God. It gives it a solidarity even with secular things with which it is contrasted. This is the basis of both the dispeace and the peace of the saints in their relationship to others. They know that the sanctification of man, of all men, is already fulfilled (like their justification) in the one man Jesus, that it is effectively and authoritatively fulfilled in Him, and that it calls for their faith and love.[293]

Nevertheless, there exists within the saints of God this particular knowledge of the man Jesus as the "first-born among many brethren" (Rom 8:29), or "the firstborn of every creature" (Col 1:15). Therefore, the one who is in Christ participates in the election of Christ in his humanity. Even so, in the particular humanity of Jesus exists this one man as the humanity of the Son of God, the humanity for which every human being is ordained, and in which every part already has a part in him. However, despite the particular knowledge of Jesus that is revealed to the saint, the relevance of the

292. Ibid., 518.
293. Ibid., 518–19.

humanity of Christ is not denied to all humanity. For Barth, what took place in Christ—the exaltation of humanity and therefore humanity's sanctification for God—took place as the new "impression" of all humanity. As such, the relevance of his being and actions is not only for the saints, but for others also who are beside and around us—in likeness with us.[294]

Barth draws a sharp contrast between the universal relevance of Christ's humanity with Calvin's doctrine of the *participatio Christi*. In his analysis Barth charges that Calvin found no place (as defined by his distinctive doctrine of predestination) for the recognition of the universal relevance of the existence of the man Jesus and the sanctification of all humanity as it was achieved in him. Barth argues that for Calvin, Jesus Christ did not die for the reprobate, neither did he humble himself as the Son of God, nor has he been exalted to fellowship with God as the Son of Man. Neither did Jesus Christ act as a representative for them as their Lord and head and shepherd.[295]

Barth argues that the sanctification which comes *de facto* on the saints does so in virtue of their participation in the sanctity of Jesus Christ, which "acquires its weight" from the sanctification that has already come on all humanity *de iure* in Jesus Christ. Barth then turns to the question of how the transition is made from this presupposition—to the participation—of the saints, of the particular people of God in the world in whom sanctification has come on them *de facto*. Barth argues that with respect to the particularity of their existence, it is not a matter of their understanding and interpreting Christ's existence and its relevance, but a matter of his self-interpretation having been revealed to them.[296] Using New Testament language Barth marks out the saint of God as the one in whom God has reached and touched them through the quickening power of the Holy Spirit.[297] It is the Holy Spirit who in his action reveals and makes himself known as the one he is—placing them under his direction and claiming them as his own—as he bears witness to his holiness. "The Holy Spirit is the living Lord Jesus Christ himself in the work of the sanctification of his particular people in the world, of his community and all its members."[298] Therefore, the sanc-

---

294. Ibid., 519.

295. Ibid., 520.

296. Ibid., 521.

297. Pannenberg argues that Barth rightly pointed out in Paul's gospel—as the message of reconciliation—the claim to the new reality by the Spirit. See Pannenberg, *Systematic Theology*, 2:461.

298. Barth, 522. It is at this point that Barth "rejoins" Calvin. Despite Barth's refusal to overlook what he understands to be the weakness introduced in Calvin's doctrine of predestination into his establishment of the *participatio Christi*, Barth cannot overlook

tification of the saints by *the* Holy One takes place in the mode appropriate to the being of the Son of God as the eternal Logos, and the relationship of the Son of Man to other human beings. Jesus speaks forcefully, not merely in words, but also in his action revealed in his existence and death. And when Jesus speaks, other human beings hear him, not only with their ears as they hear other human beings, but as a call to obedience.[299]

> Hence the sanctification of man as the work of the Holy Spirit has to be described as the giving and receiving of direction. It is in this way that the Holy One creates the saints. It is in this way that He shares with them, in supreme reality, His own holiness; man's new form of existence as the true covenant-partner of God.[300]

Barth describes the human response to the call of obedience as the awakening that takes place according to the law of divine action, but a divine action that takes place in the context and under the conditions of human action. This must be so because genuine human sanctification must take place with humanity present in its inner and outer activity. It must involve the total cooperation of human being, of the whole heart and soul and mind, which in biblical terms includes the whole physical being. Otherwise it would not be an awakening. Therefore, this awakening must be understood as an event that takes place on earth and in time, having both a historical and creaturely dimension.[301]

Moreover, this awakening is both wholly creaturely and wholly divine, where the initial shock must come from God. There is no coordination between two comparable elements, but only the absolute primacy of the divine over the creaturely. Barth explains this as the creaturely being made serviceable to the divine and therefore actually becomes the servant of God as the instrument of God. As such, without its creatureliness being impaired, God bestows to it a special character. Therefore, being qualified in this way and claimed by God for cooperation, this human being cooperates in a way that the whole is still an action that is understood to be specifically divine. Barth understands this awakening of humanity as one event with one meaning and

---

what he understands to be the exemplary determination and power with which Calvin asserted the Christ created participation of the saints in the sanctity of Jesus Christ and therefore their membership in him as their Lord as the basis of all soteriology. Barth continues that this is the center of Calvin's thinking that gives clear insight into the relationship between justification and sanctification. See Barth, *CD* IV/2, 522.

299. Ibid., 523.

300. Ibid.

301. Ibid., 556–57.

content. In this context of unity, humanity is awakened to conversion.[302] The heart of the matter is the rising up of humanity that takes place in its conversion. This is a human being awakened from sleep; that is, awakened from walking a wrong path of perversion with no recourse. Furthermore, this awakening from sleep is not simply the vertical rising from it, but a turning around and going in the opposite direction.

> That God awakens us to this is the problem set for the Church, and therefore for us, by Holy Scripture. It cannot be exchanged for the (in themselves) very interesting problems of improvement or reformation or more noble effort in our further progress along the same path.[303]

Barth argues that we don't in fact see converted human beings in the Bible, but human beings caught up in the movement of conversion. That is, they are at the very heart of the movement having formerly moved away from God—but now—can no longer proceed without God. They are compelled to come to him, and are now in the process of doing so.[304] Their former movement is halted, and they are told to proceed in the opposite direction. The two movements, which belong together in an indissoluble unity, constitute this conversion.[305]

> Revealed to him as truth, the realty that God is for him and he for God sets him in this movement, in the *conversio* which is as such his *renovatio*. In the dynamic of this twofold principle— because God is for him and he for God—he can and may cease to proceed in the old direction and turn round and begin to move in the other way.[306]

God is the subject of this universal mystery who demonstrates in this action that he is for humanity. In addition, the human engagement in this action demonstrates that the individual is also for God. This is the axis on which the individual moves in turning from its own way to God. But this conversion and renewal must not be understood as an end in itself, which in Barth's view has been interpreted as an egocentric Christianity. Therefore, the person who simply desires to be converted for his or her own sake rather than for God the Lord—to serve him and his cause on earth as his

302. Ibid., 557.
303. Ibid., 559–60.
304. Ibid., 560.
305. Ibid., 560–61.
306. Ibid., 561.

witness—is not the whole human being.[307] For Barth, conversion, which is a matter of God's omnipotent mercy through the power of his Holy Spirit, is a conversion to being and action made possible by the freedom given by God.[308] As such, in Christ, we mirror the being and action of the royal man in our union with him. "To be sure, there is a compulsion, He *must* pass from a well-known past to a future which is only just opening up, "to a land that I shall shew thee"; from himself to the old man to himself as a new man; from his own death to his own true life."[309]

Barth explains that this is a compulsion that flows out of the permission and ability granted by God, that of a free human being enabled to exercise this freedom. As such, this human being *must* turn away from those things that are behind to that which is before. In this freedom has been removed any mere choosing or self-deciding. "In the exercise of this freedom—still as the man he was, already as the man he will be—he fulfills his conversion." Therefore, the origin and basis of a person's conversion is a decision by God for him or her, which makes possible a corresponding decision of this person for God as a free act of obedience, as well as making this act and obedience a reality by causing it to take place.[310]

We draw this section to a close with what is perhaps the most significant role that *anhypostasis* and *enhypostasis* play in Karl Barth's Christology—*Barth's development of human sanctification*. For Barth, it is the exaltation of human beings in their union with the royal man that is absolutely necessary for their conversion to saints. This brings to climax the coalescence of Jesus Christ's humiliation and exaltation in becoming flesh as the royal man with Christ's justification and sanctification on behalf of his church. And out of this coalescence Barth develops the mutual relationship between justification and sanctification in God's reconciliation with humanity by working out the ontological reality of the *anhypostasis* and *enhypostasis* of Christ's human nature in direct relationship to his community of saints. Consequently, to separate justification and sanctification would result in separating the one actuality of Jesus Christ and the Holy Spirit, and thereby isolate the self-humiliating Son of God on the one side and the exalted Son of Man on the other.

For Barth, the existence of the royal man answers the question of obedience necessary for the summoning and preparing of humanity for the service of God. Therefore, sanctification cannot simply be subordinated to

---

307. Ibid., 565.
308. Barth, *CD* IV/2, 578.
309. Ibid.
310. Ibid., *CD* IV/2, 578–79.

justifying grace in view of this whole event, but must be taken into account given its meaning and purpose. While sanctification is the second in execution (*executione posterius*), it is in fact the first in intention (*intentione prius*) that God wills and effects the reconciliation of humanity with himself in the incarnate Word of God as the royal man. Barth argues that teleologically, sanctification is in fact superior to justification because sanctified humanity is awakened and empowered by the action of a holy God in becoming a saint of God. Moreover, the sanctification of humanity that has taken place in Jesus Christ *is* in fact our sanctification. This means that sanctification is originally and properly the sanctification of Jesus of Nazareth. Consequently, the sanctification which comes *de facto* on the saints does so in virtue of their participation in the sanctity of Jesus Christ, which "acquires its weight" from the sanctification that has already come on all humanity *de iure* in Jesus Christ. For the particular saints, it is not a matter of their understanding and interpreting his existence and its relevance, but a matter of its self-interpretation having been revealed to them. Therefore, the saint of God is the one in whom God has reached and touched through the quickening power of his Holy Spirit being sanctified by *the* holy one. Moreover, this takes place in the mode appropriate to the being of the Son of God as the Logos and the relationship of the Son of Man to other human beings. Such is the relationship of the saints of God with Jesus Christ, which is realized in their union together as *anhypostasis* and *enhypostasis*.

Conclusion

WE CONCLUDE THAT BARTH'S adoption of the *anhypostasis* and *enhypostasis* of Christ's human nature has far reaching implications that encompass the ontological relationships between the human nature of Jesus with the Logos and with his church. As the royal man, Jesus Christ brings the Kingdom of God to this world of sufferers that he dwells among. And in so doing he brings to these the grace and freedom to trust him for help based upon their faith in him. This faith is their confidence in his power—the power of the Kingdom of God—that he brings with him in a real and concrete way. This is genuine faith determined by the fact that the royal man *already* called them his own by virtue of their *being* having been brought into relationship with his being. This is the ontological reality of the royal man in relationship with his people, the outworking of which derives from the *anhypostasis* and *enhypostasis* relationship between them. True humanity therefore is realized in the union of the Son of Man with the Son of God, which in turn determines the reality of the church in its union with the royal man.

Barth emphasizes that the Word of God spoken through the royal man is a human word, a word spoken by the Word became flesh in Jesus of Nazareth. In this way Barth develops the critical connection between the exaltation of humanity in the royal man through whom the Word of God is spoken by this true man in his indissoluble union with true God. As such, Jesus Christ proclaims the gospel—the *kerygma*—which he alone can reveal. Therefore, the fact that the Word became flesh means the royal man became a human being for all humanity where his very existence unites all humanity with God by virtue of his exaltation of humanity in Jesus of Nazareth. As the first Adam, the royal man embodies true humanity in our own anthropological sphere as God intended, and he exalts humanity in his union with the Son of God. This marks a significant point in Barth's Christology as an expression of the *anhypostasis* and *enhypostasis* formulation where the being and action of the royal man accomplishes the reconciliation of humanity with God. That is, our knowledge of him as one of his own includes the knowledge of ourselves. This is not a self-obtained knowledge, but a knowledge that is realized in the existence of the royal man and in his relationship with humanity in this anthropological sphere. Moreover, this ontological connection between Jesus and his community is the legal basis for the *kerygma* through which he establishes and charges his church.

Grounded in this relationship between the royal man and his church, Barth marks the decisive work of Christ's Holy Spirit—his direction—in accomplishing Christ's ontological union with his community of saints. It is the direction of the Holy Spirit that enables the actual union of the royal man with his church. And in this union we see the *anhypostasis* and *enhypostasis* dynamic expressed to its fullest. It is the Holy Spirit of the royal man who enables this union. The Holy Spirit transitions Christians from their being as false humanity to true humanity as actualized beings in Christ. This is the grace of God who grants to human beings the freedom of faith as its "anthropological counterpart," which can only claim this reality given its union in the royal man.

Moreover, as our mediator the human nature of Christ establishes the point of contact, the union between a Holy God and sinful humanity. This is an ontological contact, a simultaneous union of the royal man—with the Father—and with humanity. It is this union in being which uniquely expresses of the fullness and significance of how the *anhypostasis* and *enhypostasis* of Christ's human nature accomplished the reconciliation of humanity with God. As our mediator Jesus sacrificed himself to free humanity from the evil that had invaded this world and introduce a reconciled world in this royal man. Barth emphasizes here the seriousness of sin which dominates the human condition and the misery that accompanies it. This is the sin of sloth, old humanity's evil inaction characterized by its own pride and willingness to reject God. This is human sin that the Son of Man confronts having humbled himself in becoming flesh and unmasking this sin in his revelation of God, bringing with it God's reconciling grace characterized as both justifying and sanctifying grace. Therefore, only in the being of Jesus Christ can any human being realize its true humanity. For Barth, the ontological grounding of sanctified humanity in the royal man is striking, particularly in view of its emergence from the *anhypostasis* and *enhypostasis* dynamic. This is where humanity becomes its true self in union with the royal man—through the direction of the royal man—in receiving his Holy Spirit. It is in this direction, this summons, that the Holy Spirit reveals the reality of the royal man as he confronts us in our slothfulness. This is the freedom that Jesus Christ was won for us and granted to us in himself. Therefore, the bondage of the will and the freedom from this bondage in our sanctification must be always understood christologically.

It is the direction of the royal man that brings to climax what it perhaps the most significant aspect of *anhypostasis* and *enhypostasis* in Karl Barth's Christology—human sanctification. This marks the exaltation of human beings in their union with the royal man. In this movement we see the coalescence of Jesus Christ's humiliation and exaltation in becoming flesh as the royal man together with Christ's justification and sanctification on behalf of his church. For Barth, this is the mutual relationship between justification and sanctification in God's reconciliation with humanity, which is accomplished in the ontological reality of the *anhypostasis* and *enhypostasis* of Christ's human nature. Therefore, justification and sanctification must be understood as inseparable movements of Christ's ontological relationship with his church. In return, any move to separate justification from sanctification would separate the one actuality of Jesus Christ and the Holy Spirit, and thereby isolate the self-humiliating Son of God on the one side and the exalted Son of Man on the other.

Finally, the ontological reality of the royal man speaks to the question of obedience necessary for summoning and preparing humanity for the service of God. Consequently, sanctification cannot be subordinated to justification in full view of the union of the royal man with his people. Although second in execution, sanctification is understood to be first in God's intention to reconcile humanity with himself—in the Word of God—as the royal man. Barth argues that teleologically, sanctification is in fact superior to justification because sanctified humanity is awakened and empowered by the action of a holy God in becoming a saint of God. Moreover, the sanctification of humanity that takes place in Jesus Christ *is* our sanctification that comes *de facto* on the saints by virtue of their participation in the sanctity of Jesus Christ. The saint of God is therefore one in whom God has touched through the quickening power of his Holy Spirit having been being sanctified by *the* Holy One. This is the relationship that the saints of God enjoy with Jesus Christ, which is realized in their union together as *anhypostasis* and *enhypostasis*.

Bibliography

Althaus, Paul. *The Theology of Martin Luther*. Translated by Robert C. Schultz. Philadelphia: Fortress, 1966.

Anderson, Clifford B. and Bruce L. McCormack, eds. *Karl Barth and the Making of Evangelical Theology: A Fifty-Year Perspective*. Grand Rapids: Eerdmans, 2015.

Anderson, William P. *Aspects of the Theology of Karl Barth*. Washington D. C.: University Press of America, 1981.

Anselm of Canterbury. *Anselm of Canterbury*. Edited and translated by Jasper Hopkins and Herbert Richardson. Vol. 3. New York: E. Mellen, 1976.

Baillie, D. M. *God was in Christ: An Essay on Incarnation and Atonement*. New York: Scribner, 1948.

Balthasar, Hans Urs von. *The Theology of Karl Barth: Exposition and Interpretation*. Translated by Edward T. Oakes. San Francisco: Communio, 1992.

Barth, Karl. *Anselm, Fides Quarens Intellectum: Anselm's Proof of the Existence of God in the Context of His Theological Scheme*. 1960. Reprint, Eugene, OR: Pickwick, 2009.

———. *Christ and Adam: Man and Humanity in Romans 5*. Translated by T. A. Smail. New York: Collier, 1962.

———. *Church Dogmatics*. 13 vols. Translated by G. T. Thomson and Harold Knight. Peabody, MA: Hendrickson, 2010.

———. *Come, Holy Spirit*. Sermons by Karl Barth and Eduard Thurneysen. Translated by Professor George W. Richards, Reverend Elmer G. Homrighausen, and Professor Karl J. Ernst. Grand Rapids: Eerdmans, 1933.

———. *Deliverance to the Captives*. Westport: Greenwood, 1961.

———. *Der Römerbrief (Zweite Fassung) 1922*. Edited by Cornelis van der Kooi and Katja Tolstaja. Zürich: TVZ, 2010.

———. *Die Kirchliche Dogmatik*, vol. 1, pt. 2. Zürich: TVZ, 1990.

———. *Die Kirchliche Dogmatik*, vol. 4, pt. 1. Zürich: TVZ, 1986.

———. *Die Kirchliche Dogmatik*, vol. 4, pt. 2. Zürich: TVZ, 1990.

———. *Dogmatics in Outline*. Translated by G. T. Thomson. New York: Harper, 1972.

———. *The Epistle to the Philippians*. 6th ed. Translated by James W. Leitch. Richmond: John Knox, 1962.

———. *The Epistle to the Romans*. Translated by Edwyn C. Hoskyns. London: Oxford University Press, 1963.

———. *God Here and Now*. Translated by Paul M. van Buren. New York: Harper, 1964.

———. *God in Action*. Translated by E. G. Homrighausen and Karl J. Ernst. New York: Round Table, 1963.

———. *The Göttingen Dogmatics*. Translated by Geoffrey W. Bromiley. Grand Rapids: Eerdmans, 1991.

———. *The Great Promise: Commentary on Luke 1*. Translated by Hans Freund. New York: Philosophical Library, 1963.

———. *The Heidelberg Catechism for Today*. Translated by Shirley C. Guthrie. Richmond: John Knox, 1964.

———. *How I Changed My Mind*. Richmond: John Knox, 1966.

———. *The Humanity of God*. Translated by John Newton Thomas and Thomas Wieser. Richmond: John Knox, 1964.

———. *The Knowledge of God and the Service of God According to the Teaching of the Reformation*. Translated by J. L. M. Haire and Ian Henderson. London: Hodder and Stoughton, 1960.

———. *On Religion: The Revelation of God as the Sublimation of Religion*. Translated by Garrett Green. New York: T & T Clark, 2006.

———. *Protestant Theology in the Nineteenth Century: Its Background & History*. Translated by Brian Cozens, John Bowden and SCM Editorial Staff. London: SCM, 1972.

———. *Revolutionary Theology in the Making: Barth-Thurneysen Correspondence, 1914–1925*. Translated by James D. Smart. Richmond: John Knox, 1964.

———. *Theology and Church: Shorter Writings 1920–1928*. Translated by Louise Pettibone Smith. London: SCM, 1962.

———. *The Theology of John Calvin*. Translated by Geoffrey W. Bromiley. Grand Rapids: Eerdmans, 1995.

———. *The Theology of the Reformed Confessions*. Translated and annotated by Darrell L. Guder and Judith J. Guder. Westminster: John Knox, 2002.

———. *Witness to the Word: A Commentary on John 1*. Lectures at Munster in 1925 and at Bonn in 1933. Translated by Geoffrey W. Bromiley. Grand Rapids: Eerdmans, 1986.

———. *The Word of God and the Word of Man*. Translated by Douglas Horton. New York: Harper, 1957.

———. *The Word of God and Theology*. Translated by Amy Marga. New York: T & T Clark, 2011.

Bavinck, Herman. *Reformed Dogmatics*. 4 vols. Translated by John Vriend. Grand Rapids: Baker, 2009.

Berkhof, Hendrikus. *Two Hundred Years of Theology*. Translated by John Vriend. Grand Rapids: Eerdmans, 1989.

Berkhof, Louis. *Systematic Theology*. Grand Rapids: Eerdmans, 1996.

Berkouwer, G. C. *Divine Election*. Translated by Hugo Bekker. Grand Rapids: Eerdmans, 1960.

———. *The Person of Christ*. Translated by John Vriend. Grand Rapids: Eerdmans, 1954.

———. *The Triumph of Grace in the Theology of Karl Barth*. Grand Rapids: Eerdmans, 1956.

———. *The Work of Christ*. Translated by Cornelius Lambregtse. Grand Rapids: Eerdmans, 1965.

Boettner, Lorraine. *The Reformed Doctrine of Predestination*. Phillipsburg, NJ: Presbyterian and Reformed, 1996.

Bonhoeffer, Dietrich. *Christ the Center*. Translated by Edwin H. Robertson. San Francisco: Harper, 1978.

Brazier, P. H. *Barth and Dostoevsky: A Study of the Influence of the Russian Writer Fyodor Mikhailovich Dostoevsky on the Development of the Swiss Theologian Karl Barth 1915–1922*. Colorado Springs: Paternoster, 2007.

Bromiley, Geoffrey W. *Introduction to the Theology of Karl Barth*. Grand Rapids: Eerdmans, 1979.

————. "The Karl Barth Experience." In *How Karl Barth Changed My Mind*, edited by Donald K. McKim et al., 65. Grand Rapids: Eerdmans, 1986.

Burnett, Richard E. *Karl Barth's Theological Exegesis: The Hermeneutical Principles of the Romerbrief Period*. Grand Rapids: Eerdmans 2004.

Busch, Eberhard. *Karl Barth: His life from letters and autobiographical texts*. 2nd revised edition. Translated by John Bowden. Munich: Christian Kaiser Verlag, 1976.

————. *Karl Barth and the Pietists*. Translated by Daniel W. Bloesch. Downers Grove, IL: Intervarsity, 1978.

Calvin, John. *Institutes of the Christian Religion*. 2 vols. Louisville: John Knox, 1960.

Chung, Sung Wook. *Admiration & Challenge: Karl Barth's Theological Relationship with John Calvin*. New York: Lang, 2002.

————, ed. *Karl Barth and Evangelical Theology*. Grand Rapids: Baker, 2006.

Clark, Gordon H. *Karl Barth's Theological Method*. Hobbs, NM: The Trinity Foundation, 1997.

Cortez, Marc. *Theological Anthropology: A Guide for the Perplexed*. London: T & T Clark, 2010.

Crisp, Oliver. *Divinity and Humanity: The Incarnation Reconsidered*. Cambridge: Cambridge University Press. 2007.

Cross, Terry L. *Dialectic in Karl Barth's Doctrine of God*. New York: Lang, 2001.

Cunningham, Mary Kathleen. "Karl Barth's Interpretation and Use of Ephesians 1:4 in His Doctrine of Election: An Essay in the Relation of Scripture and Theology." UMI Dissertation Information Services, 1988.

Deddo, Gary W. *Karl Barth's Theology of Relations: Trinitarian, Christological, and Human: Towards an Ethic of the Family*. New York: Lang, 1999.

Driver, Lisa D. Maugans. *Christ at the Center*. Louisville: Westminster John Knox, 2009.

Drury, John L. *The Resurrection of God: Karl Barth's Trinitarian Theology of Easter*. Minneapolis: Fortress, 2014.

Fairweather, A. M. *The Word as Truth: a Critical Examination of the Christian Doctrine of Revelation in the Writings of Thomas Aquinas and Karl Barth*. London: Lutterworth, 1944.

Fisher, Simon. *Revelatory Positivism? Barth's Earliest Theology and the Marburg School*. Oxford: Oxford University Press, 1988.

Ford, David. *Barth and God's Story: Biblical Narrative and the Theological Method of Karl Barth in the Church Dogmatics*. Frankfurt: Lang, 1985.

Gibson, David T. *Reading the Decree: Exegesis, Election and Christology in Calvin and Barth*. London: T & T Clark, 2009.

Gibson, David, and David Strange, eds. *Engaging with Barth: Contemporary Evangelical Critiques*. Nottingham, UK: Apollos, 2008.

Gockel, Matthias. "A Dubious Christological Formula? Leontius of Byzantium and the Anhypostasis–Enhypostasis Theory." *The Journal of Theological Studies*, 51.2 (2000) 515–32.

Gorringe, Timothy J. *Karl Barth: Against Hegemony*. Oxford: Oxford University Press, 1999.

Grillmeier, Aloys. *Christ in Christian Tradition*. Vol. 2, pt. 2, The Church of Constantinople in the Sixth Century. Translated by John Cawte and Pauline Allen. Louisville: Westminster John Knox 1995.

———. *Christ in Christian Tradition*. Vol. 2, pt. 4, *The Church of Alexandria with Nubia and Ethiopia after 451*. Translated by O. C. Dean Jr. Louisville: Westminster John Knox. 1996.

———. "The Understanding of the Christological Definitions of Both (Oriental Orthodox and Roman Catholic) Traditions in the Light of the Post-Chalcedonian Theology (Analysis of Terminologies in a Conceptual Framework)." In *Christ in East and West*, edited by Paul Fries and Tiran Nersoyan, 65–82. Macon, GA: Mercer University Press, 1987.

Hardy, Edward Rochie, and Cyril C. Richardson, eds. *Christology of the Later Fathers*. Philadelphia: Westminster, 1954.

Hart, Trevor. *Regarding Karl Barth: Toward a Reading of His Theology*. Downers Grove, IL: InterVarsity, 1999.

Hartwell, Herbert. *The Theology of Karl Barth: An Introduction*. Philadelphia: Westminster, 1964.

Hector, Kevin W. "God's Triunity and Self-Determination: A Conversation with Karl Barth, Bruce McCormack, and Paul Molnar." *International Journal of Systematic Theology* 7.3 (2005) 246–61.

Henry, David Paul. *The Early Development of the Hermeneutic of Karl Barth as Evidenced by His Appropriation of Romans 5:12–21*. Macon, GA: Mercer University Press, 1985.

Heppe, Heinrich. *Reformed Dogmatics*. Translated by G. T. Thomson. Grand Rapids: Baker, 1978.

Hoffmann, Peter. *The History of the German Resistance 1933–1945*. Translated by Richard Barry. Cambridge: MIT Press, 1977.

Hodge, Charles. *Systematic Theology*, vol. 1. Grand Rapids: Eerdmans, 2001.

Hunsinger, George. *Disruptive Grace: Studies in the Theology of Karl Barth*. Grand Rapids: Eerdmans, 2000.

———. *How to Read Karl Barth: The Shape of His Theology*. Oxford: Oxford University Press, 1991.

———, ed. *Karl Barth and Radical Politics*. Translated by George Hunsinger. Philadelphia: Westminster, 1976.

———, ed. *The Word is Truth: Barth on Scripture*. Grand Rapids: Eerdmans, 2012.

Jenson, Robert W. *Systematic Theology: Volume 1; The Triune God*. New York: Oxford University Press, 1997.

Johnson, Roger A. *The Origins of Demythologizing: Philosophy and Historiography in the Theology of Rudolf Bultmann*. Leiden: Brill, 1974.

Johnson, William Stacey. *The Mystery of God: Karl Barth and the Postmodern Foundations of Theology*. Louisville: Westminster John Knox, 1997.

Jones, Paul Dafydd. *The Humanity of Christ: Christology in Karl Barth's Church Dogmatics*. London: T & T Clark, 2008.

Jüngel, Eberhard, *God's Being is in Becoming: The Trinitarian Being of God in the Theology of Karl Barth*. Translated by John Webster. Grand Rapids: Eerdmans, 2001.

———. *Karl Barth: A Theological Legacy*. Translated by Garrett E. Paul. Philadelphia: Westminster, 1986.

Klooster, Fred H. *Calvin's Doctrine of Predestination*. Grand Rapids: Baker, 1977.

Knox, John. *The Humanity and Divinity of Christ*. Cambridge: Cambridge University Press, 1967.

Kooi, Cornelis van der. *As in a Mirror: John Calvin and Karl Barth on Knowing God*. Translated by Donald Mader. Boston: Brill, 2005.

Krausmüller, Dirk. "Leontius of Jerusalem: A Theologian of the Seventh Century." *The Journal of Theological Studies* 52 (2001) 637–57.

—————. "Making Sense of the Formula of Chalcedon: the Cappadocians and Aristotle in Leontius of Byzantium's *Contra Nestorianos et Eutychianos*." *Vigiliae Christianae* 65 (2011) 484–513.

Lang, U. M. "Anhypostasis–Enhypostasis: Church Fathers, Protestant Orthodoxy and Karl Barth." *The Journal of Theological Studies* 49.2 (1998) 630–57.

Lauber, David. *Barth on the Descent into Hell: God, Atonement and the Christian Life*. Aldershot, UK: Ashgate, 2004.

Leslie, Benjamin C. *Trinitarian Hermeneutics: The Hermeneutical Significance of Karl Barth's Doctrine of the Trinity*. New York: Lang, 1991.

Lohse, Bernhard. *Martin Luther's Theology*. Translated and edited by Roy A. Harrisville. Minneapolis: Fortress, 1999.

—————. *A Short History of Christian Doctrine: From the First Century to the Present*. Translated by Ernst Stoeffler. Philadelphia: Fortress, 1985.

Lynch, John J. "Leontius of Byzantium: A Cyrillan Christology." *Theological Studies* 36 (1975) 455–71.

Macken, John. *The Autonomy Theme in the Church Dogmatics: Karl Barth and His Critics*. Cambridge: Cambridge University Press, 1990.

Mangina, Joseph L. *Karl Barth on the Christian Life: The Practical Knowledge of God*. New York: Lang, 2001.

Margo, Amy. *Karl Barth's Dialogue with Catholicism in Göttingen and Munster*. Tübingen: Mohr Siebeck, 2010.

Marquardt, Friedrich-Wilhelm. *Theological Audacities: Theological Essays*. Translated by Don McCord, H. Martin Rumscheidt, and Paul S. Chung. Eugene, OR: Pickwick, 2010.

Marshall, Bruce. *Christology in Conflict: The Identity of a Saviour in Rahner and Barth*. Oxford: Blackwell, 1987.

McCormack, Bruce. "Karl Barth's Christology as a Resource for a Reformed Version of Kenoticism." *International Journal of Systematic Theology* 8.3 (2006) 243–51.

—————. *Karl Barth's Critically Realistic Dialectical Theology: Its Genesis and Development 1909–1936*. Oxford: Oxford University Press, 1995.

—————. "Historical Criticism and Dogmatic Interest in Karl Barth's Theological Exegesis of the New Testament." In *Biblical Hermeneutics in Historical Perspective*, edited by Mark Burrows and Paul Rorem, 322–26. Grand Rapids: Eerdmans, 1991.

—————. "The Ontological Presupposition of Barth's Doctrine of the Atonement." In *The Glory of the Atonement: Biblical, Theological & Practical Perspectives: Essays in Honor of Roger Nicole*, 346–66. Downers Grove, IL: InterVarsity, 2004.

—————. *Orthodox and Modern: Studies in the Theology of Karl Barth*. Grand Rapids: Baker, 2008.

—————. "Why Should Theology Be Christocentric? Christology and Metaphysics in Paul Tillich and Karl Barth." *Wesleyan Theological Journal* 45 (2010) 42–80.

McCormack, Bruce, and Clifford B. Anderson, eds. *Karl Barth and American Evangelicalism*. Grand Rapids: Eerdmans, 2011.

McCormack, Bruce, and Gerrit Neven, eds. *The Reality of Faith in Theology: Studies on Karl Barth*. Bern, CH: Lang, 2007.

MacDonald, Neil B. *Karl Barth and the Strange New World Within the Bible: Barth, Wittgenstein, and the Metadilemmas of the Enlightenment*. Waynesboro, GA: Paternoster, 2000.

McGrath, Alister E. *Iustitia Dei: A History of the Christian Doctrine of Justification*. 3rd ed. Cambridge: Cambridge University Press, 1986.

———. "Justification and Christology: The Axiomatic Correlation between the Historical Jesus and the Proclaimed Christ." *Modern Theology* 1 (1984) 45–54.

———. *The Making of Modern German Christology: From the Enlightenment to Pannenberg*. Oxford: Blackwell, 1986.

———. *The Making of Modern German Christology: 1750–1990*, 2nd ed. Eugene, OR: Wipf & Stock, 1994.

McKinney, Gerald. *The Analogy of Grace: Karl Barth's Moral Theology*. Oxford: Oxford University Press, 2010.

Metzger, Paul Louis. *The Word of Christ and the World of Culture: Sacred and Secular through the Theology of Karl Barth*. Grand Rapids: Eerdmans, 2003.

Mikkelsen, Hans Vium. *Reconciled Humanity: Karl Barth in Dialogue*. Grand Rapids: Eerdmans, 2010.

Molnar, Paul D. *Incarnation and Resurrection: Toward a contemporary understanding*. Grand Rapids: Eerdmans, 2007.

———. "The Trinity, Election, and God's Ontological Freedom: A Response to Kevin W. Hector." *International Journal of Systematic Theology* 8 (2006) 294–306.

Mueller, David L. *Foundation of Karl Barth's Doctrine of Reconciliation: Jesus Christ Crucified and Risen*. Lewiston: E. Mellen, 1990.

———. *Karl Barth: Makers of the Modern Theological Mind*. Waco, TX: Word, 1972.

Neder, Adam. *Participation in Christ: An Entry into Karl Barth's Church Dogmatics*. Louisville: Westminster John Knox, 2009.

Nimmo, Paul T. *Being in Action: The Theological Shape of Barth's Ethical Vision*. London: T & T Clark, 2007.

Oakes, Kenneth. *Karl Barth on Theology & Philosophy*. Oxford: Oxford University Press, 2012.

Oh, Peter S. *Karl Barth's Trinitarian Theology: A Study in Karl Barth's Analogical Use of the Trinitarian Relation*. London: T & T Clark, 2006.

Pannenberg, Wolfhart. *Jesus—God and man*. Translated by Lewis L. Wilkins and Duane A. Priebe. Philadelphia: Westminster, 1977.

———. *Systematic Theology*. Three vols. Translated by Geoffrey W. Bromiley. Grand Rapids: Eerdmans, 1998.

Pelikan, Jaroslav. *The Christian Tradition: A History of the Development of Doctrine*. Five volumes. Chicago: University of Chicago Press, 1989.

Percival, Henry R., ed. *Nicene and Post-Nicene Fathers*, vol. 14. Fourth printing. Peabody, MA: Hendrickson, 2004.

Pokrifka, Todd B. *Redescribing God: The Roles of Scripture, Tradition, and Reason in Karl Barth's Doctrines of Divine Unity, Constancy, and Eternity*. Eugene, OR: Pickwick, 2010.

Prestige, G. L. *God in Patristic Thought*. Eugene, OR: Wipf & Stock, 1964.

Price, Daniel J. *Karl Barth's Anthropology in Light of Modern Thought*. Grand Rapids: Eerdmans, 2002.

Rees, Silas. "Leontius of Byzantium and His Defense of the Council of Chalcedon." *Harvard Theological Review* (April 1931) 111–12.

Schaff, Philip. *The Creeds of Christendom.* Vol. 1. Grand Rapids: Baker, 2007.

Schaff, Philip, and Henry Wace, eds. *Nicene and Post-Nicene Fathers*, vol. 9. Fourth printing. Peabody, MA: Hendrickson, 2004.

Schmid, Heinrich. *The Doctrinal Theology of the Evangelical Lutheran Church*, 3rd ed. Translated by Charles A. Hay and Henry E. Jacobs. Eugene, OR: Wipf & Stock, 2008.

Sharp, Douglas R. *The Hermeneutics of Election: The Significance of the Doctrine in Barth's Church Dogmatics.* Lanham, MD: University Press of America, 1990.

Shults, LeRon F. "A Dubious Christological Formula: From Leontius of Byzantium to Karl Barth." *Theological Investigations* 57 (1996) 431–46.

Smith, James K. A., and James H. Olthuis, eds. *Radical Orthodoxy and the Reformed Tradition: Creation, Covenant, and Participation.* Grand Rapids: Baker, 2005.

Sumner, Darren O. "The Twofold Life of the Word: Karl Barth's Critical Reception of the Extra Calvinisticum." *International Journal of Systematic Theology* 15 (2013) 42–57.

Sykes, S. W. Editor. *Karl Barth: Centenary Essays.* Cambridge: Cambridge University Press, 1989.

Thompson, John. *Christ in Perspective: Christological Perspectives in the Theology of Karl Barth.* Grand Rapids: Eerdmans, 1978.

Thompson, Geoff, and Christiaan Mostert, eds. *Karl Barth: A Future for Postmodern Theology?* Hindmarsh, SA: Australian Theological Forum, 2000.

Torrance, Thomas F. *Atonement: The Person and Work of Christ.* Downers Grove, IL: InterVarsity, 2009.

———. *Karl Barth, Biblical and Evangelical Theologian.* Edinburgh: T & T Clark, 1990.

Turretin, Francis. *Institutes of Elenctic Theology.* Vol. 3. Translated by George Musgrave Giger. Phillipsburg, NJ: P & R Publishing, 1992.

Ward, Graham. *Christ and Culture.* Malden, MA: Blackwell, 2005.

Warfield, Benjamin B. *The Person and Work of Christ.* Phillipsburg, NJ: Presbyterian and Reformed, 1950.

———. *The Works of Benjamin B. Warfield.* Vol. 3. Grand Rapids: Baker, 2003.

Weber, Otto. *Karl Barth's Church Dogmatics: An Introductory Report.* Philadelphia: Westminster, 1953.

Webster, John. *Barth's Earlier Theology.* New York: T & T Clark, 2005.

———. *Barth's Ethics of Reconciliation.* Cambridge : Cambridge University Press, 1995.

———. *Barth's Moral Theology: Human Action in Barth's Thought.* Grand Rapids: Eerdmans, 1998.

———, ed. *The Cambridge Companion to Karl Barth.* Cambridge: Cambridge University Press, 2000.

———. "Karl Barth." In *Reading Romans Through the Centuries: From the Early Church to Karl Barth*, edited by Jeffrey P. Greenman and Timothy Larsen et al., Grand Rapids: Banzos, 2005.

Welker, Michael. *Creation and Reality.* Minneapolis: Fortress, 1999.

———. *God the Revealed.* Translated by Douglas W. Stott. Grand Rapids: Eerdmans, 2013.

———. "Karl Barths und Deitrich Bonhoeffers Beiträge zur zukünftigen Ekklesiologie." *Zeitschrift für Dialektische Theologie* 22 (2006) 120–37.

Welker, Michael, and Cynthia A. Jarvis, eds. *Loving God with Our Minds: The Pastor as Theologian*. Grand Rapids: Eerdmans, 2004.

Wesche, Kenneth Paul. "The Christology of Leontius of Jerusalem: Monophysite or Chalcedonian?" *St. Vladimir's Theological Quarterly* 31 (1987) 65–95.

Wigley, Stephen. *Karl Barth and Hans Urs von Balthasar: A Critical Engagement*. New York: T & T Clark, 2007.

Wingren, Gustaf. *Theology in Conflict: Nygren, Barth, Bultmann*. Philadelphia: Muhlenberg, 1958.

Wood, Donald. *Barth's Theology of Interpretation*. Burlington: Ashgate, 2007.

Young, Frances M. *From Nicaea to Chalcedon. A Guide to the Literature and its Background*. London: SCM, 1988.

Zuck, Lowell H. "Heinrich Heppe: Melanchthonian Liberal in the Nineteenth-Century German Reformed Church." *Church History* 51 (1982) 419–33.